W9-DAZ-780

PROPERTY                    OF
COLBY SCHOOL FOR GIRLS

# BINDING

## Vol. IV

The binding design on this volume is an authorized facsimile of the original art binding on the official Italian copy of the Versailles Peace Treaty, which was signed by King Victor Emmanuel and M. Tittoni and deposited in the Archives of the Italian Government.

The World's Greatest Sea Fight
The Battle of Jutland or the Skagerrak. The night of confusion, tumult and disaster which followed the battle

Painting by Willy Stower

The World's Greatest Sea Fight

The Battle of Jutland or the Skagerrak. The night of confusion, tumult and disaster which followed the battle

Painting by Willy Stower

# SOURCE RECORDS

OF

# THE GREAT WAR

A COMPREHENSIVE AND READABLE SOURCE RECORD OF THE
WORLD'S GREAT WAR, EMPHASIZING THE MORE IMPORTANT
EVENTS, AND PRESENTING THESE AS COMPLETE NARRATIVES
IN THE ACTUAL WORDS OF THE CHIEF OFFICIALS AND MOST
EMINENT LEADERS

NON-PARTISAN                    NON-SECTIONAL                    NON-SECTARIAN

PRESENTING DOCUMENTS FROM GOVERNMENT ARCHIVES AND
OTHER AUTHORITATIVE SOURCES, WITH OUTLINE NARRATIVES,
INDICES, CHRONOLOGIES, AND COURSES OF READING ON SOCIO-
LOGICAL MOVEMENTS AND INDIVIDUAL NATIONAL ACTIVITIES

EDITOR-IN-CHIEF

## CHARLES F. HORNE, Ph.D.

DIRECTING EDITOR

## WALTER F. AUSTIN, LL.M

*With a staff of specialists*

## VOLUME IV

PROPERTY OF
COLBY SCHOOL FOR GIRLS

## National Alumni

9508

D
521
.H6
vol. 4

940.3
H 8/5
V. IV

9508

Copyright, 1923, National Alumni
Printed in U. S. A.

# CONTENTS

## VOLUME IV—1916

### "THEY SHALL NOT PASS"

# CONTENTS

# CONTENTS

# ILLUSTRATIONS

## VOLUME IV

## 1916

## "THEY SHALL NOT PASS"

AN OUTLINE NARRATIVE OF

### VERDUN AND THE BLACK YEAR OF EXHAUSTION

BY CHARLES F. HORNE

THE increasing shadow of German mastery of the universe which had hung heavy upon the world toward the close of 1915 became more ominous still in 1916. For Europe this was the darkest year of the War, the year of black exhaustion, with no promise of an end in sight. Neither side would yield in the desolating struggle; and yet neither side could win. Between them, mankind, or at least the European peoples who had so long been the leaders of mankind, seemed doomed to extermination.

This was the year of the tremendous attacks upon Verdun. With tornadoes of ammunition and an endless avalanche of men, the Germans beat the staggering French line back and back, until the whole world trembled for its breaking. With each new day civilization everywhere looked eagerly to its morning news to know if the barrier had indeed broken at last. Was the flood of evil to be again let loose, to submerge France as it had submerged peaceful Belgium, and helpless Poland, and vast voiceless Western Russia, and heroic Serbia.

Then the French troops at Verdun raised their heroic counter-cry, "They shall not pass!" and the French poilus held firm, each serving at his appointed task until he perished; whereon yet another poilu would step forward steadily to endure the misery until he also fell; and—the Germans did not pass! The world has never known a period of more dramatic anxiety—nor one which should more inspire us with faith in the future of our human race.

On the whole, the year 1916 went badly for Germany; for her main efforts were put forth upon the Western front, and were symbolized by her failure to win Verdun. Yet while the German war-machine could by its utmost effort win no great triumph in the West, its victories continued with but little apparent effort in the East, and the way was prepared for the complete breakdown of Russia in the following year. Thus an impartial estimate of what this somber year meant to the world might best be summed up by that one desolating word—Exhaustion!

France, Britain and Italy, each now had reached the maximum of its strength. Each was using every available man and woman at some needful war-work. Of these exhaustive drains, that upon the man power was the worst. By the end of 1916 France had lost from her fighting hordes over a quarter of her total possible soldiers.[1] That is, of her four million sons once fit to defend her by physical force, over a million were dead or permanently crippled, or —worse still—were prisoners to the sullenly embittered Germans. France, the gay, the brilliant, the intellectual star among nations, had lost a million not of her duller, narrower and more selfish sons, but of her bravest and most eager and most loyal. Britain, similarly, had lost a fifth of her best children, and Italy a tenth of hers. As for Russia, drawing in stubborn fashion upon her seemingly limitless reserves of hapless human beings, she was nearer to the breaking point than men then guessed.

In other lands there was even worse exhaustion. Through all the regions held in German thrall the conquered peoples were perishing [2] under such massacre and starvation as our preceding volume has described. This was the year of the complete enslavement of Belgian labor, and of the shameful

[1] Readers must discriminate between permanent losses and the usually stated "casualties" of a battle. In the casualties the largest figure is made up of the wounded; and under modern surgery the greater number of the wounded are soon made well again. In the intense passion of the Great War, the recovered wounded returned almost always to the ranks. Many men were thus "casualties" four and even more times over. Western Europe, if fighting without its "hospital corps," must soon have collapsed—as Turkey did.

[2] See § VII, "The Deportations from Lille," by Gerard, Hoover, etc.

deportation of young women from their homes in Lille and the other captured regions of France.  Even among the dominant races in the new Middle-Europe Empire, the grip of want became severe.  Austria, demoralized and lacking through casualties, capture, or desertion fully a third of her original fighting strength, saw the gaunt specter of starvation creeping appreciably close.  Germany, by the end of 1916, had lost nearly two million men from her armies, a fifth of her possible strength, and was by no means the Germany which had so eagerly welcomed war two and a half years before.

### THE PEACE TALK AND THE DEEPENING SHADOW

To the German people the goal of world-conquest no longer glowed with such alluring colors.  Now that they had for over two years plodded the awful road which they had been told would lead to glory, they found it wholly unlike their expectations.  They had pictured Conquest as a wondrous goddess of beauty; they had been promised that she would bring with her pleasure and honor and boundless wealth.  Instead, she had given to their victorious hands only wasted and ruined regions, only nations of decaying corpses, only hollow faced and useless captives, who cursed Germany even as they died.[1]  "Conquest destroys the thing conquered."  Vaguely the deluded German people began to recognize their dream goddess as the devil-hag she is.  And always her false face and her distorted smile remained as distant from them, and as difficult to win, as ever.

The German nation could scarcely have been held longer to its painful and exhaustive task, had the war been still set before them as a struggle for the winning of more land or wealth or fame.  Not until July of 1917 did the German parliament pass its notable resolution declaring that it wanted peace without any annexations of territory whatever; and this parliament, it must be remembered, was only a talking body, a powerless voice for expressing a restricted amount of public sentiment.  Yet from 1916 onward the German

[1] See § XXVII, "German Treatment of Prisoners," by Vierorde, McCarthy, etc.

Government found it necessary to convince its people that they were really fighting in self-defense, that the world was bent on destroying them, as they themselves had destroyed Serbia and Poland. Elusive peace proposals filled the air. But always when these were sifted down they were found to include Germany's demand that she be allowed to keep her plunder, that her victims should remain victims, and "frightfulness" become thus the established code of war.

Western Europe considered the first peace proposals seriously; for men knew the frightful price they still must pay before victory was possible. Doubters had even begun to fear that with their utmost effort and sacrifice they could not outlast Germany. But when the Allies learned what the German Government really demanded, as opposed to the fair words of its powerless parliament, there was a general grim refusal of her terms. A widespread saying arose among men, in America as well as Europe, that if such deeds as Germany had perpetrated could pass without redress in this world, then the world was not worth living in anyway; and they would fight their way out of it. In such stern mood did Western Europe approach the ending of this somber year. Hope was dying from the world.

In its place came the flaming spirit of martyrdom,[1] the spirit of the old crusades. Even among neutrals there were those who would no longer endure in patience the approach of the German terror. Many Americans both with voice and pen urged their country to go to Europe's aid. Many would not wait for the doubtful national action, but went individually as volunteers into the French or British armies. There they died as men should die, as the poet Alan Seeger died, cheering on his comrades with his death song through the last bleak night.[2] Death had indeed come to be but a little thing in the minds of men, as compared with freedom and with justice. And to console the survivors of the youthful heroes everywhere falling, there spread over the civilized world a great religious revival. Its full meaning, its depth

[1] See § I, "Belgium's Martyrdom," by Whitlock, Mercier, etc.
[2] See § XVI, "The First Americans to Pay the Debt," by Hervier, etc.

and richness can only be measured by a later age when it looks back on them.

Let us trace the chronological steps by which 1916 brought these changes in the outer fortunes and the inward spirit of the world. The close of 1915 had seen the Middle-Europe Empire fully established by the defeat of Russia, the crushing of Serbia, and Bulgaria's union with the seekers for dominion over subject races. But Russia's defeat had been incomplete, and she was now beginning to make ammunition for herself and to receive more from Japan. Moreover, in the Balkans the Allies had still one army strongly sheltered at Salonika and another possible army being rebuilt from the escaped Serbs, who were protected in their Adriatic refuge by the navy of Italy.

### THE WAR SPREADS IN ASIA

At the opening of 1916 Russia signalized her returning strength by a successful campaign against Turkey in the Caucasus. Here, where in the preceding winter she had driven the Turks from her frontier, she signalized this second winter by overthrowing another army and capturing Erzerum, the chief fortress city of Armenia. Soon she held all the northern section of Armenia, and so checked the Turkish massacres in that unhappy region.[1]

But now the immeasurable devastation of the War, which in the last year had hung only on the borders of Asia, began spreading its wings of death over the interior of that continent also. The Russian forces advanced through Persia and occupied Ispahan, its capital. They then drove the Turks out of Persia and over the border mountains into the Turkish domain of Mesopotamia, the Bible region of the childhood of mankind. By June the advancing Russians were within seventy miles of Bagdad, the ancient Asiatic city which loomed so large in German minds.

Bagdad, however, was not yet to fall. The tide of fortune turned against the daring Russian column which had penetrated so far into these ancient wilds. The Russians

[1] See § III, "Russia's Conquest of Armenia," by Gen. Yudenitch, etc.

were compelled to retreat by the gathering masses of Turks, who had become available through their triumph over a similar British expedition against Bagdad.

This British expedition stands high among the many tragedies of the War. From the opening days of 1914, Germany had encouraged the Turks in the vicinity of the ancient Holy Lands to attack the British in Egypt. Such an effort could not fail to be as disastrous to the Turks as it was profitable to Germany by holding large British forces in Egypt on the defensive. It was quite beyond Turkey's powers of organization to carry an army successfully across the deserts which separate Egypt from Asia. Twice she broke down in the attempt. Then Britain determined to block the influence of the Turks over her millions of Mohammedan subjects in Egypt and India by striking at the center of Turkey's Asiatic power. Hence, in April of 1915, with but little preliminary study or labor, she started an army to invade Mesopotamia from the South. Marching from the head of the Persian Gulf, this gallant column fought its way slowly northward up the course of the Tigris and Euphrates Rivers until by the end of November, 1915, an advance guard was within twenty miles of Bagdad. Here, however, the van was held up by a strong Turkish army and driven back upon the main British column at Kut-el-Amarna.

At Kut the Britons were surrounded and besieged by the Turks during the early months of 1916. A second British army tried to fight its way up the river valley to rescue the first. But the Turks were now in such heavy force that they blocked the way of the relieving army, and on April 29th compelled the surrender of the beleaguered troops in Kut. Some nine thousand British soldiers, mostly from India, thus became captive to the Turks. Such a surrender of an entire army had not dimmed Britain's proud record since the day of Cornwallis' surrender to Washington. The Indian soldiers captured at Kut were well treated, but of some three thousand Britons barely a thousand survived the rigors of the barbarous captivity in which they were held until the end of the War.[1]

[1] See § IX, "British Disaster at Kut," by Gen. Townshend, etc.

This impressive Turkish success, coming upon top of the triumph over Britain at the Dardanelles, was doubly disastrous. It quite convinced the Turks of their own glory; and it went far toward restoring the Asiatic tradition of their prowess. A spark now might have set the whole Moslem world in flame against the Christians.

Not until December of 1916 were the dogged Britons able to reassert themselves so far from home, and send sufficient reënforcements to their troops upon the Persian Gulf. Then these began a new advance up the marsh-covered, fever-swept Euphrates valley. Meanwhile, as we have seen, the Turks turned upon the Russians with eager dash, and swept them back into Persia. That was the last of the Russian advance. For the second time Bagdad had been successfully defended against the European invaders.

What perhaps saved the world from the added horror of a "holy war" of the Moslems in 1916 was the formation in the spring, before the Mesopotamian disasters had developed, of an independent religious government in Arabia. The submission of desert Arabia to its Turkish overlords had long been merely nominal. Moreover, the religious chieftain of the Moslem holy Arabian cities, Mecca and Medina, was regarded by many Arabs as the true head of their faith, rather than the Turkish high-priest. In June, 1916, under British encouragement, this Arab high-priest declared his independence of Turkey. His people joined him, and thus the Moslem world became divided. If Emperor William of Germany had his own usually obedient Mohammedan high-priest in Constantinople, King George of England, lord of the Empire of India, had his in Arabia. Such was the Asiatic situation in 1916.[1]

### VERDUN

In the nearer East, the Balkans and the Russian front, there was no very heavy fighting until June. In January the Serbian overthrow of the preceding year was completed by the Austrian capture of Cettinje, the last point of resistance in Montenegro, the lesser Serb state which had

[1] See § XIV, "Arab Independence Proclaimed," by King Hussein, etc.

shared Serbia's fortunes.[1] But this was but a minor step in the tremendous moves of the War. The Allied army at Salonika was not strong enough to leave its secure position; so Montenegro fell unaided. After that Russia was only too glad to snatch the breathing spell she so sorely needed; and Germany and Austria saw no profit in pursuing the stubborn Russians further through the vast empty spaces of the Russian swamps. Moreover they thought their Eastern European foes so exhausted that they might well be ignored. Hence the Central Powers turned attention to the West. Austria made ready for an attack on Italy, and Germany hurled her full strength against Verdun.

Verdun was obviously intended to be the seat of Germany's main operation of the year and of the War. She planned to break France, as she had broken the Russian front, by such a concentration of artillery as should be absolutely irresistible. Then, when she had the French fleeing from Verdun, there were in France no such vast empty spaces as had saved Russia by offering a hiding and rallying place for the defeated troops. With France crushed and Russia exhausted, Britain could soon be driven back into her island home.

The German plan for 1914 had been to win by a sudden rush; and it had been checked at the Marne. The plan for 1915 had been to win by crushing the East; and it had halfway succeeded—only that the beaten foes refused, one and all, to recognize defeat. Russia still staggered on behind her marshes; the Britons still clung to their desperate footing upon the Persian Gulf; and the French general with his beleaguered forces at Salonika delayed the complete surrender of the Balkans. The plan for 1916 turned again to the West. Germany now resolved to win by grinding France into atoms at Verdun; and this plan had at least as promising an outlook as either of the earlier ones.[2]

How near the attack came to succeeding we have already told. The Crown Prince of Germany was placed at its head,

[1] See § II, "Little Montenegro's Last Stand," by Wallace and Muskovitch.
[2] See § IV, "The First Assault on Verdun," by De Souza, Ludendorff, etc.

so that he might become a Hohenzollern hero for his countrymen. His first assault on Verdun developed suddenly on February 21st. Fort Douaumont, one of the main defenses, fell on the 25th; but the French resisted desperately and by the end of February had hurried to the spot such reënforcements as enabled them to meet the foe upon more equal terms. Huge battles were fought almost every day up to April 11th. Then came a breathing space. The Germans, staggered and dazed by a resistance as stubborn as was their attack, had to pause, to reorganize, to make new plans. Their losses had been tremendous; and their loudly vaunted attack, which was to have annihilated the foe, had carried them onward practically not at all.

Apparently, however, their High Staff could devise no better plan; for in May their assaults began again. This second series of Verdun battles lasted in full intensity for over two months; but again the French resistance proved unbreakable.[1] In July the weight of the assault decreased, and by September it had almost died away; for by this time two things had happened. On their side, the Germans, long losing faith in their Crown Prince and in the possibility of any serious Verdun success, sought excuse to abandon the too costly enterprise. The Allies on their side, knowing how the Verdun defense was shaken, endeavored to relieve it by forcing Germany to turn her attention elsewhere. Hence the month of June saw a general renewal of active warfare in many places; and by mid-July Verdun had ceased to be one of the chief centers of battle. The unsuccessful assault had cost the Germans at least half a million casualties. The defense had cost the French not quite so heavily, but they could afford these terrible losses even less than the Germans.

### THE COUNTER-ATTACKS IN THE WEST

The three main counter-assaults were that of the Italians, that of the Russians, and most tremendous of all, that of the British and French along the Somme River. Heavy fighting began first in Italy, though not from the Italian side. Austria, fresh from the conquest of little Montenegro,

[1] See § XIII, "The Climax of the Verdun Assault," by Hanotaux, Joffre, etc.

planned a spring assault on Italy to parallel the Verdun drive. But the Austrians were slower of movement than the Germans and only opened their offensive in mid-May. Attacking suddenly from the Alpine summits of the Trentino, four hundred thousand Austrian troops hammered the Italians back from the mountain heights to the edge of the Italian lakes. These, too, were anxious days for civilization. Would the western line of defense be broken here rather than in France? By June, however, the Italians, like the French at Verdun, had brought their full strength to meet the attack. The Austrian advance slowed up. By June 6th it was completely blocked. Then the Italian counter-attacks began.[1]

Cadorna, the Italian commander, had no intention of trying to fight his way across the Alps in face of a foe so strong in artillery. Contenting himself with blocking the Austrians on the Trentino front, he on August 6th launched his main attack at the head of the Adriatic, along the Isonzo River where the Italians had vainly endeavored to advance during the preceding year. The new assault was gallant, deadly, and long continued. On August 9th the city of Gorizia, the center of the Austrian defense, was carried in a great assault.[2] The Austrians were driven from one steep mountain summit after another. In the end, however, their natural defense of mountains proved too strong for the assailants. Winter found the Italians still but a few miles beyond the Isonzo River. Through all the summer and fall along this frontier more than a million men fought actively on either side without any large success for either. The sole appreciable result was the same as at Verdun, death, and desolation, and the exhaustion of the world's supplies, of men, of money, and of the treasured sources of food, the herds and farms and hoarded grains.

Similar, only in yet more stupendous measure of desolation, is the story of the Somme battle.[3] Britain by her thorough preparation in 1915 had been able by the summer

[1] See § X, "Austria's First Great Attack on Italy," by Low, etc.
[2] See § XIX, "The Storming of Gorizia," by Cadorna, Oertel, etc.
[3] See § XV, "The Battle of the Somme," by Gibbs, Prince Rupprecht, etc.

of 1916 to place in France an active army of over two million men. Their store of ammunition equaled even that of the Germans at Verdun. On July 1st this greatest British army that had ever existed began a tremendous attack upon the western front about midway between Paris and the northern coast, where once the city of Péronne had stood upon the banks of the Somme. The French in somewhat lesser numbers joined in the assault, advancing up the actual valley of the Somme, while the Britons fought along the higher ground to the north of the river.

General Haig had succeeded General French in supreme command of the British forces in December of 1915, so the Somme was Haig's battle. General Foch commanded the French. Day after day the struggle continued all through the summer. There was the usual advance at first, before the Germans gathered in sufficient numbers to resist. Then came the old deadlock. Every foot of ground was fought for. A German cartoon of the time represents the British commander as reporting "We have gained ground again to-day—just enough to make graves for the day's dead."

Here, on September 5th, the Britons sprang one of the most successful surprises of the War, the first "tank" attack. So successful were these new "moving forts," these "land cruisers," that they soon became an essential feature of armament. The Germans, dismayed by them at first, soon copied them, and found ways to meet them; and the balance of fighting strength was restored.

The Somme battle can scarcely be said to have ended. It faded out, as did the fighting on the Italian front, with the approach of winter. Up to mid-November the Britons were still doggedly attacking, and their newspapers were still recording each slight advance as a new victory. But the German line remained seemingly as firm as ever. Not until after the War did we learn from the German leaders how terribly their forces were worn down by the "Somme fighting," how anxiously they discussed ways of preventing its renewal in the next year. The total casualties of the Germans at the Somme approached three-quarters of a million men. The casualties of the British and French were even higher; since theirs was the constant attack, and since they never achieved the ultimate "breaking through" which means wholesale losses to the shattered defense.

Until the great final campaign of the War, these twin battles of Verdun and the Somme stood as the longest, the most hard fought, the most exhaustive, in human annals. Verdun also continued to exact its heavy toll of lives all through the autumn. But now it was the French who triumphantly attacked the wearied Teutons. In a series of dashing assaults the French won back almost all the ground they had lost in the spring.[1] Indeed, the worst sorrow of these awful battles lay, like all the sorrow of 1916, in that they were without decisive result. They left the main opponents about as these had stood before. The issue was still unsettled, and the contestants had still to struggle on, bleeding, gasping, reeling, ever nearer to mutual destruction and the utter downfall of the European races.

### THE RUSSIAN BETRAYAL AND RUMANIAN DOWNFALL

Turn now to the Russian counter-offensive and the second half of the year in eastern Europe. Here the operations offered a strange and striking parallel to those of 1915, with Rumania as the victim instead of Serbia. Russia, as we have seen, was somewhat recovering from her defeats of 1915; and in June of 1916 she sought to do her share toward relieving Verdun. Her most successful general, Brusiloff, was in command along the Austrian front, and he began an advance similar to those which had twice before carried him to the Hungarian border amid the peaks of the Carpathian Mountains.[2]

On a front of over two hundred miles from Poland south to the Rumanian border, Brusiloff made a sudden simultaneous advance with almost a million men. The Austrians broke before him like straw. The strong fortress city of Czernovitz was taken on June 18th. Hundreds of thousands of Austrian prisoners were captured. Before the end of July southern Galicia was again overrun, and Hun-

---

[1] See § XXIV, "The Verdun Counter-attack," by Ludendorff, etc.
[2] See § XII, "Brusiloff Breaks the Austrian Line," by Brusiloff, etc.

gary for the third time was in danger. This attack had a large share in stopping the May assault of the Austrians against Italy. They had to hurry all available forces to the east to meet the Russians.

The tale of what followed is among the blackest of the War. The Russian court had long been a strange confusion of loyal Russian nobles and selfish schemers, many of them raised to highest places by German influence. Even the Czarina, originally a German princess, was suspected of acting as a German spy. The closest military secrets constantly reached German ears. Now came one of the most dramatic and terrible triumphs of court intrigue.

Sturmer, a new Prime Minister, was appointed in Russia. He was regarded as a German tool and was afterward executed on the charge of having plotted to accomplish three things: to stop the Brusiloff attack, to make a separate Russo-German peace, and to betray neutral Rumania into German hands. Thus might Russia escape the disastrous War, and some further millions of starving serfs and their plundered Rumanian land be added to the glorious Empire of Middle Europe. Two-thirds of Sturmer's plan succeeded, but not what was to his own career the most essential third, the Russian peace.[1]

Brusiloff's offensive was blocked by sending him the wrong ammunition for his guns and by generally confusing his supplies. It is difficult to conceive Sturmer's treachery as extending beyond this, though at his trial he was also accused of actually disclosing Brusiloff's plans to the enemy. He thus caused the deaths of thousands of the unhappy people he was supposed to be governing.

His betrayal of Rumania was equally abominable. Her sympathy with the Allies had always been strong; but her lack of preparation and her exposed position in face of the united power of Austria, Bulgaria and Turkey would have made it almost suicidal for her to have entered the War at any previous period. In August of 1916, however, with Brusiloff still advancing in Galicia and taking 300,000 Austrain prisoners, Rumania might supposedly count on Rus-

[1] See § XX, "The Black Betrayal," by Milyukof, etc.

sian protection against Austria at least. Moreover, Germany had failed at Verdun; the Britons and French were holding all her attention with their advance along the Somme; and Italy was apparently winning upon the Isonzo front. Had things been all as they seemed, this might well have been the hour for Rumania to make a triumphal entry into the War. So Sturmer seized this moment to send Rumania a secret ultimatum. If she would join Russia at once and take a share in the great Brusiloff advance, Russia would lend her ammunition, and an army to protect her. If not, Russia would abandon her to the devouring maw of Middle Europe, both now and at the peace conference to follow.[1]

Rumania selected war, proclaimed it on August 27th, and launched her army in an attack on Hungary. Then came the closing of the trap. The exhausted Brusiloff fell back. Neither ammunition nor army was sent to Rumania's aid. Instead a powerful German-Austrian army, secretly ready in advance, was hurled against her as it had been against Serbia the year before. Moreover, Mackensen, the conqueror of Serbia, was placed in command against Rumania, and in addition to the army advancing against her through Hungary, he organized another composed mainly of Bulgarians. He himself led the Bulgarian army to attack Rumania from the rear, just as the Bulgarians had before attacked Serbia.[2]

In face of this overwhelming combination of force and treachery, Rumania was helpless as a babe. Her troops fought valiantly, but hopelessly. They were soon driven out of Hungary, defeated in their border mountain passes, and driven back upon Bucharest, their capital. Mackensen, advancing from the south, fought his way across the Danube to join the northern army, and Bucharest was captured on December 6th.[3]

[1] See § XXI, "Rumania joins the Allies," by Jonescu, King Ferdinand, etc.
[2] See § XXV, "Mackensen's Brilliant Rumanian Campaign," by Wollman, Mackensen, etc.
[3] See § XXVI, "Capture of Bucharest," by Queen Marie, Angelscu, etc.

Rumania's destruction, however, was never so complete as that of Serbia. The remnant of her soldiers maintained themselves in the mountain region along the Russian border where they were still in touch with Brusiloff. Then Sturmer, suspected of treason, lost his control of Russia; and early in the next year came the first Russian Revolution to sweep him and all his evil crew from power. Rumania, saved for the moment by a more genuine Russian aid, was able to make a sort of peace treaty with the Teutons, which left her some shadow of self-government.

What, now, of the Allies' army at Salonika? Could it not have saved Rumania? It made what effort it could. In August an advance from Salonika was begun; and in September the reconstructed Serbian army rushed eagerly into action upon this front. The Serbs fought their way back across the Serbian border, and set up a new Serbian government in the town of Monastir.[1] But the Bulgarian and Austrian resistance to this Salonika advance was strong; and conditions in Greece soon checked it altogether.

Greece, the nominal owner of the port of Salonika, was in much the same position as Rumania. Her sympathies with the Allies had been strong; but the fate of Serbia naturally terrified her. When Rumania entered the War, Greece almost entered too. Her Prime Minister, Venizelos, had for years been keen for her to take this vigorous course; but her king, Constantine, was pro-German, was indeed of German descent, and had held her at peace. Now the two factions flared into open contest; and Venizelos, driven from the capital, set up a pro-Ally Greek Government at Salonika.[2] For the moment the Allies had their hands full in supporting him. They could not possibly advance to an attack leaving revolution in their rear.

Thus in reviewing the whole European theater of the War for 1916, we see only the one struggle that could be called other than indecisive. That was the Rumanian campaign. The Middle-Europe Empire had been increased by

[1] See § XXV, "Serbia Reborn," by Price.
[2] See § XXII, "Revolution in Greece," by Duggan, King Constantine, etc.

the crushing of this one more Balkan state; German prestige had been augmented by one more victorious campaign; and Germany's source of supplies had been slightly extended by the capture of Rumania's oil wells and her grain fields.

### THE WAR AT SEA

On the seas this was the year of the great Jutland battle, in size the foremost naval combat of the world.[1] Dreadnaughts fought with super-dreadnaughts; and huge steel cruisers, once the pride of their nations, proved too feeble for the giant fray. Yet this combat, too, was indecisive of result. It left affairs where it had found them. Each side lost several ships and many valuable lives of expert naval men. Three huge British ships were blown up; and Germany, hiding her own losses, boasted of having won a mighty victory. But the end of the fight, after a day and night of thunderous battle, was only that the Germans returned to their harbors, keeping sheltered there as before, and the Britons continued in control of the North Sea.

So too the German U-boat campaign continued without definite result. It was exhaustive, but not sufficiently so to be in any way decisive in its influence on the War. America's persistent agitation of the *Lusitania* question led in April, after a year of patient discussion, to President Wilson's refusal to await further evasions. He sent Germany what amounted to an ultimatum.[2] Facing this, Germany promised to abandon the methods of blind attack which had menaced American lives. For a time she kept her word, and the U-boat became consequently less destructive.

German ingenuity, however, carried her U-boat construction forward to two points which would have been much noted achievements in time of peace. She made her U-boats so much bigger and stronger that they could carry heavy guns, became in fact "cruisers" above water. In this fashion they were able to defend themselves against merchant ships and even to seize and search them, thus extending the possi-

[1] See § XI, "The Mightiest of all Naval Fights," by von Capelle, Jellicoe, etc.

[2] See § VI, "Germany Yields to America's Ultimatum," by Wilson and von Jagow.

bilities of a legitimate U-boat war on commerce. More impressive still was the building of the *Deutschland*, a submarine so big that it crossed the Atlantic and appeared as a merchant ship upon the American coast.[1]  A second similar submarine followed the *Deutschland;* but the tireless British navy soon put an end to even these secret voyages.

Naval bitterness between Britain and Germany was still further increased during the year by the execution of Captain Fryatt.  He was a British merchant-ship captain who had escaped a German submarine by boldly ramming at it.  The Germans pointed to the fact that under International Law a merchant ship was forbidden to resist capture after a search.  This law had been established on the principle that men-of-war must not destroy merchant ships without investigation and preservation of the crew, and that therefore a ship which submitted to the investigation must not suddenly burst into treacherous attack.  But by one of those extraordinary twists of the German reasoning power under stress of passion, the Germans argued that this law should still have held Captain Fryatt from fighting their U-boats, though the U-boats had already rejected the basis on which the law was built.  They had left the merchant skippers no alternative except successful resistance or death.  Now they declared that resistance should also mean death.  That is, they captured Captain Fryatt on a later voyage, held a form of trial, and executed him.  To Britons this seemed a far more evil thing than even the sinking of the *Lusitania*.  To condemn a man for defending his own life!  The Germans could have discovered no surer way to add to the indignation of neutrals, and to have made Britain fight them to the death.[2]

### GERMAN INTRIGUE AND AMERICAN ANXIETY

Two other doubtful successes of German intrigue of the year were the Sinn Fein (shin fane) Revolt in Ireland, and the Mexican troubles of the United States.  The members of the Sinn Fein were encouraged to revolt by promises of

[1] See § XVIII, "The First Submarine to Cross the Atlantic," by Captain Koenig, etc.
[2] See § XVIII, "Execution of Captain Fryatt," by Balfour, etc.

German aid, and for a week they held control of Dublin.
But the German aid failed them, and the mass of the Irish
people refused to link hands with the German betrayers of
civilization. So upon the whole, Britain's difficulties were
rather lessened than increased by the easy suppression of the
revolt.[1]

The Mexican trouble culminated in a United States
army being gathered on the Mexican border under Generals Funston and Pershing. Thus the army men received
a training which helped prepare them for the Great War.
So far as the German intent went, of giving the United
States such trouble at home as would distract her attention
from the larger war, Mexico was far too feeble to be ever
seriously regarded in America as an opponent.[2]

On the contrary, the ever-deepening interest and anxiety
of the United States as to the Great War can be traced
through all this disastrous year. Not only did she deliver
her ultimatum in the submarine dispute, but she made frequent protests against the mistreatment of the Belgians.
She declared her readiness to aid in forming a League of
Nations; and in December President Wilson made a formal
effort to bring the exhausted foes together for an honorable
peace. Germany unhappily was still too hopeful of victory
to be willing either to admit her crimes or to abandon her
spoils. So the seemingly hopeless War dragged on into 1917.

### THE CHANGING LEADERSHIP

The strife in the next year was to be resumed with Amer-
ica's aid and under leaders almost wholly new. Odd indeed
in its completeness was the shifting of the individuals in the
War command during 1916, and especially in its closing
months. Britain's commander on the battlefield, General
French, gave way to General Haig at the close of 1915.
Then Britain lost her great organizing hero warrior, Lord
Kitchener. He was drowned June 7, 1916, while voyaging
to Russia to lend her the aid of his power and prestige.
Britain's war cabinet also became almost wholly changed,

[1] See § VIII, "The Sinn-Fein Uprising," by Pearse, Casement, etc.
[2] See § V, "Armed Intervention in Mexico," by Funston, Carranza, etc.

the old-time leaders, both Liberal and Conservative, gradually yielding before the new Democratic leader, Lloyd George. He was made Prime Minister in December of 1916, with his former opponents accepting positions under him in a coalition government.

In France in 1916, the heroic and well-loved minister of war, General Gallieni, the defender of Paris, died. Marshal Joffre, the most prominent figure among Ally leaders during the first two years of war, was retired in December. The "Radical" Premier, M. Briand, though still supported by the masses of the people, had repeatedly to meet the protest of Clemenceau and other leaders who felt Briand too lax in forcing on the war preparations. Early in 1917 he too was driven to resign; and in November, 1917, Clemenceau himself took the helm, "the tiger of France." He was a fierce and partly discredited old man of seventy, disliked by the Radicals, who were still in the majority, but accepted by every one as a fighter and a devoted lover of France.

In Italy Prime Minister Salandra, who had led his country into the War, was also driven to resign in 1916. He had lost the confidence of his impatient people, because of the continued ill-success of their arms. His cabinet was replaced in June by a coalition ministry headed by an aged, honored, and trusted scholar, Signor Boselli. Other coalition ministries soon superseded that of Boselli. Thus the War was carried beyond 1916 by new and strangely composite Ally governments, by leaders who had been farthest from men's thoughts when war began.

Equally complete was the 1916 shift of leadership within the Central Empires. The outworn but still vigorous Austrian Emperor, Franz Josef, died rather suddenly on November 21st, at the age of 88. He was succeeded by his grand-nephew, the Emperor Charles I., son of a younger brother of that Archduke Franz whose murder at Serajevo had been made the pretext for the War. The Prime Minister, not of Austro-Hungary but of Austria itself, Count Sturgkh, was shot by a Socialistic Austrian in October; and in December the new Emperor dismissed Sturgkh's successor and appointed a Prime Minister of his own choosing.

This was Count Clam-Martinitz, a court favorite, but of Slav ancestry, and hence presumably opposed to the domination of either Germans or Hungarians. The Minister of War of the older generation, General Krobatin, was dropped soon afterward. Only the Hungarian leaders, Burián and Tisza, remained from the previous régime.

In Germany von Tirpitz, the champion of ruthless U-boat warfare, was temporarily dismissed from the cabinet in March, though recalled to power with the reacceptance of his plans the following year. Von Jagow, the Minister of Foreign Affairs, was superseded by Alfred Zimmermann, soon to become of equal ill-repute in his dealings with America. Far more wide-reaching than these minor changes was the fact that both the Kaiser and his son, after the Verdun failure, were eclipsed in popular esteem by von Hindenburg, the victor over Russia. On August 29, 1916, Hindenburg was made "Chief-of-Staff"; and soon afterward the Kaiser even bent his pride so far as to confer upon the new Chief-of-Staff the rank previously reserved solely for himself, that of Commander-in-Chief of all the German armies. Moreover, Hindenburg was allowed to name as head of his own staff, his chosen lieutenant, the sternly able General von Ludendorff. The latter remained Germany's real organizer of the War until its close.

Under Ludendorff and Hindenburg, the army chiefs of Germany assumed complete control of the nation. Even the smooth and pertinacious Imperial Chancellor, Bethmann-Hollweg, was compelled by them to resign in 1917 and his place was filled by one puppet chancellor after another. It is impressive indeed to note that not one of the men who had led the Central Powers into the War remained to lead them out of it—save only the Kaiser himself; and he had sunk to be a mere querulous figurehead. The War of 1916 had grown too terrible to be controlled by any vain poseur or any self-seeking politician. Verdun and the Somme could be survived only by the strong, by those who could endure all things, grim chieftains such as the once unknown von Ludendorff, and the once disgraced von Hindenburg.

# BELGIUM'S MARTYRDOM

## THE ENSLAVEMENT OF LABOR

### OCTOBER, 1915-NOVEMBER, 1916

BRAND WHITLOCK            CARDINAL MERCIER
BARON VON BISSING
APPEAL OF THE BELGIAN WORKMEN
APPEAL OF THE BELGIAN WOMEN

Conquest, plunder, slaughter! These the Belgians had suffered in the first year of the War. But from the time of the German decree of October 12, 1915, a disaster yet more complete began to threaten them. This decree declared that the German military commanders might compel the Belgians to work in any way the military wanted. It was the beginning of possible enslavement. Such compulsory labor did not, however, become common until 1916. Then it gradually increased in severity. At first the people were set to tasks in their own neighborhood and were paid for the work. Next, they were ordered to do war work, aiding the German army against their own countrymen. Next, refusals to work were punished by deportation to Germany and enforced prison labor there. Next, the enforced labor was paid for in such absurdly small sums as made it practically unpaid slavery. Finally, in October of 1916 the deportations to Germany became wholesale. People of all classes were carried off and compelled by force to toil and starve and perish absolutely as slaves.

There arose a storm of neutral protest, to which Germany gave but scant attention. Her rulers blandly asserted that they were engaged in a work of charity, that the deported Belgians would be much better off in Germany. But the tales of such exhausted survivors as ultimately regained their homes show not only how badly they were treated but how utterly they were forced into the degradation of unquestioning submission to their taskmaster's will.

General von Bissing, the German governor, here states the German side of the matter, in answer to the celebrated protests of Cardinal Mercier, the Roman Catholic Archbishop of Malines. The neutral view is first given by the United States Minister, Brand Whitlock. Then the Belgians are summoned to speak for themselves in two noted protests, the first by the Belgian workmen, the second by the shamed and agonized women of Belgium.     C. F. H.

## BY BRAND WHITLOCK

I HAVE had it in mind, and I might say, on my conscience, since the Germans began to deport Belgian workmen early in November of 1916, to prepare for the Department a detailed report on this latest instance of brutality, but there have been so many obstacles in the way of obtaining evidence on which a calm and judicious opinion could be based, and one is so overwhelmed with the horror of the thing itself, that it has been, and even now is, difficult to write calmly and justly about it. I have had to content myself with the fragmentary dispatches I have from time to time sent to the Department and with doing what I could, little as that can be, to alleviate the distress that this gratuitous cruelty has caused the population of this unhappy land.

In order to understand fully the situation it is necessary to go back to the autumn of 1914. At the time we were organizing the relief work, the Comité National—the Belgian relief organization that collaborates with the Commission for Relief in Belgium—proposed an arrangement by which the Belgian Government should pay to its own employees left in Belgium, and other unemployed men besides, the wages they had been accustomed to receive. The Belgians wished to do this both for humanitarian and patriotic purposes; they wished to provide the unemployed with the means of livelihood, and, at the same time, to prevent their working for the Germans. I refused to be connected in any way with this plan, and told the Belgian committee that it had many possibilities of danger; that not only would it place a premium on idleness, but that it would ultimately exasperate the Germans. However, the policy was adopted, and has been continued in practice, and on the rolls of the Comité National have been borne the names of hundreds of thousands—some 700,000, I believe—of idle men receiving this dole, distributed throughout the communes.

The presence of these unemployed, however, was a constant temptation to German cupidity. Many times they sought to obtain the lists of the *chômeurs,* but were always foiled by the claim that under the guarantees covering the relief work, the records of the Comité National and its various suborganizations were immune. Rather than risk any interruption of the *ravitaillement,* for which, while loath to own any obligation to America, the Germans have always been grateful, since it has had the effect of keeping the population calm, the authorities never pressed the point, other than with the burgomasters of the communes.

Finally, however, the military party, always brutal and with an astounding ignorance of public opinion and of moral sentiment, determined to put these idle men to work.

In August of 1916 von Hindenburg was appointed to the supreme command. He is said to have criticised von Bissing's policy as too mild; there was a quarrel; von Bissing went to Berlin to protest, threatened to resign, but did not. He returned, and a German official here said that Belgium would now be subjected to a more terrible régime, would learn what war was. The prophecy has been vindicated.

The deportations began in October in the étape, at Ghent and at Bruges. The policy spread; the rich industrial districts of Hainaut, the mines and steel works about Charleroi were next attacked; next they were seizing men in Brabant, even in Brussels, despite some indications, and even predictions of the civil authorities, that the policy was about to be abandoned.

Their seizures in Brussels were made evidently with much greater care than in the provinces, with more regard for the appearances. There was no public announcement of the intention to deport, but suddenly certain men in towns whose names were on the list of *chômeurs* received summonses notifying them to report at one of the railway stations on a given day and penalties were fixed for failure to respond to the summons, and there was printed on the card an offer of employment by the German Government, either in Germany or Belgium.

On the first day, out of about 1,500 men ordered to present themselves at the Gare du Midi, about 750 responded. These were examined by German physicians and 300 were taken. There was no disorder, a large force of mounted Uhlans keeping back the crowds and barring access to the station to all but those who had been summoned to appear. The Commission for Relief in Belgium had secured permission to give to each deported man a loaf of bread, and some of the communes provided warm clothing for those who had none, and in addition a small financial allowance.

As by one of the ironies of life, the winter had been more excessively cold than Belgium has ever known it, and while many of those who presented themselves were adequately protected against the cold, many of them were without overcoats. The men shivering from cold and fear, the parting from weeping wives and children, the barriers of brutal Uhlans, all this made the scene a pitiable and distressing one.

The rage, the terror, and despair excited by this measure all over Belgium were beyond anything we had witnessed since the day the Germans poured into Brussels. The delegates of the Commission for Relief in Belgium, returning to Brussels, told the most distressing stories of the scenes of cruelty and sorrow attending the seizures. And daily, hourly, almost, since that time, appalling stories have been related by Belgians coming to the legation. It is impossible for us to verify them, first because it is necessary for us to exercise all possible tact in dealing with the subject at all, and, secondly, because there is no means of communication between the *Occupations Gebiet* and the *Etappen Gebiet*.

Transportation everywhere in Belgium is difficult, the vicinal railways scarcely operating any more because of the lack of oil, while all the horses have been taken. The people who are forced to go from one village to another must do so on foot or in vans drawn by the few miserable horses that are left. The wagons of the breweries, the one institution that the Germans have scrupulously respected, are hauled by oxen.

The well-known tendency of sensational reports to exaggerate themselves, especially in time of war, and in a situation like that existing here, with no newspapers to serve as a daily clearing house for all the rumors that are as avidly believed as they are eagerly repeated, should, of course, be considered, but even if a modicum of all that is told is true, there still remains enough to stamp this deed as one of the foulest that history records.

I am constantly in receipt of reports from all over Belgium that tend to bear out the stories one constantly hears of brutality and cruelty. A number of men sent back to Mons were in a dying condition, many of them tubercular. At Malines and at Antwerp returned men died, their friends asserting that they had been victims of neglect and cruelty, of cold, of exposure, of hunger.

I have had requests from the Burgomasters of ten communes from La Louvière, asking that permission be obtained to send to the deported men in Germany packages of food similar to those that are being sent to prisoners of war. Thus far the German authorities have refused to permit this except in special instances, and returning Belgians claim that even when such packages are received they are used by the camp authorities only as another means of coercing them to sign the agreements to work.

It is said that in spite of the liberal salary promised those who would sign voluntarily no money has as yet been received in Belgium from workmen in Germany.

One interesting result of the deportations remains to be noted, a result that once more places in relief the German capacity for blundering almost as great as the German capacity for cruelty.

They have dealt a mortal blow to any prospect they may ever have had of being tolerated by the population of Flanders; in tearing away from nearly every humble home in the land a husband and a father or a son and brother, they have lighted a fire of hatred that will never go out; they have brought home to every heart in the land, in a way that will impress its horror indelibly on the memory of three generations, a realization of what German methods mean, not, as with the early atrocities in the heat of passion and the first lust of war, but by one of those deeds that make one despair of the future of the human race, a deed coldly planned, studiously matured, and deliberately and systematically executed, a deed so cruel that German soldiers are said to have wept in its execution and so monstrous that even German officers are now said to be ashamed.

BY CARDINAL DESIRÉE MERCIER

MALINES, November 7, 1916.

Every day the military authorities deport from Belgium into Germany thousands of inoffensive citizens to oblige them there to perform forced labor.

As early as October 19th we sent to the Governor General a protest, a copy of which was handed to the representatives of the Holy See, of Spain, the United States, and Holland, in Brussels, but the Governor General replied to it that nothing could be done.

At the time of our protest the orders of the occupying power threatened only the unemployed; to-day every able-bodied man is carried off, pellmell, assembled in freight cars, and carried off to unknown parts, like a herd of slaves. The enemy proceeds by regions. Vague rumors had come to our ears that arrests had been made in Tournau, Ghent, and Alost, but we were not aware of the conditions under which they had been made. Between October 24th and November 2nd deportations took place in the region of Mons, Quievrain, Saint Guislain, Jemappes, in bunches of 800 to 1,200 men a day. The next and the following days they were extended to the Arrondissement of Nivelles. Here is a specimen of the announcement concerning the proceedings:

"By order of the Kreischef every male person over 17 years old shall present himself, Place Saint Paul, in Nivelles, on November 8, 1916, at 8 o'clock (Belgian time), 9 o'clock (Central time), bringing with him his identification card and eventually his card from the Meldeamt.

"Only small hand baggage is permitted.

"Those not presenting themselves will be forcibly deported into Germany, and will besides be liable to a heavy fine and to long imprisonment.

"Ecclesiastics, physicians, lawyers, and teachers are exempt from this order.

"The Mayors will be held responsible for the proper execution of this order, which must be brought immediately to the knowledge of the inhabitants."

Between the announcement and the deportation there is an interval of only twenty-four hours.

Under pretext of public works to be performed on Belgian soil, the occupying power had attempted to obtain from the communities the lists of workingmen out of work. Most of the communities proudly refused.

Three decrees from the General Government prepared the way for the execution which is in force to-day.

Under date of August 15, 1915, a first decree imposes, under penalty of imprisonment and fine, forced work on the idle, but adds that the work is to be executed in Belgium, and that noncompliance will be adjudged by Belgian tribunals.

A second decree, dated May 2, 1916, reserves the right of the German authorities to supply work to the idle, and threatens a fine of three years' imprisonment and 20,000 marks imposable on anybody executing or ordering to be executed work not approved of by the General Government.

Under the same decree, the right to judge infractions which had remained with the Belgian tribunals passed from the Belgian to the German tribunals.

A third decree, dated May 13, 1916, "authorizes the governors, the military commanders, and the chiefs of arrondissements to order that the unemployed be conducted by force to the places where they must work." This was already forcible working, although in Belgium.

Now it is no longer a question of forcible working in Belgium, but in Germany, and for the benefit of the Germans.

To give an appearance of plausibility to these violent measures, the occupying power insisted in the German press, both in Germany and Belgium, on these two pretexts: the unemployed constitute a danger to public order and a burden on official benevolence.

To this we replied in a letter addressed to the Governor General and to the head of the Political Department on October 16th, as follows:

"You are well aware that public order is in no wise threatened and that all influences, moral and civil, would support you spontaneously were it in danger. The unemployed are not a burden on official benevolence; it is not from your funds that they receive assistance."

In his reply the Governor General no longer urges these two first considerations, but he alleges that "doles to the unemployed, from whatever source they may come at present, must finally be a charge upon our finances, and that it is

the duty of a good administrator to lighten such charges";
he adds that "prolonged unemployment would cause our
workmen to lose their technical proficiency, and that in the
time of peace to come they would be useless to industry."

True, there were other ways in which our finances might
have been protected. We might have been spared those war
levies which have now reached the sum of one billion francs,
and are still mounting up at the rate of forty millions a
month; we might have been spared those requisitions in kind,
which amount to several thousands of millions, and are ex-
hausting us.

There are other ways of providing for the maintenance
of professional skill among our workpeople, such as leaving
to Belgian industry its machinery and accessories, its raw materials, and its manufactured goods, which have passed from
Belgium into Germany. And it is neither to the quarries nor
to the lime kilns to which the Germans themselves declare
our specialists will go to complete their professional education.

The naked truth is that every deported workman is
another soldier for the German army. He will take the
place of a German workman, who will be made into a soldier. Thus the situation which we denounce to the civilized
world may be reduced to these terms: Four hundred thousand workmen have been thrown out of work by no fault of
their own, and largely on account of the régime of the occupation. Sons, husbands, and fathers of families, they bear
their unhappy lot without murmuring, respectful of public
order; national solidarity provides their most pressing wants;
by dint of unselfish thrift and self-denial they escape extreme
destitution, and they await with dignity and in a mutual
affection which our national sorrows have intensified, the
end of our common ordeal.

Groups of soldiers introduced themselves forcibly in the
homes of these people, tearing the young people out of the
arms of their parents, the husband from his wife, the father
from his children; at the point of the bayonet they block the
entrances to the homes, preventing wives and mothers from
rushing out to say a last farewell to them; they align the cap-

tives in groups of forty or fifty and push them forcibly into freight cars; the locomotive is under steam, and as soon as a trainload is ready, an officer gives the signal and they depart. Thus are another thousand Belgians reduced to slavery, without previous trial, condemned to the penalty which comes next in cruelty to the death penalty—deportation. They do not know how long their exile is going to last, neither do they know where they are going. All they know is that their work will benefit the enemy. Several of them have been brought to sign—by coercion or by threats—an engagement which their oppressors dare to call "voluntary."

While they certainly take the unemployed, they also take a large number in the proportion of one-quarter for the Arrondissement of Mons—of men who were never out of work and who belong to diversified professions—butchers, bakers, tailors, brewery workers, electricians, farmers; they even take the youngest men, college and university students, or young men from other high schools.

This in spite of the fact that two high authorities of the German Empire had formally guaranteed the liberty of our compatriots.

The day after the capitulation of Antwerp the frightened populace asked itself what would become of the Belgians of military age or those which would arrive at that age before the end of the siege. Baron von Huene, Military Governor of Antwerp, authorized me to reassure in his name the frightened parents. However, as rumors were running that in Antwerp, Liege, Namur, and Charleroi young men had been seized and forcibly carried off to Germany, I asked Governor von Huene to confirm to me in writing the verbal guarantees which he had given me. He replied that the rumors pertaining to deportations were without foundation, and he gave me without hesitancy the written declaration which was read on Sunday, October 18, 1914, in all the parochial churches of the Arrondissement of Antwerp: "Young men need have no fear of being carried off to Germany, either for enrollment in the army or for forcible employment."

Immediately after the arrival of Baron von der Goltz in the capacity of Governor General at Brussels, I went to ask him to ratify the guarantees given by Governor von Huene to the Province of Antwerp extending them to the whole country without any time limit. The Governor General retained my petition in order to consider it at his leisure. The following day he was good enough to come in person to Malines to express his approval and in the presence of two aides de camp and of my private secretary to confirm the promise that the liberty of the Belgian citizens would be respected.

In my letter of October 16th last to Baron von Bissing after reminding him of the undertaking given by his predecessor, I concluded: "Your Excellency will understand how painful would be the burden of responsibility that I have incurred toward families if the confidence they placed in you through me and at my earnest entreaty should be so lamentably disappointed."

The Governor General replied: "The employment of the Belgian unemployed in Germany, which has only been initiated after two years of war, differs essentially from the captivity of men fit for military service. Moreover, the measure is not related to the conduct of the war, properly speaking, but it is determined by social and economic causes."

As if the word of an honest man were terminable at the end of a year or two! As if the declaration confirmed in 1914 did not explicitly exclude both military operations and forced labor! As if, in fine, every Belgian workman who takes the place of a German workman did not enable the latter to fill a gap in the German army!

We, the shepherds of these sheep who are torn from us by brutal force, full of anguish at the thought of the moral and religious isolation in which they are about to languish, impotent witnesses of the grief and terror in the numerous homes shattered or threatened, appeal to all souls, believers or unbelievers, in allied countries, in neutral countries, and even in enemy countries, who have a respect for human dignity.

When Cardinal Lavigerie embarked on his anti-slavery campaign, Pope Leo XIII., as he blessed his mission, remarked: "Opinion is more than ever the queen of the world.

It is on this you must work. You will only conquer by means of opinion."

May Divine Providence deign to inspire all who have any authority, all who are masters of speech and pen, to rally around our humble Belgian flag for the abolition of European slavery.

May human conscience triumph over all sophisms and remain steadfastly faithful to the great precept of St. Ambrose: Honor above everything! *Nihil præferendum honestati!*

In the name of the Belgian Bishops,

D. J. (Cardinal) MERCIER,
Archbishop of Malines.

BY GOVERNOR VON BISSING

BRUSSELS, November 23, 1916.

Most Honored Cardinal:

I acknowledge receipt of your honored letter, dated November 10th, and of the manuscript letter dated November 15th, concerning the delay in delivery. This is the answer which I have to give:

Your Eminence wrote to me on October 19th last requesting that the utilization of Belgian unemployed in Germany should come to an end. In my answer dated October 28th, I have, in spite of my appreciation of your point of view in the matter, indicated the reasons and the ideas which have inspired the decisions of the occupying power with relation to the question of labor. These decisions were not arbitrary or hastily taken without sufficient consideration for the difficulties of the problem; they were the outcome of ripe reflection bearing on the circumstances and the necessity recognized as unavoidable.

The extensive unemployment which prevails in Belgium is a great social evil, and the employment of idle Belgians in Germany brings them great benefit. I said to your Eminence, on my arrival in Belgium, that I wanted to heal the wounds inflicted by the war upon the Belgian people; the recent measures are not in the least in contradiction with this declaration. I must also consider as a misrepresentation of facts the way your Eminence sets aside the many and often successful efforts which I have made to revive Belgium's economic life with the remark that, on the contrary, unemployment has been artificially created.

Regarding the importation of raw materials into Belgium and the exportation of manufactured articles, England has made unacceptable conditions. There were some time ago negotiations between neutral and Belgian organizations on this question; to dwell on them would lead me too far. I can only repeat here that the present regrettable circumstances are the result, fundamentally, of England's policy of isolation, just as the seizure by us of all raw material was only, after all, a forced consequence of the same policy.

I must also firmly maintain that the occupation affords the country, from the economic point of view, all the advantages which can be provided, considering the conditions enforced on us by England.

In the execution of the measures taken concerning the unemployed, my administration has met with a series of difficulties which cause some inconvenience to the population. All this might have been avoided if the communal authorities had made their execution more simple and more effective by their attitude toward them. Under the present circumstances, we are obliged to use a more involved procedure, into which a wider circle of people are necessarily drawn.

Measures, however, have been taken in order to avoid mistakes as much as possible. Some definite classes of professions have been exempted beforehand from submitting to control, and the individual claims, if they are well founded, will be either immediately considered or submitted to further examination.

Your Eminence will understand from what is stated above that it is impossible to comply with the desire concerning the stoppage of the measures which have been adopted, and that, in spite of the difficulties which we have met, their execution is pursued in the interest of all.

BY CARDINAL MERCIER

November 29, 1916.

To the Governor General, Sir:

The letter which your Excellency did me the honor to write to me, under date of November 23rd, is a disappointment to me. In various circles, which I had reason to believe were correctly informed, it was said, your Excellency, that you had felt it your duty to protest to the highest authorities of the empire against the measures which you were constrained to apply in Belgium. I counted on at least a delay in the application of these measures, while they were being submitted to fresh examination, and also on some relaxation of the rigor with which they are applied.

And now, your Excellency, without replying one word to any of the arguments by which I established the illegal and anti-social character of the condemnation of the Belgian working classes to forced labor and to deportation, you confine yourself to repeating, in your telegram of November 23rd, the very text of your letter of October 26th. These two letters are, really, identical in matter and almost in word.

On the other hand, the recruiting of the so-called unemployed continues, generally without any regard for the observations of the local authorities. Several reports which I have in hand prove that the clergy are brutally thrust aside, burgomasters and town councilors reduced to silence; the recruiters then find themselves face to face with unknown men, among whom they arbitrarily make their choice. There are abundant examples to prove this statement. I will give two recent ones, chosen from a quantity of others which I hold at the disposal of your Excellency.

On November 21st recruiting began in the commune of Kersbeek-Miscom. From the 1,325 inhabitants of this commune the recruiters took away altogether, without any distinction of social position or profession, farmers' sons, men who were supporting aged and infirm parents, fathers of families who left wives and families in misery, each of them as necessary to his family as its daily bread. Two families found themselves deprived each of four sons at once.

Among ninety-four deportees there were only two unemployed.

In the region of Aerschot recruiting began on November 23rd; at Rillaer, at Gebrede, at Rotselaer, young men, supporting their widowed mothers; farmers at the head of large families (one of these, who is over 50 years of age, has ten children working on the land), who possess cattle and have never touched a penny of public money, were taken away by force in spite of all their protestations. In the little commune of Rillaer they actually took twenty-five boys of 17.

Your Excellency wished that the communal councils should become the accomplices of this odious recruiting. By their legal situation and by reason of conscience, they could not do so. But they could have advised the recruiters and are entitled to do so. The priests, who know the working people better than any one else, might have been of the utmost assistance to the recruiters. Why is their help refused?

At the end of your letter, your Excellency, you remind me that men belonging to liberal professions are not interfered with. If only the unemployed were removed I could understand this exception. But if all able-bodied men continue to be enrolled indiscriminately the exception is unjustifiable. It would be iniquitous to make the whole weight of the deportations fall upon the working classes. The middle classes must have their part in the sacrifice, however cruel it may be, and just because it is cruel, that the occupying power imposes on the nation. A great many members of my clergy have asked me to beg for them a place in the van of the persecuted. I register their offer and submit it to you with pride.

I would wish to believe that the authorities of the empire have not said their last word. They will think of our undeserved sorrows, of the reprobation of the civilized world, of the judgment of history, and of the chastisement of God.

### THE APPEAL OF THE BELGIAN WORKMEN
This Proclamation was sent out by the Belgian Labor Unions in 1916

Workers,—In the name of the international bonds that unite all workmen, the working classes of Belgium—threatened, without exception, with slavery, deportation, and forced labor for the enemy's gain—send to the working classes in other lands a supreme appeal.

Germany, as you know, attacked and terrorized Belgium in 1914 for having defended her right to neutrality and her faith and honor.

Germany has been martyrizing Belgium. She has from that moment onwards turned the land into a prison: the frontiers are armed against Belgians like a battle front. . . . All our constitutional liberties have been abolished. There is no longer safety anywhere; the life of our citizens is at the mercy of the policeman,—arbitrary, limitless, pitiless. . . . Belgian industrial idleness has been the creation of the Germans, maintained by them for their own profit.[1] To these 500,000 unemployed they have for the last month been saying: "Either you will sign a contract to work for Germany, or you will be reduced to slavery." In either case, it means exile, deportation, forced labor in the interests of the enemy, and against the interests of our country: formidable punishments, the cruellest ever invented by tyranny for the punishment of crimes—and what *are* the crimes alleged? . . . On the western front, Belgian workmen—your brothers and ours—are being forced to dig trenches, to build aviation camps, to fortify the German lines, and when the victims, in spite of everything, are firm in their refusal to take part in work forbidden by International Law, they are starved and beaten into illness, wounded, and sometimes even *killed*.

In Germany, they are turned on to work in mines, and at lime-kilns, quite regardless of their age, profession, or trade. Youths of seventeen, old men of seventy, are deported in haphazard masses. *Is not this a revival of ancient Slavery with all its horrors?* Do you know, brothers, what

---

[1] By levying on Belgium a war contribution which exceeded $200,-000,000—by transporting to Germany food, merchandise and various products to the value of more than $1,000,000,000—by seizing and dispatching to their own country the greater portion of raw material, machines and accessories—by issuing threatening edicts to prevent localities from using the unemployed on their own important works of public utility.

the Germans throw to their victims by way of pay? **Thirty pfennigs (six cents) a day!**

Workers: *Never forget that the soldiers who are acting as the torturers of our Belgian workmen are themselves German workers!*

In the depths of our distress, we count on you. It is for you to act! For ourselves, even if brute force succeeds for the moment in reducing our bodies to servitude, we shall never give our consent.

A final word: Whatever tortures we may undergo, we do not wish for Peace except with the independence of our country and the triumph of justice.

THE WORKMEN OF BELGIUM.

### THE APPEAL OF THE BELGIUM WOMEN

This appeal signed by many women's societies, and individual women of Brussels, was sent to the U. S. Minister, Mr. Brand Whitlock, on November 18, 1916.

From the depths of our well of misery our supplication rises to you.

In addressing ourselves to you, we denounce to your Government, as well as to our sisters, the women of the nation which you represent in our midst, the criminal abuse of force of which our unhappy and defenseless people is a victim.

Since the beginning of this atrocious war we have looked on impotently and with our hearts torn with every sorrow at terrible events which put our civilization back into the ages of the barbarian hordes.

Mr. Minister, the crime which is now being committed under your eyes, namely, the deportation of thousands of men compelled to work on enemy soil against the interests of their country, can not find any shadow of excuse on the ground of military necessity, for it constitutes a violation by force of a sacred right of human conscience.

Whatever may be the motive it can not be admitted that citizens may be compelled to work directly or indirectly *for* the enemy *against* their brothers who are fighting.

The Convention of The Hague has consecrated this principle.

Nevertheless, the occupying power is forcing thousands of men to this monstrous extremity, which is contrary to morals and international law, both these men who have already been taken to Germany and those who to-morrow will undergo the same fate, if from the outside, from neutral Europe and the United States, no help is offered.

Oh! The Belgian women have also known how to carry out their duty in the hour of danger; they have not weakened the courage of the soldiers of honor by their tears.

They have bravely given to their country those whom they loved. . . . The blood of mothers is flowing on the battlefields.

Those who are taken away to-day do not go to perform a glorious duty. They are slaves in chains who, in a dark exile, threatened by hunger, prison, death, will be called upon to perform the most odious work—service to the enemy against the fatherland.

The mothers can not stand by while such an abomination is taking place without making their voices heard in protest.

They are not thinking of their own sufferings, their own moral torture, the abandonment and the misery in which they are to be placed with their children.

They address you in the name of the inalterable rights of honor and conscience.

It has been said that women are "all powerful suppliants."

We have felt authorized by this saying, Mr. Minister, to extend our hands to you and to address to your country a last appeal.

We trust that in reading these lines you will feel at each word the unhappy heartbeats of the Belgian women and will find in your broad and humane sympathy imperative reasons for intervention.

Only the united will of the neutral peoples energetically expressed can counterbalance that of the German authorities.

This assistance which the neutral nations can and, therefore, ought to lend us, will it be refused to the oppressed Belgians?

# LITTLE MONTENEGRO'S LAST STAND

## THE AUSTRIANS CAPTURE ITS CAPITAL, CETTINJE

### JANUARY 13, 1916

**EDGAR WALLACE**                    **LAZARE MUSKOVITCH**

The little state of Montenegro, whose name means the Black Mountain, might have remained neutral on its stormy mountain heights;
but its people were Serbs, and they loyally cast in their lot with
Serbia from the beginning of the War. Hence when Serbia was
crushed at the end of 1915, an Austrian army under General Koevess
at once turned upon Montenegro. Its tiny army of thirty thousand
men was overwhelmed in a desperate battle in the Tara valley at
the beginning of January, and the last remaining resistance was from
the garrison on Mount Lovcen, a supposedly impregnable fortress
overlooking the capital, Cettinje. Lovcen, however, fell easily before the Austrian guns; indeed, the despairing Montenegrin royal
family had already begun negotiations with Austria. With Lovcen
gone, the capital had then no choice except to surrender.

The sturdy old King Nicholas then found the Austrian terms too
hard to bear. He fled with his court to Italy; and a temporary government patched up a peace with Austria. Many of the "Black Moun-
taineers," however, refused to acknowledge Austria's mastery and continued a guerrilla warfare from their fastnesses.

The man who actually made the peace with Austria here tells why
he felt compelled to do so. He was the Prime Minister of Montenegro, M. Muskovitch, who had always been inclined to urge his
country to lean on Austria for protection. Hence the Montenegrins
hoped he could secure for them more favorable terms than he did.
The view of the Allied Powers, that Montenegro should have held
out to the bitter end, as Serbia did, is here voiced by the historian,
Edgar Wallace.


### BY EDGAR WALLACE

BEFORE we turn again to events in the larger fields of
war we may spare a moment to note briefly the tragic
position of the smallest of the Allies, Montenegro. Normally
some 30,000 strong, but at the beginning of 1916 reduced to
about 15,000, the Montenegrin army since the beginning of
the war had been protecting the left of the retiring Serbians
and had themselves been driven back and were now, in the

beginning of January, 1916, holding on desperately to Mount Lovcen, the last stronghold defending the capital, Cettinje.

They were short of artillery and munitions, short of all kinds of supplies, but it was clearly impossible for the Entente to offer them material relief. Montenegro is a mountainous country, unserved by any seaport, and even the Italians who had landed at Durazzo could not hope to open up communications to bring them the material they needed.

Lovcen was the hill which dominated the Austrian port of Cattaro. The Italian Minister Barzilai explained at once Italy's attitude and the importance or non-importance of Mount Lovcen in a terse but remarkable statement:

"Cattaro was, and remains, a natural harbor of the first order, capable of accommodating the whole Austrian fleet in spite of a possible menace from the top of Mount Lovcen. The barracks at Cattaro are visible from Mount Lovcen, but during the sixteen months of the war artillery of medium caliber (guns of large caliber could never be brought there because there were no proper roads) placed on the mountain never succeeded in doing any damage to them. If the means for completely saving Montenegro were wanting (and such an operation would require two or three hundred thousand men, and an effort six times greater than that necessary to convey the same forces on national territory), Lovcen, armed or unarmed, would anyhow have fallen with the rest of the territory into the hands of the enemy."

About January 12th the great hill was stormed by Austrian infantry, and the remnants of the heroic Montenegrin Army—30,000 at its strongest—began its retreat upon Cettinje. It is said that the Montenegrins' resistance was cut short when the troops learnt that, behind their backs, the Government was in negotiation for a separate peace with Austria.

On the 17th it was announced in the Austrian Parliament by Count Tisza that Montenegro had surrendered, and Montenegro's official explanation for that surrender was given in a Note issued by the Consulate-General for Montenegro in Paris.

"The newspapers announce that unhappy Montenegro has had to submit to the inevitable after having struggled

heroically under particularly disadvantageous conditions
against an enemy much superior in numbers and formidably
armed.  It may be considered as certain that if the King and
Government have yielded it is because the Army had exhausted its last munitions.

"Even flight was impossible.  The enemies were on the
frontiers; there was no escape by the sea; inveterate hostility
was to be encountered in Albania.  If the Serbian army was
able to escape from Serbia, the weak contingents of Montenegrins, exhausted by the superhuman efforts of their long
and desperate but effective resistance, and by privations of
all kinds, were not able to seek refuge on friendly territory.
It is possible to discuss *ad infinitum* the conditions of the
suspension of hostilities, the details of which, it is to be observed, come from enemy sources; it is even possible to heap
insults on the unfortunate conquered, but that will in no way
detract from the reputation of valiant little Montenegro nor
from the sublime rôle of heroism which she is proud of having played in the great war."

The story of Montenegro's "surrender," so eagerly ac-
claimed in Germany, is difficult to recapitulate.

Who was responsible—the King or his Minister—for
opening up negotiations for surrender?  Muskovitch, who
was frankly Austrophil, had become Premier at a critical moment in Montenegro's fate, and negotiations were proceeding
even whilst the fighting on Mount Lovcen was in progress.
As a result of this, some of the troops abandoned their positions after twenty-four hours' bombardment.

The Austrians, however, made a crowning mistake.
Thinking that the surrender of Montenegro was inevitable,
they put forward peace terms which were wholly unacceptable.  This produced a reaction, in the course of which King
Nicholas escaped from his country and the heroic remnants
of the army fell back upon Albania.  The peace terms were
such as would be offered, not to an honorably conquered nation, but to brigands who had been crushed by the superior
forces of the law, and they could not have been accepted by
any nation which desired to retain its self-respect.

The old King reached Italy, where he was met by his son-in-law, the King of Italy, and from thence he went on to France. Though a large number of Montenegrin troops were captured, a much larger number reached Albania in safety, and, joining hands with Assad Pasha, an Albanian leader, who favored the cause of the Allies, were able to hold up the advancing Austrians.

Montenegro itself was overrun, but this country, the poorest in Europe, offered the Central Empires very little reward for their enterprise. Cettinje was unharmed and the King's palace, which was visited by an Austrian journalist, was found intact.

"In the reception-room two great oil-paintings occupied the position of honor. One was that of the Emperor of Austria and the other was of Queen Elizabeth of Hungary. In the study of King Nicholas, on one of the writing-tables, there was a portrait of Francis Joseph, and in other rooms we also came across his picture."

### BY LAZARE MUSKOVITCH

When Montenegro entered the war on the side of the Allies she was promised everything necessary for the army, and also for the civil population, because even in ordinary times they imported wheat. Russia and France were to furnish supplies, but, unfortunately, this promise could not be carried out. They did what they could, but it was much less than Montenegro needed, alike in arms, artillery, and munitions, and, above all, in food.

Montenegro was given the task of protecting the rear of the Serbian army, and its battalions defended the Sandjak frontier with such success that on this side the Serbians were given time to retire. But when the Serbians were unexpectedly obliged to fall back on Montenegro and Albania, their arrival precipitated events. The Montenegrins had still some supplies, but with 120,000 to 130,000 mouths to feed, and with soldiers as well as civil population arriving in the country famished and denuded of everything, it was necessary to provide for their subsistence.

Many times the Montenegrin soldiers did not receive food for a whole week, and when they did the ration was only half a pound a day, for the most part maize flour, and not baked bread. They were very dejected, discontented, and fatigued. Montenegro had already informed the Foreign Ministers that it would be attacked, and counted upon an Allied Fleet attacking the Austrian Fleet, but it did not arrive. Shells from the Austrian Fleet came over the mountain almost as far as Cettinje.

Five or six days' march was necessary for the arrival of reënforcements at Lovcen, and to gain time for the arrival of forces from the other fronts the Montenegrins were obliged to demand an armistice of six days. Reënforcements were thus brought up from the Sandjak front to the number of twelve battalions, who fought very well on the Lovcen front.

We have, therefore, used this expedient in the *pourparlers* for no other purpose than to gain time, since their conditions were not acceptable, namely, that men from sixteen to fifty must all be interned in Austria, with the occupation of our country, the laying down of arms, to submit to requisitions, to administer the country themselves, to give them passage through the country to Albania, to deliver up all the members of the Royal Family having a command in the Army. It was impossible to accept those conditions, and it was, therefore, a peace absolutely impossible.

The King left his son behind in order to organize the resistance, and the Montenegrin army had received orders to retire towards Scutari behind the Serbian army, and to follow it in the direction of Durazzo. The King had barely time to escape. He sent the following order to his troops from Brindisi:

"To General Vukovitch, commanding the Montenegrin Army:—I order you anew to resist the enemy in the most energetic way possible. In the event of a retreat, follow the direction of the Serbian army towards Durazzo. The Serbian commanders have been informed of this. I hope that you will obtain food supplies at Medua and farther on.

"Prince Mirko and all the other Ministers who have remained cannot in any case open negotiations with any one whatever. The French Government have promised our retreating army all possible facilities, such as they have given to the Serbian army. Prince Mirko and the other Ministers must in no case remain, but make every possible effort to escape."

The newspapers had spoken of a secret treaty with Austria. It can be said now that Montenegro had been crushed by Austria under conditions the most difficult for her. If we had a secret treaty, the conditions imposed by Austria must have been much more favorable than those actually proposed. I do not understand how any one can any longer be in doubt as to what we have done. We have the right to demand that our Allies should respect our honor in not lending faith to the inaccurate statements of any Austrian origin. I can affirm again that the soldiers of no European army could have resisted more than the Montenegrins, neither at Lovcen nor on any of the other fronts, with the equipment, the supplies, the arms and the munitions at the disposal of our soldiers.

The so-called "surrender" of Montenegro was hailed with much rejoicing in Berlin and Vienna. "Surrender will follow," said a German newspaper, "till every one of the Allies has yielded, and the last will pay the piper." There was, indeed, little to justify the fantastic joy of the people, the event had no significance whatever as regards the outcome of the War, and the rejoicing was quickly damped down when it became known that there was no unconditional capitulation after all of this, the weakest and the smallest of all the countries at war. Montenegro refused to bow the knee, and the Government was transferred to Lyons and decided to continue the struggle.

# RUSSIA'S TEMPORARY CONQUEST OF ARMENIA

## THE CAPTURE OF ERZERUM

### FEBRUARY 16TH

GENERAL YUDENITCH                    MORGAN PRICE

In 1915, as our previous volume told, the Russians drove back a Turkish army from their Asiatic frontier among the Caucasus Mountains, the so-called "roof of the world." Late in that year Grand Duke Nicholas, certainly the ablest member of the Russian royal family, arrived on the Caucasus front as its commander. With the aid of his Chief of Staff, General Yudenitch, Nicholas promptly planned an aggressive campaign against the Turks. In this the Turkish army was driven back through the Armenian regions, the scene of the awful massacres which began in 1915. The outline of the campaign is here sketched by General Yudenitch; its details are given by Mr. Price, the official British observer with the Russians.

The capture of Erzerum, the chief city and stronghold of the region, was the military climax of the campaign. The capture of Trebizond, the second important city, followed naturally from the complete disorganization of the Turkish army at Erzerum. Following upon these successes the Russians penetrated Persia; but unfortunately for them the British reverses at the Dardanelles and later at Kut-el-Amara allowed almost the entire Turkish forces to turn their strength against the Russians. The latter were compelled to retire from Armenia, leaving that unhappy land to another series of massacres. Thus the entire 1916 campaign in the Caucasus ended, as did most of the battling of the year, with no decisive victory for either side. It was marked only by unending slaughter.

## BY GENERAL YUDENITCH

THE fortress of Erzerum was the only fortified point in the interior of Asia Minor, protecting Western Armenia and Anatolia and commanding all the best roads of Transcaucasia and the interior of Asia Minor. For many years past great improvements had been carried out in the works by the Turks, with the assistance of the Germans. The *terrain* in front rendered it naturally strong, while it was covered on the flanks by mountain masses most difficult of approach and with their passes protected by powerful forts.

24

Such was the formidable barrier on the path of our offensive, with enormous defensive advantages on the northeast and east.  During the five days' assault the fortress was defended by the Turks with a stubbornness to which the enormous quantity of killed and frozen corpses gives testimony.  The Caucasus army succeeded in surmounting steep mountains protected not only by frost but by wire entanglements and other defenses, and assaulted the fortress after an artillery preparation.

The assault on the forts and the principal position lasted from February 11th till February 15th inclusive.  After we had taken the forts on the left flank of the principal Turkish line of defense, extending about 27 miles, the fate of the forts in the center and on the right flank, and, after them of the second line forts and the principal defensive position, was decided on February 16th after short attacks.  These fortifications, which were full of Turkish dead, remained in our possession.

During the assault on the fortress several Turkish regiments were annihilated or made prisoners with all their officers.  On the line of forts alone we took 197 pieces of artillery of various calibers in good condition.  In the defense works of the central fortress we took another 126 pieces of artillery.  In the fortified region of Erzerum we took a large number of depots of various kinds, which have already been mentioned by the Headquarters Staff.  The exact number of Turkish prisoners is 235 officers and 12,753 men.

It is possible to estimate the force of the blow which we dealt the Turkish army, whose demoralized remnants are now withdrawing in disorder towards the west, if only by the fact that some Army Corps of three divisions now only number from 3,000 to 5,000 men with a few guns.  All the remainder have either fallen into our hands or perished in the fighting, or from the cold.

According to latest information received, Turkish officer and soldier prisoners, who were captured in the fortified district of Erzerum and in the course of the pursuit, complain bitterly that their Headquarters Staff was concentrated in the hands of Germans.  The latter during the assault on the fortress of Erzerum were the first to abandon the fortified positions, causing a panic and disorder among the already shaken Turkish troops.

The great Russian advance west of Erzerum came to an end only with the exhaustion of the pursuers. In the south, Mush, eighty miles beyond Erzerum, fell on February 19th; and on March 1st the Russians were at Kamak, only seven miles northeast of Bitlis. On the following day Bitlis itself was taken, the mountain pass opening up the whole of the Tigris valley, and only 100 miles from the Turkish railhead at Nisibin, thus coming into the possession of the victorious invaders. Here again the Russians found themselves confronted with terrible obstacles owing to continual snowstorms and severe frost at an altitude of nearly 5,000 feet. Bitlis had been an important Armenian center, but there were few of the oppressed race left to welcome their liberators, the Turks and Kurds, under Djevdet Pasha, having massacred some 15,000 of them in the previous June. With this success the whole of the Van region passed into Russian hands, and the connection between the Turks in Anatolia and their forces across the Persian frontier and south of Lake Urmia was severed.

### BY MORGAN PRICE

This success had been due to errors by the Turks, who did not feel insecure in Armenia, and would take risks to save Bagdad. They must have been ill-informed as to the nature of the Russian reënforcements, for in December they gave leave of absence to a number of officers in the Erzerum garrison, while they made no haste to send back to Erzerum the heavy artillery from the Dardanelles. Instead, they concentrated all their efforts on Mesopotamia, where they succeeded in surrounding General Townsend in Kut, and in threatening the whole British expedition with breakdown. Thus it was clear that a Russian offensive on the Caucasus front would not only relieve the situation in Mesopotamia, but would stand a good chance of driving the Turks back on their last line of defense round the fortress of Erzerum, and possibly even of taking it. The Russians were now superior

by about 50,000 men along the whole of the Asiatic front
from the Black Sea to Persia.   This enabled them to undertake flanking movements, which always count for so much in
Asiatic warfare.   In Asia, with its wide expanses, the chances
of an enemy digging himself into positions which cannot
be outflanked are very much less than in Europe.   Everything, therefore, favored an offensive in the direction of
Erzerum, and a series of maneuvers and flanking movements in the mountains and valleys at the head-waters of the
Araxes and the Euphrates.

The eastern approach to Erzerum lies along the Passan
plain.   Its outer chain of forts lies on the Deve-Boyun, a
range of rolling hills from 7,000 to 8,000 feet high, dividing
the head-waters of the Araxes from those of the western
Euphrates.   Bounding the Passan and upper Euphrates plain
on the south is the great range of the Palan-teken, rising
to 10,000 feet, and running east and west like most of the
ridges of Armenia outside the volcanic zone.   To the north
of the plain lies a confused area, where volcanic effusions
have overlaid the original plateau ranges.   To the east, not
far from the Russo-Turkish frontier, lie the masses of the
Djelli-Gel and Kodjut-Dag, which to the west merge into the
great uplift of the Kargar-bazar.   Further west still rise the
Giaur and Dumlu Dags, between which and the Kargar-
bazar is the only gap in the whole length of the mountain-
wall that shields Erzerum on the north.   This gap is the
defile of Gurji-Bogaz,[1] and the road through it, at the height
of 7,000 feet, is the only approach to Erzerum from this
side.   Coming up from the south and passing through this
defile, one enters the valley of the Tortum River and descends
into the relative depression of Olti Chai and the middle Chorokh.   The problem for the Turks was to hold the approaches
to Erzerum along the Passan plain on the east (this was
effected by the 9th and part of the 10th Army Corps), and to
block the narrow gap in the mountains on the northeast (this
was done by the 11th Army Corps, which had entrenched
itself some months previously on the mountain mass of the

[1] Turkish for "Georgian Gates."

Gey Dag, just southwest of Olti). To the south of Erzerum, across the Palan-teken, lay a part of the 10th Army
Corps, protecting the road leading into the Van basin and on
to Mesopotamia.

The Russian plan, worked out by General Yudenitch, the
Grand Duke Nicholas's commander in the field, was to attack the Turkish positions in three columns. The 2nd Turkestan Army Corps at Olti in the Chorokh depression was to
attack the Turks guarding the Gurji-Bogaz defiles in the positions on the Gey Dag, and by this demonstration to draw
off their strength from the Passan plain, where the main
blow was to be struck by the 1st Army Corps, which was to
make a frontal attack on the Azap Keui positions between
Hassan Kaleh and the old Russo-Turkish frontier. These
positions had been carefully prepared for some months, and
had all the signs of permanent field-fortifications. To make
them untenable, a third force, the 4th Rifle Division, was to
be sent into the mountain country of the Djelli-Gel, to hold
the line between the 1st Army Corps and the Turkestans,
and to threaten the flanks of the Turks at Azap Keui and
on the Gey Dag. It is interesting to note that this was the
same sort of plan as that which Enver Pasha adopted, when
he attacked the Russians just twelve months before. He,
however, demonstrated on the Passan plain, and made his
main attack on the Olti and Chorokh basins. His plan ultimately failed, because he could not guarantee supplies to his
advanced forces in the country that they had occupied. But
the Russians were brilliantly successful, because they had
given the necessary attention to roads and transport for their
main advance along the Passan plain.

On January 13th the Russian advance began. The 2nd
Turkestan Army Corps attacked the Turkish 11th Army
Corps, which was strongly entrenched on the Gey Dag west
of Olti. The Russian losses were heavy, and they did not
succeed in dislodging the Turks; but the real object of the
attack was obtained by causing the Turks to draw off forces
for the defense of the northeast (Gurji-Bogaz) gateway to
Erzerum, and by masking the main blow, which was delivered on the Passan plain. Information brought by airmen,

who flew over Erzerum during these days, showed that Abdulla Kerim Pasha, the Turkish commander, had withdrawn one regiment to the north to protect his left flank in the defiles. This gave the necessary opportunity for the Russian 1st Army Corps to carry the main Turkish position, and on January 13th the Azap Keui line was attacked.

In spite of the withdrawal of a regiment, the Turks made a very stubborn resistance, and for three days there was severe fighting with great losses on both sides. But on January 15th the 4th Composite Division, which had been given the task of connecting the 2nd Turkestans with the 1st Army Corps, crossed the high rugged country of the Djelli Gel at a level of 9,000 feet, and joined up with the Turkestans in the valleys of the upper Olti Chai. The Turkish 11th Army Corps on the Gey Dag, and the 9th and 10th in the Passan plain, were thus in danger of being outflanked. Moreover, the Russians had so severely pounded the Azap Keui positions that they were now practically untenable. So on January 16th Abdulla Kerim Pasha ordered a general retreat to the last line of defense on the Erzerum forts.

Then followed what is frequently met with in Turkish retreats, and is very characteristic of that race. The Turk has all the stubbornness and endurance of a highlander and an agriculturist. He does not see at once when he is outmastered: but when he does, then the untrained Oriental comes out strong in him; he throws everything away and bolts in a general *sauve qui peut*. In this case he just ran till he reached Erzerum. The Russians reached Kupri Keui on the 18th, and the next day were in Hassan Kaleh, thus getting into their hands the whole of the east Passan plain and the basin of the Araxes right up to the outer forts of Erzerum. On January 19th the last Turkish column was seen disappearing behind the rolling banks of the Deve-Boyun. The Cossacks pursued right up to the outer chain of forts under cover of darkness, and cut off 1,000 prisoners. Next day field artillery shelled the outer forts, and so after thirty-nine years Erzerum saw a Russian shell again within its precincts.

Up to this time it was not really part of the Russian plan

to attack Erzerum. The original plan was to break the
Turkish line on the Passan plain, and to put such pressure
on the Turks along the whole line from the Chorokh to
Bitlis that the pressure on the English at Bagdad would
be relieved. The extraordinary success of the advance in the
second week of January took no one more by surprise than
the Russians themselves. The Grank Duke Nicholas would
not believe the news when he heard that Hassan Kaleh and
Kupri Keui had fallen. Indeed, it was not until January
23rd that General Yudenitch informed him that he thought
it possible to take Erzerum, and asked for permission to
work out a plan. This was done in the next few days. Meanwhile, information which strengthened this decision came to
hand in the shape of a wireless telegram, intercepted between Abdulla Kerim Pasha and Enver Pasha, in which it
was stated that "the condition of the 3rd Army is serious;
reënforcements must be sent at once, or else Erzerum cannot be held."

On January 31st a demonstration was made from Hassan
Kaleh by the Russians against the outer forts of the Deve-
Boyun to test the strength of the Turks. The bombardment
continued all day, and by evening it was seen that the Turks
had poured water down the slopes in front of the forts, which
on freezing covered the mountain sides with icy sheets. According to accounts given me by some officers, as the sun was
setting that evening the sign of a cross appeared in the clouds
of white smoke that accompanied the bombardment and lay
over the forts.

During the first week of February heavy artillery was
brought up, and the Russian dispositions were made and
developed with extraordinary skill. General Paskevitch,
when he captured Erzerum in 1828, confined his attentions
solely to the approach from the Passan plain. Meeting with
slight Turkish resistance and with primitive forts, he had no
great difficulty in breaking through the Deve-Boyun. He
had not to trouble about the defiles and the northern approaches to Erzerum, nor had he to force a passage across
immense mountainous tracts of snowy wastes in order to
keep his line of advance intact. But in these days the meth-

ods of modern warfare have to some degree overcome nature. The Gurji-Bogaz defiles were now passable for artillery, and moreover the Turks had built two forts there. On their extreme left wing a whole Turkish Army Corps held positions far away in the isolated valleys of the upper Chorokh Su, where it had before been impossible to keep and feed a battalion. The devices of the engineer and transport services had made all this possible. The Russians therefore were threatened with the danger that, if they should make a frontal attack on the Deve-Boyun forts and carry them, the Turks in the upper Chorokh might suddenly make a great counter-move, break into the Olti depression, reach the Kars plateau, and so get into the rear of the whole Russian army, as they did in December, 1914.

This in fact is exactly what Abdulla Kerim Pasha tried to do. He ordered Halid Bey (the exceedingly brave, if somewhat rash, commander of the frontier regiment which had retreated from before Artvin through Southern Lazistan when the Azap Keui positions were captured) to call up reenforcements from Baiburt, break through the narrow Tortum valley and cut off the 2nd Turkestan Army Corps at Olti. During the first ten days of February severe fighting took place on the passes of the Kabak-tepe east of Igdir, and on more than one occasion Halid Bey seemed on the point of outflanking General Prejvalsky. By February 10th, however, the Russian Turkestans had succeeded in repulsing him and were secure in the Tortum valley, and it was safe for General Yudenitch to begin his advance on Erzerum.

The plan was to form the whole of the Russian forces in this part of Armenia into a great semicircular line stretching from the Upper Chorokh Su across the great volcanic chains of the Dumlu and Giaur Dags and the Kargar-bazar, across the Passan plain, and the heights of the Palan-teken to the valley of Khunus. The line was some 130 miles long, and it had to be covered by two Army Corps and some detached forces. All the different sections of the line had to keep in touch with each other, and to advance over snow-bound plateau or icy mountain skree, whichever fell to their lot, thus gradually converging upon the great fortress, and threatening to surround it. The object of General Yudenitch, in this most ably conceived and brilliantly executed plan, was to force Abdulla Kerim Pasha either to evacuate Erzerum, or else to be locked up in it with no hope of relief.

It is safe to say that the struggle was much greater in this operation with the natural enemies, cold and hunger, than it was with the Turks. The Russian troops had to cross mountain ranges with deep snow-drifts at 10,000 feet, and to go for at least three days cut off from supplies of food, with nothing but the few crusts of bread they could carry with them. No other race of human beings, except those accustomed to the cold of sub-arctic climates like that of Russia, could have performed this feat. The Anatolian Turk is in no degree inferior to the Russian in physical endurance, but he lacks the habit of husbanding his resources. The Russian, whenever he gets the smallest chance, sets himself down in some little hollow, and somehow or other makes himself a cup of tea by burning bits of grass or moss. But the Turkish soldier literally goes without anything for two or three days, and then eats a whole sheep or a perfect mountain of "pilaff," so that he cannot move for hours. Moreover, the Turkish army has in it Arabs and Syrians, who can ill endure a winter campaign in Armenia.

On February 11th the order for the general Russian advance was given. The Elizabetopol and Baku regiments attacked Forts Chaban-dede and Dolan-gyoz respectively. The latter fort is situated on a little knoll which juts out into the Passan plain, and is, as it were, the advanced guard of the outer chain. By 5 a. m. on the 12th Dolan-gyoz was surrounded, but the battalion of Turks holding the fort managed to retreat to the Uzun Ahmet fort, a powerful redoubt which rests upon a trapeze-like rocky mass with cliffs on three sides. At the same time the 2nd Turkestans, advancing through the defiles of the Gurji-Bogaz, surrounded the advanced fort of Kara-gyubek. Two outposts were already in the hands of the Russians; but the main struggle was yet to come.

On the Kargar-bazar heights to the north all through the day and night of the 10th and 11th of February the 4th Composite Division attacked the Turks across snow-fields and

skrees of rock.  The summit of the range was in the hands
of the Russians, but the Turks held stubbornly on to the
snow-fields to the west of the summit which connected Forts
Chaban-dede and Tufta.  Here they had made snow-trenches,
which were invisible to the naked eye at a distance of more
than a hundred yards.  On the night of the 12th the right
wing of the 39th Division was ordered to attack Fort Chaban-dede, which, with Tufta, was the key to Erzerum.  The
Baku regiment, which had taken Dolan-gyoz, now joined the
Elizabetopols, and together they advanced from the village
of Buyuk Tuy on the Passan plain up the rocky valley of the
Tuy towards the towering cliffs, on which Fort Chaban-dede
rested.  The Russian soldiers were clad in white coats, so
that in the darkness and against the snow they were invisible.
Silently creeping up the rocky slopes to the fort, they got to
within 250 yards of it before the Turkish searchlights discovered them.  At once from the Uzun Ahmet and Chaban-
dede forts a murderous cross-fire was poured upon them,
which in two hours caused them to lose one-third of their
number.  However, one battalion of the Elizabetopols
pushed right up, till they got underneath the cliffs of Fort
Chaban-dede.  Here the guns from the fort could not fire at
them, the angle being too high : but the guns from Uzun Ahmet could still rake their lines.  At this moment also the
108th regiment of the 11th Turkish Army Corps on the
Olugli heights at the head of the Tuy defile began a flanking
movement.  The right wing of the Elizabetopol regiment was
exposed, and as there was no sign of the 4th Division, whose
appearance alone could fill the gap, the position was critical.

The 4th Division was in fact at this moment struggling
under almost more terrible conditions at the height of 10,000
feet on the Kargar-bazar.  The men were engaged not with
the Turks, but with the frost and snow.  During the nights
of the 12th and 13th they lost 2,000 of their number from
frost-bite alone.  In addition to their sufferings from cold,
they had the Herculean task of carrying their artillery across
the snow and rocks, which alone was enough to account for
their delay.  Accordingly, there was nothing for the Elizabetopol and Bakintsi regiments to do but to retreat to the bot-

PROPERTY  9508  OF
COLBY SCHOOL FOR GIRLS

tom of the Tuy valley, where respite could be obtained, and this they did on the morning of the 13th. All that day they waited in vain for the 4th Division; but when evening came and no one appeared, it was seen to be useless to wait any longer, for time only aided the Turks, whose reënforcements were being hurried up from Erzerum. So it was decided that the Derbent regiment, which had hitherto been held in reserve, should come up on the right wing and try to turn the flank of the 108th Turkish regiment, which was now occupying the heights of the Sergy-kaya, a desolate knoll on the rocky mass of Olugli.

At 7 p. m. the advance began. The Derbent regiment left its position in the rear, and crossing in the darkness the head of the Tuy valley, ascended a defile and reached the snow-fields round the Olugli mass. Immense difficulty was experienced in the advance. The snow lay in drifts often five to six feet deep, and in places the soldiers in order to move had to take off their coats and walk on them in the snow, throwing them forward every three feet to avoid sinking in up to their necks. In this way they advanced painfully all night. The Turks, suspecting nothing, were lying in their snow trenches, their attention chiefly concentrated on how to prevent themselves from freezing to death. At last daylight began to break upon this arctic scene, and through scuds of snow broken by the icy wind, the Turks saw a chain of dark forms slowly closing in on them. They could hardly believe their eyes, for it seemed to them impossible that a human army with rifles and ammunition could cross the country that lay in front of them.

By 5.30 a. m. the Turks saw that their trenches on the Sergy-kaya were being surrounded from the northeast and east, and only a narrow neck of snow-field to the south connected them with the fort of Chaban-dede. So they hastily left their trenches and retreated as fast as the drifts would allow them across the Olugli snow-field till they reached the fort. Chaban-dede was now surrounded on the northeast, but the retreat of the Turkish garrison was not cut off on the south and west, and the Turks with characteristic stubbornness and bravery continued their deadly cross-fire from

Forts Uzun Ahmet and Chaban-dede, as if nothing had happened. Thus the Derbent regiment had by this maneuver gained important ground; but the Russians had not yet broken the Turkish cordon that united the forts, nor did the three regiments of the 39th Division dare to advance farther for fear of becoming separated from the Russians to the right and left of them, and so giving the Turks a chance to break through in a counter-attack.

But what had happened meanwhile to the 4th Composite Division and the 2nd Turkestans? They alone could save the situation by piercing the plateau between Forts Chaban-dede and Tufta, and so joining up with the Derbent regiment on the heights of Olugli. The critical question was whether they had been equal to their stupendous task of penetrating the 50 miles of rugged snow-bound ridges and plateau. The morning of February 14th showed that they had accomplished this task, and so sealed the fate of Erzerum.

During the previous day the 4th Composite Division had been finishing the transport of their artillery to the summit of the Kargar-bazar ridge. The guns had again been dismembered, and carried to positions whence they could drop shells on the Turks defending the right flank of Fort Tufta. The Turkestans had also prepared their artillery to sweep the fort from the north. On the morning of February the 14th the infantry of the 4th Division descended the northwestern slopes of the Kargar-bazar, sliding down the snow on their coats to the open plateau, out of which the Tuy River rises. From here they moved on to the northwest and reached the foot of the Grobovoye heights, which form the eastern side of the Gurji-Bogaz defile. This is the northeastern "gateway" to Erzerum through which the 2nd Turkestans were to advance, and which the Turkish 10th Army Corps was defending from Forts Kara-gyubek and Tufta. The plan was that the Turkish positions on the Grobovoye heights, connecting Forts Kara-gyubek and Tufta, should be attacked simultaneously by the Turkestans coming through the northern defiles, and by the 4th Division coming down from the Kargar-bazar on the south.

The critical moment for the Russians had arrived.

Would these forces unite and press their attack together, or had one of them failed and been overwhelmed in the snow-fields or defiles? About midday the artillery of the 4th Division began to drop shells on the Turkish snow-trenches on the Grobovoye heights. The bombardment went on for half an hour and then stopped, the commanders waiting in suspense to hear whether there was any reply from their comrades, the Turkestans, who should by this time be attacking from the north. Hope was beginning to wane, and they were faced by the prospect either of a single-handed encounter with a greatly superior enemy or of a disastrous retreat. But about one o'clock a faint rumble was heard, and a few minutes later shells were seen dropping on the Grobovoye heights. They were Russian shells, yet not fired by the 4th Division. The situation was saved, for the Turkestans had forced their way through the Gurji-Bogaz defile, capturing Fort Kara-gyubek, and pressing on to the Grobovoye heights and towards Fort Tufta.

The Turks now on the Grobovoye heights were in danger of being surrounded from the north, south and east. They could see that Kara-gyubek was already in Russian hands. The left wing of the 4th Division, moreover, was pressing on to the heights of Kuni-tepe, a mass lying north of the Olugli and commanding Fort Tufta from the south. This they occupied at three o'clock, and the Turks on the Grobovoye heights retired at once on Fort Tufta. In another half-hour the Turkestans appeared upon the sky-line; and here, on this desolate Grobovoye height, at this historic moment, they greeted their brothers of the 4th Division. The gap in the Russian line was now filled; the mountains and the snow-fields had been overcome, and it was now only a question of a few hours before the Turks would be overcome too.

Just as this memorable meeting was taking place, the Russian artillery observation posts at Ketchk noticed a great stir in the Turkish lines surrounding Fort Tufta. The Staff of the 10th Army Corps knew that the game was up, and, to escape being surrounded, at once began the evacuation of Fort Tufta. That night also Abdulla Kerim Pasha ordered the evacuation of all the forts of the Deve-Boyun. The reserves of the 11th Army Corps were the first to leave, followed by those of the 9th.    Then explosions in Forts Kaburgar, Ortayuk, Uzun Ahmet and Sivishli were observed from the Russian lines.   The evacuation of Fort Chaban-dede was begun at 2 p. m., and by four o'clock the Russians were in possession of all the forts of the Deve-Boyun, while the 4th Composite Division and the Turkestans were pouring into the Erzerum plain, in the hope of cutting off the Turkish retreat.    But here they met with less success.   The 4th Division, with orders to advance south, were ten miles ahead of the Turkestans, who had orders to advance west.   The confusion caused by columns crossing on the march gave a good start to the Turks, who had speedily evacuated the forts, as soon as danger was imminent.   Yet one of their divisions, the 34th, was captured at Ilidja, and a large part of their artillery was lost.

It is curious that the Russians lost much less in the operations before Erzerum than they did in the fighting before the Azap Keui positions in the previous month, when they lost not less than 30,000 killed and wounded in four days' fighting.   But in the five days' fighting along the whole length of the Erzerum forts from the Deve-Boyun to the Gurji-Bogaz defiles their losses were not more than 12,000, a large part of which were deaths or injuries due to exposure.

The capture of the great fortress, hitherto considered impregnable, sent a thrill through the whole continent.   Every bazaar from Shiraz to Samarkand, from Konia to Kuldja, began talking of the great Urus, who had taken Erzerum from the Osmanli.    Russian military prestige in the East had fallen very low since the Sarikamish battle and Enver Pasha's advance into the Caucasus in December, 1914.    But the Dardanelles expedition had given the Turks something else to think of than conquering the Caucasus, and had thus afforded the Russians the necessary respite to prepare for their attack on Erzerum, which in its turn saved the British from being driven completely out of Mesopotamia.

The capture of Erzerum was the first great success that came to the Allies in Asia.   It might be regarded as the turning point of the war in the East.

# THE FIRST ASSAULT ON VERDUN

## THE MIGHTIEST EFFORT OF GERMANY'S ARTILLERY

### FEBRUARY 21ST

COUNT DE SOUZA       GENERAL VON FALKENHAYN
CROWN PRINCE FREDERICK WILLIAM
LORD NORTHCLIFFE      GENERAL VON LUDENDORFF

The long continued assault upon Verdun will remain to most minds the great typical battle of the War. The first series of attacks began abruptly on February 21st, and lasted almost without a day of pause for over a month. During the first week of this terrific onslaught, the German advance was sufficient to encourage its commanders to hope for an early success not only in taking Verdun, which in itself meant nothing, but in breaking completely through the battered line of defense. The French even contemplated abandoning Verdun.

By March 1st, however, French reënforcements had arrived in sufficient numbers to make the battle equal, and General Pétain took command of the defense. His cheery battle cry to his men: "Now, we shall have them!" has become almost as noted as that other Verdun battle-cry of the later months, "They shall not pass!"

The general summary of the strategic situation is given by the noted French military authority, De Souza, whose faith in his countrymen and in the great Marshal Joffre makes him confident that their final victory never for a moment wavered in the balance. The February assault is pictured by the great British newspaper director who witnessed it, Lord Northcliffe. Other glimpses are also given from the personal narratives of participants.

The German viewpoint is presented by the man then in control of the entire German plans of war, the Head of the High Staff, Falkenhayn, and also by the Crown Prince, who was the general in actual command at Verdun and so received the main blame for its final failure. Falkenhayn's "defense" has a special interest because he lost his place as military director on account of Verdun. He was succeeded by Ludendorff; so our section closes with Ludendorff's own contemptuous summary of his predecessor's effort.

In briefest outline the chief events of the first six weeks' battle were as follows: Verdun lies on the Meuse River, which here winds in loops through a network of hills. The first German attacks were made well to the eastward of the river, and in five days carried the assailants half way to Verdun, close to the strong French defenses around Forts Douaumont and Vaux. On February 26th one German regiment reached an outer section of Douaumont and for a time maintained itself among the ruins; but no more Germans could fight their way to this isolated group and the French afterward retook the position. Here the French line resisted all further assaults. Meanwhile, early in March, the Germans began attacking the hills west of the

Meuse. Here they were equally firmly resisted, and very gradually won their way until they reached "Dead Man's Hill." Against this they made a tremendous assault on April 7th, gaining some slopes of the hill, but being beaten back from its main summit. After this repulse they were obliged to pause and use a considerable period for the reorganizing and reënforcing of their terribly battered troops. Except for the first few days of French unreadiness, the Germans' most stupendous efforts had won for them no appreciable advance toward Verdun.

This, however, was only the first stage of the struggle. In May, as a later section of this volume describes, the stupendous battle burst into new flame.

### BY COUNT DE SOUZA

I N dealing with the great battles and operations which developed and were prolonged for months around the Verdun salient, one must naturally dwell chiefly on the opening stages, as these initial movements, like those of the general conflict itself, decided both the course and the issue of the struggle.

The first action started on February 21st, that is if one dates it from the opening of the German infantry assaults, the preliminary bombardment of the foe having been in full swing some time before. It increased in intensity and violence until the moment appointed for the infantry movements; then the German troops which were massed opposite the sector of the salient to be attacked, advanced and deployed on a line stretching from Consenvoye, on the Meuse, to a point facing Ornes, at the opening of the Spincourt forest. There were altogether three full army corps (or, roughly, 120,000 men) with subsidiary columns in support; and others flanking them towards the Woevre, and on the left bank of the Meuse; they moved forward and swarmed in compact masses over the French advanced positions which had been battered, plowed and destroyed by their guns, and they forthwith assaulted the various *points d'appui*—farms, hills, woods and villages—which, in spite of the terrible fire to which they were subjected and to which they could not as yet adequately reply, the French still held with grim and stubborn determination. And in these localities—Brabant, Haumont, Herbebois, the woods of Wavrille and Des Caures —which suddenly assumed a sinister fame, there were desperate and fearful encounters, the whole region around becoming a blazing furnace, a roaring volcano.

The French advance elements were weak ones; on that sector of the salient they totaled barely 12,000 men; and the powerful *barrage* fire which the enemy through intense gun concentration was able to establish behind them, made it difficult, if not actually impossible in every instance, for the forces more to the rear to lend them any support. Nevertheless, they did what they could to maintain the illusion which the assailants evidently entertained as to their strength in numbers. For the latter acted there as on former and similar occasions, their plan of attack, which they carried out to the letter, being based on the assumption that their opponents held the Verdun salient in full force. Neither through their aircraft reconnoissances nor by other means of obtaining information, had they succeeded in finding out the real numbers and dispositions of the French; and their massive tactics and ponderous and deliberate movements clearly showed that they were under the impression that a strong army was opposing them.

During five days the heroic Fantassins, the Chasseurs and the Zouaves held on against the surging masses. Plied with shot and shell, scorched by liquid fire, and suffering besides all the torments which troops in their position must endure, they defended stubbornly every inch of the ground, delivered telling blows, and by their efficiency and spirit of fortitude they held back and delayed the enemy columns which were endeavoring to reach Verdun and to turn from the north the Heights of the Meuse. Their action besides rendered possible the defense of the salient.

For some little time the French generals, puzzled as to the true designs of the foe, could not make up their minds to undertake a counter-movement across the Meuse; and in view of the possible—and probable—development of the German offensive on the left bank of the river—a movement which would have threatened the communications of the troops on the right bank—they had taken into serious consideration the eventuality of having to evacuate Verdun; preliminary steps had been taken in that direction; from the very opening of the German bombardment the civilian population had been withdrawn; and some of the outer forts had been dismantled so that they should not serve as *points d'appui* to the enemy during the progress of his advance; a contingency, however, which made it more difficult in the course of time for the defenders to hold the salient when, owing to unforeseen circumstances and the blunder committed by the foe, they at length resolved to keep the positions on the right bank in their possession.

In regard to this, and lest a wrong view of affairs should be taken, it is as well to repeat here that the French Staff wisely subordinated everything to sound strategy, and above all, to their inflexible system of man-economy. General Joffre's primary consideration was to spare his men as much as technical requirements permitted, and he would not have occupied in force and held a position if his calculations had showed him that the margin of casualties would be to the profit of the enemy.

It was chiefly the manner in which the Germans carried out their onslaughts which altered the minds of the French Staff in regard to the value of the Verdun salient as a point of general and decisive contact.

When the preliminary bombardment began, they had been expecting and somewhat fearing an enemy attack on the *western* side of the Meuse from Montfaucon, which would have endangered the position of the troops on the right bank. The enemy's artillery was almost as active in that region and was centering its fire on the railway line to Ste. Menehould and Clermont. The Germans, there is no doubt, wished to mislead the French, but they committed a considerable error in omitting to carry out a more substantial threat, this being due, as has been said, to one of their leaders' views on the matter. The French, who were fairly well informed as to the objective and purpose of the coming German attempt—an attempt which, moreover, they had foreseen and made ready for for months—had mapped out their scheme of concentration in view of forestalling a German offensive on *both* sides of the Meuse; the right of de Langle de Cary's troops, who were operating in the Argonne, had

been reënforced on the Avoncourt-Bethincourt line; and so
certain the French generals felt about it that it was not until
two days after the opening of the enemy's infantry movement to the northeast of Verdun that definite orders were
sent to the commanding officer on the spot (General Herr)
to hold the positions on the eastern bank at all cost (February 23rd).  Even then, thinking of a ruse on the part of the
foe, General Joffre felt diffident as to throwing too many of
his forces on that side of the river, as it would be difficult
and probably costly to withdraw them should this, for reasons of strategy, become necessary.  On the 25th, only when
it was realized that the German attack was not a feint, and
that they had as yet no intention of assaulting the French
positions on the opposite side, the French Staff took ample
dispositions to keep the salient, and Verdun, in their possession.  It was then that General Pétain, a gifted and experienced tactician, was appointed, and that considerable reenforcements were thrown across the river.

This opened the second stage of the action; but ere one
proceeds with the narrative of the battle, one may touch on
a sidelight of the event which produced much stir at the time.

This was the nomination of General Pétain to take
charge of matters at Verdun.

By the overawed public, the appointment of this general was interpreted as a sign of unreadiness and weakness
on the part of the French, and in consequence General Joffre
himself did not escape censure from malcontent quarters.
The newspaper *Le Matin* published on the Verdun operations
a criticism which was based on contorted facts, and which
elicited a strong rebuke from high quarters.  It was thought
then—as usual (re battle of Soissons; battle of Ypres, etc.)
—that the situation of France and of the Allies was critical;
and the enemies of the Republic took advantage of the opportunity to injure the good name, and lower the prestige,
of the existing authorities, their views on the matter corre-
sponding naturally with those of the foe.

General Pétain's nomination, however, was a question of
pure technicalities and the fuss which was made about it in
some quarters was quite out of keeping with the character of

the event.  A tactical job had to be done, and that job was naturally given to the man who was best tried in the kind of operation which was about to be undertaken.

The French troops which were thrown across the Meuse on February 25th-26th consisted in several divisions belonging to the 1st, the 3rd, the 7th, and the 20th Army Corps, most of these first-rate elements having been brought over from northwestern France after the fresh extension of the British front there.  They were placed under the immediate direction of Generals Herr, Nivelle and Balfourier; and whilst they moved forward to occupy the commanding positions around Verdun, and to link them with those which were held by other divisions (5th and 6th Corps) on the Heights of the Meuse, a flanking movement was carried out from the western bank of the river, near Forges and Cumières by units of the 2nd Corps who had been battling for months in the Argonne.  This movement, which was combined with an infantry attack from the Talou Heights, brought to a standstill in the valley of the Meuse, near Champneuville, the enemy column (VIIth Corps) which had carried Brabant and Samogneux, and which from the latter place was advancing to the attack of the main French line.  Caught between two fires and vigorously charged with the bayonet, the enemy in that quarter gave way and retired, the support given him on the western bank being too meager to allow him to resume his forward movement with success.  Thus the French reënforcements were enabled to establish themselves and make good their positions on the range of low-lying heights which cover Verdun from the north.

The crowning operation which rendered the position of the French secure at Verdun was carried out by General Balfourier with troops öf the 20th Corps.  The notable feature about this operation was that General Balfourier could only dispose at the moment of one brigade of the division which he had brought forward across the Meuse, the other at the time being still on the way.  His task was not only to check the German forces (XVIIIth Corps) which had entered Louvemont and were advancing from that direction against the eastern flank of the Pepper ridge position, but also to storm and recapture the Douaumont plateau, village and fort, which another enemy contingent (IIIrd Corps) had taken. Happily, Balfourier's battalions were crack troops, and they were at full strength and comparatively fresh. Furthermore, their leader was an officer of talent. Without hesitation, as the brigade issued from Bras, on the Meuse, he threw it forward to the west of Douaumont, his action there resembling that of Sir Douglas Haig at Ypres on October 21, 1914, when the English general had stopped the dangerous gap, north of the town. At the battle of Verdun Balfourier stopped the gap which then existed (February 26th) between the Pepper ridge and the Douaumont position; he outflanked and overthrew the Germans at Louvemont; and then his battalions stormed and carried the Douaumont position, where they cut off and surrounded a famous German unit, the Brandenburg regiment, who had set foot into the partially dismantled and battered fort. This incident, of little interest in itself, created the widest sensation by the value which was universally attached to the enemy's pet units; and the curious facts concerning it were firstly: that few observers showed any interest in knowing who were the men who had beaten and cornered the smartest troops of the Kaiser; and secondly: that the real noteworthy incident of the day passed off practically unnoticed by the world at large. Yet this latter episode marked the true character of the battle, and the moral significance of the whole conflict since the cocksure and insolent aggressors had set foot in France.

It occurred at the moment when the recapture of Douaumont by the "iron division" of the 20th Corps was announced. Spontaneously, the troops which were coming on in the rear, in and around Verdun, burst into song; and the martial and triumphant strains of the *Marseillaise,* issuing from 80,000 throats, covered with their clamor the thunder of the guns.

It was the old spirit of Valmy reasserting itself. It was the voice of proud and unconquerable France. It was the trumpet of victory over a field of carnage; the willful expression of a people whose destiny was not at an end, and who meant to continue in the pursuit of the highest ideals of the human race—talent, honor, freedom.

That the victory was real and incontestable, there is no denying; for from the moment that the French reoccupied in strength their main lines around Verdun and connected them firmly with the rest of the front, a condition of affairs was created such as Joffre had been seeking all along with his policy of patience and economy. He had forced the Germans to undertake a new offensive with no military prospects for them whatever; and they were now condemned by their own action, their swaggering endurance, their *braggadocio* and Joffre's persistent refusal to attack them to squander the rest of their forces in a mad and hopeless endeavor; and this in the manner which their opponents most desired.

During three days (February 26th-29th) after their initial advance over devastated and useless ground, they assaulted with the greatest dash and determination the main French positions. But the defenders were now in strength; and the French guns at length took matters in hand. The German assaulting waves dashed themselves in vain against the Talou heights, the Pepper ridge, and the Vaux position. They were ripped open with cannon, broken by the French bayonets, and driven back with fearful slaughter, time and again. Finally the mauled and battered German columns collapsed, and they were withdrawn from the fray; the casualties of the assailants for the first full week of uninterrupted fighting being estimated, on the lowest computation, at 60,000.

For such heavy sacrifice the enemy technically had won nothing, although, as usual, he indulged in much boasting and he magnified tremendously the barren results he had obtained from the action—an insignificant and useless gain of ground, a few prisoners, and some disabled guns; this was really all he could show as the outcome of his plan which was meant to open to him the gates of Verdun and to place him in possession of the Heights of the Meuse. The French, who had only lost 20,000 men, continued to hold Verdun and the main positions surrounding it, including the above-mentioned Heights, the key to the whole region.

BY GENERAL VON FALKENHAYN

For the assault on Verdun the supply of ammunition considerably exceeded the quantity which all previous experience suggested as likely to be needed. Similarly, every demand for labor and equipment was complied with.

In order to divert the attention of the enemy from all these preparations, the other armies in the West were charged with the task of keeping him busy by small enterprises on their sectors. In this they acquitted themselves in exemplary fashion. On the 9th of January the Third Army attacked at Maisons de Champagne, on the 12th of February at Ste. Marie à Py, and on the 13th of the same month at Tahure. On the 28th and 29th of January the Second Army had a fine success at Frise, south of the Somme. The Sixth Army struck on the 26th of January at Neuville, on the 8th of February to the west of Vimy, and on the 21st of February east of Souchez. Gaede's Army Detachment pushed forward into the French lines near Obersept on the 13th of February. Everywhere the appointed objectives were reached, and the enemy suffered heavy losses.

The relatively slight German losses sustained on these occasions were justified, for it is highly probable that these operations materially contributed to mask our plans. In return, it was only in the nature of things that larger operations other than the main attack already planned should be discountenanced. When the Third Army inquired whether it was still to undertake a big attack on its sector, it was informed accordingly, and the following remarks were added in explanation of the plans to be followed in the Meuse sector: "Our precise problem is how to inflict heavy damage on the enemy at critical points at relatively small cost to ourselves. But we must not overlook the fact that previous experience of mass attacks in this war offers little inducement to imitate them. It would almost seem as if the questions of command and supply in these attacks were insoluble."

On the day appointed for the opening of the attack

the condition of the ground in the Meuse district, soaked with continuous rain, prevented any movement of the troops, while the poor visibility in the cloud-laden sky made artillery work impossible. Not till the middle of the month did the weather improve sufficiently to admit of the bombardment starting on the 21st of February.

The successful infantry attack on the following day was carried out with an irresistible impetus, and the enemy's first lines were simply overrun. Nor could the advanced fortifications, constructed in peace, stop the brave attackers, although these works were not much damaged by our artillery. On February 25th the 24th (Brandenburg) Infantry Regiment stormed the Fort Douaumont, the strong and reputedly impregnable north-eastern pillar of the Verdun defence system. Simultaneously the enemy gave way in the Orne valley as far as south of the Metz-Verdun road, so that the German front here also moved forward to the foot of the Heights of the Meuse. From many signs it was clear that this powerful German thrust had not only shaken the whole enemy front in the West very severely, but that its effects had not been lost on the peoples and the Governments of the Entente.

However, the Headquarters Staffs of the Army Groups considered it necessary to stay the forward movement against the Heights. Violent—one may say desperate—counter-attacks by troops collected in extreme haste from all parts of the front had begun. They were repulsed everywhere with very heavy loss to the enemy. The situation might have changed, however, had we not brought up our artillery, which had been unable to follow fast enough over the still barely passable roads, and assured the supply of ammunition and food.

Meanwhile the enemy had with astonishing rapidity brought a number of powerful batteries of artillery into position behind the Marre ridge, on the western bank of the river. Their half-flanking effect made itself severely felt on our assault troops. The discomfort caused by these guns had to be stopped. This could not possibly be effected from the right bank of the Meuse, for here we had our hands full in dealing with the enemy forces immediately confronting us. The only means available—as had been forseen and prepared for—was to push forward the German front on the left bank so far that its artillery could deal with the Franco-British guns on the Marre ridge more effectively than before. We now had troops available to carry out this necessary movement.

Apart from a weak attempt in Champagne, there had been no relief attacks by the enemy in any other sectors, and our observations showed that no preparations for any immediate attack of this sort were in hand. Indeed, it had become highly improbable. The French had nearly got together the whole of their reserves from the rest of their front, and had quickly handed over to the English the sector near Arras, formerly held by them, in order to provide the wherewithal to hold their positions in the Meuse sector. The English had been compelled, by taking over the Arras sector, to extend their line so much, that nothing on a big scale from this direction was to be apprehended. To be sure, the formation of Kitchener's conscript armies in England was proceeding vigorously. Thus it was to be anticipated that the forty to forty-two English divisions, whose presence on the Continent had been established, would be nearly doubled at no very distant date. Whether, and when, these new troops would become fit for use in an offensive was still, however, a matter of uncertainty.

In these circumstances the question that had to be considered by G. H. Q. was whether to intimate that the continuance of the operation on the Meuse would be abandoned, and a new enterprise started on another front. This measure would have meant a complete departure from the views on which the attack north of Verdun was based. Nor was there any reason for doing so. We had hitherto achieved what we had set out to achieve, and there was every reason to hope we should do so again in the future. As a matter of fact, that is what actually happened. No offensive elsewhere had particularly good prospects. The enemy still held their line in great strength. The English, for example, had from seven to eight men to every yard of their front.

Success was to be gained against positions so strongly held as these only by employing the artillery we had concentrated on the Meuse. Further, it would have meant a great loss of time, and the enemy would assuredly have taken advantage of this to transfer his reserves likewise. It was therefore decided to renounce the idea of changing the scene of operations.

The attack carried out on the 6th of March and in the succeeding weeks on the west bank succeeded to this extent, that the French were thrown out of their foremost lines with heavy casualties every time. Owing to the peculiar confirmation of the country we could not use these successes to bring our artillery far enough forward, and consequently the preparatory work here had to be continued. Intense fighting lasted for the whole month of April on the western bank. Not till our occupation of the main portion of Hill 304, on the 7th of May, was there any momentary pause in our attack in this sector.

The conduct of the actions in the Meuse sector was at first directly in the hands of the H. Q. Staff of the Crown Prince's Army Group itself. But with the extension of operations some relief of the burden on this Staff became necessary. Accordingly, in March, while preserving its control, we put General von Mudra in command on the right bank, and on the left General von Gallwitz, whose command of the Eleventh Army in Macedonia was taken over by Lieutenant-General von Winckler.

As already stated, there had been a temporary cessation of our attack in the western sector; but it must not be assumed from this that things had become absolutely quiet there. Here, as on the eastern bank, the fighting raged continuously and more fiercely than ever. The French saw to that with their practically incessant counter-attacks. The artillery battle never stopped. The raids of the defenders were generally relieved by big thrusts carried out by forces far superior to those of the attackers. For example, a particularly resolute thrust was made on the 22nd and 23rd of May, in the region of Douaumont, and for a time our hold on the armored fort was in danger.

For our part, we usually confined ourselves to sending our opponents home with bloody pates, recovering from him such small patches of ground as he might have gained here and there, and, where necessary, effecting slight improvements in our positions. Nevertheless, this fighting without visible or—for the man at the front—tangible result afforded the sternest test imaginable of the capabilities of the troops. With very few exceptions they stood the test most brilliantly. The enemy nowhere secured any permanent advantages; nowhere could he free himself from the German pressure. On the other hand, the losses he sustained were very severe. They were carefully noted and compared with our own which, unhappily, were not light. The result was that the comparison worked out at something like two and a half to one: that is to say, for two Germans put out of action five Frenchmen had to shed their blood. But deplorable as were the German sacrifices, they were certainly made in a most promising cause.

### BY CROWN PRINCE FREDERICK WILLIAM

The attack on Verdun began on February 21th, 1916, and the huge successes of the first three days are well known. The infantry of the Third, Eighteenth and Seventh Reserve Corps performed marvels of courage. The taking of Fort Douaumont crowned everything. Indeed, we should, after all, have succeeded in rushing the entire east front of Verdun, if the reserves promised us had arrived on time. Why they failed to do so is not within my knowledge.

I was told by Captain von Brandis, who stormed Fort Douaumont, that, on the fourth day, he had observed a complete absence of Frenchmen in the whole district of Douaumont-Souville-Tavannes. But our own troops had exhausted their strength; the weather was horrible, and rations could not everywhere be brought up as needed. That it would have been possible to take the entire east front of Verdun by at once continuing the attack is clear from the fact that the local leaders of the French had already ordered the evacuation. Only later was this order countermanded by General Joffre.

The fatigue of our troops after a huge military performance and the lack of reserves despoiled us of the prize of victory. I bring no accusation; I merely record the fact.

From that day onward, surprises were no longer possible; and the early impetuous advances by storm gave place to a gigantic wrestle and struggle for every foot of ground. Within a few weeks, I perceived clearly that it would not be feasible to break through the stubborn defense, and that our own losses would ultimately be quite out of proportion to the gains. Consequently, I soon did everything in my power to stop the attacks; and I repeatedly gave expression to my views and the deductions to be drawn from them. In this matter I stood somewhat opposed to my then Chief of Staff, General Schmidt von Knobelsdorf, and my representations were at first put aside; the orders ran, "Continue to attack."

### NARRATIVES BY EYE-WITNESSES

*Lord Northcliffe, the great British newspaper owner,*
*writes from the French Headquarters on the field,*
*March 4th.*

What is the secret motive underlying the German attempt to break the French line at Verdun, in which the Crown Prince's Army is incurring such appalling losses? Is it financial, in view of the coming war loan? Is it dynastic? Or is it intended to influence doubting neutrals? From the evidence of German deserters it is known that the attack was originally intended to take place a month or two hence, when the ground was dry. Premature spring caused the Germans to accelerate their plans. There were two final delays owing to bad weather, and then came the colossal onslaught of February 21st.

The Germans made a good many of the mistakes we made at Gallipoli. They announced that something large was pending by closing the Swiss frontier. The French, who were not ready, were also warned by their own astute Intelligence Department. Their *avions* were not idle, and, if confirmation were needed, it was given by deserters, who, surmising the horrors that were to come, crept out of the trenches at night, lay down by the edge of the Meuse till the morning, and then gave themselves up, together with information that has since proved to be accurate.

The district of Verdun lies in one of the coldest and also the most misty sectors in the long line between Nieuport and Switzerland. Changes of temperature, too, are somewhat more frequent here than elsewhere; and so sudden are these changes that not long ago here occurred, on a part of the front, one of nature's furious and romantic reminders of her power to impose her will. The opposing French and German trenches, their parapets hard frozen, were so close that they were actually within hearing of each other. Towards dawn a rapid thaw set in. The parapets melted and subsided, and two long lines of men stood up naked, as it were, before each other, face to face with only two possibilities—wholesale murder on the one side or the other, or a temporary unofficial peace for the making of fresh parapet protections. The situation was astounding and unique in the history of trench warfare. The French and German officers, without conferring and unwilling to negotiate, turned their backs so that they might not see officially so unwarlike a scene, and the men on each side rebuilt their parapets without the firing of a single shot.

This instance serves to illustrate the precarious weather in which the Germans undertook an adventure in the quick success of which the elements play such a part. That the attack would certainly prove more costly to them than to the French the German Staff must have known. That the sufferings of the wounded lying out through the long nights of icy wind in the No Man's Land between the lines would be great did not probably disturb the Crown Prince. It is one of the most grewsome facts in the history of the War that the French, peering through the moonlight at what they thought to be stealthily crawling Germans, found them to be wounded men frozen to death.

During the War, in France and in Flanders, in camps and in hospitals, I have conserved with at least 100 Germans. Prisoners' talk is always to be accepted with great reserve, but the prisoners of the Verdun campaign have so plainly horror and misery depicted upon their countenances that I need no other evidence as to the tragedy through which they have passed.

The town is being made into a second Ypres by the Germans. Yet, as it stands out in the sunlight, it is difficult to realize that it is a place whose people have all gone, save a few of the faithful who live below ground. The tall tower of Verdun still stands. Close by us is a hidden French battery, and it is pretty to see the promptitude with which it sends its screaming shells back to the Germans within a few seconds of the dispatch of a missive from the Huns. One speedily grows accustomed to the sound and the scene, and can follow the position of the villages about which the Germans endeavor to mislead the world by wireless every morning.

We journey farther afield, and the famous fort of Douaumont is pointed out. The storming of Fort Douaumont, gunless and unmanned, was a military operation of little value. A number of the Brandenburgers climbed into the gunless fort, and some of them were still there on March 6th, supplied precariously with food by their comrades at night. They were practically surrounded by the French, whose Headquarters Staff regarded the whole incident as a simple episode in the give-and-take of war. The announcement of the fall of Fort Douaumont to the world evinces the great anxiety of the Germans to magnify anything concerning Verdun into a great event. It should also cause people to apply a grain of salt to German official *communiqués* before swallowing them.

### A Neutral Eye-witness Pictures the Preparations of the German Artillery

Over the roads leading towards Verdun artillery and ammunition were brought up in such quantities as the history of war has never seen on such a small space. The country was covered with guns. We could hardly believe what we saw round Verdun. Long rows of guns as in old battle pictures, set up in open fields with gunners standing about them, and on the hill-tops observation-posts with their great telescopes uncovered. When I shut my eyes I still see before me those curved lines, row upon row in endless array, with gunners moving about them in the open battlefield.

### The First Attack, February 21st, described by a French Staff Officer

Thousands of projectiles are flying in all directions, some whistling, others howling, others moaning low, and all uniting in one infernal roar. From time to time an aërial torpedo passes, making a noise like a gigantic motor car. With a tremendous thud a giant shell bursts quite close to our observation post, breaking the telephone wire and interrupting all communication with our batteries.

A man gets out at once for repairs, crawling along on his stomach through all this place of bursting mines and shells. It seems quite impossible that he should escape in the rain of shell, which exceeds anything imaginable; there has never been such a bombardment in war. Our man seems to be enveloped in explosions, and shelters himself from time to time in the shell craters which honeycomb the ground; finally he reaches a less stormy spot, mends his wires, and then, as it would be madness to try to return, settles down in a big crater and waits for the storm to pass.

Beyond, in the valley, dark masses are moving over the snow-covered ground. It is German infantry advancing in packed formation along the valley to the attack. They look like a big gray carpet being unrolled over the country. We telephone through to the batteries and the ball begins. The sight is hellish. In the distance, in the valley and upon the slopes, regiments spread out, and as they deploy fresh troops come pouring in.

There is a whistle over our heads. It is our first shell. It falls right in the middle of the enemy infantry. We telephone through, telling our batteries of their hit, and a deluge of heavy shells is poured on the enemy. Their position becomes critical. Through glasses we can see men maddened, men covered with earth and blood, falling one upon the other. When the first wave of the assault is decimated, the ground is dotted with heaps of corpses, but the second wave is al-

ready pressing on.   Once more our shells carve awful gaps
in their ranks.   Nevertheless, like an army of rats the Boches
continue to advance in spite of our "marmites."   Then our
heavy artillery bursts forth in fury.   The whole valley is
turned into a volcano, and its exit is stopped by the barrier
of the slain.

*A French Officer pictures a Scene from the French With-
drawal*

In the afternoon of February 23rd, while we had not retired a single foot, order was given us to withdraw carefully, for, the Waville wood having been taken, we ran the
risk of being surrounded.   We waited for the night to come.
Some of our men, when they learned that we were to leave,
protested, asking to be allowed to fight and die on the spot.
However, tactical reasons obliged us to evacuate Herbebois,
and we had to reckon with the general situation.

The retirement order was executed, and we went to take
a position in front of La Chaume wood, in communication
with the units on our right and left.

The defense of Herbebois will certainly remain one of
the most glorious pages in the annals of our regiment.   More
than 3,000 Germans came in successive waves to smash themselves against our ranks, although we were in a fighting position of the most disadvantageous kind.   We voluntarily
abandoned the ground, where hundreds and hundreds of German corpses show sufficiently how effective was our resistance.

Neither the bombardment, nor the snow, nor the difficulties of obtaining provisions, nor fatigue could overcome
the stubborn bravery of our infantry.   By thus holding firm
in this corner of Herbebois they for their part contributed
to win time for the arrival of the necessary reserves, and they
seriously interfered with the advance of the Germans.   It
was sacrifices of this kind, repeated at numerous points on
our front, which held back the enemy flood.

*The Destruction of Fort Douaumont on February 26th,*
*described by a French Soldier*

Despite the horror of it, despite the ceaseless flow of blood, one wants to see. One's soul wants to feed on the sight of the brute Boches falling. I stopped on the ground for hours, and when I closed my eyes I saw the whole picture again. The guns are firing at 200 and 300 yards, and shrapnel is exploding with a crash, scything them down. Our men hold their ground; our machine guns keep to their work, and yet they advance.

Near me, as I lie in the mud, there is a giant wrapped in one of our uniforms with a steel helmet on his head. He seems to be dead, he is so absolutely still. At a given moment the Boches are quite close to us. Despite the noise of the guns one can hear their oaths and their shouts as they strike. Then the giant next to me jumps up, and with a voice like a stentor shouts in German, *"Hier da! Hier da!"* Mechanically some of us get up. My wound, which had been dressed, left me free and I had forgotten it. I was unarmed, and so I struck him with my steel helmet and he dropped, with his head broken. An officer who was passing sees the incident and takes off the man's coat. Below is a German uniform. Where had the spy come from and how had he got there?

But the Boches are returning again massed to the assault, and they are being killed in bulk. It makes one think that in declaring war the Kaiser had sworn the destruction of his race, and he would have shown good taste in doing so. Their gunfire is slackening now, and ours redoubles. The fort has gone, and if under its ruins there are left a few guns and gunners the bulk of the guns are firing from outside. The machine guns are coming up and getting in position, and our men are moving on in numerous waves.

I find a rifle belonging to a comrade who has fallen and join the Chasseurs with the fifty cartridges that I have left. What a fight it is, and what troops! From time to time a man falls, rises, shoots, runs, shoots again, keeps on firing, fights with his bayonet, and then, worn out, falls, to be trampled on without raising a cry. The storm of fire continues. Everything is on fire—the wood near by, the village of Douaumont, Verdun, the front of Bezonvaux, and the back of Thiaumont. There is fire everywhere. The acrid smell of carbonic acid and blood catches at our throats, but the battle goes on.

They are brave, but one of our men is worth two of theirs, especially in hand-to-hand fighting. They bend and fall back, and the sound of the song they sing to order, *"Heil dir im Siegerkranz,"* only reaches us in hiccoughs. Our reënforcements continue to arrive. We are the masters. Our officers, with wonderful coolness, control the ardor of the troops. The infantry action is over. By its *tirs de barrage* the artillery is holding that of the enemy, and we keep awaiting the fresh order for action in silence.

### German Advance of April 2nd from Caillette toward Fort Vaux described by a French Staff Officer

A wonderful work was accomplished that Sunday forenoon in the livid, Londonlike fog and twilight produced by the lowering clouds and battle smoke. While the German assault columns in the van fought the French hand to hand, picked corps of workers behind them formed an amazing human chain from the woods to the east over the shoulder of the center of the Douaumont slope to the crossroads of a network of communication trenches, 600 yards in the rear.

Four deep was this chain, and along its line of nearly 3,000 men passed an unending stream of wooden billets, sandbags, chevaux-de-frise, steel shelters, and light mitrailleuses, in a word, all the material for defensive fortifications, like buckets at a country fire.

Despite the hurricane of French artillery fire, the German commander had adopted the only possible means of rapid transport over the shell-torn ground, covered with débris, over which neither horse nor cart could go. Every moment counted. Unless barriers rose swiftly the French counterattacks, already massing, would sweep the assailants back into the wood.

Cover was disdained. The workers stood at full height,

and the chain stretched openly across the hollows and hillocks, a fair target for the French gunners. The latter missed no chance. Again and again great rents were torn in the line by the bursting melinite, but as coolly as at maneuvers the iron-disciplined soldiers of Germany sprang forward from shelters to take the places of the fallen, and the work went apace.

Gradually another line doubled the chain of the workers, as the upheaved corpses formed a continuous embankment, each additional dead man giving greater protection to his comrades, until the barrier began to form shape along the diameter of the wood. There others were digging and burying logs deep into the earth, installing shelters and mitrailleuses, or feverishly building fortifications.

At last the work was ended at fearful cost, but as the vanguard sullenly withdrew behind it, from the whole length burst a havoc of flame upon the advancing Frenchmen. Vainly the latter dashed forward. They could not pass, and as the evening fell the barrier still held, covering the German working parties, burrowing like moles in the maze of trenches and boyaux.

So solid was the barricade, padded with sandbags and earthworks, that the artillery fire fell practically unavailing, and the French General realized that the barrier must be breached by explosives as in Napoleon's battles.

It was 8 o'clock and already pitch dark in that blighted atmosphere as a special blasting corps, as devoted as the German chain workers, crept forward toward the German position. The rest of the French waited, sheltered in the ravine east of Douaumont, until an explosion should signal the assault.

In Indian file, to give the least possible sign of their presence to the hostile sentinels, the blasting corps advanced in a long line, at first with comparative rapidity, only stiffening into the grotesque rigidity of simulated death when the searchlights played upon them, and resuming progress when the beam shifted; then as they approached the barrier they moved slowly and more slowly.

When they arrived within fifty yards the movement of

the crawling men became imperceptible; the German star-shells and sentinels surpassed the searchlights in vigilance.

The blasting corps lay at full length, just like hundreds of other motionless forms about them, but all were working busily. With a short trowel each file leader scuffled the earth from under the body, taking care not to raise his arms, and gradually making a shallow trench deep enough to hide him. The others followed his example until the whole line had sunk below the surface. Then the leader began scooping gently forward while his followers deepened the furrow already made.

Thus literally, inch by inch, the files stole forward, sheltered in a narrow ditch from the gusts of German mitrailleuse fire that constantly swept the terrain. Here and there the sentinels' eye caught a suspicious movement and an incautiously raised head sank down, pierced by a bullet. But the stealthily mole-like advance continued.

Hours passed. It was nearly dawn when the remnant of the blasting corps reached the barricade at last, and hurriedly put their explosives in position. Back they wriggled breathlessly. An over-hasty movement meant death, yet they must needs hurry lest the imminent explosions overwhelm them.

Suddenly there comes a roar that dwarfs the cannonade, and along the barrier fountains of fire rise skyward, hurling a rain of fragments upon what was left of the blasting party.

The barricade was breached, but 75 per cent. of the devoted corps had given their lives to do it.

As the survivors lay exhausted, the attackers charged over them, cheering. In the mêlée that followed there was no room to shoot or wield the rifle.

Some of the French fought with unfixed bayonets like the stabbing swords of the Roman legions. Others had knives or clubs. All were battle-frenzied, as only Frenchmen can be.

The Germans broke, and as the first rays of dawn streaked the sky, only a small northern section of the wood was still in their hands. There a similar barrier stopped progress, and it was evident that the night's work must be repeated.  But the hearts of the French soldiers were leaping with victory as they dug furiously to consolidate the ground they had gained, strewn with German bodies as thick as leaves.

Over 6,000 Germans were counted in a section a quarter of a mile square, and the conquerors saw why their cannonade had been so ineffective.  The enemy had piled a second barrier of corpses close behind the first, so that the soft human flesh would act as a buffer to neutralize the force of the shells.

### BY GENERAL VON LUDENDORFF

Verdun from the viewpoint of general strategy was well chosen as the place for our attack; for Verdun was a particularly threatening starting-point for a French counter-assault.  It very seriously threatened our main line of railroad communication with Germany.  This was disastrously proved by the attack launched from there in the fall of 1918.[1]  Had we been able to drive the French wholly from the east bank of the Meuse, our victory would have been complete, as this would have materially strengthened our position along the whole western front.

The first days of the Verdun assault were very successful, made so by the brilliant qualities of our men.  The advantage, however, was insufficiently exploited and our advance soon came to a standstill.  At the beginning of March the world was still under the impression that the Germans had won a victory at Verdun.

[1] This refers to Pershing's Argonne-Meuse attack.

U-Boat 53 off Nantucket Lightship, met by the United States

The U-Boat Raid off New
England

U-Boat 53 off Nantucket Lightship, met by the United States
"Destroyer Benham"

Painting by Willy Stower

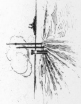

# ARMED INTERVENTION IN MEXICO

## THE UNITED STATES VOLUNTEER ARMY GATHERED AND TRAINED

### MARCH 15TH-JUNE 18TH

GENERAL JOHN PERSHING          VENUSTIANO CARRANZA
GENERAL FREDERICK FUNSTON          ROBERT LANSING

The troubles of the United States with Mexico in 1916 are now known to have been deliberately fomented by the German Government. Even while America was opposing the Allies for Germany's sake in the matter of the new merchant submarines, Germany knowing that she meant to break her submarine pact with the Americans if she found it advisable, was plotting to embroil them in difficulties at home which should make them powerless against her. Hence she stirred up the rival Mexican leaders, Carranza and Villa, to insult and defy their great northern neighbor.

Villa began on January 11, 1916, by seizing a train in the State of Chihuahua, taking from it nineteen United States citizens and shooting them. On March 9th, with 1,500 troops, he attacked the town of Columbus in New Mexico, plundered it and slew eleven civilians before the nearest U. S. troops could reach the town. The troopers put Villa's bandits to flight and killed about thirty of them, but with a loss of nine troopers slain. These two outrages roused the United States people and Government to a just resentment which insisted upon decisive action. The Mexican President, Carranza, insisted that his own soldiers would punish the Villistas and that the United States must not interfere. But patience with this helpless and empty worded braggart, puffed up with German promises, had ceased to be longer possible. General Funston, the U. S. commander along the border, was authorized to send a strong American column into Mexico to pursue Villa, capture him "alive or dead," and disperse his murderous followers. General Pershing was placed in command of the invading column.

Pershing's force of over 4,000 men entered Mexico on March 15th, and remained there until early in 1917. On March 29th a genuine small-scale battle occurred near Parral in Chihuahua between some 400 U. S. troops and a larger force of Villistas. These were completely defeated and many of them killed, with only a single death on the side of the well-armed U. S. troops. Villa himself had been wounded by Carranza's troops previously, and now his entire forces were dispersed or took refuge in the inaccessible mountains.

The U. S. soldiers continued in pursuit of the scattered Villistas, and were brought into serious clashes with the Carranza troops who, now that Villa was disposed of, began to appear in Chihuahua in ever-increasing numbers. The first armed conflict was at Parral on April

61

12th, when the Mexicans endeavored to ambush and entrap a force of 150 U. S. soldiers who approached them in amity. Two of the U. S. troops were slain, but the force turned upon its would-be destroyers and drove them off with heavy losses. On June 24th a more serious affray occurred at Carrizal. Eighty-four U. S. cavalrymen under Captain Boyd were encircled by an entire Mexican army under General Gomez, while Gomez himself engaged in an apparently amicable parley with Boyd. Then the Mexican general withdrew, and without any warning the Mexicans suddenly attacked their peaceful visitors. About half the U. S. troopers succeeded in fighting their way through the encircling foes, but Captain Boyd and about fourteen others were killed and twenty-four captured.

War trembled in the balance. The danger was the more serious because just before this, President Wilson had decided that the Mexican difficulty had become too menacing to be left to the small U. S. army of "regulars." So on June 18th he called out the volunteer army, the National Guard of all the States. These were already gathering on the Mexican border.

President Carranza now, however, awakened to the folly of which he had been guilty. The captured U. S. troops were restored, and on July 4th an apologetic note requested a conference to prevent further warlike difficulties. This conference continued to sit until the end of the year. Meanwhile the U. S. militia all along the border had a season of excellent training which prepared them for the sterner warfare they were soon to undertake in Europe.

C. F. H.

## BY GENERAL PERSHING
### Official Report of the Dispersal of Villa's Forces

SAN GERONIMO RANCH, March 30, 1916.

DODD struck Villa's command, consisting of 500, 6 o'clock, March 29th, at Guerrero. Villa, who is suffering from a broken leg and lame hip, was not present. Number Villa's dead known to be thirty, probably others carried away dead. Dodd captured two machine guns, large number horses, saddles, and arms. Our casualties, four enlisted men wounded, none seriously.

Attack was surprise, the Villa troops being driven in a ten-mile running fight and retreated to mountains northeast of railroad, where they separated into small bands. Large number Carranzista prisoners, who were being held for execution, were liberated during the fight. In order to reach Guerrero, Dodd marched fifty-five miles in seventeen hours and carried on fight for five hours.

Eliseo Hernandez, who commanded Villa's troops, was killed in fight. With Villa permanently disabled, Lopez wounded, and Hernandez dead, the blow administered is a serious one to Villa's band.

### BY GENERAL FUNSTON
#### Official Report of April 15th on the Mexican Attack at Parral

Frank Tompkins's column, Troop K, Thirteenth Cavalry, and Troop M, Thirteenth Cavalry, entered Parral 11 a. m., 12th instant. Proceeding was cordially received by higher civil and military authorities. Military Commander General Lozano accompanied Major Frank Tompkins on way to camp.

In the outskirts of the town groups of native troops and civilians, following, jeered, threw stones, and fired on column. Major Frank Tompkins took defensive position north of railroad, but was soon flanked by native troops and forced to further retire.

About 300 Carranza troops joined in pursuit, and Major Frank Tompkins continued to withdraw to avoid further complications until he reached Santa Cruz, eight miles from Parral. Fighting ceased about fifteen miles from town. Major Frank Tompkins deserves great praise for his forbearance. General Lozano attempted to control his men when fight first began, but failed to.

Colonel Brown, with Major Charles Young, Tenth Cavalry, squadron of Tenth Cavalry, eight miles away when notified, and joined Major Frank Tompkins 7 p. m. Reported privately forty Mexicans killed, all soldiers, including one major. One civilian wounded. Americans killed, two; wounded, six; missing, one.

Major R. L. Howze, Eleventh Cavalry, arrived Parral yesterday from San Berja and Ballesea, having had several skirmishes with Villa men. One man killed, two wounded.

### BY PRESIDENT CARRANZA
#### Protest Transmitted, Through His Secretary, to the U. S. Government[1]

MEXICO, D. F., May 22, 1916.

1. The Mexican Government has just been informed

---

[1] The somewhat unusual phraseology of this protest has not been altered, as it is the semi-official translation presented to the U. S. Government.

that a group of American troops, crossing the international boundary, has entered Mexican territory and is at the present time near a place called El Pino, located about sixty miles south of the line.

The crossing of these troops effected again without the consent of the Mexican Government gravely endangers the harmony and good relations which should exist between the Governments of the United States and Mexico.

This Government must consider the above action as a violation of the sovereignty of Mexico, and therefore it requests in a most urgent manner that the Washington Government should consider the case carefully in order to definitely outline the policy it should follow with regard to the Mexican Nation.

In order to afford a clear understanding of the basis of the request involved in this note, it becomes necessary to carefully review the incidents which have occurred up to the present time.

2.   On account of the incursion at Columbus, N. M., by a band led by Francisco Villa on the morning of March 9, 1916, the Mexican Government, sincerely deploring the occurrence, and for the purpose of affording efficacious protection to the frontier, advanced its desire that the Governments of the United States and Mexico should enter into an agreement for the pursuit of bandits. The above proposal was made by the Government of Mexico guided by the precedent established under similar conditions obtaining in the years 1880 to 1884, and requested, in concrete, a permission for Mexican forces to cross into American territory in pursuit of bandits, under a condition of reciprocity which would permit American forces to cross into Mexican territory, if the Columbus incident should be repeated in any other point of the frontier line.

As a consequence of this proposal made in the Mexican note of March 10th the Government of the United States, through error or haste, considered that the good disposition shown by the Mexican Government was sufficient to authorize the crossing of the boundary, and to that effect, without awaiting the conclusion of a formal agreement on the matter, ordered that a column of American forces should cross into Mexican territory in pursuit of Villa and his band.

3. The American Government, on this account, made emphatic declarations, assuring the Mexican Government that it was acting with entire good faith and stating that its only purpose in crossing the frontier was to pursue and capture or destroy the Villa band that had assaulted Columbus; that this action did not mean an invasion of our territory, nor any intention to impair Mexican sovereignty, and that as soon as a practical result should be obtained the American troops would withdraw from Mexican territory.

4. The Mexican Government was not informed that the American troops had crossed the frontier until March 17th, at which time it was unofficially known, through private channels from El Paso, that the American troops had entered into Mexican territory. This Government then addressed a note to the Government of the United States stating that, inasmuch as the precise terms and conventions of an agreement which should be formally entered into between both countries for the crossing of troops had not been stipulated, the American Government should not consider itself authorized to send the expedition.

The Washington Government explained the sending of such expedition, expressing its regret that a misinterpretation had occurred in regard to the attitude of the Mexican Government concerning the crossing of American troops over the boundary line in pursuit of Villa, but that this had been done under the impression that the previous exchange of messages implied the full consent of the Mexican Government, without the necessity of further formalities.

The American Government explained also that its attitude was due to the necessity of quick action, and stated that it was disposed to receive any suggestions the Mexican Government would wish to make in regard to the terms of a definite agreement covering the operations of troops on either side of the boundary.

5. Both Governments then began to discuss the terms of an agreement in accordance to which the reciprocal crossing of troops should be arranged, and to this end two projects

from the Mexican Government and two counter-projects from the American Government were exchanged. During the discussion of this agreement the Mexican Government constantly insisted that the above-mentioned crossing should be limited within a zone of operations for the troops in foreign territory, that the time the troops should remain within it, the number of soldiers of an expedition and the class of arms they should pertain to should be fixed.

The Government of the United States objected to the above limitations, and when at last the American Government submitted the last counter-draft, accepting them in part, it stated, nevertheless, that while agreeing to sign the agreement, the latter would not apply on the Columbus expedition.

6. This attitude of the American Government brought forth the Mexican note of April 12th, in which, deferring the discussion of the agreement, since the latter was not to apply to the Columbus case, the Mexican Government requested the American Government to withdraw its troops, since the stay of them was not based on any agreement, and the expedition was then unnecessary, inasmuch as the Villa bandits had been dispersed and reduced to impotency.

7. While the American Government was delaying its reply to the aforesaid note of April 12th, and took no action to withdraw its troops, it was considered convenient that military commanders of both countries should meet in some point of the frontier to review the military aspect of the situation and endeavor through this channel to arrive at a satisfactory solution, which on the part of Mexico consisted in the withdrawal of American troops from its territory.

To this end Generals Hugh L. Scott and Frederick Funston, representing the American Government, and General Alvaro Obregon, Secretary of War and Marine, representing Mexico, met, at Ciudad Juarez and El Paso, where they held a series of conferences within an open spirit of cordiality. During these conferences full explanations and data were exchanged concerning the military situation on the frontier.

As a result of these conferences a draft of a memorandum was submitted to the approval of the Washington and Mexican Governments in accordance with which General Scott declared that the destruction and dispersion of the Villa band had been completed, and, therefore, the American Government has decided to begin the withdrawal of its troops under the promise that the Mexican Government would endeavor to maintain efficacious guard on the frontier against new incursions similar to that at Columbus.

8. The Mexican Government refused to approve that sort of agreement, because it was stated in it, besides, that the American Government could suspend the withdrawal of its troops if any other incident should occur which would serve to change the belief of the Washington Government in the ability of the Mexican Government to protect the frontier.

The Mexican Government could not accept this condition to suspend the withdrawal, because the evacuation of its territory is a matter entirely affecting the sovereignty of the country, which should at no time be subjected to the discretion of the American Government, it being possible on the other hand that another incident might occur which would give the indefinite stay of the American troops in Mexican territory a certain color of legality.

9. General Scott, General Funston, and General Obregon were discussing this point, when on the 5th of the present month of May a band of outlaws assaulted an American garrison at Glenn Springs, on the American side, crossing the Rio Grande immediately after to enter into Mexican territory via Boquillas.

10. On this account, and fearing that the American Government would hasten the crossing of new troops into Mexican territory in pursuit of the outlaws, the Mexican Government instructed General Obregon to notify the United States that the crossing of American soldiers on this new account would not be permitted to enter into Mexico, and that orders had already been given to all military commanders on the frontier to prevent it.

11. When the attitude of the Mexican Government became known Generals Scott and Funston assured General

Obregon that no movement of American troops had been ordered to cross the frontier on account of the Boquillas incident, and that no more American soldiers would enter into our territory.

This assurance, which was personally made by Generals Scott and Funston to General Obregon when the conferences were about to be adjourned, was reiterated by General Scott himself in a later private conversation he had with Licenciado Juan Neftali Amador, Sub-Secretary for Foreign Affairs, who had had the opportunity to take part in the conferences between the American and the Mexican military commanders.

12.   On account of the same incident of Glenn Springs, or Boquillas, fearing that the various bands of outlaws which are organized or armed near the frontier might repeat their incursions, and with a view to procuring an effective military coöperation between American and Mexican forces, this Government suggested through its representative, General Obregon, to Generals Scott and Funston, representing the United States, the convenience of reaching an understanding on a military plan of distribution of troops along the frontier in order that an effective watch could be kept over the whole region, and avoiding in this way, so far as possible, the recurrence of similar assaults.  The Mexican Government showed by this action not only its good faith and good wishes, but also its frank willingness to arrive at an effective coöperation with the Government of the United States to avoid all further sense of friction between the two countries.

This plan for the distribution of American and Mexican forces in their respective territories along the frontier was proposed as a means to prevent immediately any new difficulty, and always with the idea of arriving later at the celebration of an agreement for the reciprocal crossing of troops, as long as the abnormal conditions exist in our territory.

13.   The conferences between Generals Scott, Funston, and Obregon adjourned on May 11th without reaching any agreement concerning the unconditional withdrawal of the

American troops.  General Scott insisted in the form of the memorandum concerning the conditional withdrawal of the American forces, but did not take into consideration the plan proposed by the Mexican Government for the protection of the frontier by means of detachments along the same.

Under these conditions it was left for the Governments of Washington and Mexico to conclude the arrangements initiated during the conferences of Ciudad Juarez and El Paso.  Up to that time no complication had occurred on account of the new Boquillas incident, and all the assurances given by Generals Scott and Funston led us to suppose that the above incident would not bring about new difficulties.

14.  The Mexican Government, however, has just been informed that 400 men of the Eighth Regiment of the American Army are in Mexican territory, having crossed the line in the direction of Boquillas approximately between the 10th and 11th of May, and are at present near a place called El Pino, about sixty miles south of the frontier.  This fact was brought to the attention of the Mexican authorities by the commander himself of the American troops which crossed the frontier, who gave advice to the Mexican military commander at Esmeraldo, Sierra Mojada, by a communication in which he informed him that he crossed the frontier in pursuit of the band of outlaws which had assaulted Glenn Springs, and in accordance with an agreement existing between the American and the Mexican Governments regarding the crossing of troops, and with the consent of a Mexican Consular official in Del Rio, Texas, to whom the commander alleged he had announced the entry of his expedition.

15.  The Mexican Government cannot assume that an error has been committed a second time by the American Government ordering the crossing of its troops without the consent of the Government of Mexico.  It fails to understand also that a commander of troops of the United States Army would enter into Mexican territory without the due authority from his superiors, and believing that he could secure permission for the crossing of his troops from a Consular agent.

The explanation given by the American Government in regard to the crossing of troops at Columbus has never been satisfactory to the Mexican Government; but the new invasion of our territory is no longer an isolated fact and tends to convince the Mexican Government that something more than a mere error is involved.

16. This latter act of the American forces causes new complications for the Mexican Government in the possibility of a satisfactory solution and increases the tenseness of the international situation between both countries.

The Mexican Government cannot consider this last incident except as an invasion of our territory, made by American forces against the expressed will of the Mexican Government, and it is its duty to request, as it does, the American Government to order the immediate withdrawal of these new forces and to abstain completely from sending any other expedition of a similar character.

17. The Mexican Government understands its obligation to protect the frontier; but this obligation is not exclusively its own, and it expects that the American Government, which is subject to an equal obligation, will appreciate the material difficulties with which this task is met, inasmuch as the American troops themselves, notwithstanding their number and in spite of the fact that their attention is not shared by other military operations, are physically unable to effectively protect the frontier on the American side.

The Mexican Government has made every effort on its part to protect the frontier without disregarding, on the other hand, the considerable task of pacification which is being performed in the rest of the country, and the American Government should understand that if now and then any lamentable incursions into American territory committed by irresponsible bands of outlaws might occur, this should be a case of pecuniary reparation and a reason to adopt a combined defense, but never a cause for the American authorities to invade our national territory.

The incursion of bands of outlaws into American territory is a deplorable incident, to say the least, but in no way can the Mexican Government be made responsible for them, inasmuch as it is doing everything possible to prevent them. The crossing of regular American troops into Mexican territory, against the express will of the Mexican Government, does constitute an act of which the American Government is responsible.

18. The Mexican Government, therefore, believes that the time has come for it to insist with the American Government that in withdrawing at once the new Boquillas expedition it should abstain in the future from sending new troops. In any case, the Mexican Government after having made clear its unwillingness to permit the crossing of new American troops into Mexican territory, will have to consider the latter as an act of invasion of its territory, and therefore it will be forced to defend itself against any group of American troops which may be found within it.

19. With reference to the troops which are now interned in the State of Chihuahua on account of the Columbus incident, the Mexican Government is compelled to insist on their withdrawal.

The Mexican Government understands that, in the face of the unwillingness of the American Government to withdraw the above forces, it would be left no other recourse than to procure the defense of its territory by means of arms, but it understands at the same time its duty to avoid as far as possible an armed conflict between both countries; and, acting in accordance with Article 21 of the treaty of February 2, 1848, it considers it its duty to resort to all means of a peaceful character to find a solution of the international conflict in which both countries are involved.

20. The Mexican Government considers it necessary to avail itself of this opportunity to request the American Government to give a more categorical explanation of its real intentions toward Mexico. To this end it hopes that in speaking with entire frankness its words may not be interpreted as tending to wound the sensibility of the American Government; but that it finds itself in the condition to set aside all diplomatic euphemism, in order to express its ideas with entire frankness. If in the expression of the grievances hereinafter mentioned the Mexican Government

makes use of the most perfect frankness, it is because it considers its duty to convey the most perfect clearness to the mind of the Government and the people of the United States concerning the Mexican point of view.

21.    The American Government has for some time been making protests of friendship to Latin-American countries, and it has availed itself of all possible efforts to convince the same that it is its desire to respect their sovereignty absolutely.

With respect to Mexico especially, the American Government has stated on various occasions that it has no intention to intervene in any way in its internal affairs and that it wishes to leave our country to decide by itself its difficult problems of political and social transformation.    It is still reasoned when, on account of the Columbus expedition, the American Government, through the voice of its President, has made the declaration that it does not intend to interfere in the affairs of Mexico nor to invade it, that it does not desire to acquire a single inch of its territory, and that it will in no way impair its sovereignty.

The Washington Government and its representatives on the frontier have also expressly declared that it is not the will of the American people to go into war or have an armed conflict with Mexico.

Summing up all of the above, and judging from the official declarations which have been made for some time past by the Washington Government, there should appear to be an honest purpose on the part of the Government and people of the United States not to launch into a conflict with Mexico.

22.    The Mexican Government, however, regrets to remark that the acts of the American military authorities are in absolute conflict with the above statements, and therefore finds itself constrained to appeal to the President, the Department of State, the Senate, the American people to the end that once and for all time the true political tendency of the United States toward Mexico be defined.

23.    It is equally necessary that on this account the Government of the United States should define in a precise man-

ner its purposes toward Mexico, in order that the other Latin-American nations may be able to judge the sincerity of such purposes and be able to appreciate the proper value of the protests of amity and fraternity which have been made to them during many years.

24.   The American Government, through the voice of its own President, stated that the punitive expedition from Columbus would withdraw from Mexican territory as soon as the bands of the Villa outlaws could have been destroyed or dispersed.   More than two months have elapsed since this expedition entered into Mexican territory; Generals Scott and Funston declared in Ciudad Juarez that the Villa band has been entirely dispersed, and, knowing this, the American troops are not withdrawn from the territory of Mexico.

The American Government is convinced and has accepted the fact that no military task is now left for the Columbus expedition, and nevertheless the promise made by President Wilson that the forces would withdraw as soon as the purpose which caused them to go in would have been reached has not been complied with.

The causes of any internal political order which may exist not to withdraw the American troops from Mexican territory, however justified they may appear, cannot justify the above attitude, but on the contrary they accentuate the discrepancy between the protests of respect to the sovereignty of Mexico and the actual fact that on account of reasons of internal policy of the United States a status should be maintained which is utterly unjust with regard to the Mexican Republic.

25.   The American Government stated that its purpose in causing the American troops to enter Mexico was only to defend the frontier against probable incursions.   This statement, however, is in conflict with the attitude assumed by the same American Government in discussing the agreement concerning the reciprocal crossing of the frontier, because while the Mexican Government maintained that said agreement should limit the zone of operations of the troops of one and the other country, as well as the time which the expeditions should last, the number of soldiers and the arm to which

they should belong, the American Government constantly eluded these limitations. This attitude of the American Government, which is the one expecting to have frequent occasion to cross the frontier on account of incursions of outlaws, is clearly indicating the purpose of having power to enter Mexican territory beyond the limit which the necessities of defense could require.

26. The Columbus punitive expedition, as it has been called, had not, according to the statements of President Wilson, any other purpose than to reach and punish the band of outlaws which had committed the outrage, and it was organized under the supposition that the Mexican Government had given its consent to it. Such expedition, however, has had a character of such clear distrust toward Mexico and of such absolute independence, that it cannot justly be considered as anything but an invasion made without the consent, without the knowledge, and without the coöperation of the Mexican authorities.

It was a known fact that the Columbus expedition crossed the frontier without the consent of the Mexican Government. The American military authorities have carried this expedition into effect without awaiting for the consent of the Government of Mexico, and even after they were officially informed that this Government had not given its consent for it, they nevertheless continued it, causing more troops to cross the line without informing the Mexican authorities of this fact.

The expedition has entered and operated within Mexican territory without procuring the coöperation of the Mexican authorities. The American military authorities have always maintained complete secrecy regarding their movements without informing the Mexican Government about them, such as they would have done if they really had tried to obtain coöperation. This lack of advice and agreement was the cause of the clash which occurred in Parral between American forces and Mexican citizens.

In conclusion, the Columbus expedition has been carried into effect without any spirit of harmony, but, on the contrary, under a spirit of distrust with respect to our authorities, as our coöperation was not only unsought, nor were we informed with regard to military operations affected, besides the expedition was organized, carrying artillery and infantry forces.

Now, then, the protests of friendly coöperation made by the American authorities are not in keeping with the use of infantry and artillery exclusively destined to be employed against the regular Mexican forces.

If the Columbus expedition had taken place with the consent of the Mexican Government and its coöperation had been sought, the use of artillery and infantry would have been considered an insult to the Mexican authorities because of the supposition that they might feloniously assault the American forces which would have entered Mexico in pursuit of a common enemy confiding in the friendship of the former. Nevertheless, it is preferable to interpret this act as a proof that the American forces entered into Mexican territory without the consent of the Mexican Government, and, therefore, ready to repel any aggression on the part of regular Mexican forces who were ignorant of their presence.

All of the above facts demonstrate that there has been a great discrepancy between the protests of sincere friendly coöperation on the part of the American authorities and the actual attitude of the expedition, which, on account of its distrust, its secrecy regarding its movements and the arms at its disposal, clearly indicated that it was a hostile expedition and a real invasion of our territory.

27. The American Government has stated on different occasions that the Columbus expedition had no other object than to pursue and destroy the Villa bandits, and that as soon as this would be accomplished the expedition would be withdrawn. The facts, however, have shown that the intention of the American Government was not the same during the conference at Ciudad Juarez and El Paso. It cannot be explained otherwise that General Scott should have insisted so emphatically on the signing of a memorandum stating that the American forces would not finish their withdrawal, if any other incident occurred which would mortify the belief

of the American Government in the ability of the Mexican Government to protect the frontier.

The conclusion to be drawn from this insistency of General Scott regarding the signing of this memorandum is that the Columbus expedition entered into Mexico promising to withdraw as soon as it should have destroyed the Villa band, but that it is the purpose to make use of it afterward as an instrument to guarantee the protection of the frontier.

28.  The American Government justly desires that the frontier should be protected.  If the frontier should be properly protected against incursions from Mexico there would be no reason then for the existing difficulty.  The American Government knows of the difficulties obtaining in the protection of a frontier line in which there are no natural facilities to aid in its defense, and, notwithstanding its immense resources, the American Government itself has not been able to render an effective protection along a line of more than 2,000 kilometers to be guarded.

The Mexican Government proposed that the military chiefs in charge of the troops in one and the other country should discuss a plan of cantonments along the boundary line, and, notwithstanding the protestations of the American Government of its desire to solve its difficulties with Mexico, General Scott did not approve the above plan of cantonments, which is the only thing rational and the only plan that could be carried into effect without involving the sovereignty or territory of one or the other country.  The American Government prefers to keep its troops inactive and idle within the territory of Mexico, instead of withdrawing them to post them along the frontier in accord with Mexican authorities who would do likewise on their side.  By this action the American Government gives room for the supposition that its true intention is to keep the troops it already has interned in Mexico anticipating that it may make use of them later for future operations.

29.  The American Government has on all occasions declared its desire to help the Constitutionalist Government to complete the work of pacification and its desire that this task should be carried into effect within the least time pos-

sible.  The true attitude of the American Government in relation with these desires appears to be entirely incongruous, inasmuch as for some time back it has been doing things indicating that it does not only render any assistance to the work of pacification of Mexico, but that, on the contrary, it appears to place all possible obstacles to the execution of this task.  As a matter of fact, without considering the great number of diplomatic representations made under the pretext of protection to American interests in Mexico, which are constantly embarrassing the task of the new Government, whose intention it is to reorganize the political, economic, and social conditions of the country on a new basis, there is a great number of facts which cause the influence of the American Government to be felt against the consolidation of the present Government of Mexico.

The decided support given at one time to Villa by General Scott and the Department of State itself was the principal cause for the prolongation of civil war in Mexico for many months.  Later on the continuous aid which the American Catholic clergy has rendered to the Mexican Catholic clergy, which is incessantly working against the Constitutionalist Government, and the constant activities of the American interventionist press and business men of that country, are, to say the least, an indication that the present American Government does not wish or is unable to prevent all the works of conspiracy against the Constitutionalist Government carried into effect in the United States.

30.  The American Government claims constantly from the Mexican Government an effective protection of the frontiers, and, nevertheless, the greater number of the bands which take the name of rebels against this Government is provided and armed, and perhaps also organized, on the American side under the tolerance of the authorities of the State of Texas, and, it may be said, even of the Federal authorities of the United States.  The leniency of the American authorities toward such bands is such that in the majority of cases the conspirators, who are well known, and wherever they have been discovered and imprisoned, are re-

leased under insignificant bonds, permitting them to continue in their efforts.

Mexican emigrants, who are plotting and organizing incursions on the American side, have now more facilities to cause injury than before, because knowing that any new difficulty between Mexico and the United States will prolong the stay of American troops, they endeavor to increase the occasions for a conflict and friction.

31.  The American Government claims to help the Constitutionalist Government in its task of pacification and urges that such a work be done within the least time possible, and that the protection of the frontiers be effected in the most efficacious way.   And nevertheless, on various occasions, the American Government has detained shipments of arms and ammunition purchased by the Mexican Government in the United States, which should be employed to hasten the task of pacification and to more efficaciously protect the frontier.   The pretexts given to detain the shipment of munitions consigned to this Government have always been futile and never have we been given a frank reason; it has been said, for example, that the munitions were embargoed because it was not known who the owner might be, or because of the fear that they might fall into the hands of Villista bands.

The embargo of war material consigned to the Mexican Government can have no other interpretation than that the Government of the United States wishes to protect itself against the emergency of a future conflict, and therefore it is endeavoring to prevent arms and ammunition which might be used against American troops from reaching the hands of the Mexican Government.   The American Government would have the right to take this precaution against such emergency, but in that case it ought not to say that it is endeavoring to coöperate with the Mexican Government, and it would be preferable to give out a more frank statement concerning its procedure.

The American Government either desires to decidedly and frankly help the Mexican Government to reëstablish peace, and in this case it ought not to prevent the exportation of arms, or the true purposes of the American Government are to get ready so that in the case of future war with Mexico the latter may find itself less provided with arms and ammunition. If this is the case, it would be preferable to say so.

In any case, the embargo on arms and ammunition consigned to the Mexican authorities, under the frivolous pretext of preventing these arms and ammunition from falling into the hands of Villista bands, is an indication that the actual acts of the American military authorities are entirely in conflict with the purposes of peace of the American Government.

The Mexican Government cannot wish war with the United States, and if this should occur it would undoubtedly be as a consequence of a deliberate purpose of the United States. For the time being the above precautionary acts of the American Government indicate that there is a purpose of preparedness for such emergency, or that, which is the same, the beginning of hostility on the part of the United States toward Mexico.

32. In conclusion, the New York American authorities, alleging that they act at the suggestion of a neutral peaceful society, have ordered the detention of several parts of machinery which the Mexican Government was forwarding to Mexico for its ammunition factory. It could not be conceived that this machinery could be used before several months after it had reached its destination. This action of the American Government, tending to prevent the manufacturing of munitions in a remote future, is another clear indication that its true purposes toward Mexico are not peaceful, because while millions and millions of dollars' worth of arms and ammunition are being daily exported for the European war without peace societies becoming impressed by the spectacle of that war, the New York authorities are showing exceedingly marked interest in seconding the purposes of the above-mentioned humanitarian societies whenever it is a matter of exporting to Mexico any machinery for the manufacture of arms and ammunition.

Mexico has the indisputable right just like the United

States and all other nations in the world to provide for its military necessities, especially so when it is confronting so vast a task as that of insuring the pacification of the interior of this country; and the action of the Government of the United States in detaining machinery destined for the manufacture of ammunitions is indicative either that the United States wishes to place obstacles to its complete pacification, or that this action is one of the series carried into effect by the American authorities as a matter of precaution in case of a projected war with Mexico.

33.   All of the above-mentioned circumstances indicate that the true purpose of the military authorities of the United States are in absolute contradiction with the continuous protestations of amity of the American Government toward Mexico.

34.   The Mexican people and Government are absolutely sure that the American people do not wish war with Mexico. There are, nevertheless, strong American interests and strong Mexican interests laboring to secure a conflict between the two countries.   The Mexican Government firmly desires to preserve peace with the American Government, but to that effect it is indispensable that the American Government should frankly explain its true purposes toward Mexico.

The Mexican Government, therefore, formally invites the Government of the United States to cause the situation of uncertainty between the two countries to cease and to support its declarations and protests of amity with real and effective action which will convince the Mexican people of the sincerity of its purposes.   This action, in the present situation, cannot be other than the immediate withdrawal of the American troops which are now in Mexican territory.

BY ROBERT LANSING
U. S. Official Reply to the Above Protest

WASHINGTON, June 20, 1916.

SIR: I have read your communication, which was delivered to me on May 22, 1916, under instructions of the Chief Executive of the de facto Government of Mexico, on the subject of the presence of American troops in Mexican territory, and I would be wanting in candor if I did not, before making answer to the allegations of fact and the conclusions reached by your Government, express the surprise and regret which have been caused this Government by the discourteous tone and temper of this last communication of the de facto Government of Mexico.

The Government of the United States has viewed with deep concern and increasing disappointment the progress of the revolution in Mexico.  Continuous bloodshed and disorders have marked its progress.  For three years the Mexican Republic has been torn with civil strife; the lives of Americans and other aliens have been sacrificed; vast properties developed by American capital and enterprise have been destroyed or rendered non-productive; bandits have been permitted to roam at will through the territory contiguous to the United States and to seize, without punishment or without effective attempt at punishment, the property of Americans, while the lives of citizens of the United States, who ventured to remain in Mexican territory or to return there to protect their interests, have been taken, in some cases barbarously taken, and the murderers have neither been apprehended nor brought to justice.  It would be difficult to find in the annals of the history of Mexico conditions more deplorable than those which have existed there during these recent years of civil war.

It would be tedious to recount instance after instance, outrage after outrage, atrocity after atrocity, to illustrate the true nature and extent of the widespread conditions of lawlessness and violence which have prevailed.  During the past nine months in particular, the frontier of the United States along the lower Rio Grande has been thrown into a state of constant apprehension and turmoil because of frequent and sudden incursions into American territory and depredations and murders on American soil by Mexican bandits, who have taken the lives and destroyed the property of American citizens, sometimes carrying American citizens across the international boundary with the booty seized.

American garrisons have been attacked at night, American soldiers killed, and their equipment and horses stolen. American ranches have been raided, property stolen and destroyed, and American trains wrecked and plundered. The attacks on Brownsville, Red House Ferry, Progreso Post Office, and Las Peladas, all occurring during September last, are typical. In these attacks on American territory, Carranzista adherents and even Carranzista soldiers took part in the looting, burning, and killing. Not only were these murders characterized by ruthless brutality, but un-civilized acts of mutilation were perpetrated. Representations were made to General Carranza, and he was emphati-cally requested to stop these reprehensible acts in a section which he has long claimed to be under the complete domina-tion of his authority.

Notwithstanding these representations and the promise of General Nafarrete to prevent attacks along the interna-tional boundary, in the following month of October a passen-ger train was wrecked by bandits and several persons killed seven miles north of Brownsville, and an attack was made upon United States troops at the same place several days later. Since these attacks, leaders of the bandits well known both to Mexican civil and military authorities, as well as to American officers, have been enjoying with impunity the liberty of the towns of Northern Mexico. So far has the indifference of the de facto Government to these atrocities gone that some of these leaders, as I am advised, have re-ceived not only the protection of that Government, but en-couragement and aid as well.

Depredations upon American persons and property within Mexican jurisdiction have been still more numerous. This Government has repeatedly requested in the strongest terms that the de facto Government safeguard the lives and homes of American citizens and furnish the protection which international obligation imposes, to American interests in the northern States of Tamaulipas, Nuevo Leon, Coahuila, Chihuahua, and Sonora, and also in the States to the south.

For example, on January 3rd, troops were requested to punish the bands of outlaws which looted the Cusi mining property, eighty miles west of Chihuahua, but no effective results came from this request.  During the following week the bandit, Villa, with his band of about 200 men, was operating without opposition between Rubio and Santa Ysabel, a fact well known to Carranzista authorities.  Meanwhile a party of unfortunate Americans started by train from Chihuahua to visit the Cusi mines, after having received assurances from the Carranzista authorities in the State of Chihuahua that the country was safe and that a guard on the train was not necessary.  The Americans held passports or safe conducts issued by authorities of the de facto Government.  On January 10th the train was stopped by Villa bandits, and eighteen of the American party were stripped of their clothing and shot in cold blood, in what is now known as the "Santa Ysabel massacre."  General Carranza stated to the agent of the Department of State that he had issued orders for the immediate pursuit, capture, and punishment of those responsible for this atrocious crime, and appealed to this Government and to the American people to consider the difficulties of according protection along the railroad where the massacre occurred.  Assurances were also given by Mr. Arredondo, presumably under instructions from the de facto Government, that the murderers would be brought to justice, and that steps would also be taken to remedy the lawless conditions existing in the State of Durango.

It is true that Villa, Castro, and Lopez were publicly declared to be outlaws and subject to apprehension and execution, but so far as known only a single man personally connected with this massacre has been brought to justice by Mexican authorities.  Within a month after this barbarous slaughter of inoffensive Americans, it was notorious that Villa was operating within twenty miles of Cusihuiriachic and publicly stated that his purpose was to destroy American lives and property.  Despite repeated and insistent demands that military protection should be furnished to Americans, Villa openly carried on his operations, constantly approaching closer and closer to the border.  He was not intercepted nor were his movements impeded by troops of the de facto Government and no effectual attempt was made to

frustrate his hostile designs against Americans.   In fact, as
I am informed, while Villa and his band were slowly moving toward the American frontier in the neighborhood of
Columbus, N. M., not a single Mexican soldier was seen
in this vicinity.   Yet the Mexican authorities were fully
cognizant of his movements, for on March 6, as General
Gavira publicly announced, he advised the American military
authorities of the outlaw's approach to the border, so that
they might be prepared to prevent him from crossing the
boundary.

Villa's unhindered activities culminated in the unprovoked and cold-blooded attack upon American soldiers and
citizens in the town of Columbus on the night of March
9th, the details of which do not need repetition here in order
to refresh your memory with the heinousness of the crime.
After murdering, burning, and plundering, Villa and his
bandits, fleeing south, passed within sight of the Carranzista military post at Casas Grandes, and no effort was
made to stop him by the officers and garrison of the de facto
Government stationed there.

In the face of these depredations, not only on American
lives and property on Mexican soil, but on American soldiers, citizens, and homes on American territory, the perpetrators of which General Carranza was unable or possibly
considered it inadvisable to apprehend and punish, the United
States had no recourse other than to employ force to disperse the bands of Mexican outlaws who were with increasing boldness systematically raiding across the international
boundary.

The maurauders engaged in the attack on Columbus
were driven back across the border by American cavalry,
and subsequently, as soon as a sufficient force to cope with
the band could be collected, were pursued into Mexico in an
effort to capture or destroy them.   Without coöperation
or assistance in the field on the part of the de facto Government, despite repeated requests by the United States, and
without apparent recognition on its part of the desirability of
putting an end to these systematic raids, or of punishing the
chief perpetrators of the crimes committed, because they

menaced the good relations of the two countries, American
forces pursued the lawless bands as far as Parral, where
the pursuit was halted by the hostility of Mexicans, presumed
to be loyal to the de facto Government, who arrayed themselves on the side of outlawry and became in effect the protectors of Villa and his band.

In this manner and for these reasons have the American forces entered Mexican territory.  Knowing fully the
circumstances set forth, the de facto Government cannot be
blind to the necessity which compelled this Government to
act, and yet it has seen fit to recite groundless sentiments of
hostility toward the expedition and to impute to this Government ulterior motives for the continued presence of American troops on Mexican soil.  It is charged that these troops
crossed the frontier without first obtaining the consent or permission of the de facto Government.  Obviously, as immediate action alone could avail, there was no opportunity to
reach an agreement (other than that of March 10th-13th,
now repudiated by General Carranza) prior to the entrance
of such an expedition into Mexico if the expedition was to
be effective.  Subsequent events and correspondence have
demonstrated to the satisfaction of this Government that
General Carranza would not have entered into any agreement providing for an effective plan for the capture and
destruction of the Villa bands.

While the American troops were moving rapidly southward in pursuit of the raiders, it was the form and nature of
the agreement that occupied the attention of General Carranza, rather than the practical object which it was to obtain—the number of limitations that could be imposed upon
the American forces to impede their progress, rather than
the obstacles that could be raised to prevent the escape of
the outlaws.  It was General Carranza who suspended
through your note of April 12th all discussions and negotiations for an agreement along the lines of the protocols between the United States and Mexico concluded during the
period 1882-1896, under which the two countries had so
successfully restored peace on their common boundary.

It may be mentioned here that, notwithstanding the

statement in your note that "the American Government gave no answer to the note of April 12th," this note was replied to on April 14th, when the department instructed Mr. Rodgers by telegraph to deliver this Government's answer to General Carranza.

Shortly after this reply the conferences between Generals Scott, Funston, and Obregon began at El Paso, during which they signed on May 2nd a project of a memorandum ad referendum, regarding the withdrawal of American troops. As an indication of the alleged bad faith of the American Government, you state that though General Scott declared in this memorandum that the destruction and dispersion of the Villa band "had been accomplished," yet American forces are not withdrawn from Mexico. It is only necessary to read the memorandum, which is in the English language, to ascertain that this is clearly a misstatement, for the memorandum states that "the American punitive expeditionary forces have destroyed or dispersed many of the lawless elements and bandits . . . or have driven them far into the interior of the Republic of Mexico," and, further, that the United States forces were then "carrying on a vigorous pursuit of such small numbers of bandits or lawless elements as may have escaped."

The context of your note gives the impression that the object of the expedition being admittedly accomplished, the United States had agreed in the memorandum to begin the withdrawal of its troops. The memorandum shows, however, that it was not alone on account of partial dispersion of the bandits that it was decided to begin the withdrawal of American forces, but equally on account of the assurances of the Mexican Government that their forces were "at the present time being augmented and strengthened to such an extent that they will be able to prevent any disorders occurring in Mexico that would in any way endanger American territory," and that they would "continue to diligently pursue, capture, or destroy any lawless bands of bandits that may still exist or hereafter exist in the northern part of Mexico," and that it would "make a proper distribution of such of its forces as may be necessary to prevent the possibility of invasion of American territory from Mexico." It was because of these assurances and because of General Scott's confidence that they would be carried out that he said that American forces would be "gradually withdrawn."

It is to be noted that, while the American Government was willing to ratify this agreement, General Carranza refused to do so, as General Obregon stated, because, among other things, it imposed improper conditions upon Mexico.

Notwithstanding the assurances in the memorandum, it is well known that the forces of the de facto Government have not carried on a vigorous pursuit of the remaining bandits, and that no proper distribution of forces to prevent the invasion of American territory has been made. I am reluctant to be forced to the conclusion which might be drawn from these circumstances that the de facto Government, in spite of the crimes committed and the sinister designs of Villa and his followers, did not and does not now intend or desire that these outlaws should be captured, destroyed, or dispersed by American troops or, at the request of this Government, by Mexican troops.

### BY NEWTON BAKER
#### Proclamation of June 18th, the Calling of the National Guard

In view of the disturbed conditions on the Mexican border, and in order to assure complete protection for all Americans, the President has called out substantially all the State militia, and will send them to the border wherever and as fully as General Funston determines them to be needed for the purpose stated.

If all are not needed an effort will be made to relieve those on duty there from time to time so as to distribute the duty.

This call for militia is wholly unrelated to General Pershing's expedition, and contemplates no additional entry into Mexico, except as may be necessary to pursue bandits who attempt outrages on American soil.

The militia are being called out so as to leave some troops in the several States. They will be mobilized at their home stations, where necessary recruiting can be done.

# GERMANY YIELDS TO AMERICA'S ULTIMATUM

## ABANDONMENT OF UNRESTRICTED SUBMARINE WARFARE

APRIL 18TH

WOODROW WILSON                    GOTTLIEB VON JAGOW

In looking for the decisive moment of the Great War, Admiral Tirpitz, director of Germany's U-boat warfare, declared that his country's defeat was decided by the United States ultimatum of April 18, 1916, or rather by Germany's yielding to that ultimatum, as she did in Von Jagow's note of May 4th. Both of these historically celebrated notes are here given, and also President Wilson's brief speech of April 19th, explaining to Congress what he had done.

The dispute reached back to the submarine controversies of the preceding year, which had culminated in the sinking of the *Lusitania*. After that Germany procrastinated, apologized and continued suggesting modifications of international law at sea. Meanwhile her U-boats torpedoed an occasional American ship, or slew an American citizen on some Ally merchant ship. Such attacks were denied or explained away, until President Wilson after almost a year of patient expostulation seized upon a clear and undeniable case and made it the basis of his ultimatum.

The case thus emphasized was that of the *Sussex*, a British passenger ship of obviously pacific character, which was torpedoed while crossing the English Channel. Among the slain passengers were several United States citizens. Germany at first denied the torpedoing, but afterward admitted it. In the interim, the Von Jagow note, here given, made the required promise that thereafter U-boats would sink no peaceful ship without giving warning and providing for the safety of passengers and crew.

This restriction so far reduced the destructiveness of the U-boats that during the remainder of 1916 they ceased to be a serious factor in the War. This in reality was only a temporary pause. One main cause for Germany's apparent yielding was that her old-style submarines were proving too feeble, and so many of them had been destroyed that the remainder could not have continued a very vigorous attack. German ship-yards employed the year to complete at top speed a fleet of new and far stronger submarines. Hence Von Tirpitz's lament over the fatal surrender of April 18th was not because of the temporarily decreased destruction of neutral and enemy merchant ships, but rather because of the weakness of seeming to yield anything whatsoever. According to the U-boat admiral's view, this yielding only encouraged the United States to demand more and more,

**and so at length** led her into the War; had the American people been sufficiently bullied from the start, they would never have dared to take up arms against so terrible a Germany.        **C. F. H.**

BY PRESIDENT WILSON
Address to Congress on April 19, 1916

IN pursuance of the policy of submarine warfare against the commerce of its adversaries, announced and entered upon by the Imperial German Government, despite the solemn protest of this Government, the commanders of German undersea vessels have attacked merchant ships with greater and greater activity, not only upon the high seas surrounding Great Britain and Ireland, but wherever they could encounter them, in a way that has grown more and more ruthless, more and more indiscriminate, as the months have gone by, less and less observant of restraints of any kind; and they have delivered their attacks without compunction against vessels of every nationality and bound upon every sort of errand. Vessels of neutral ownership, even vessels of neutral ownership bound from neutral port to neutral port, have been destroyed along with vessels of belligerent ownership, in constantly increasing numbers. Sometimes the merchantman attacked has been warned and summoned to surrender before being fired on or torpedoed; sometimes passengers or crews have been vouchsafed the poor security of being allowed to take to the ship's boats before she was sent to the bottom. But again and again no warning has been given, no escape even to the ship's boats allowed to those on board. What this Government foresaw must happen has happened. Tragedy has followed tragedy on the seas in such fashion, with such attendant circumstances, as to make it grossly evident that warfare of such a sort, if warfare it be, cannot be carried on without the most palpable violation of the dictates alike of right and of humanity. Whatever the disposition and intention of the Imperial German Government, it has manifestly proved impossible for it to keep such methods of attack upon the commerce of its enemies within the bounds set by either the reason or the heart of mankind. . . .

I have deemed it my duty, therefore, to say to the Imperial German Government that if it is still its purpose to prosecute relentless and indiscriminate warfare against vessels of commerce by the use of submarines, notwithstanding the now demonstrated impossibility of conducting that warfare in accordance with what the Government of the United States must consider the sacred and indisputable rules of international law and the universally recognized dictates of humanity, the Government of the United States is at last forced to the conclusion that there is but one course it can pursue and that unless the Imperial German Government should now immediately declare and effect an abandonment of its present methods of warfare against passenger and freight-carrying vessels, this Government can have no choice but to sever diplomatic relations with the Government of the German Empire altogether.

This decision I have arrived at with the keenest regret; the possibility of the action contemplated I am sure all thoughtful Americans will look forward to with unaffected reluctance. But we cannot forget that we are in some sort and by the force of circumstances the responsible spokesmen of the rights of humanity, and that we cannot remain silent while those rights seem in process of being swept utterly away in the maelstrom of this terrible war. We owe it to a due regard for our own rights as a nation, to our sense of duty as a representative of the rights of neutrals the world over, and to a just conception of the rights of mankind to take this stand now with the utmost solemnity and firmness.

I have taken it, and taken it in the confidence that it will meet with your approval and support. All sober-minded men must unite in hoping that the Imperial German Government, which has in other circumstances stood as the champion of all that we are now contending for in the interest of humanity, may recognize the justice of our demands and meet them in the spirit in which they are made.

### Ultimatum Delivered to Germany's Secretary of Foreign Affairs, April 18th

Information now in the possession of the Government of the United States fully establishes the facts in the case of the *Sussex,* and the inferences which the Government has drawn from that information it regards as confirmed by the circumstances set forth in your Excellency's note of the 10th inst.  On the 24th of March, 1916, at about 2.50 o'clock in the afternoon, the unarmed steamer *Sussex,* with 325 or more passengers on board, among whom were a number of American citizens, was torpedoed while crossing from Folkestone to Dieppe.  The *Sussex* had never been armed; was a vessel known to be habitually used only for the conveyance of passengers across the English Channel; and was not following the route taken by troop ships or supply ships. About eighty of her passengers, noncombatants of all ages and sexes, including citizens of the United States, were killed or injured.

A careful, detailed, and scrupulously impartial investigation by naval and military officers of the United States has conclusively established the fact that the *Sussex* was torpedoed without warning or summons to surrender, and that the torpedo by which she was struck was of German manufacture.  In the view of the Government of the United States these facts from the first made the conclusion that the torpedo was fired by a German submarine unavoidable.  It now considers that conclusion substantiated by the statements of Your Excellency's note.  A full statement of the facts upon which the Government of the United States has based its conclusion, is inclosed.

The Government of the United States, after having given careful consideration to the note of the Imperial Government of the 10th of April, regrets to state that the impression made upon it by the statements and proposals contained in that note is that the Imperial Government has failed to appreciate the gravity of the situation which has resulted, not alone from the attack on the *Sussex,* but from the whole method and character of submarine warfare as disclosed by the unrestrained practice of the commanders of German undersea craft during the past twelvemonth and more in the indiscriminate destruction of merchant vessels of all sorts, nationalities, and destinations.  If the sinking of the *Sussex* had been an isolated case the Government of the

United States might find it possible to hope that the officer who was responsible for that act had willfully violated his orders or had been criminally negligent in taking none of the precautions they prescribed, and that the ends of justice might be satisfied by imposing upon him an adequate punishment, coupled with a formal disavowal of the act and payment of a suitable indemnity by the Imperial Government. But, though the attack upon the *Sussex* was manifestly indefensible and caused a loss of life so tragical as to make it stand forth as one of the most terrible examples of the inhumanity of submarine warfare as the commanders of German vessels are conducting it, it unhappily does not stand alone.

On the contrary, the Government of the United States is forced by recent events to conclude that it is only one instance, even though one of the most extreme and most distressing instances, of the deliberate method and spirit of indiscriminate destruction of merchant vessels of all sorts, nationalities, and destinations which have become more and more unmistakable as the activity of German undersea vessels of war has in recent months been quickened and extended.

The Imperial Government will recall that when, in February, 1915, it announced its intention of treating the waters surrounding Great Britain and Ireland as embraced within the seat of war and of destroying all merchant ships owned by its enemies that might be found within that zone of danger, and warned all vessels, neutral as well as belligerent, to keep out of the waters thus proscribed or to enter them at their peril, the Government of the United States earnestly protested. It took the position that such a policy could not be pursued without constant gross and palpable violations of the accepted law of nations, particularly if submarine craft were to be employed as its instruments, inasmuch as the rules prescribed by that law, rules founded on the principles of humanity and established for the protection of the lives of noncombatants at sea, could not in the nature of the case be observed by such vessels. It based its protest on the ground that persons of neutral nationality and vessels of neutral ownership would be exposed to extreme and intolerable risks, and that no right to close any part of the high seas could lawfully be asserted by the Imperial Government in the circumstances then existing.

The law of nations in these matters, upon which the Government of the United States based that protest, is not of recent origin or founded upon merely arbitrary principles set up by convention. It is based, on the contrary, upon manifest principles of humanity and has long been established with the approval and by the express assent of all civilized nations.

The Imperial Government, notwithstanding, persisted in carrying out the policy announced, expressing the hope that the dangers involved, at any rate to neutral vessels, would be reduced to a minimum by the instructions which it had issued to the commanders of its submarines, and assuring the Government of the United States that it would take every possible precaution both to respect the rights of neutrals and to safeguard the lives of noncombatants.

In pursuance of this policy of submarine warfare against the commerce of its adversaries, thus announced and thus entered upon in despite of the solemn protest of the Government of the United States, the commanders of the Imperial Government's undersea vessels have carried on practices of such ruthless destruction, which have made it more and more evident as the months have gone by that the Imperial Government has found it impracticable to put any such restraints upon them as it had hoped and promised to put. Again and again the Imperial Government has given its solemn assurances to the Government of the United States that at least passenger ships would not be thus dealt with, and yet it has repeatedly permitted its undersea commanders to disregard those assurances with entire impunity. As recently as February last it gave notice that it would regard all armed merchantmen owned by its enemies as part of the armed naval forces of its adversaries and deal with them as with men-of-war, thus, at least by implication, pledging itself to give warning to vessels which were not armed and to accord security of life to their passengers and crews; but even this limitation their submarine commanders have recklessly ignored.

Vessels of neutral ownership, even vessels of neutral ownership bound from neutral port to neutral port, have been destroyed, along with vessels of belligerent ownership, in constantly increasing numbers. Sometimes the merchant-men attacked have been warned and summoned to surrender before being fired on or torpedoed; sometimes their pas-sengers and crews have been vouchsafed the poor security of being allowed to take to the ship's boats before the ship was sent to the bottom. But again and again no warning has been given, no escape even to the ship's boats allowed to those on board. Great liners like the *Lusitania* and *Arabic,* and mere passenger boats like the *Sussex,* have been attacked without a moment's warning, often before they have even become aware that they were in the presence of an armed ship of the enemy, and the lives of noncombatants, passen-gers and crew, have been destroyed wholesale and in a man-ner which the Government of the United States cannot but regard as wanton and without the slightest color of justifica-tion. No limit of any kind has, in fact, been set to their indiscriminate pursuit and destruction of merchantmen of all kinds and nationalities within the waters which the Imperial Government has chosen to designate as lying within the seat of war. The roll of Americans who have lost their lives upon ships thus attacked and destroyed has grown month by month until the ominous toll has mounted into the hundreds.

The Government of the United States has been very pa-tient. At every stage of this distressing experience of trag-edy after tragedy it has sought to be governed by the most thoughtful consideration of the extraordinary circumstances of an unprecedented war and to be guided by sentiments of very genuine friendship for the people and Government of Germany. It has accepted the successive explanations and assurances of the Imperial Government as, of course, given in entire sincerity and good faith, and has hoped, even against hope, that it would prove to be possible for the Imperial Government so to order and control the acts of its naval commanders as to square its policy with the recognized prin-ciples of humanity as embodied in the law of nations. It has made every allowance for unprecedented conditions and has been willing to wait until the facts became unmistakable and were susceptible of only one interpretation.

It now owes it to a just regard for its own rights to say to the Imperial Government that that time has come. It has become painfully evident to it that the position which it took at the very outset is inevitable, namely, the use of submarines for the destruction of an enemy's commerce, is, of necessity, because of the very character of the vessels employed and the very methods of attack which their employment of course involves, utterly incompatible with the principles of humanity, the long-established and incontrovertible rights of neutrals, and the sacred immunities of non-combatants.

If it is still the purpose of the Imperial Government to prosecute relentless and indiscriminate warfare against vessels of commerce by the use of submarines, without regard to what the Government of the United States must consider the sacred and indisputable rules of international law and the universally recognized dictates of humanity, the Government of the United States is at last forced to the conclusion that there is but one course it can pursue. Unless the Imperial Government should now immediately declare and effect an abandonment of its present methods of submarine warfare against passenger and freight-carrying vessels, the Government of the United States can have no choice but to sever diplomatic relations with the German Empire altogether. This action the Government of the United States contemplates with the greatest reluctance, but feels constrained to take in behalf of humanity and the rights of neutral nations.

### BY GOTTLIEB VON JAGOW
Reply of May 4th, by the German Secretary of Foreign Affairs

The German Government handed over to the proper naval authorities for early investigation the evidence concerning the *Sussex,* as communicated by the Government of the United States. Judging by the results that the investigation has hitherto yielded, the German Government is alive to the possibility that the ship mentioned in the note of April 10th as having been torpedoed by a German submarine is actually identical with the *Sussex*. The German Government begs to reserve further communication on the matter until certain points are ascertained, which are of decisive importance for establishing the facts of the case. Should it turn out that the commander was wrong in assuming the vessel to be a man-of-war, the German Government will not fail to draw the consequence therefrom.

In connection with the case of the *Sussex* the Government of the United States made a series of statements, the gist of which is the assertion that the incident is to be considered but one instance of a deliberate method of indiscriminate destruction of vessels of all sorts, nationalities, and destinations by German submarine commanders.

The German Government must emphatically repudiate the assertion. The German Government, however, thinks it of little avail to enter into details in the present stage of affairs, more particularly as the Government of the United States omitted to substantiate the assertion by reference to concrete facts.

The German Government will only state that it has imposed far-reaching restraints upon the use of the submarine weapon, solely in consideration of neutrals' interests, in spite of the fact that these restrictions are necessarily of advantage to Germany's enemies. No such consideration has ever been shown neutrals by Great Britain and her allies.[1]

The German submarine forces have had, in fact, orders to conduct the submarine warfare in accordance with the general principles of visit and search and the destruction of merchant vessels recognized by international law, the sole exception being the conduct of warfare against enemy trade carried on enemy freight ships encountered in the war zone surrounding Great Britain. With regard to these, no assurances have ever been given to the Government of the United States. No such assurances are contained in the declaration of February 8, 1916.

[1] Unfortunately this entire document must be read as a typical product of the policy of misstatement and deception adopted by the German Government in the War. Britain encroached somewhat on the rights of neutrals, but never to anything like the extent that Germany did.

The German Government cannot admit any doubt that these orders were given or are executed in good faith. Errors actually occurred. They can in no kind of warfare be avoided altogether. Allowances must be made in the conduct of naval warfare against an enemy resorting to all kinds of ruses, whether permissible or illicit.

But apart from the possibility of errors, naval warfare, just like warfare on land, implies unavoidable dangers for neutral persons and goods entering the fighting zone. Even in cases where the naval action is confined to ordinary forms of cruiser warfare, neutral persons and goods repeatedly come to grief. The German Government has repeatedly and explicitly pointed out the dangers from mines that have led to the loss of numerous ships.

The German Government has made several proposals to the Government of the United States in order to reduce to a minimum for American travelers and goods the inherent dangers of naval warfare. Unfortunately the Government of the United States decided not to accept the proposals. Had it accepted, the Government of the United States would have been instrumental in preventing the greater part of the accidents that American citizens have met with in the meantime.

The German Government still stands by its offer to come to an agreement along these lines.

As the German Government repeatedly declared, it cannot dispense with the use of the submarine weapon in the conduct of warfare against enemy trade. The German Government, however, has now decided to make a further concession, adapting methods of submarine war to the interests of neutrals. In reaching its decision the German Government is actuated by considerations which are above the level of the disputed question.

The German Government attaches no less importance to the sacred principles of humanity than the Government of the United States. It again fully takes into account that both Governments for many years coöperated in developing international law in conformity with these principles, the ultimate object of which has always been to confine warfare on sea and land to armed forces of belligerents and safeguard as far as possible noncombatants against the horrors of war.

But although these considerations are of great weight, they alone would not under present circumstances have determined the attitude of the German Government. For in answer to the appeal by the Government of the United States on behalf of the sacred principles of humanity and international law, the German Government must repeat once more, with all emphasis, that it was not the German, but the British, Government which ignored all accepted rules of international law and extended this terrible war to the lives and property of noncombatants, having no regard whatever for the interests and rights of neutrals and noncombatants that through this method of warfare have been severely injured.

In self-defense against the illegal conduct of British warfare, while fighting a bitter struggle for national existence, Germany had to resort to the hard but effective weapon of submarine warfare.

As matters stand, the German Government cannot but reiterate regret that the sentiments of humanity, which the Government of the United States extends with such fervor to the unhappy victims of submarine warfare, are not extended with the same warmth of feeling to many millions of women and children who, according to the avowed intention of the British Government, shall be starved, and who by sufferings shall force the victorious armies of the Central Powers into ignominious capitulation.

The German Government, in agreement with the German people, fails to understand this discrimination,[2] all the

---

[2] This statement is an obvious absurdity. Every human Government that ever existed has been more active in defending its own citizens than in defending those of other countries. Hence Von Jagow's words are presumably intended not to sway the U. S. Government, but to arouse angry and unreasoning Germans. The appeal is typical. Germany having herself declared war, and destroyed her victims with an unparalleled rigor, Von Jagow now assumes that it is the duty of the United States to protect the German people from any sufferings caused by that war; and he sneeringly implies hypocrisy in America because Americans prefer to devote their first consideration to protecting Americans, and their next to protecting other neutrals. How could any people honestly prefer to help a starving Belgian or Pole, or an Armenian shrieking under physical torture, when they might instead be giving help to a well-fed German!

Moreover, readers need to keep in mind that the picture of German

more as it has repeatedly and explicitly declared itself ready
to use the submarine weapon in strict conformity with the
rules of international law as recognized before the outbreak
of the war, if Great Britain likewise was ready to adapt
the conduct of warfare to these rules.

Several attempts made by the Government of the United
States to prevail upon the British Government to act accordingly failed because of flat refusal on the part of the
British Government. Moreover, Great Britain again and
again has violated international law, surpassing all bounds
in outraging neutral rights. The latest measure adopted by
Great Britain, declaring German bunker coal contraband and
establishing conditions under which English bunker coal
alone is supplied to neutrals, is nothing but an unheard-of
attempt by way of exaction to force neutral tonnage into
the service of British trade war.

The German people know that the Government of the
United States has the power to confine the war to armed
forces of the belligerent countries, in the interest of humanity and maintenance of international law. The Government of the United States would have been certain of attaining this end had it been determined to insist, against
Great Britain, on the incontrovertible rights to freedom of
the seas. But, as matters stand, the German people is under the impression that the Government of the United States,
while demanding that Germany, struggling for existence,
shall restrain the use of an effective weapon and while
making compliance with these demands a condition for maintenance of relations with Germany, confines itself to protests
against illegal methods adopted by Germany's enemies.
Moreover, the German people knows to what considerable
extent its enemies are supplied with all kinds of war material from the United States.

It will, therefore, be understood that the appeal made by
the Government of the United States to sentiments of hu-

starvation as constantly drawn in German documents is merely a
poetic metaphor. It is sketched by anticipatory fear, not drawn from
facts. At the close of the War the mass of the German people were
in better physical condition than those of even the unconquered districts of France, and in infinitely better condition than the miserable
remnant left by the Germans in any conquered or co-conspiring land.

manity and principles of international law cannot, under
the circumstances, meet the same hearty response from the
German people which such an appeal otherwise always is
certain to find here.   If the German Government, nevertheless, is resolved to go to the utmost limit of concessions,
it has been guided not alone by the friendship connecting
the two great nations for over one hundred years, but also
by the thought of the great doom which threatens the entire
civilized world should the cruel and sanguinary war be extended and prolonged.

The German Government, conscious of Germany's
strength, twice within the last few months announced before
the world its readiness to make peace on a basis safeguarding
Germany's vital interests, thus indicating that it is not Germany's fault if peace is still withheld from the nations of
Europe.[3]   The German Government feels all the more justified in declaring that responsibility could not be borne before the forum of mankind and in history if after twenty-
one months of the war's duration the submarine question, under discussion between the German Government and the Government of the United States, were to take a turn seriously
threatening maintenance of peace between the two nations.

As far as lies with the German Government, it wishes
to prevent things from taking such a course.   The German
Government, moreover, is prepared to do its utmost to confine operations of the war for the rest of its duration to
the fighting forces of the belligerents, thereby also insuring
the freedom of the seas, a principle upon which the German
Government believes, now as before, that it is in agreement
with the Government of the United States.

The German Government, guided by this idea, notifies the
Government of the United States that German naval forces
have received the following order:

*In accordance with the general principles of visit and
search and the destruction of merchant vessels, recognized
by international law, such vessels, both within and without*

[3] These German offers of peace, as we have previously noted, were
always based on the demand that Germany was to keep the plunder
she had won.

*the area declared a naval war zone, shall not be sunk without warning and without saving human lives unless the ship attempts to escape or offer resistance.*

But neutrals cannot expect that Germany, forced to fight for existence, shall, for the sake of neutral interests, restrict the use of an effective weapon, if the enemy is permitted to continue to apply at will methods of warfare violating rules of international law. Such a demand would be incompatible with the character of neutrality, and the German Government is convinced that the Government of the United States does not think of making such a demand, knowing that the Government of the United States repeatedly declares that it is determined to restore the principle of freedom of the seas, from whatever quarter it has been violated.

Accordingly, the German Government is confident that in consequence of the new orders issued to the naval forces the Government of the United States will also now consider all impediments removed which may have been in the way of a mutual coöperation toward restoration of the freedom of the seas during the war, as suggested in the note of July 23, 1915, and it does not doubt that the Government of the United States will now demand and insist that the British Government shall forthwith observe the rules of international law universally recognized before the war, as are laid down in the notes presented by the Government of the United States to the British Government December 28, 1914, and November 5, 1915.[4]

Should steps taken by the Government of the United States not attain the object it desires, to have the laws of humanity followed by all belligerent nations, the German Government would then be facing a new situation in which it must reserve to itself complete liberty of decision.

[4] What this paragraph, when stripped of its verbiage, really asks is that because Germany has yielded a very small fraction of her many and obvious breakings of international law, therefore America should insist on Britain's yielding everything. The U. S. Government immediately and positively rejected this suggestion or request, declaring that her dispute with Britain must be settled on its own merits. She was not going to bargain with Germany and pay her for sparing American lives. Germany did not press the suggestion further.

# THE DEPORTATIONS FROM LILLE

## ENSLAVEMENT EXTENDED OVER THE CAPTURED RE-GION OF FRANCE

### APRIL 22ND

JAMES W. GERARD          ARISTIDE BRIAND
GENERAL VON GRAEVENITZ   BISHOP CHAROST OF LILLE
HERBERT HOOVER

In grim contrast to Germany's appeal to "humanity" in the preceding section of our volume, was her own conduct—and her own hypocrisy—in dealing with the people of northern France. She sought to force them to work for her and even to do war-work in opposition to their own countrymen. The methods which we have already shown her as employing in Belgium, she employed with even more severity in France, because in France there were no neutral officials to watch and to protest.

Germany tried to compel this work first by falsehood and afterward by blows, by starvation and even by death. These terrors were employed everywhere; but as Lille was the largest city of the captured region, Lille suffered most, and its name has become chiefly associated with the tragedy. Moreover, the number of young women deported from Lille was unusually large. The German Government reckoned the captured populace only as so many human bodies to be used in whatever way her military leaders saw fit.

The charge of falsehood against the German Government happens in this case to be particularly glaring. It is implied in the brief statement of the American Ambassador at Berlin, James W. Gerard; and this becomes more clear when we learn that the Spanish Ambassador at Berlin also protested as a neutral against these deportations, and sent the following telegraphic report giving the German Government's attitude:

"The German Minister of Foreign Affairs has declared to me verbally that the persons referred to in the telegram of June 29th—to a number with which he is not acquainted—are employed on harvest work, for the benefit of the occupied provinces, in order to procure food for the inhabitants, who would otherwise die of starvation as a result of the policy pursued against Germany by France and Eng-land."

In face of this telegram stands the fact that in the preceding year the French people had been similarly persuaded to raise their crops and then these had all been taken from them for Germany's use. That is why every official German knew that it was useless to tell any Frenchman of the most ordinary intelligence that the crops of this second year would be given to the French. Moreover, the mass of statements summed up in the accounts here given make it beyond denial (except a German denial) that these deported people were forced into labor of every sort, whatever was most wanted by their taskmasters. M. Briand, then Prime Minister of France, speaks officially of the deportations; so does General Graevenitz, the German commander; so does the Bishop of Lille, Alexis Charost. For a general summing up of the case Americans will ask no more secure word than that of Herbert Hoover. Yet, months after full reports of the matter had reached the German Government, its Imperial Chancellor and Von Jagow, its Imperial Secretary, put off neutral ambassadors with bland assurances of ignorance and benevolence.

Note that the constantly repeated reference to the Allies' "policy," which appears in the Spanish Ambassador's telegram, is really a covert threat which meant: "If the Allies do not give us all the food [and everything else, including all war munitions] we want, we will starve and destroy our captives." That is exactly what Germany meant, and what except for American intervention she might have accomplished."

C. F. H.

## BY JAMES W. GERARD

IT seems that the Germans had endeavored to get volunteers from the great industrial towns of Lille, Roubaix, and Tourcoing to work these fields; that after the posting of the notices calling for volunteers only fourteen had appeared. The Germans then gave orders to seize a certain number of inhabitants and send them out to farms in the outlying districts to engage in agricultural work. The Americans told me that this order was carried out with the greatest barbarity; that a man would come home at night and find that his wife or children had disappeared and no one could tell him where they had gone except that the neighbors would relate that German non-commissioned officers and a file of soldiers had carried them off. For instance, in a house of a well-to-do merchant who had perhaps two daughters of fifteen and seventeen and a man servant, the two daughters and the servant would be seized and sent off together to work for the Germans in some little farmhouse whose location was not disclosed to the parents. The Americans told me that this sort of thing was causing such indignation among the population of these towns that they feared a great uprising and a consequent slaughter and burning by the Germans.

That night at dinner I spoke to the Chancellor about

this and told him that it seemed to me absolutely outrageous; and that, without consulting with my Government, I was prepared to protest in the name of humanity against a continuance of this treatment of the civil population of occupied France. The Chancellor told me that he had not known of it, that it was the result of orders given by the military, that he would speak to the Emperor about it, and that he hoped to be able to stop further deportations. I believe that they were stopped, but twenty thousand or more who had been taken from their homes were not returned until months afterwards. I said in a speech that I made in May on my return to America that it required the joint efforts of the Pope, the King of Spain, and our President to cause the return of these people to their homes; and I then saw that some German press agency had come out with an article that I had made false statements about this matter because these people were not returned to their homes as a result of the representations of the Pope, the King of Spain, and our President, but were sent back because the Germans had no further use for them. It seems to me that this denial makes the case rather worse than before.

### BY ARISTIDE BRIAND
#### Official Statement of the French Government

On several occasions the Government of the Republic has had occasion to bring to the notice of neutral Powers the action of the German military authorities towards the population of the French territory temporarily occupied by them as being in conflict with treaty rights.

The Government of the Republic finds itself to-day obliged to lay before foreign governments documents which will establish that our enemies have put in force measures still more inconsistent with humanity.

By order of General von Graevenitz, and with the support of Infantry Regiment No. 64, detailed for the purpose by the German General Headquarters, about 25,000 French —consisting of girls between 16 and 20 years of age, young women, and men up to the age of 55—without regard to social position, were torn from their homes at Roubaix, Tourcoing, and Lille, separated ruthlessly from their families, and compelled to do agricultural work in the Departments of the Aisne and the Ardennes.

Better than any comment which we can make, the official notices of the German authorities, the despairing protests of the Mayor and the Bishop of Lille, and extracts from the letters received from these localities will throw light upon this new outrage committed by the Imperial German Government.

The Minister of War, under date of June 30, 1916, gives us the following accounts of these occurrences:

"Not content with subjecting our people in the North to every kind of oppression, the Germans have recently treated them in the most iniquitous way.

"In contempt of rules universally recognized and of their own express promises not to molest the civil population, they have taken women and girls away from their families; they have sent them off, mixed up with men, to destinations unknown, to work unknown.

"In the early days of April, official notices offered to families needing work a settlement in the country—in the Department of the Nord—with work in the fields or at tree-felling.

"Finding this overture unsuccessful, the Germans decided to have recourse to compulsion. From April 9th onwards they resorted to raids—in the streets, in the houses—carrying off men and girls indiscriminately, and sending them Heaven knows where.

"A wider scope and a more methodical application were soon given to the measure. A General and a large force arrived at Lille, among others the 64th Regiment from Verdun.

"On April 19th and 20th, the public were warned by proclamation to be prepared for a compulsory evacuation.

"The Mayor entered an immediate protest, the Bishop tried to gain access to the local Commandant, local worthies wrote letters of protest.

"No effect! On Holy Saturday, at three in the morning, methodical raids began at Lille in the Fives quarter, in the Marlière quarter of Tourcoing, and at Roubaix. After a suspension on Easter Sunday, the work went on all the week, ending up in the Saint Maurice quarter of Lille.

"About three in the morning, troops, with fixed bayonets, barred the streets, machine guns commanded the road, against unarmed people.

"Soldiers made their way into the houses. The officer pointed out the people who were to go, and, half an hour later, everybody was marched pell-mell into an adjacent factory, and from there to the station, whence the departure took place.

"Mothers with children under 14 were spared.

"Girls under 20 were deported only when accompanied by one of their family. This in no way relieves the barbarity of the proceeding. Soldiers of the Landsturm blushed to be employed on such work.

"The victims of this brutal act displayed the greatest courage. They were heard crying *'Vive la France,'* and singing the *Marseillaise* in the cattle-trucks in which they were carried off.

"It is said that the men are employed in agriculture, road-mending, the making of munitions and trench digging.

"The women are employed in cooking and laundry-work for the soldiers and as substitutes for officers' servants.

"For this severe work, housemaids, domestic servants and factory women have been taken by preference.

"No servants are left in the Rue Royale at Lille.

"But some brave girls of the upper middle-class have come forward and refused to allow the working-class girls to go alone. The names of Mlles. B—— and de B—— are mentioned as having insisted on accompanying the girls of their district.

"The unfortunate people, thus requisitioned, have been scattered from Seclin and Templeuve, as far as the Ardennes.

"Their number is estimated at about 25,000, from the towns of Lille, Roubaix, and Tourcoing.

"The Quartier de la Place at Lille, the communes of Loos, Haubourdin, la Madeleine, and Lambersart are said to have been spared."

Unequaled emotion was felt by the population of the

north of France, without distinction of classes, during these days of Holy Week.

These measures surpassed in inhumanity those previously adopted. It is, however, necessary to return to the latter.

It appears necessary to compare the documents annexed to this Note with a reply given by the German Government to a previous complaint relating to work enforced, in violation of the Convention, on the civil population of Landrecies and Hancourt.

After declaring that at Landrecies the French who are liable to military service have work suitable to their profession assigned to them, the German Government asserts that at Landrecies, Hancourt, and everywhere else the population of the occupied French districts is treated with justice and perfect humanity.

The documents annexed to the present Note will show the value of this assertion. It is not a matter of men liable to military service having been forced to work; women, and girls between 16 and 20, have been taken into captivity and sent into exile.

Does the German Government, denying the principles, the sanctity of which it accepted in the Hague Convention, maintain that a belligerent has the right to compel enemy civilians to work?

In a Note dated March 22, 1916, it stated that it felt compelled to "request the French Government to issue orders to all commandants of internment camps on the subject of forced labor, and to require a formal declaration with regard to the matter."

This declaration was made to the Imperial Government on several occasions and in the most definite form. How can that Government reconcile its claim in respect to interned German civilians—whom it declares not to be liable to forced labor—with its admission that French civilians, liable to military service, but at liberty, are constrained to labor, or with the disgraceful measures taken at Roubaix and Lille with regard to women and girls?

In orders placarded at Lille the German military authority has endeavored to justify the wholesale deportations ordered at Lille and Roubaix as a retaliation for the attitude of England in making the provisioning of the population increasingly difficult. Nothing, however, can justify such a barbarous measure. Seizure of contraband and interference with enemy commerce are acts of war; deportation of the population without military necessity is not an act of war. Moreover, to dispose of this pretended justification, it is sufficient to show that Germany has not only stripped—for her own profit—the occupied districts of all the products which would have insured the subsistence of the inhabitants, but also, previously to any interference with enemy commerce, organized for her own benefit the exploitation of the labor of French civilians.

To show this, extracts from the depositions of French citizens who have been evacuated from the invaded Departments are annexed to the present Note.

These depositions were made on oath before the magistrates of the districts where the evacuated people found asylum in all parts of France, by refugees from all points of the invaded Departments.

They were made in response to a form of inquiry in which the question of forced labor was not in contemplation—it was too much at variance with international law. They emanate from persons of all ages and conditions, and their absolute agreement (more than two hundred have been taken) proves that the civil population of the Departments occupied by the German troops has been reduced to absolute servitude by the army of occupation.

Article 52 of the regulations annexed to the Fourth Convention of the Hague permits requisitions in kind and in services for the needs of the army of occupation. In the recorded depositions there is no question of any regular form of requisitions. Services, sometimes of a most repulsive nature, have been forcibly imposed on the entire civil population, without distinction of sex, age, or social position. These unhappy people had to present themselves for the work imposed on them by night or by day, at all sorts of places and at great distances from their homes, sometimes even under artillery fire, in most cases without any kind of remuneration, in others for a few crusts of bread.

The German military authority has never concerned itself with the care of the population which the war has brought under its provisional administration. The products of the forced labor of the population have been transported to Germany in spite of the absolute destitution of the workers.

Finally, it can be established from these depositions that the German authorities have not hesitated to compel the population to take part in military operations against their own country; they have even obliged them to assist in pillaging their own countryside!

They have employed them as direct auxiliaries of the combatant forces, either by placing them in front of the German troops to serve as shields or by compelling them to do work in connection with military operations.

Where this working material—for there is no more a question of human beings but of mere machines moved from place to place as required—where this human material gives out in certain districts of the occupied territory, the German authorities draw without limit either on the internment camps where, contrary to all law, the mobilizable men belonging to this territory have been confined, or on the other invaded districts. The people are not sent back to their former homes. These civilians are formed into regiments and, although the Germans themselves acknowledge that they ought not to be compelled to work, they are sent to any point of the districts occupied by the German army and compelled to perform the most severe labor. And when France demands, in the name of some agonized family, information as to the fate of an unhappy exile, the German Government replies that the military authorities do not consider themselves under any obligation to explain their reasons for these transferences. For entire months it is impossible to find out what has become of the unhappy people.

The indisputable result of the following declarations, read as a whole, is that, without any immediate necessity, not in the excitement of battle—moments which might excuse the violations of international law committed by the German authorities—those authorities, in pursuance of a deliberate purpose and according to a predetermined method, have reduced the unfortunate population of the invaded districts to a condition which can be likened only to slavery.

### BY GENERAL VON GRAEVENITZ
Proclamation of April, 1916, by the German Military Commandant of Lille

The attitude of England makes the provisioning of the population more and more difficult.

In order to relieve the distress, the German Government has recently asked for volunteers to go to work in the country. This offer has not had the success anticipated.

Consequently, the inhabitants will be evacuated by order and removed to the country. The evacuated persons will be sent to the interior of the occupied French territory, far behind the front, where they will be employed in agriculture, and in no way on military works.

This measure will give them the opportunity of making better provision for their subsistence.

In case of necessity, it will be possible to obtain provisions from the German depots.

Each evacuated person will be allowed 30 kilograms of luggage (household utensils, clothes, etc.), which it would be well to prepare immediately.

I therefore order as follows: Pending further orders, no person shall change his residence. No person may be absent from his declared legal residence between the hours of 9 p. m. and 6 a. m. (German time) unless he is in possession of a permit.

Since this measure cannot be recalled, it is in the interest of the population itself to remain calm and obedient.

### Notice Issued to Individuals With the Above

All the inhabitants of the house, with the exception of children under fourteen and their mothers, and of the aged, must prepare themselves to be transported within an hour and a half.

An officer will decide definitely what persons are to be

taken to the concentration camps. For this purpose, all the inhabitants of the house must assemble in front of the house; in case of bad weather they may remain in the passage. The door of the house must remain open. No protest will be listened to. No inhabitant of the house (even including those who are not to be transported) may leave it before 8 a. m. (German time).

Each person will be entitled to 30 kilograms of luggage; if the weight is excessive, the whole of the luggage of the person concerned will be peremptorily refused. The packages must be packed separately for each person, and provided with an address legibly written and firmly affixed. The address must bear the surname, first name, and the number of the identity card.

It is absolutely necessary that each person should, in his own interest, provide himself with eating and drinking utensils, with a woolen blanket, with good shoes and with body linen. Every person must bring his identity card. Any person endeavoring to avoid transportation will be punished without mercy.

### BY THE BISHOP OF LILLE
#### Appeal to General von Graevenitz

*Monsieur le Général:*

It is my duty to bring to your notice the fact that a very agitated state of mind exists among the population.

Numerous removals of women and girls, certain transfers of men and youths, and even of children, have been carried out in the districts of Tourcoing and Roubaix without judicial procedure or trial.

The unfortunate people have been sent to unknown places. Measures equally extreme and on a larger scale are contemplated at Lille. You will not be surprised, Monsieur le Général, that I intercede with you in the name of the religious mission confided to me. That mission lays on me the burden of defending, with respect but with courage, the Law of Nations, which the law of war must never infringe, and that eternal morality, whose rules nothing can suspend. It makes it my duty to protect the feeble and the unarmed, who are as my family to me and whose burdens and sorrows are mine.

You are a father; you know that there is not in the order of humanity a right more honorable or more holy than that of the family. For every Christian the inviolability of God, who created the family, attaches to it. The German officers who have been billeted for a long time in our homes know how deep in our hearts we of the North hold family affection and that it is the sweetest thing in life to us. Thus, to dismember the family, by tearing youths and girls from their homes, is not war; it is for us torture and the worst of tortures—unlimited moral torture. The violation of family rights is doubled by a violation of the sacred demands of morality. Morality is exposed to perils, the mere idea of which revolts every honest man, from the promiscuity which inevitably accompanies removals *en masse,* involving mixture of the sexes, or, at all events, of persons of very unequal moral standing. Young girls of irreproachable life—who have never committed any worse offense than that of trying to pick up some bread or a few potatoes to feed a numerous family, and who have, besides, paid the light penalty for such trespass—have been carried off. Their mothers, who have watched so closely over them, and had no other joy than that of keeping their daughters beside them, in the absence of father and sons fighting or killed at the front—these mothers are now alone. They bring to me their despair and their anguish. I am speaking of what I have seen and heard. I know that you have no part in these harsh measures. You are by nature inclined towards justice; that is why I venture to turn to you; I beg you to be good enough to forward without delay to the German High Military Command this letter from a Bishop, whose deep grief they will easily imagine. We have suffered much for the last twenty months, but no stroke of fortune could be comparable to this; it would be as undeserved as it is cruel and would produce in all France an indelible impression. I cannot believe that the blow will fall. I have faith in the human conscience and I preserve the hope that the young men and girls of respectable families will be restored to their homes in answer to the demand for their return and that sentiments of justice and honor will prevail over all lower considerations.

### BY HERBERT HOOVER
#### Statement Issued in September, 1917

I have been often called upon for a statement of my observation of German rule in Belgium and northern France.

I have neither the desire nor the adequate pen to picture the scenes which have heated my blood through the two and a half years that I have spent in work for the relief of these 10,000,000 people.

The sight of the destroyed homes and cities, the widowed and fatherless, the destitute, the physical misery of a people but partially nourished at best, the deportation of men by tens of thousands to slavery in German mines and factories, the execution of men and women for paltry effusions of their loyalty to their country, the sacking of every resource through financial robbery, the battening of armies on the slender produce of the country, the denudation of the country of cattle, horses and textiles; all these things we had to witness, dumb to help other than by protest and sympathy, during this long and terrible time—and still these are not the events of battle heat, but the effects of the grinding heel of a race demanding the mastership of the world.

All these things are well known to the world—but what can never be known is the dumb agony of the people, the expressionless faces of millions whose souls have passed the whole gamut of emotions.  And why?  Because these, a free and democratic people, dared plunge their bodies before the march of autocracy.

I myself believe that if we do not fight and fight now, all these things are possible to us—but even should the broad Atlantic prove our present defender, there is still Belgium. Is it worth while for us to live in a world where this free and unoffending people is to be trampled into the earth and to raise no sword in protest?

# THE SINN FEIN UPRISING IN DUBLIN

## GERMANY LENDS AID TO AN IRISH REVOLT

### APRIL 24TH-MAY 1ST

PADRAIC PEARSE                          JOHN REDMOND
GENERAL MAXWELL              SIR ROGER CASEMENT
              LORD ROBERT CECIL

American sympathy with the Irish demand for complete self-government has always been so strong that even so ill-advised an uprising as that of the Sinn Fein in 1916 aroused some degree of pity and even of approval. The central and bitterly accusing fact of the uprisal is, however, undeniable, and undenied. It was undertaken at Germany's instigation and its leaders allied themselves with Germany. At a time when Germany had been for two years revealing to the world her utter scorn of Democracy and her trampling on the rights and bodies of smaller peoples in Belgium, Poland and Serbia, these Irish leaders declared that they believed Germany to be the noble and trusty friend of Ireland and of freedom and Democracy. At a time when hundreds of thousands of Irishmen were fighting for the cause of Civilization in France, these few thousand Irish at home struck a blow which if successful would have gone far to ruin that cause by paralyzing the strength of Britons and Irishmen in France.

What happened was, briefly, this: Sir Roger Casement since the opening of the War had been trying to convince his Irish countrymen that now was the time for them to fight England and win freedom by German aid. Chiefly he had tried to raise an army for this purpose in Germany from among the Irish prisoners there. In this he failed conspicuously; but in April of 1916 he left Germany on a secret German ship. Another secret German ship brought arms and ammunition. Both he and the munitions were captured by British ships. At the same moment seven leaders of the Sinn Fein published in Dublin a proclamation declaring themselves the heads of a free Irish Republic and summoning their followers to aid them in revolt. Padraic Pearse, one of the signers, was declared president, and James Connolly was made the general in command in Dublin. Some thousands of Irishmen joined them, chiefly in Dublin. They seized the Dublin post-office and custom house as fortresses and slew a number of unarmed policemen and of British officers caught unprepared in the streets.

For two days the police and the small garrison of British troops could only hold their own; then a large force of troops under General Maxwell reached Dublin, surrounded the revolters, and attacked them with artillery. Three days later, April 29th, the Sinn Fein leaders abandoned the struggle, but fighting continued in sections of the burning city for yet a day or two longer. By that time all who could not escape had surrendered. Some eighteen hundred were thus made prisoners. Of the revolters and other civilians slain with or by them, two or three hundred were killed, and of the troops an even larger number, beside many wounded on both sides.

Pearse and fourteen other leaders were condemned as traitors by a military court and were shot. Casement was later tried by a full British court and was hanged on August 3rd. His final speech is here given, as also the original announcement of their purpose by Pearse and his colleagues. John Redmond, the noted leader of the Irish "Nationalists" or main body of patriots, voices the condemnation of the reckless revolt by the great mass of Irishmen; and the British view of Casement is voiced by Lord Cecil, a noted lawyer and Minister for the Blockade. General Maxwell depicts the actual fighting in which he commanded. C. F. H.

## PROCLAMATION ISSUED IN DUBLIN APRIL 24, 1916, AND SIGNED BY PADRAIC PEARSE AND SIX OTHERS

*THE Provisional Government of the Irish Republic to the people of Ireland:*

Irishmen and Irishwomen, in the name of God and of the dead generations from which you received the old traditions of nationhood, Ireland, through us, summons her children to her flag and strikes for her freedom, having organized and trained her manhood through her secret revolutionary organization, the Irish Republican Brotherhood, and through her open military organization, the Irish Volunteers, and the Irish citizen army.

Having patiently perfected their discipline and resolutely waited for the right moment to reveal itself, she now seizes that moment, and, supported by her exiled children in America, and by her gallant allies in Europe, by relying on her own strength, she strikes, in full confidence of victory.

We declare the right of the people of Ireland to the ownership of Ireland and to the unfettered control of Irish destinies to be sovereign and indefeasible. Long usurpation of that right by a foreign people and Government has not extinguished that right, nor can it ever be extinguished except by the destruction of the Irish people.

In every generation the Irish people have asserted their right to national freedom and sovereignty. Six times during the past 300 years they have asserted it in arms. Standing on that fundamental right, and again asserting it in arms in the face of the world, we hereby proclaim the Irish Republic as a sovereign, independent State and we pledge our lives and the lives of our comrades in arms to the cause of its freedom, its welfare, and its exaltation among nations.

The Irish Republic is entitled to, and hereby claims, the allegiance of every Irishman and Irishwoman. The republic guarantees religious and civil liberty, equal rights and equal opportunities to all its citizens, and declares its resolve to pursue the happiness and prosperity of the whole nation, and of all its parts, cherishing all the children of the nation equally, and oblivious of the differences, carefully fostered by an alien Government, which have divided the minority from the majority in the past.

Until our arms have brought the opportune moment for the establishment of a permanent National Government, representative of the whole people of Ireland and elected by the suffrage of all her men and women, the Provisional Government hereby constituted will administer the civil and military affairs of the republic, in trust for the people.

We place the cause of the Irish Republic under the protection of the Most High God, whose blessing we invoke upon our arms, and we pray that no one who serves that cause will dishonor it by cowardice, inhumanity, or rapine. In this supreme hour the Irish Nation must, by its valor and discipline and by the readiness of its children to sacrifice themselves for the common good, prove itself worthy of the august destiny to which it is called.

### BY JOHN REDMOND

My first feeling, of course, on hearing of this insane movement was one of horror, discouragement, almost despair. I asked myself whether Ireland, as so often before in her tragic history, was to dash the cup of liberty from her lips; was the insanity of a small section of her people once again to turn all her marvelous victories of the last few years into irreparable defeat, and to send her back, on the very eve of her final recognition as a free nation, into another long night of slavery, incalculable suffering, weary and uncertain struggle?

Look at the Irish position to-day. In the short space of forty years she has by a Constitutional movement made an almost unbrokenly triumphant march from pauperism and slavery to prosperity and freedom. She has won back the possession of the Irish land; she has stayed emigration; she at last began an era of national prosperity. Finally, she succeeded in placing on the Statute Book the greatest charter of freedom ever offered her since the days of Grattan. Is all this to be lost?

When the war came she made a choice which was inevitable, if she was to be true to all the principles which she had held through all her history, and which she had just so completely vindicated on her own soil—namely, the rights of small nations; the sacred principle of nationality; liberty and democracy. Moreover, the nations for which through all her history she had felt the sympathy that came from common principles and common aspirations were trampled, as she in her time had been trampled, under the iron heel of arrogant force. What has Ireland suffered in the past which Poland, Alsace, Belgium and Serbia have not suffered at the hands of Germany, and, I may add also, that portion of the soil of France, her old friend and ally, which is in the hands of Germany? What has been the record of Germany but the suppression of nationality, of freedom, and of language—in short, the suppression of all the things for which for centuries Ireland has struggled, the victory of which Ireland has achieved? Take the case of Belgium. Has there not been there that same ruthless shedding of the blood of priests and people that is part of Ireland's own history?

Leave the question of principle out, and consider the question only of the mere interests of Ireland herself. What did the situation demand? Neutrality? That was impossible. Hostility to the just cause of the Allies? Is there a sane man in Ireland who does not see this meant the drowning of the newly-won liberties of Ireland in Irish blood? Be these views right or wrong, this was the opinion of the overwhelming majority of the Irish people; it was the opinion which thousands of Irish soldiers have sealed with their blood by dying in the cause of the liberty of Ireland and of the world.   But anyhow it was the opinion of Ireland, and surely I need not argue the principle, especially with anybody who professes himself to be a Home Ruler, that the policy of Ireland must be decided by Ireland herself. That is a principle which has been accepted by the Irish race everywhere.   The millions of our people in the United States and elsewhere whose generous devotion has helped us so largely to win our victories for the Motherland of the race have always accepted it.   However bounteous their help, never have they denied the right of Ireland to choose her policy for herself.

That doctrine has been contested only by the very same men who to-day have tried to make Ireland the cat's-paw of Germany.   In all our long and successful struggle to obtain Home Rule we have been thwarted and opposed by that same section.   We have won Home Rule, not through them, but in spite of them.   This wicked move of theirs was their last blow at Home Rule.   It was not half as much treason to the cause of the Allies as treason to the cause of Home Rule.

This attempted deadly blow at Home Rule, carried on through this section, is made the more wicked and the more insolent by this fact—that Germany plotted it, Germany organized it, Germany paid for it.   So far as Germany's share in it is concerned, it is a German invasion of Ireland, as brutal, as selfish, as cynical as Germany's invasion of Belgium.   Blood has been shed, and if Ireland has not been reduced to the same horrors as Belgium, with her starving people, her massacred priests, her violated convents, it is not the fault of Germany.

And a final aggravation of the movement is this.   The misguided and insane young men who have taken part in this movement in Ireland have risked, and some of them lost, their lives.   But what am I to say of those men who have sent them into this insane and anti-patriotic movement while they have remained in the safe remoteness of American cities? I might add that this movement has been set in motion by this same class of men at the very moment when America is demanding reparation for the blood of innocent American men and women and children shed by Germans; they thus are guilty of double treason—treason to the generous land that received them, as well as to the land which gave them birth.

Is it not an additional horror that on the very day when we hear that men of the Dublin Fusiliers have been killed by Irishmen in the streets of Dublin, we receive the news of how the men of the 16th Division—our own Irish Brigade, and of the same Dublin Fusiliers—had dashed forward and by their unconquerable bravery retaken the trenches that the Germans had won at Hulluch? Was there ever such a picture of the tragedy which a small section of Irish faction had so often inflicted on the fairest hopes and the bravest deeds of Ireland?

As to the final result. I do not believe that this wicked and insane movement will achieve its ends. The German plot has failed. The majority of the people of Ireland retain their calmness, fortitude and unity. They abhor this attack on their interests, their rights, their hopes, their principles. Home Rule has not been destroyed; it remains indestructible.

## BY GENERAL SIR JOHN MAXWELL

The rebellion began by Sinn Feiners, presumably acting under orders, shooting in cold blood certain soldiers and policemen. Simultaneously they took possession of various important buildings and occupied houses along the routes in the City of Dublin which were likely to be used by troops taking up posts.

Most of the rebels were not in any uniform, and by mixing with peaceful citizens made it almost impossible for the troops to distinguish between friend and foe until fire was opened.

In many cases troops having passed along a street seemingly occupied by harmless people were suddenly fired upon from behind from windows and roof tops. Such were the conditions when reënforcements commenced to arrive in Dublin.

Whilst fighting continued under conditions at once so confused and so trying, it is possible that some innocent citizens were shot. It must be remembered that the struggle was in many cases of a house-to-house character, that sniping was continuous and very persistent, and that it was often extremely difficult to distinguish between those who were or had been firing upon the troops and those who had for various reasons chosen to remain on the scene of the fighting, instead of leaving the houses and passing through the cordons.

The number of such incidents that has been brought to notice is very insignificant.

Once the rebellion started the members of the Dublin Metropolitan Police—an unarmed uniformed force—had to be withdrawn, or they would have been mercilessly shot down, as, indeed, were all who had the bad luck to meet the rebels. In their absence a number of the worst elements of the city joined the rebels and were armed by them. The daily record of the Dublin Magistrates' Court proves that such looting as there was was done by such elements.

There have been numerous incidents of deliberate shooting on ambulances and those courageous people who voluntarily came out to tend to the wounded. The City Fire Brigade, when turned out in consequence of incendiary fires, were fired on and had to retire.

As soon as it was ascertained that the rebels had established themselves in various centers, the first phase of operations was conducted with a view to isolate them by forming a cordon of troops round each.

To carry out this streets were selected along which the cordon could be drawn. Some of these streets, for instance, North King Street, were found to be strongly held, rebels occupying the roofs of houses, upper windows, and strongly constructed barricades.

Artillery fire was only used to reduce the barricades, or against a particular house known to be strongly held.

The troops suffered severe losses in establishing these

cordons, and, once established, the troops were subjected to a continuous fire from all directions, especially at night time, and invariably from persons concealed in houses.

To give an idea of the opposition offered to his Majesty's troops in the execution of their duty, the following losses occurred:

|  | Killed | Wounded |
|---|---|---|
| Officers .................. | 17 | 46 |
| Other ranks .............. | 89 | 288 |

I wish to draw attention to the fact that, when it became known that the leaders of the rebellion wished to surrender, the officers used every endeavor to prevent further bloodshed; emissaries were sent in to the various isolated bands, and time was given them to consider their position.

I cannot imagine a more difficult situation than that in which the troops were placed; most of those employed were draft-finding battalions, or young Territorials from England, who had no knowledge of Dublin.

The surrenders, which began on April 30th, were continued until late on May 1st, during which time there was a considerable amount of isolated sniping.

Under the circumstances related above I consider the troops as a whole behaved with the greatest restraint, and carried out their disagreeable and distasteful duties in a manner which reflects the greatest credit on their discipline.

Allegations on the behavior of the troops brought to my notice are being most carefully inquired into. I am glad to say they are few in number, and these are not all borne out by direct evidence.

Numerous cases of unarmed persons killed by rebels during the outbreak have been reported to me. As instances, I may select the following: J. Brien, a constable of the Dublin Metropolitan Police, was shot while on duty at Castle Gate on April 24th. On the same day another constable of the same force named M. Lahiff was shot while on duty at St. Stephen's Green. On April 25th R. Waters of Recess, Monkstown, County Dublin, was shot at Mount Street Bridge while being driven into Dublin by Captain Scovell, R.A.M.C.

All these were unarmed, as was Captain Scovell. In the last case the car was not challenged or asked to stop.

I wish to emphasize that the responsibility for the loss of life, however it occurred, the destruction of property and other losses, rests entirely with those who engineered this revolt, and who, at a time when the empire is engaged in a gigantic struggle, invited the assistance and coöperation of the Germans.

### BY SIR ROGER CASEMENT
#### His Speech in Court When Condemned as a Traitor

As I wish my words to reach a much wider audience than I see before me here, I intend to read all that I propose to say. What I shall read now is something I wrote more than twenty days ago. There is an objection possibly not good in law but surely good on moral grounds against the application to me here of this English statute, 565 years old, that seeks to deprive an Irishman to-day of life and honor, not for "adhering to the King's enemies" but for adhering to his own people. When this statute was passed, in 1351, what was the state of men's minds on the question of a far higher allegiance—that of man to God and His Kingdom? The law of that day did not permit a man to forsake his Church or deny his God save with his life. The heretic then had the same doom as the traitor. To-day a man may forswear God and His Heavenly Realm without fear or penalty, all earlier statutes having gone the way of Nero's edicts against the Christians; but that constitutional phantom the King can still dig up from the dungeons and torture chambers of the Dark Ages a law that takes a man's life and limb for an exercise of conscience.

Loyalty is a sentiment, not a law. It rests on Love, not on restraint. The government of Ireland by England rests on restraint and not on law; and, since it demands no love, it can evoke no loyalty. Judicial assassination to-day is reserved only for one race of the King's subjects, for Irishmen; for those who cannot forget their allegiance to the realm of Ireland. What is the fundamental charter of an Englishman's liberty? That he shall be tried by his peers. With all respect I assert that this court is to me, an Irishman, a foreign court—this jury is for me, an Irishman, not a jury of my peers.   It is patent to every man of conscience that I have an indefeasible right, if tried at all under this statute of high treason, to be tried in Ireland, before an Irish court, and by an Irish jury.   This court, this jury, the public opinion of this country, England, cannot but be prejudiced in varying degree against me, most of all in time of war.   From this court and its jurisdiction I appeal to those I am alleged to have wronged, and to those I am alleged to have injured by my "evil example," and claim that they alone are competent to decide my guilt or my innocence.

This is so fundamental a right, so natural a right, so obvious a right, that it is clear the Crown were aware of it when they brought me by force and by stealth from Ireland to this country.   It was not I who landed in England, but the Crown who dragged me here, away from my own country, to which I had returned with a price upon my head, away from my own countrymen, whose loyalty is not in doubt, and safe from the judgment of my peers, whose judgment I do not shrink from.   I admit no other judgment but theirs.   I accept no verdict save at their hands.

I assert from this dock that I am being tried here not because it is just, but because it is unjust.   My counsel has referred to the Ulster Volunteer movement, and I will not touch at length upon that ground, save only to say that neither I nor any of the leaders of the Irish Volunteers, who were founded in Dublin in November, 1913, had quarrel with the Ulster Volunteers as such, who were born a year earlier. Our movement was not directed against them, but against the men who misused and misdirected the courage, the sincerity, and the local patriotism of the men of the North of Ireland. On the contrary, we welcomed the coming of the Ulster Volunteers, even while we deprecated the aims and intentions of those Englishmen who sought to pervert to an English party use—to the mean purposes of their own bid for place and power in England—the armed activities of simple Irishmen. We aimed at winning the Ulster Volunteers to the cause of a united Ireland—we aimed at uniting all Irishmen in a natural and national bond of cohesion based on mutual self-respect. Our hope was a natural one, and, if left to ourselves, not hard to accomplish. If external influences of disintegration would but leave us alone, we were sure that nature itself must bring us together. It was not the Irish Volunteers who broke the law, but a British party.

The Government had permitted the Ulster Volunteers to be armed by Englishmen to threaten not merely an English party in its hold on office, but to threaten that party through the lives and blood of Irishmen. Our choice lay between submitting to foreign lawlessness and resisting it, and we did not hesitate. I for one was determined that Ireland was much more to me than empire, and that if charity begins at home so must loyalty.

Since arms were so necessary to make our organization a reality and to give to the minds of Irishmen menaced with the most outrageous threats a sense of security, it was our bounden duty to get arms before all else. I decided with this end in view to go to America. If, as the right honorable gentleman, the present Attorney General, asserted in a speech at Manchester, Nationalists would neither fight for home rule nor pay for it, it was our duty to show him that we knew how to do both.

Then came the war. As Mr. Birrell said in his evidence recently laid before the Commission of Inquiry into the causes of the late rebellion in Ireland, "The war upset all our calculations." It upset mine no less than Mr. Birrell's, and put an end to my mission of peaceful effort in America. War between Great Britain and Germany meant, as I believed, ruin for all the hopes we had founded on the enrollment of the Irish Volunteers. I felt over there in America that my first duty was to keep Irishmen at home in the only army that could safeguard our national existence. If small nationalities were to be the pawns in this game of embattled giants, I saw no reason why Ireland should shed her blood in any cause but her own, and if that be treason beyond the seas I am not ashamed to avow it or to answer for it here with my life.

And when we had the doctrine of Unionist loyalty at

last, "Mausers and Kaisers and any King you like," I felt I needed no other warrant than that these words conveyed—to go forth and do likewise. The difference between us was that the Unionist champions chose a path which they felt would lead to the Woolsack, while I went a road that I knew must lead to the dock. And the event proves that we were both right. But let me say that I am prouder to stand here to-day in the traitor's dock to answer this impeachment than to fill the place of my accusers. If there be no right of rebellion against a state of things that no savage tribe would endure without resistance, then am I sure that it is better for men to fight and die without right than to live in such a state of right as this. Where all your rights become only an accumulated wrong; where men must beg with bated breath for leave to subsist in their own land, to think their own thoughts, to sing their own songs, to garner the fruit of their own labors—and even while they beg to see these things inexorably withdrawn from them—then surely it is a braver, a saner, and a truer thing to be a rebel in act and deed against such circumstances as this than tamely to accept it as the natural lot of men.

My Lord, I have done. Gentlemen of the Jury, I wish to thank you for your verdict. I hope you will not think that I made any imputation upon your truthfulness or your integrity when I said that this was not a trial by my peers.

## BY LORD ROBERT CECIL
### Official British Government Statement

No doubt of Casement's guilt exists. No one doubts that the court and jury arrived at the right verdict. The only ground for a reprieve would be political expediency, a difficult ground to put forward in this country. This country never could strain the law to punish a man for the same reason that it could not strain the law to let one off.

The Irish rebellion began with the murder of unarmed people, both soldiers and police. No grievance justified it, and it was purely a political movement organized by a small section of Irish people who still hate England and were assisted by Germany. There was and is in this country the greatest possible indignation against these people.   There is no doubt that Casement did everything possible to assist this rebellion in coöperation with the Germans.   There can be no doubt that he was moved by enmity for this country. The contention that he landed in Ireland for the purpose of preventing the rebellion is demonstrably false.   No such assertion was made by counsel at the trial.

Casement was much more malignant and hostile to this country than were the leaders of the rising, who were caught with arms in their hands.   He visited military prisons in Germany with the intention of persuading Irish soldiers to throw off their allegiance.   All sorts of promises were made for the improvement of the conditions of these men to induce them to join the Irish legion.   An enormous majority thus approached refused and thereafter were subjected to increased hardships by the Germans.   From among these Irish soldiers a number have since been repatriated as hopeless invalids, and they subsequently died.   They looked upon Casement as their murderer.

Nor is there any ground, public or private, so far as we know, which can be quoted in mitigation of Casement's crime, and I do not think any Government doing its duty could interfere with the sentence which has been passed on him.

The British Disaster at Kut

The hand-to-hand struggle in which the Turks turned back the British Column at Ctesiphon

From a sketch by a German eye-witness
Max Ellie

The British Disaster at Kut

The hand-to-hand struggle in which the Turks turned back the British Column at Ctesiphon

From a sketch by a German eye-witness, Max Filke

# BRITISH DISASTER IN KUT-EL-AMARA

## THE SURRENDER OF A BRITISH ARMY

### APRIL 29TH

GASTON BODART  
GENERAL TOWNSHEND

EDMUND CANDLER  
MAJOR CHARLES BARBER

The surrender of the British army at Kut-el-Amara was impressive to the world not because of the number of the captives—they were but a tiny body as compared with the masses captured by either side on the Russian front—but because this was a British army, and the victors were Asiatics. For two centuries mere handfuls of Britons had been extending their rule over the swarming millions of the Orient. This surrender broke the tradition of their power upon land, as the defeat at the Dardanelles had revealed the limit of their naval strength.

Any Briton will tell you now that the Bagdad expedition was unwisely undertaken. The British held the Persian Gulf region securely, but had no sufficient force with which to penetrate over three hundred miles up the almost impassable marsh country of the Euphrates river-valley. Leaders in Britain itself disputed with leaders in India as to which should spare troops for such an advance, and the authorities in India only yielded under protest. Even then the commander in the region, General Nixon, declared his forces too small for an advance beyond Kut, to which some troops under General Townshend won their way in September, 1915, struggling against the natural difficulties of the land rather than against severe Turkish opposition.

It was this lack of Turkish resistance that lured General Nixon to attempt to capture Bagdad. General Townshend was given command of a larger column for this purpose, and fought his way against an ever-increasing resistance from Kut onward as far as Ctesiphon, a group of ancient ruins some twenty miles below Bagdad. Here Townshend fought a stiff and indecisive battle in November, and realized that the mass of Turks had grown too strong to be pushed further back. To the Britons, to stop so far from their base of supplies in a hostile land, was equivalent to defeat. Townshend knew he had no course left except to withdraw. He conducted his retreat in a masterly way; but it became more difficult with every step. When his outworn troops reached Kut on December 3rd, Townshend was glad indeed to let them rest behind the secure defenses which its position afforded.

In Kut the Britons had ample stores and at first regarded themselves merely as defenders of the outer line of the British front. The Turks, however, in ever-increasing numbers gathered round them until they were shut off from the world. By January of 1916 Britain became fully roused to their danger, and sought to rescue them. General Nixon was superseded by Sir Percy Lake. He dispatched a strong force to break through to Townshend's rescue; but the Turkish commander, Nur-ed-Din, fought the relievers so vigorously that in battle after battle the Britons did little more than hold their own.

One column under General Aylmer was driven back; another under General Gorringe won its way up the Euphrates to within twenty miles of Kut. Here, on April 22nd, it was hurled back from a desperate attack upon the Turkish entrenchments which barred its way at Sanna-i-yat. The repulse sealed Townshend's fate; he surrendered April 29th.

Townshend's own statement is given here, as well as the picture drawn by one of his officers, Major Barber. The Teuton view is supplied by the official Austrian investigator, Dr. Bodart. The story of the relieving columns is told by Edmund Candler, the official British observer, who marched with them.

BY GASTON BODART

In order to fasten the bolt against the "German impulse toward the East," England converted the fiction of 1912, regarding the independence of the Sultanate of Koweit into an actual title of possession and, in the beginning of November, 1914, from this base brought the Persian Gulf under British dominion.

An Anglo-Indian expeditionary corps, under General Nixon, consisting originally of 6 Indian infantry brigades and one of cavalry, marched up the Shatt-el-Arab, seized Basra, the former port of Bagdad and the starting point for the Arab incursions into India. In this exploit the corps was supported by the British warships. In addition to military and political motives, economic interests also came into consideration as regards this expedition, inasmuch as the concession regarding the renewed irrigation of Irak and the exploitation of the rich petroleum and naphtha wells, which lay on nearby Persian territory along the Karun River, were in the hands of English companies.

From Basra a group of the expeditionary corps marched to the Karun region in order to occupy it, although this was neutral Persian ground. After fights with the Turkish vanguard, which, however, could not prevent the capture of Korna at the junction of the Euphrates and Tigris (December 9th), the British were held up by Turkish counter-

attacks on January 20th, 21st ond 30th, 1915.  Not until
the middle of April were they able to break down the
resistance (at Shaiba and Sobeir) by reason of the vigorous
participation of their gunboats.   Thereupon one column
marched up the Euphrates and another up the Tigris, always accompanied by gunboats and steamers.  The Turkish
military command had meanwhile, in the face of great
difficulties, concentrated its Sixth Army under Nur-ed-Din
(later under Khalif Pasha) and met the advance on both
rivers.   The Tigris column under Townshend advanced
with relatively good speed, forced back the Turks before
Amara, and, on September 29th, 1915, occupied the important point Kut-el-Amara.  The Euphrates columns of
the English under Gorringe met with defeat at two places,
but subsequently captured Nasariyeh on July 24th.

Made overconfident by his easily won successes, Townshend, underrating his enemy and without awaiting reinforcements, advanced impetuously against Bagdad, encountered, on November 22nd, near the ruins of Ctesiphon, 4
well-intrenched Turkish divisions and suffered a severe
defeat.   Hard pressed by the pursuing Turks, who were
now commanded by Field-Marshal Von der Goltz, who had
hurried here from the Dardanelles, Townshend was compelled to retreat to his point of support, Kut-el-Amara,
where he was surrounded by the superior forces of the
Turkish army.

General Percy Lake, who had superseded General Nixon
in the chief command of the expeditionary corps, from his
base at El Garbi did all in his power to relieve Townshend.
In a surprisingly short time five divisions, including the
Thirteenth under General Maude, which had shortly before
arrived from the Dardanelles, were put in readiness, and,
as the Tigris corps, were placed under the command of
General Aylmer.

The latter, at the beginning of January, 1916, encountered the Turkish besiegers of Kut-el-Amara at Sheick-Saad
and succeeded, after continuous fighting, in forcing them
back to a point near El Gussa, one day's march from the
positions occupied by Townshend's division.  Aylmer suc-

ceeded, after penetrating the first Turkish line of defense, in reaching Fellahieh, while the column of Younghusband, which was advancing along the southern bank, advanced about an equal distance and threatened the second Turkish line at Sanaaiyat. But the English forces, weakened by heavy losses, unfavorable weather and camp diseases, were not equal to the task of breaking this second line.

Although within ten miles of their goal, they were forced to relinquish all the positions captured and to fall back to their point of departure, Amara, leaving the brave defenders of Kut-el-Amara to their inevitable fate. Forced by hunger, Townshend, on April 26th, 1916, surrendered with 13,000 men at Kut-el-Amara. This was the worst blow which English prestige suffered in the war.

### BY EDMUND CANDLER

#### Official British Observer With the Relieving Force

The last communications from Townshend reached us [the relieving force] by wireless on the morning of April 29th. "Have destroyed my guns and am destroying most of my munitions, and have sent out officers to Khalil to say am ready to surrender. Khalil is at Madug. I am unable to hold on any more. I must have some food here. I have told Khalil to-day, and have sent launch with deputation to bring food from *Julnar*." The next message told us that a Turkish regiment was approaching the fort to take over guards in Kut. "I have hoisted white flag over town and fort. Troops commence going into camp near Shumran 2 P. M. I shall shortly destroy wireless." At 1 P. M. a pre-arranged signal by wireless indicated that Townshend's last message had gone through.

Wireless, guns, revolvers, rifles, aëroplane, ammunition, compasses, glasses—everything that might be useful to the enemy, was destroyed and we were near enough to see the blaze. There was no Hunnish fury or obscenity in the last scene. We left the Turks our gramophone and records and anything that might contribute to the civil uses of life.

Nine thousand fighting men, 3,000 British and 6,000 Indians, exclusive of followers, surrendered at Kut; and it is useless to try and gloss over the disgrace which is attached, not to our soldiers, but to the politicians responsible for the disaster. There has been no surrender on the same scale in the history of the British army. The nearest parallel to it is that of Cornwallis with 7,073 officers and men in the American War of Independence. But in Mesopotamia the relieving force lost more than twice the number of the garrison in their attempt to save them,[1] apart from the loss of prestige in the one theater of the war where we could least afford a fluctuating standard. The Arabs believed Townshend invincible. Until the retirement from Ctesiphon the 6th Division had never attacked a position which they had not taken. The mere abstract record of their achievement was worth the substance of a new division in establishing our security on the Tigris. The British flag had never been associated with reverse. But this one setback showed the Arab that we were fallible like other people. Upon the fall of Kut the Medjidieh and Turkish paper money fetched its old value in the bazaar. But the respect for Townshend was not greatly diminished, and it was admitted that nothing short of starvation could have defeated him.

Townshend impressed his personality deeply on the Turk. He was permitted to retain his sword; his progress to the Bosphorus was almost triumphal; and when he arrived at his island he became the lion of the place. Khalil Bey, the Turkish Commander, spoke of him with the most profound admiration when he received our *parlementaires* on the evening of the surrender   "We will give him as good a time as the Russians gave Osman Pasha," he said; and he was evidently anxious that he should receive every comfort and attention after the privations he had endured so gallantly. He regretted that his supplies were so scanty, and welcomed our proposal to send stores to the garrison. Two barges with a day and a half's iron rations left our camp the next morning. These were followed by a hospital ship and a paddle-steamer with lighters attached loaded with food and canteen stores. The hospital ship *Sikhim* returned with the first batch of sick and wounded, whom we exchanged for Turkish prisoners.

[1] The total casualties in the advance from Ali Gharbi (Jan. 6th— April 22nd) amounted to 21,973.

The Kut garrison at the time of the surrender were well treated by the enemy. Turkish officers gave every British soldier a handful of cigarettes as he left the camp, and British and Ottoman privates were observed fraternizing with friendly and explanatory gestures. Rough fare, primitive medical arrangements, and a wretched sanitary system were inevitable in the conditions existing in Bagdad. These hardships were shared with the Turkish troops.

To turn to the diary of the siege. During the first month the garrison were fighting for their lives and were only afraid that ammunition would give out before the relieving column could reach them. They reckoned it a certainty that the reënforcements collecting at Basra would be able to join hands with Townshend and drive out the Turk. All this time the troops in Kut were receiving full rations, and the question of supplies seems to have afforded no anxiety. In the meanwhile the relieving force advancing from Ali Gharbi in the first week of January believed that Townshend was near the end of his resources. Aylmer's force was far from fully organized, and there was a whole new division on its way upstream which would have doubled our power of offensive. But, as we have seen, every hour's delay was regarded as vital, and we wasted our strength by throwing in our troops in detail as they came up the river.

As soon as we advanced from Ali Gharbi the enemy relaxed their hold on Townshend. There was no longer any danger of ammunition running short, but the check at Orah made the question of supplies serious. The civil population had remained in Kut. Upon Townshend's arrival they had been given their choice—to stay or leave; they had a bare twenty-four hours to evacuate. They elected to stay. Neither they nor we foresaw the dark days ahead. The few who left the town in the first days of the investment were tied up by the enemy and shot, and the Turks made it quite clear that they would execute any who tried to escape. To expel them now would mean the wholesale murder of the Arab inhabitants of the town. Thus the garrison was burdened with 6,000 additional mouths.

But on January 24th, after our repulse at El Hannah,

the discovery of considerable grain stores hidden away in the houses, mostly underground, opened a new phase in the investment. These were commandeered and paid for, and they afforded the garrison three months' supplies on a gradually reduced scale. The Arabs, who had previously been self-supporting, now received rations as issued to British soldiers and sepoys. Thus the story of Kut resolves itself into two distinct phases, at first a determined siege, and then a protracted investment. And in both of these, whether in the gallantry of the defense or in the endurance of privations, whether in combating the Turk or hunger, the garrison was tried and proved in a measure worthy of the most glorious traditions of the British army.

On December 3rd, when Townshend arrived at Kut, the force opposing him consisted of four infantry divisions totaling some 15,000 rifles, 1,000 camelry, 400 cavalry, thirty-one mobile guns, seven heavy guns and some thousands of Arab tribesmen. On the 4th he reported himself on the point of being invested. The enemy's advance guard were ten miles off, the main body five miles behind. The position Townshend held was a peninsula formed by a loop of the Tigris, 3,200 yards north to south and 1,700 yards wide; and on the right bank he held the licorice factory and village, which he fortified, and garrisoned with two battalions. He was invested on all sides except the west. His troops were worn out with their long fighting march from Ctesiphon, but they began at once to form a strongly entrenched camp. If any one could save Kut it was Townshend. He had all the resourcefulness and personal magnetism which is so essential in the commander of a beleaguered garrison. He and his division were bound together by the strongest ties. They were undefeated, and the retirement from Ctesiphon had demanded and proved even higher qualities in both leader and men than had been called for in the victorious advance towards Bagdad. Also Townshend had had experience of sieges. From the beginning he prepared to defend Kut with the same resolution and resource as he had defended Chitral in 1895, and with more confidence in the issue.

On December 4th and 5th he sent the steamers and barges

and most of the *mahailas* downstream, retaining one steamer
only, the *Sumana,* for use as a ferry.   On the 6th he sent off
the cavalry brigade to Ali Gharbi, holding back one squadron; they fought a rearguard action all the way, but got
through with trifling casualties.   The Turkish prisoners taken
at Ctesiphon, 1,400 in number, were cleared just in time.   On
December 7th one of the Turkish divisions had moved round
his flank four miles to the south on the opposite bank of
the river, and two other divisions had taken up a position
on the left bank west of Kut.   On the 9th Nur-ed-Din sent a
letter demanding the garrison's surrender.   Our refusal was
followed by a heavy bombardment from northwest and
southeast.   The camp was attacked from all points of the
compass and shelled all day.   The bridgehead detachment
was driven in.   At night a gallant young sapper, Lieutenant
Matthews, R.E., swam the river and blew up the bridge on
the Turkish side in the teeth of the enemy.   On the 10th
and 11th attacks were pressed severely all day.   Our casualties on the 10th were 129; on the 11th, 202.   The enemy had
now dug up to within 600 yards, and was strengthening his
works with sandbags and timber.   Townshend's tactics were
to keep a central mass in hand with a minimum force observing each avenue of approach.   In artillery duels the garrison suffered the disadvantage of concentrated hostile fire
from all sides, while their own gunfire directed from the center to the circumference had to be divergent and dissemi-
nated.   The Turks' 5-centimeter guns fired rapidly and ac-
curately at 7,500 yards; our own 5-inch guns were very old,
and little use over 6,000 yards owing to error.

On December 14th our casualties dropped to eighty-
seven, on the 15th to sixty-four.   The Turks were becoming tired of these ineffectual attacks, and on the 16th a general apathy was apparent amongst the enemy.   They had
lost at least a thousand men killed and wounded in their
attacks on the 11th and 12th.   During all this time the
garrison made repeated sorties.   On the 14th the small force
in the licorice factory drove the enemy out of their trenches
250 yards away.   On the 17th, in two small sorties, thirty

Turks were bayoneted; our casualties were one man slightly wounded.

Townshend estimated that his garrison was being contained by 10,000 men; but on the 24th an increased boldness in the attack indicated that the enemy had received reënforcements. The famous 52nd Division had arrived from the Caucasus front. The fort was heavily shelled. Large breaches were made in the wall. The fort garrison was driven in beyond the first line, and up to the second line, of the defense. But here the wave was held up. The Oxford and Buckinghamshire Light Infantry flung in a gallant counterattack, and the Turks were expelled. In another fierce attack at midnight the enemy again effected a lodgment in the northeast bastion, but were again driven out, and, though ejected, came on at breaches in the walls, bombing us at close quarters. At daylight they had retired from the bastion to their trenches 500 yards from the fort. Our casualties on the 24th and 25th were 315. Prisoners said that the enemy believed Townshend's ammunition was giving out and that the garrison must fall if the attack was pressed hotly. Hence the fury of the assault. They described our fort as a cemetery of Turkish dead, and said that the 52nd Division had been annihilated. On the 29th the enemy asked for an armistice to bury his dead and remove the wounded who lay in numbers outside the bastions. Our casualties during the first month of the siege amounted to 1,840 killed and wounded. The enemy must have lost 4,000.

The failure of the Turkish attacks on December 24th and 25th introduced a new phase. The enemy now turned his siege into a blockade investment. There were no more infantry attacks; only the daily bombardment and raids by aëroplane. The artillery fire was fairly consistent until March 22nd, when the Turks fired some thousand rounds in quick succession. After this they reserved their ammunition for the evening "strafe," generally between four and eight o'clock. The shelling was mostly confined to the town and the fort, where the Union Jack and the observation post, with a battery of 5-inch guns and the Headquarters adjacent, offered good targets. The Turks had some naval guns, but the majority were 40-pounders. On the right bank they had a species of trench mortar christened by our soldiers "Petulant Fanny." She fired very noisy 15-inch bronze shells, always in the same place, but never hit anybody.

On January 2nd the first hostile aëroplane was sighted. From February 13th to March 22nd the aviator's bombs caused more damage than shell-fire. On March 18th one bomb, falling on a hospital, killed six British soldiers on the spot and wounded twenty-eight, fourteen severely, of whom twelve died within a few days. On March 21st four bombs were dropped in the neighborhood of Headquarters, killing many Arab women and children, and the aviators sank a horse-boat on the river, which carried a 4.7-inch gun. After this the aërial bombardment slackened, probably through lack of ammunition. The bomb that exploded on the hospital with such appalling fatality was no doubt aimed at Townshend's Headquarters, a favorite target of the enemy's heavies. The Turkish airman who dropped it expressed the most profound regret and cannot be held guilty of the intention. Osmanli "frightfulness" has much to answer for, but the sinking of hospital ships and firing at the Red Cross is not part of the code.

The advance of our relieving column in the first week of January drew off the greater part of the Turkish army, leaving a minimum force to carry on the work of investment. From this period the diary of the siege is concerned more with fighting hunger, and the postponement of date which was given from time to time as the last day the garrison could hold out indicated in each case a reduction in the scale of rations. Horse-meat at first was plentiful, but very few of the Indian troops were willing to eat it. Their loathing was more physical than spiritual, for Townshend communicated through wireless with the leaders of the chief religious communities in India and obtained from them a ruling that this siege meat was lawful. Nevertheless, the sepoys' reluctance could not be overcome, and Townshend hesitated to coerce them. In lieu of horse-meat they were given a larger flour ration than the British troops.

The days following the setback at El Hannah were a grim foretaste to the besieged of the evil days in front of them. With the further reduction in rations the Force became familiar with hunger. The continued suspense was hard to bear. But at this time, and two months afterwards for that matter, there was no question in their minds as to the ultimate issue. They only asked "How long?" Townshend himself was the chief fountain of optimism. He was always on his rounds, visiting the sick, chatting with the men, inspiring confidence and cheerfulness everywhere. He was a born commander in a siege, as great with his back to the wall parrying calamity as in the thrust of an offensive. The personality of the man may be read in his *communiqués*. On January 26th he issued an address to the garrison, taking them into his confidence, explaining how things stood, and exactly what part they were playing.

### General Townshend's Announcement

"The relieving force under General Aylmer has been unsuccessful in its efforts to dislodge the Turks entrenched on the left bank of the river some fourteen miles below the position at Sinn, where we defeated them in September last.

"Our relieving force suffered severe loss and had very bad weather to contend against; they are entrenched close to the Turkish position. More reënforcements are on their way up-river, and I confidently expect to be relieved some day during the first half of the month of February. I desire all ranks to know why I decided to make a stand at Kut during our retirement from Ctesiphon. It was because, as long as we hold Kut, the Turks cannot get their ships, barges, stores and munitions past this place, and so cannot move down to attack Amara, and thus we are holding up the whole of the Turkish advance. It also gives time for our reënforcements to come up-river from Basra, and so restore success to our arms.

"It gives time to our allies, the Russians, to move towards Bagdad, which a large force is now doing. I had a personal message from General Baratoff, in command of the Russian Expeditionary Force in Persia, telling me of his ad-

miration of what you men of the 6th Division and troops
attached have done in the past few months, and telling of
his own progress on the road from Kermanshah towards
Bagdad. By standing at Kut I maintain the territory we
have won in the past year at the expense of much blood,
commencing with your glorious victory at Shaiba, and thus
we maintain the campaign as a glorious one, instead of letting disaster pursue its course down to Amara, and perhaps beyond.

"I have ample food for eighty-four days, and that is
not counting the 3,000 animals which can be eaten. When I
defended Chitral some twenty years ago we lived well on
*atta* and horse-flesh; but, as I repeat, I expect confidently
to be relieved in the first half of the month of February.
Our duty stands out clear and simple. It is our duty to our
Empire, to our beloved King and country, to stand here
and hold up the Turkish advance as we are doing now, and
with the help of all, heart and soul together, we will make
this defense to be remembered in history as a glorious one.
All in India and England are watching us now, and are
proud of the splendid courage you have shown; and I tell
you let all remember the glorious defense of Plevna, for
that is what is in my mind.

"I am absolutely calm and confident as to the result.
The Turk, though good behind the trench, is of little value
in the attack. They have tried it once, and their losses in
one night in their attempt on the fort were 2,000 alone.

"They have already had very heavy losses from General Aylmer's musketry and guns, and I have no doubt they
have had enough.

"I have done my duty. You know the result, and whether
I was right or not, and your name will go down in history
as the heroes of Ctesiphon, for heroes you proved yourselves
in the battle. I, perhaps, by right, should not have told you
of the above; but I feel I owe it to you all to speak straight
and openly and to take you into my confidence, for, God
knows, I felt our heavy losses and the suffering of my poor
brave wounded, and shall remember it as long as I live, and
I may truly say that no general I know of has been more loy-

ally obeyed and served than I have been in command of the Sixth Division.

"These words are long, I am afraid, but I speak straight from the heart, and you will see that I have thrown all officialdom overboard. We will succeed—mark my words!— but save your ammunition as if it were gold!"

The different units saw very little of each other during the siege. At the beginning indirect machine gun and rifle fire, in addition to shells, swept the whole area day and night. The troops only left the dug-outs for important defense works. During the latter phase, when the fire slackened, the officers and men had very little strength to break the monotony of the siege in the way of games, exercise and amusements, but on the right bank the two battalions in the licorice factory, the 110th Mahrattas and the 121st Infantry, were better off, and there was some dead ground here, a pitch of about fifty yards by twenty, where they could play hockey and cricket with pick handles and a rag ball. Also they fished, and did so with success, supplementing the rations at the same time. Two companies of the Norfolks joined them in turn, crossing by the ferry at night. They appreciated the relief.

On March 2nd, owing to the shortage of fuel for the mill, the barley meal ration was reduced from a pound to three-quarters for the Indian troops, but 6 ounces were issued for parching. The death-rate now increased. The vitality of the troops was very low; the recuperative power of the sick was at a minimum; those suffering from serious diseases could not hope to survive; before the end trivial ailments were often fatal, and wounds would not heal. Skin and flesh lost the power of renovation, and the surgeons could do nothing where nature would not play her part. The scurvy trouble among the Indians became more and more aggravated. As many as 1,050 cases were admitted to hospital during the siege, besides those treated regimentally. The sepoy's horror of horse-flesh in many cases cost him his life, for in the end, when he was driven by starvation to eat it, he was so weak that the power of digestion and assimilation had gone. Those who ate it at the beginning fared better, and the Gurkhas, who never had any scruples in the matter, best of all.

On March 9th, after the unsuccessful attack on the Dujaila Redoubt, the British ration loaf was reduced from 12 to 10 ounces. The Dujaila failure was an even greater disappointment than the reverses in January. The garrison were waiting expectantly for the relief. It was understood that another great effort was being made by Aylmer's column, who were to strike in the morning, and that they were striking with all their force. At 4.30 a. m. the men besieged in Kut were standing to arms. The sound of guns grew nearer. All day they waited with eyes strained on the other bank. But Aylmer's force did not appear. Once more their hopes were kindled only to flicker and die out; and the suspense and strain left them weary with an exhaustion which infected the body through the mind.

On the 10th Townshend issued another *communiqué*:

### General Townshend's Second Announcement

"As on a former occasion, I take the troops of all ranks into my confidence again. We have now stood a three months' siege in a manner which has called upon you the praise of our beloved King and our fellow-countrymen in England, Scotland, Ireland and India, and all this after your brilliant battles of Kut-el-Amara and Ctesiphon and your retirement to Kut, all of which feats of arms are now famous. Since December 5, 1915, you have spent three months of cruel uncertainty, and to all men and all people uncertainty is intolerable. As I say, on the top of all this comes the second failure to relieve us. And I ask you also to give a little sympathy to me who have commanded you in these battles referred to, and who, having come to you as a stranger, now love my command with a depth of feeling I have never known in my life before. When I mention myself I would also mention the names of the generals under me, whose names are distinguished in the army as leaders of men.

"I am speaking to you as I did before, straight from the

heart, and, as I say, I ask your sympathy for my feelings, having promised you relief on certain dates on the promise of those ordered to relieve us. Not their fault, no doubt. Do not think that I blame them; they are giving their lives freely, and deserve our gratitude and admiration. But I want you to help me again, as before. I have asked General Aylmer for the next attempt to bring such numbers as will break down all resistance and leave no doubt as to the issue. In order, then, to hold out, I am killing a large number of horses so as to reduce the quantity of grain eaten every day, and I have had to reduce your ration. It is necessary to do this in order to keep our flag flying. I am determined to hold out, and I know you are with me heart and soul."

On March 31st rations were again reduced. On April 8th the mill stopped working for want of fuel; flour had been ground to last until April 15th. On April 16th the flour ration was reduced to 4 ounces for British and Indian. Small opium pills were distributed among the sepoys by the medical staff to stay the pangs of hunger. By this time all Indians were eating horse-flesh. On April 21st the 4-ounce ration gave out. From the 22nd to the 25th the garrison subsisted on two days' reserve rations issued in January. After our third repulse at Sannaiyat, on April 22nd, immediate relief was hopeless. The only chance for the garrison lay in the *Julnar,* which on the night of the 24th attempted to force the blockade and failed. In the meanwhile Kut was fed by aëroplane. This air service gave the garrison another four days, but the carriage of such heavy freight was too great a tax on the machines. Previously they had been employed for dropping light articles into camp, such as rifle cleaners, spare parts for wireless, drugs and medical dressings, saccharin, seine nets for fishing, and at one time cigarettes and tobacco. But as it was impossible to supply all, Townshend ruled out these luxuries as introducing a form of privilege. He himself shared every privation with his troops.

After April 20th many of the Arabs in the town, feeling the pinch of hunger, made attempts to escape by river. These men are splendid swimmers. Two of them got through to our camp with the help of the strong current. One, supported by skin bladders, made the journey by night in eight hours; the other concealed himself during the day and arrived on the second night. A third, the sole survivor of a party of eighteen, came through on a raft with a bullet in his leg. The Turks fired on them from the bank; four had been killed; the others, many of them wounded, dived into the river, and it is doubtful if any of them escaped. These Arabs spoke of the cheerfulness of the garrison, who they said looked thin, but hard and strong. The inhabitants of Kut were still confident that the place would be relieved; this confidence in Townshend, based on his personality and the achievements of the troops under his command, amounted to something like superstition. They abandoned the town out of sheer hunger.

Before the end the garrison were on the verge of starvation. During the last week of the siege the daily death-rate averaged eight British and twenty-one Indians. The troops were so exhausted that the regiments who were holding the front line remained there a fortnight without being relieved. They were too weak to dig. Men on sentry-go would drop at their posts. Colonel Hehir, the senior medical officer, has recorded cases of Indians returning from the trenches in the evening, seemingly with nothing the matter, who lay down and were found dead in the morning, dead of exhaustion; they simply had not strength for the effort of life. He doubted whether the strongest man in the garrison was equal to a five-mile march carrying his equipment. Still, hope was not yet dead. Our machine gun and rifle fire were heard at Beit Aieesa; the flashes of our guns were seen at night; and on April 20th General Aylmer wired: "Stick to it. Gorringe will relieve you in a few days." They stuck to it. They hung on. On the day of surrender the men in the trenches were too weak to carry back their kit.

The bitterness of the end may perhaps have been softened by the knowledge that they had done everything within mortal bounds that could be done. They must have had some inward sense of their long devotion under trial. It could not be otherwise; for messages had reached them before the wire-

less was destroyed which bore witness to the recognition of
it by their countrymen in no uncertain terms.   But another
crushing disappointment was in store.   A passage in Towns-
shend's last *communiqué*, dated April 28th, offered hopes of
release:

"These considerations alone, namely, that I can help my
comrades of all ranks to the end, have decided me to overcome my bodily illness and the anguish of mind which I am
suffering now, and I have interviewed the Turkish General-
in-Chief yesterday, who is full of admiration at 'an heroic
defense of five months,' as he puts it.   Negotiations are
still in progress, but I hope to be able to announce your departure for India, on parole not to serve against the Turks,
since the Turkish Commander says he thinks it will be allowed, and has wired to Constantinople to ask for this, and
that the *Julnar,* which is lying with food for us at Magasis
now, may be permitted to come to us.   Whatever has happened, my comrades, you can only be proud of yourselves.
We have done our duty to King and Empire; the whole world
knows that we have done our duty.   I ask you to stand by
me with your steady and splendid discipline, shown throughout, in the next few days for the expedition of all service I
demand of you."

Instead of release on parole, captivity awaited them with
all its hardships and humiliations.   The long-drawn months
ran into years, and more than half of the rank and file succumbed to the hard conditions of exile.   When the armistice
was concluded it was found that of 2,680 British N.C.O.s
and privates taken at Kut, 1,306 had died and 449 remained
untraced: that is, over 65 per cent. perished.   Of the 10,486
Indians, combatants and followers, 1,290 died and 1,773
were untraced.   "These figures," says the report, "give the
exact measure of the meaning of captivity in Turkey."   Most
of the Kut prisoners perished in the terrible crossing of the
desert between Samarrah and Aleppo in June.   They were
separated from their officers, and those who were too weak
to march were left to die by the roadside, stripped of their
clothes by the Arabs, exhausted with dysentery and starvation, and with no medical attendance.   It was a history of

brutal callousness and neglect which, if we had known it at the time, would have left us no illusions about the Turk.

### BY MAJOR CHARLES BARBER

On the 22nd there was a heavy cannonade in the morning, and we could see the bursts of H.E. over a long line of a mile or more; but the result was another disappointment, for the next day we got a *communiqué* to say that the R.F. had not taken Sanaaiyat, but had advanced a little on the right bank. As a set-off the aëroplanes made fourteen or fifteen trips and dropped food.

It was Easter Sunday, and Trixie and I went to church in the morning. The two little rooms, still intact, were crowded with officers. Why had so many come that day? Was it to share in the joyous festival of Easter, of the resurrection of the God-man, or was it the growing fear in our hearts that the service would be the last of its kind in Kut, and that the future was so full of uncertainty?

Be that as it may, there was a very good attendance, and after the morning service the Communion was held. One by one, in a silence that could be felt, the gaunt and war-worn defenders, with the thoughtful eyes of those who had seen much, went up each in his turn and knelt before the padre. A deep hush fell over us all, and in those few moments men got near to their God. . . .

On the 24th a quiver of excitement went through us when we got wind of the impending attempt of the R.F. to run the blockade that night by a boat full of food. We could hardly sleep for thinking about it, and were up on the H.Q. roof as the sun rose. There she was, the gallant *Fulnar*, over against Megasis Fort, stuck in the mud just within range of our longest guns, with her splendid captain on her bridge lying dead in a pool of his own blood. So pleased were the Turks—so one of their officers who was there told me afterwards—with the gallant bravery of poor Cowley and the other man with him on the *Fulnar*, that they, then and there, gave them a special military funeral in recognition of their magnificent effort, which so nearly succeeded. But the enemy had her, and her capture sealed our fate. Deep down within us we knew we were now done for, that our people couldn't get through, and that for us it meant Bagdad, or Mosul, or God only knew where! We did not acknowledge it yet, however, and that day another auction was held, at which prices ruled higher than ever: a box of cheroots fetched 206 rupees, and a tin of fifty Wills' cigarettes were sold for over £3—surely the biggest money ever paid for "Three Castles"!

That night, after leaving us almost alone for a day or two, the Turks gave us a bad "strafing," and followed it up by an evening hate next day and another night bombardment, much to the discomfort of a Turkish envoy who stayed the night in the town. They also accounted for at least one of the aëroplanes of the R.F. that had been working very hard at our food supply, but now got interfered with by the Fokkers, that had the wings of them.

On the 23rd and 24th we had eaten our first day's emergency ration split into two; on the 25th and 26th we fed on the aëroplane supply, and on the 27th we broached half of our last day's reserve ration.

The following message was received from the Army Commander: "The C.-in-C. has desired me to convey to you and your brave and devoted troops his appreciation of the manner in which you together have undergone the suffering and hardships of the siege, which he knows has been due to the high spirit of devotion to duty in which you have met the call of your Sovereign and Empire. The C.-in-C.'s sentiments are shared by myself, General Gorringe, and all the troops of the Tigris Column. We can only express extreme disappointment, and regret our effort to relieve you should not have been crowned with success."

And so, with a farewell from our friends below, we went into captivity.

# AUSTRIA'S FIRST GREAT ATTACK ON ITALY

## REPULSE OF THE AUSTRIAN INVASION AT ASIAGO

### MAY 15TH-JUNE 3RD

### OFFICIAL ITALIAN STATEMENT

THOMAS NELSON PAGE          GENERAL VON CRAMON

For almost a year following Italy's entry into the War, the Austrians had allowed her to wear out her strength against their well-nigh impregnable mountain frontiers. In May of 1916 Austria suddenly assumed the offensive. She was facing the Italians on two lines. To the north of Italy lay the Austrian Alps, the region known as the Tyrol. Here the Italian "Alpini" had been fighting their way slowly northward over the mighty mountains, seizing the semi-Italian district called the Trentino. To the east of Italy at the head of the Adriatic lay the Isonzo River section of Austria. There the Italians had been making their chief attack and gathering their main armies.

In attacking along the less powerfully held line in the Trentino, the Austrians might hope to break into Italy from the north, get behind the Isonzo army, and so break its line of supplies and compel its surrender. The attack is here described, first, by the official statement issued by Italy for the use of the American troops who were sent there, second, by the sober judgment of the honored U. S. Ambassador to Italy, Mr. Page, and third by the General who acted the part of "liaison" officer and official observer for the Germans.

The heavy attack at first swept away the smaller bodies of Italians. Mountain peak after peak was stormed and captured. By the end of May the Italians were driven back across their own border; and the Italian cities of Arsiero and Asiago, the latter some seven miles behind the frontier, were in Austrian hands. This, however, marked the high tide of the invasion. Count Cadorna, the Italian general, had by this time strengthened his loosely guarded defenses and gathered his forces. His line stretched along the last and lowest series of hills by which the Alps sink into the Italian plain. Vicenza and the main railroad for supplying the Isonzo army were only twenty miles away. On June 3rd Cadorna issued a general order to stop the retreat before the foe, saying, "Remember that here we defend the soil of our country and the honor of our army. These positions are to be defended to the death."

They were thus held. More than one Italian regiment lost two-thirds of its men without giving way. The Austrian advance was completely checked. The main fighting was around Mounts Ciove, Pasubio and Sette Communi. A final assault was delivered against the latter on June 18th, and was repulsed with heavy losses. Gradually the Austrians withdrew to secure entrenchments, and the struggle shifted, as described in a later section, to the Isonzo front. Austria had attacked bravely; Italy had resisted with even greater strength and self-devotion.

OFFICIAL ITALIAN STATEMENT

The plan of the invasion of Italy on these weak frontiers was the most familiar to Austria in all its military manoeuvres, the most studied and thought over by the Supreme Command, and especially by the Commander in Chief, General Conrad von Hoetzendorf, who was wholly in favour of the campaign in the Trentino. Germany had decided on the destruction of France and the British Army, and Austria had decided on her "Punitive Campaign."

Conrad's choice to attack by way of the Trentino, under snow until spring was well advanced, and the necessity of regulating the Balkan disturbances, prevented simultaneous attacks. The undertaking against Italy, which would be invaded and forced to a separate peace, was a foregone conclusion in the mind of the Austrian General who had long boasted of the merits of this "Decisive Blow." The certainty of Conrad's plan was such that the Austrian Command ordered a prolonged and careful preparation of the offensive. This certainty was based on two decisions which later proved themselves grossly erroneous.

The first was based on the presumption of feeble resistance on the part of the Italian army which was deemed incapable of facing a broad and decisive frontal attack, incapable not only on account of defects in preparation, but more on account of a want of moral strength, whereby any retreat from a good position would have speedily become a rout. The second was based on the impossibility of the Russians to attempt a grand offensive after the actions of January, which were promptly frustrated.

Strong in these conceptions, the Austrian Command, deeming its eastern front secure, drew therefrom her finest, most warlike and most faithful troops, with a vast quantity of artillery, and these with others selected from the Balkan front, constituted the 18 divisions destined to attack the Trentino.

This force of 400,000 men supported by more than 2,000 cannon the half of which were of medium calibre, with 40 pieces of 305, four of 380, and four of 420, was entitled the "Punitive Expedition," a title which breathed assurance and contempt. This, with the aid of a concentrated artillery fire and with the aggression of battalions massed on a restricted front defended by mountain ranges, would rapidly descend on the Paduan plains, thus obtaining a position in the rear of the Italians on the Isonzo, who, caught between two fires would be driven to a hasty retreat. The successful invasion of these valuable and populous regions of Italy was so certain, that many officials, with manuals of art and history and Baedekers, were appointed to follow the victorious troops and to collect the most precious treasures of the country from Italian museums and churches, etc., and pack them off to Austria.

The scheme failed rapidly and utterly. The attack chosen by the Austrians comprised the zone between the Adige and the Brenta. The bombardment opening on May 12 became terrific on the 14th. An apparent offensive spread rapidly from the Val Giudicaria to the sea in order to deceive the Italians. This the enemy could well afford to do, as the massing of artillery for the real attack was not interfered with by those feigned elsewhere. It revealed the tremendous superiority of their guns. On May 15 the infantry assault followed, very fierce and impetuous on the lines chosen for the real attack.

The assault by their right wing was most impetuous, because they wished to drive the Italians from the positions dominating Rovereto, which were already threatened, especially as a swift success in this zone would have decided the offensive. Their forces, conquering the Vallarsa, would have attained by the road from Rovereto to Schio, the nearest points from which they could descend to the plains, and they would have established themselves on the rear of the Italians who were defending the tableland of Asiago. Instead, four days after the attack, the right wing of the Austrians was absolutely blocked. After an orderly and tenacious retreat from the most advanced positions, the Italian resistance grew more and more stubborn on the Coni-Zugna-Passo di Buole lines, and maintained itself vigorously in hostile territory some 12 kilometres beyond the old frontiers. Until the end of May the Austrians, realising the deep value of the defence offered by the 37th Division, harried them with ceaseless attacks, but after 12 days of incessant combat, the Buole Pass and the swollen stream of the Adige were filled with Austrian dead. The swift invasion was thus arrested on the right, not only through this, but because of the stubborn resistance on the Pasubio that had become one of the strongest bulwarks against the desperate hostile assaults in this same month.

The left wing suffered much the same fate in the Val Sugana. Here, to gain the end desired, the Austrians had need of a rapid victory along the course of the river Brenta. The Italians had to be thrust back from Borgo beyond the former boundaries, to secure their left flank from ulterior menace. Instead from May 15 to May 25 the Italians retired ever fighting from the most open positions and selected a line of defence slightly to the rear of Borgo, still in hostile territory at about 18 kilometres from the frontier. Here, every attack was repulsed.

Thus four days after the offensive or on May 19, the Austrian right wing was held up; later on May 26 their left wing was also held. Both wings thus weakening, the advance of the Austrian centre necessarily lost its value, and this on the tableland of Asiago where battalions and artillery, crushed in a restricted zone, were all but smothered by their own advance. Arsiero and Asiago, the chief inhabited spots of this mountainous and wooded region, relinquished by the Italian troops, suffered the rage and fury of the enemy that had failed in victory, and were sacked and burned. On June 2, thanks to 18 days' gallant defence, the Italian Supreme Command, as announced by Cadorna in the Bulletin of the succeeding day, could consider the Austrian offensive absolutely arrested all along the front.

## BY THOMAS NELSON PAGE[1]

It was to Italy that many eyes were turned in the early part of 1916, amid the gloom of the destruction of Serbia, Montenegro, and Albania; the invigoration of Turkey and Bulgaria; the obscurity of Greece; the increase in the sub-

[1] Copyright and reprinted by permission of Charles Scribners' Sons.

marine campaign, and the murderous persistence of the attack on Verdun—Italy, without coal, grain, or metal save what she could obtain with difficulty; with scarcely anything in sufficient quantity—Italy not yet at war with Germany, nor certain that she would be; with her Sphinx-like Minister for Foreign Affairs, and her strong political antiwar element; with her men, amid the measureless snows of the Trentine and Carnic and Julian Alps, driving, in Arctic cold, under incredible hardships, tunnels through mountains of ice and rock, scaling icy precipices, swinging their cables across vast gorges.—Would she stand it? Could she stand it?

As the spring drew nearer it was evident that Italy was irrevocably bent on getting Gorizia and Trieste, and Austria-Hungary began to feel the need of some action that would weaken the incessant drive that Italy was making on the Isonzo front, and relieve herself from the ever-increasing pressure toward Gorizia and Trieste. Moreover, the "gradual advance of the Italians into the Trentino, which was approaching closer and closer to the main lines of his defense, aroused in the enemy a desire to free himself from a pressure which was growing more threatening." Russia had been driven back sufficiently to give Austria a freer hand on her western and southern front, but was preparing for another attempt later on. Germany was being held up at Verdun. The time appeared ripe for a blow at Italy before Russia should be ready. Austria accordingly made carefully elaborate secret preparations for an offensive against Italy through the Trentino.

The offensive began on May 14, with an artillery bombardment of great violence along the entire Italian front, from East to West, from the Carso to the Giudicaria. It soon became evident, however, that the real assault was on the Trentino front, on the sector between the Val Lagarina and the Val Sugana. Here, after a terrific bombardment, the Infantry in great masses were launched to the attack under an artillery cover unprecedented on that front in violence or effectiveness. Eighteen divisions, or some 400,000 men and some 2,000 guns, were employed in the offensive.

The Austrians knew every foot of ground: mountain and valley, and their attack was admirably planned and well carried out. Both Artillery and Infantry were skilfully handled. The Italian advanced positions were swept away by the flood of shell poured out on them. Then, under the tremendous bombardment of the great guns, moved forward as required, other positions were rendered untenable. From point after point, position after position, the Italians were driven, with increasing losses in men and guns. Austria's dream appeared on the eve of realization.

When June came in the Italians, after two weeks of as fierce and unremitting battle as had taken place in the war, with every advantage save one against them, had made their last stand above and across the mouths of the valleys that opened on the Venetian Plain; and the Austrians, believing themselves victorious, were pressing forward with all the ardor born of success and lust of loot, and heightened by the furious desire to wreak their vengeance on an enemy whom their Emperor had denounced to them as having betrayed Austria.

A few days later (June 3) General Cadorna, confident of the stability of his army, now strung to the highest pitch by the peril to their Patria, announced to his Government that the immediate danger of invasion of Italy was past. The Italians had stopped the Austrians. The latter were now dashing in impotent rage against the Italian lines. The Italians had been ordered to hold them to the death, and they held them.

The Italians knew now that Italy herself was at stake, and all Italy was now in the fight. For some time, notwithstanding Cadorna's encouraging announcement, the issue appeared to hang in the balance. Austria, balked at the very moment of seizing the prize, as she deemed it, was loath to relinquish her aim, and continued to hurl her masses against the Italian positions, only to break in foam against them. Their force was spent, and as the Italians grew stronger the tide turned.

BY GENERAL A. VON CRAMON

The attack had originally been planned for the 10th of April. High snow, however, made the realization of this plan impossible. The same occurred on the 20th of April and the 1st of May. Von Hoetzendorff raged; he claimed never to have seen so much snow on the heights of Southern Tyrol as in the spring of that year. Others, however, who also knew the ground well, declared that, even with normal conditions of temperature, the date decided upon would have been premature.

The damage resulting from the constant postponement of the date of attack was naturally great. The assembling of troops in all villages of Southern Tyrol could not be concealed from the enemy. Moreover, a deserter of Italian descent, who went over to the enemy on the plateau of Vielgereuth, made valuable disclosures to the enemy regarding the intentions of the Austrians. Under such conditions it could not be asserted that the confidence of the Tyrolean leaders was particularly great. The reports of the German officers in charge of communications verified this. Powerful counter-measures on the part of the Italians were to be expected.

When, at the beginning of May, the day of the attack had again been postponed, General von Falkenhayn commissioned me to ask General von Hoetzendorff whether it would not be better to dispense altogether with the offensive—which would no longer come as a surprise and would therefore be problematical—and place a portion of the troops stationed in Southern Tyrol at the disposal of the Western Front. This proposition was somewhat of a surprise to me as Falkenhayn, during the winter, had been averse to utilizing Austro-Hungarian troops on the front in France. Manifestly, this change of opinion was due to the doubtful situation at Verdun.

General von Hoetzendorff declined on the ground that the offensive, prepared to the minutest detail, could not be abandoned now, more particularly as the artillery, permanently placed for the attack, could not readily be withdrawn again.

Finally, on May 15th, the avalanche of Vielgereuth-Lafraun was launched, the first attack being made by the corps of the Austrian Crown-prince Charles, to be followed two days later by the army corps of Graz, operating on the eastern wing and commanded by General Krautwald. The beginning was magnificent. The German-Austrian picked troops of the attacking group recorded a great achievement and within a few days brought in 30,000 prisoners and 300 guns. Asiago was taken. Von Falkenhayn sent a cordial telegram of congratulation to von Hoetzendorff, whose acknowledgment was equally hearty. At Teschen general headquarters everyone was beside himself with delight. We German officers also frankly rejoiced over the victory won by our ally.

On the 24th of May, however, the corps of the Austrian Crown-prince came to a standstill. The enemy meanwhile utilized the situation and brought up all the artillery and infantry that could possibly be placed on the "Terra ferma," covered in every direction by lines of railroad and highways. I was informed subsequently that the troops of the 20th Army Corps had begged to be permitted to make the leap to the edge of the mountains, without "drawing breath," and before the enemy could recover. But the corps command would not permit this because it believed that the heavy artillery would first have to be brought up. In this way the Italians had been able to gain a footing once more on the Priafora and the towering rocks nearby, thus setting at naught a continuation of the Austrian attacks.

On the other hand it was asserted that the command of the various army groups had so placed in rank the reserve divisions that it was impossible for them to participate at the right time. It cannot be our purpose here to enter into an investigation as to the accuracy of these charges. It is my opinion, however, that it did not require an entry into the campaign on the part of the Russians in the East to bring the Austrian offensive launched from Southern Tyrol to a standstill. This had already been checked and could only have been continued with new forces, which, however, were not available.

# THE MIGHTIEST OF NAVAL FIGHTS

## THE BATTLE OF JUTLAND OR OF THE SKAGERRAK

### MAY 31ST

#### W. MACNEILE DIXON
#### GERMAN AND BRITISH OFFICIAL REPORTS
#### ADMIRAL VON CAPELLE          ADMIRAL JELLICOE
#### LETTERS OF GERMAN AND BRITISH PARTICIPANTS

In the number of ships engaged, the Jutland battle was about equal to Trafalgar, that greatest sea-fight of past centuries, in which Nelson destroyed the fleets of France and Spain. In the tonnage of these ships, however, Jutland was some fifteen times as great as Trafalgar, and in number of men about twice as great. Of modern battles between ships of iron, instead of the old "wooden walls" of Nelson's day, the nearest in size to Jutland was that fought by Japan and Russia in the Tsushima Straits in 1905. At Tsushima, however, the Russians were wholly out of condition, beaten before they entered the fight, and Japan had only to choose her firing range and batter the enemy to pieces. At Jutland both sides fought splendidly and with not unequal skill.

The size of the opposing fleets at Jutland was also more equal than is usually realized; for while the British navy was much the larger, by no means all of its ships were concentrated for this battle, while the German biggest ships were practically all on hand. The British had at Jutland twenty-eight big battleships and nine "battle-cruisers" almost equaling the dreadnoughts in power; the Germans had twenty-two battleships and five battle-cruisers. Each side had a host of lesser cruisers, torpedo boats and destroyers, useful against the giants of the fleet only when they could creep close enough to launch a torpedo before being blown out of water by the huge guns which could reach a target fifteen miles away. Of the main ships, the British had been designed more for attack and less for defense than the Germans. That is to say, the British had bigger guns and greater speed, but the Germans had heavier armor.

The results of this showed strikingly in the battle. The German main ships took a terrible pounding, many of them were badly damaged, yet only one was lost, the *Lutzow,* and she did not sink until several hours after the battle. The British ships were much less pounded, yet three of the main ships were destroyed. They blew up and sank swiftly, with the loss of almost all their crews. In men the Germans lost between two and three thousand, the Britons twice as many. Among the lesser vessels also the British loss was the heavier.

The fight consisted of an attack by the British van, which retreated when it encountered the main German fleet. This in turn followed the British van until they reached the main British fleet, which endeavored to encircle the Germans. Then night closed in, and the Germans withdrew silently from the closing circle. A wierd and monstrous death-dance followed in the dark. The lesser ships of each side, seeking to keep track of the foe, hid their own lights and stumbled one upon the other in the blackness, burst into sudden flaming volleys, and fled away.    Men fought with shadows and perished in the unknown.

As to the net result of the great battle during the night, the German admiral withdrew his battered fleet cautiously toward its home ports, while the British admiral held back from pursuit for fear of terrible losses in the dark, either from mines or torpedoes.    Hence there was no decision on the field.    The British fleet, however, continued in even more complete control of the seas than before, for never again did the Germans risk a similar combat.

Immediately after the battle Germany proclaimed that she had won a tremendous naval triumph, basing her statement on the admitted British losses and the denial of her own.    As the claim was never withdrawn, there are doubtless Germans who still believe in the splendor of their victory and wonder why nothing further ever came of it.    C. F. H.

### BY W. MACNEILE DIXON

THAT stern and decisive conflict, which clinched, as it were, the naval situation, the battle of Jutland, was in respect of all particulars that make a battle great, the magnitude of the forces engaged, the scale of the operations, and the significance of the results, the fiercest clash of fleets since Trafalgar.

At extreme range, to avoid the deadly torpedo attacks, the great war-vessels pounded each other amid haze and smoke screens, behind which the Germans when pressed withdrew from sight.    Wounded vessels drifted out of the scene and left their fate in doubt; destroyers dashed to and fro attacking and retreating; ships, the flames licking their iron masts a hundred feet aloft, loomed up for a few moments only to vanish in the mist.    As "was anticipated," the Germans put their trust chiefly in torpedo attacks, easily made against approaching, difficult to direct against retiring, vessels.    Throughout destroyers on both sides played a magnificent and conspicuous part, the "hussar" tactics of a naval action.    But so numerous were the vessels engaged and so dim the weather that a certain confusion inseparable from the conditions reigned the entire day.    Indubitably a long-hoped-for opportunity had come to the British; the German fleet had actually emerged in strength and "upon an enterprise."    Yet emerged only to withdraw, to tantalize, and, if possible, to lure the pursuers into fatal areas.

The annoyance which Nelson suffered from the French Admiral Latouche Treville, who used *"to play bo-peep in and out of Toulon, like a mouse at the edge of her hole,"* as the British Admiral expressed it, was the lot also of Sir John Jellicoe. Von Scheer repeated the tactics of Latouche. His orders were, no doubt, the same, to show the "greatest circumspection," to risk nothing. But this "fettered and timid" warfare, as a French writer once complained, must always fail. The chief hope and aim of the British fleet in the present war has been the same as Nelson's, to compel a decisive engagement; the aim of the enemy's fleet to avoid one, a perfectly legitimate and perfectly intelligible policy, with which no one can quarrel.

Germany consistently refuses all actions except on chosen ground at her own front door, where she can, when the odds are against her, withdraw her ships immediately within her protected ports and slam the door in the face of her antagonist. There only will she fight, within a few miles of her own coast, in shallow waters suitable for the operation of underwater craft, and in the immediate neighborhood of her own mine fields. Had Nelson been alive to-day he could have done no more than the British Admirals have done— offer battle to the unwilling enemy on his own terms. Germany takes only as much of the war as she wishes, Britain takes the whole, everywhere and all the time. Repeatedly Sir David Beatty has faced this situation with its attendant risks. Repeatedly with his cruising squadron he appeared within sight of the German defenses, four hundred miles from his own base. If he could engage the Germans even at heavy cost to himself, "cling to them as long as his teeth would hold," in an entangling and detaining action the Grand Fleet might reach him in time to secure an overwhelming victory. That was his hope. And let it be frankly admitted the hope was not fulfilled. At Jutland once more he took the risks—some say unwisely, for why do more than contain the German Navy useless in its ports?—he incurred the inevitable losses, the main British fleet arrived in time to strike a shattering blow, but failed to administer the *coup de grâce*. "I can fully sympathize with his feelings," wrote

Sir John Jellicoe, "when the evening mist and fading light robbed the fleet of that complete victory for which he had maneuvered, and for which the vessels in company with him had striven so hard."

To understand, even in a measure, this immense conflict, one must bear in mind that the British Grand Fleet under Sir John Jellicoe was on May 30th actually at sea, to the north of Sir David Beatty's battle-cruisers, who on the 31st, having completed his sweep, turned away from the south to rejoin the Commander-in-Chief. About half-past two Beatty received signals from his light-cruiser squadron that the enemy was out and in force. A seaplane scout went aloft and confirmed the signals. German battle-cruisers were in sight, but falling back upon probably still stronger forces. To engage or not to engage was hardly Beatty's problem. Should he at all cost pursue, encounter, and detain the foe, or, avoiding more than a mere exchange of shots, continue on his course to join Admiral Jellicoe? Faint heart never won a great decision. He chose the heroic, the British, way, and determined to force the battle, "to engage the enemy in sight."

We may, perhaps, best understand the action if we divide it into three stages, (a) pursuit, (b) retreat, (c) again pursuit; the first, that in which Beatty was engaged with the enemy's battle-cruisers falling back upon their main fleet, which lasted about an hour, from 3.48 when the opening shots were fired till the German High Seas Fleet showed itself at 4.38. At this point Beatty swung round to draw the enemy toward Jellicoe approaching from the north, and the second stage of the battle began in which the British were heavily engaged with a greatly superior force, in fact, the whole German Navy. They had, however, the assistance of the Fifth Battle Squadron under Evan Thomas, four powerful battle-ships which had come up during the first phase, fired a few shots at the extreme range of about twelve miles and took the first fire of Von Scheer's battleships. Steaming north now instead of south, Beatty slackened speed to keep in touch with the heavy ships. This stage of the action also lasted about an hour or more, when about six o'clock Jellicoe came

in sight five miles to the north, and the third phase began.
Beatty toward the end of the second stage had drawn ahead
of the enemy, pressing in upon and curving round his line,
and now drove straight across it to the east, closing the range
to twelve thousand yards, with two objects—first, to bring
the leading German ships under concentrated fire, and second, to allow a clear space for Jellicoe to come down and
complete their destruction. It was a masterly maneuver
which enabled the Third Battle-cruiser Squadron, in advance
of Jellicoe, under Admiral Hood, to join at once in the battle,
and assist in "crumpling up" the head of the German line.

The supreme moment had come. Jellicoe's great fleet was
in line behind Hood, bearing down on Von Scheer in overwhelming force. By beautiful handling the British Admiral
effected the junction of his fleets in very difficult conditions.
There still remains in naval warfare much of the splendid
pageantry of old, which in land operations is gone beyond
recall. "The grandest sight I have ever seen," wrote an officer in the fleet, "was the sight of our battle line—miles of it
fading into mist—taking up their positions like clock-work
and then belching forth great sheets of fire and clouds of
smoke." But the prize was snatched from the British grasp.
It was already seven o'clock and the evening brought with it
the thick North Sea haze behind which and his own smoke
screens Von Scheer turned and fled for his ports. "Great
care was necessary," wrote Sir John Jellicoe, "to insure that
our own ships were not mistaken for enemy vessels." By
half-past eight or nine practically all was over, save for the
British destroyer attacks, which lasted far into the darkness,
on the scattered and fleeing enemy. Only two hours of a
misty daylight had been left to Sir John Jellicoe to accomplish
his task.

Then came night, and in the night the shattered and
shaken Germans crept—one is not quite clear by what route
—through their mine fields to the blessed security of protected harbors. Had the weather been different—well, who
knows whether in that case the German fleet would have put
to sea? Now as ever in naval warfare commanders must
choose conditions the most favorable to their designs. The

British Admiral remained on the scene of the battle, picking up survivors from some of the smaller craft till after midday (1.15 p. m.) on June 1st. On that day not one German ship was in sight on a sea strewn with the tangled and shapeless wreckage of proud vessels, the melancholy litter of war.

Perhaps Jutland, inconclusive as it seemed, may be judged by the world the true crisis of the struggle. While Germany, after her manner, poured forth to the skeptical world tidings of amazing victory, Britain, too, after her manner, said little save bluntly to record her losses, and later published merely the reports of the admirals engaged. They are very plain and matter-of-fact, these documents without brag. So they can be recommended to the attention of seekers after truth. For lovers of romance, of course, the German versions will afford brighter reading.

Here, however, is the unofficial account of a midshipman on board one of the battleships: "We were all as cheery as Punch when action was sounded off. The battle-cruisers, which, by the way, were first sighted by your eldest son, who went without his tea to look out in the foretop, were away on the bow, firing like blazes, and doing a colossal turn of speed. I expect they were very pleased to see us. The battle fleet put it across them properly. We personally "strafed" a large battleship, which we left badly bent, and very much on fire. They fired stink shells at us, which fortunately burst some distance away. They looked as if they smelt horrible. We engaged a Zepp which showed an inclination to become pally. I think it thought we were Germans. Altogether it was some stunt.

"Yes, you were right, I was up in the foretop and saw the whole show. I told you I was seventeen hours up there, didn't I? Simply bristling with glasses, revolvers, respirators, ear-protectors, and what-nots. I cannot imagine anything more intensely dramatic than our final junction with the battle-cruisers. They appeared on the starboard bow going a tremendous speed and firing like blazes at an enemy we could not see. Even before we opened first the colossal noise was nearly deafening. The Grand Fleet opened fire. We commenced by "strafing" one of the "Kaisers" that was only just visible on the horizon, going hell for leather. The whole High Sea Fleet were firing like blazes.

"It is the most extraordinary sensation I know to be sitting up there in the foretop gazing at a comparatively unruffled bit of sea, when suddenly about five immense columns of water about a hundred feet high shoot up as if from nowhere, and bits of shell go rattling down into the water, or else, with a noise like an express train, the projectiles go screeching overhead and fall about a mile the other side of you. You watch the enemy firing six great flashes about as many miles away, and then for fifteen seconds or so you reflect that there is about two tons of sudden death hurtling toward you. Then with a sigh of relief the splashes rise up, all six of them, away on the starboard bow. On the other hand, there is a most savage exultation in firing at another ship.

"You hear the order 'Fire!' the foretop gets up and hits you in the face, an enormous yellow cloud of cordite smoke—the charge weighs two thousand pounds—rises up and blows away just as the gentleman with the stop-watch says, "Time!" and then you see the splashes go up, perhaps between you and the enemy, behind the enemy, perhaps, or, if you are lucky, a great flash breaks out on the enemy, and when the smoke has rolled away you just have time to see that she is well and truly blazing before the next salvo goes off. I had the extreme satisfaction of seeing the *Lützow* get a salvo which must have caused her furiously to sink. There are minor side-shows, too, which contribute greatly to the excitement.

"We also discharged our large pieces at the *Rostock,* but she was getting such a thin time from somebody else that we refrained from pressing the question. Her mainmast and after-funnel had gone. She was quite stationary, and badly on fire. We sighted submarines, two in number, and also large numbers of enemy destroyers, one of which we soundly 'strafed.' So soundly, in fact, that it gave up the ghost.

"Well, when I climbed down from the foretop late that night I was as black as a nigger, very tired, and as hungry as a hunter, I having missed my tea. I wish you could have seen the state we were in between the decks. Water every-where, chairs, stools, radiators, tin baths, boots, shoes, clothes, books, and every conceivable article, chucked all over the place. We didn't care a fig, because we all thought of 'Der Tag' on the morrow which we all expected. Destroyers and light cruisers were attacking like fury all night, and when I got up at the bugle 'Action!' at 2 a. m. I felt as if I had slept about three and a half minutes."

Look now a little more closely at the details and epi-sodes of this engagement. Picture a calm and hazy sea and spread over an immense area the fleets of larger ships surrounded by screens of light cruisers and destroyers furi-ously engaged in encounters of their own, battles within the greater battle, and one sees how entirely this action lacks the classic simplicity of such engagements as the battle of the Nile or Trafalgar. But the main movements are clear enough. The heaviest losses of the British were sustained in the earlier, of the Germans in the later, stages, when the efficiency of their gunnery "became rapidly reduced under punishment, while ours was maintained throughout." Hardly was Beatty in action before he lost two battle-cruisers, the *Indefatigable* and the *Queen Mary*. Later, the *Invincible*, the flagship of the Third Cruiser Squadron, went down with Admiral Hood, who had brought his ships into "action ahead in a most inspiring manner worthy of his great naval an-cestors." One may note here two difficulties of pursuit in a modern action: first, that the enemy fire is concentrated on the leading ship, which can hardly escape punishment, and second, that his fast smaller craft, continually present on your engaged bow, discharge torpedoes and drop mines if you attempt to close him. Three armored cruisers and eight destroyers shared the fate of the larger vessels. The Ger-man losses, on a conservative estimate, were still more severe, especially when "the head of their line was crumpled up, leav-ing battleships as targets for the majority of our battle-cruisers." The enemy constantly "turned away" in the last stage and under cover of smoke screens endeavored to avoid the withering fifteen-inch gunfire, but at least four or five battleships and battle-cruisers, as many light cruisers, and six or eight destroyers were finally lost, probably twenty vessels in all and ten thousand men.[1]

Throughout the day of thunderous war the destroyers dashed to the torpedo attacks on the great ships, careless of the heart-shaking deluge of shells, utterly careless of life and youth, and all else save the mighty business in hand, and when night put an end to the main action, continued their work in the uncanny darkness, under the momentary glare of searchlights or the spouting flames from some wounded vessel. And all the while the unruffled sea appeared, we are told, like a marble surface when the searchlights swept it, and moving there the destroyers looked like venomous insects—"black as cockroaches on a floor." Never in the proud history of her navy have English sailors fought with more inspiring dash, more superb intrepidity.

So ended the battle of Jutland. But this, you may naturally say, is very different from the German story. There is no denying it, the discrepancy exists. Make the most liberal allowance for national prejudices and you cannot harmonize the versions. Which, then, are we to believe? There are no independent witnesses that can be summoned into court. How can one decide between statements so conflicting? There is one way and one way only. Victories, like everything else in the world, have results; a tree is known by its fruits. If, indeed, therefore, the Germans won, as they claim, a great victory,—they were certainly first in the field with the news, and, lest there should be any mistake in the matter, made the announcement at express speed,—how, the announcement apart, do we know of it? We have, of course, the Kaiser's assurances to his people, and that is of great importance. But did he also announce that the British blockade would no longer harass Germany? Oddly enough it was not mentioned and since the battle has become much more stringent.

On the other hand, let us ponder these facts: Immediately after the engagement the great naval port, Wilhelmshaven, was sealed with seven seals, so that no patriotic Ger-

[1] The final German report of losses was: 1 battle cruiser (the *Lutzow*), 1 old style battleship (the *Pommern*), 4 light cruisers, 5 torpedo boats and 2,800 men.

man could look upon his victorious ships.  Britain proclaimed her losses, Germany concealed her wounds.  Later
she discovered that she had accidentally in her haste overlooked the loss of a few trifling vessels.  And meanwhile,
steadily and without even momentary interruption, British
merchantmen and liners pursued, as they had hitherto pursued, their accustomed journeys; the transport of soldiers
by the hundred thousand, of supplies by the million ton, of
artillery, heavy artillery, by the shipload proceeded in the
Channel, the Mediterranean, the Indian and Atlantic Oceans.
If these results are possible after "defeat," how magnificent
must be the fruits of "victory."  One inquires for them without much success.  They are very disappointing in fruit,
these paper trees.

### FIRST GERMAN OFFICIAL REPORT

BERLIN, June 1, 1916.

During an enterprise directed to the northward our high
sea fleet on May 31st encountered the main part of the
English fighting fleet, which was considerably superior to
our forces.

During the afternoon, between Skagerrak and Horn Reef,
a heavy engagement developed, which was successful to us,
and which continued during the whole night.

In this engagement, so far as known up to the present,
there were destroyed by us the large battleship *Warspite,*
the battle-cruisers *Queen Mary* and *Indefatigable,* two armored cruisers, apparently of the *Achilles* type; one small
cruiser, the new flagships of destroyer squadrons, the *Turbulent, Nestor,* and *Alcaster,* a large number of torpedo-boat
destroyers, and one submarine.

By observation, which was free and clear of clouds, it
was stated that a large number of English battleships suffered damage from our ships and the attacks of our torpedo-
boat flotilla during the day engagement and throughout the
night.  Among others, the large battleship *Marlborough* was
hit by a torpedo.  This was confirmed by prisoners.

Several of our ships rescued parts of the crews of the

sunken English ships, among them being two and the only survivors of the *Indefatigable*.

On our side the small cruiser *Wiesbaden,* by hostile gun-fire during the day engagement, and his Majesty's ship *Pommern,* during the night, as the result of a torpedo, were sunk.

The fate of his Majesty's ship *Frauenlob,* which is missing, and of some torpedo boats, which have not returned yet, is unknown.

The High Sea Fleet returned to-day [Thursday] into our port.

### FIRST BRITISH OFFICIAL REPORT

LONDON, June 2, 1916.

On the afternoon of Wednesday, the 31st of May, a naval engagement took place off the coast of Jutland.

The British ships on which the brunt of the fighting fell were the battle-cruiser fleet and some cruisers and light cruisers, supported by four fast battleships. Among these the losses were heavy.

The German battle fleet, aided by low visibility, avoided a prolonged action with our main forces. As soon as these appeared on the scene the enemy returned to port, though not before receiving severe damage from our battleships.

The battle-cruisers *Queen Mary, Indefatigable,* and *Invincible,* and the cruisers *Defense* and *Black Prince* were sunk.

The *Warrior* was disabled, and after being towed for some time had to be abandoned by her crew.

It is also known that the destroyers *Tipperary, Turbulent, Fortune, Sparrowhawk,* and *Ardent* were lost, and six others are not yet accounted for.

No British battleships or light cruisers were sunk.

The enemy's losses were serious. At least one battle cruiser was destroyed and one was severely damaged. One battleship is reported to have been sunk by our destroyers.

During the night attack two light cruisers were disabled and probably sunk.

The exact number of enemy destroyers disposed of during the action cannot be ascertained with any certainty, but must have been large.

### Further Statement

Since the foregoing communication was issued a further report has been received from the Commander-in-Chief of the Grand Fleet stating that it has now been ascertained that our total losses in destroyers amount to eight boats in all.

The Commander-in-Chief also reports that it is now possible to form a closer estimate of the losses and the damage sustained by the enemy fleet.

One dreadnought battleship of the *Kaiser* class was blown up in an attack by British destroyers and another dreadnought battleship of the *Kaiser* class is believed to have been sunk by gunfire. Of three German battle-cruisers, two of which are believed were the *Derfflinger* and the *Lützow,* one was blown up, another was heavily engaged by our battle fleet and was seen to be disabled and stopping, and the third was observed to be seriously damaged.

One German light cruiser and six German destroyers were sunk, and at least two more German light cruisers were seen to be disabled. Further repeated hits were observed on three other German battleships that were engaged.

Finally, a German submarine was rammed and sunk.

BY ADMIRAL EDWARD VON CAPELLE
Official Statement Issued by the German Ministry of Marine on June 29th

The High Sea Fleet, consisting of three battleship squadrons, five battle-cruisers, and a large number of small cruisers, with several destroyer flotillas, was cruising in the Skagerrak on May 31st for the purpose, as on earlier occasions, of offering battle to the British fleet. The vanguard of small cruisers at 4.30 o'clock in the afternoon suddenly encountered ninety miles west of Hanstholm, a group of eight of the newest cruisers of the *Calliope* class and fifteen or twenty of the most modern destroyers.[1]

While the German light forces and the first cruiser squad-

---

[1] German time, which is an hour later than British, is rather nearer true time for the battle's location.

ron under Vice-Admiral Hipper were following the British, who were retiring northwestward, the German battle-cruisers sighted to the westward Vice-Admiral Beatty's battle-cruiser squadron of six ships, including four of the *Lion* type and two of the *Indefatigable* type. Beatty's squadron developed a battle line on a southeasterly course and Vice-Admiral Hipper formed his line ahead of the same general course and approached for a running fight. He opened fire at 5.49 o'clock in the afternoon with heavy artillery at a range of 13,000 meters against the superior enemy. The weather was clear and light, and the sea was light with a northwest wind.

After about a quarter of an hour a violent explosion occurred on the last cruiser of the *Indefatigable* type. It was caused by a heavy shell, and destroyed the vessel.

About 6.20 o'clock in the afternoon five warships of the *Queen Elizabeth* type came from the west and joined the British battle-cruiser line, powerfully reënforcing with their fifteen-inch guns the five British battle-cruisers remaining after 6.20 o'clock. To equalize this superiority Vice-Admiral Hipper ordered the destroyers to attack the enemy. The British destroyers and small cruisers interposed, and a bitter engagement at close range ensued, in the course of which a light cruiser participated.

The Germans lost two torpedo boats, the crews of which were rescued by sister ships under a heavy fire. Two British destroyers were sunk by artillery, and two others—the *Nestor* and *Nomad*—remained on the scene in a crippled condition. These later were destroyed by the main fleet after German torpedo boats had rescued all the survivors.

While this engagement was in progress a mighty explosion, caused by a big shell, broke the *Queen Mary,* the third ship in line, asunder at 6.30 o'clock.

Soon thereafter the German main battleship fleet was sighted to the southward, steering north. The hostile fast squadrons thereupon turned northward, closing the first part of the fight, which lasted about an hour.

The British retired at high speed before the German fleet, which followed closely. The German battle-cruisers continued the artillery combat with increasing intensity, particularly with the division of the vessels of the *Queen Eliza-beth* type, and in this the leading German battleship division participated intermittently. The hostile ships showed a de-sire to run in a flat curve ahead of the point of our line and to cross it.

At 7.45 o'clock in the evening British small cruisers and destroyers launched an attack against our battle-cruisers, who avoided the torpedoes by maneuvering, while the British bat-tle-cruisers retired from the engagement, in which they did not participate further as far as can be established. Shortly thereafter a German reconnoitering group, which was parry-ing the destroyer attack, received an attack from the north-east. The cruiser *Wiesbaden* was soon put out of action in this attack. The German torpedo flotillas immediately at-tacked the heavy ships.

Appearing shadow-like from the haze bank to the north-east was made out a long line of at least twenty-five battle-ships, which at first sought a junction with the British battle-cruisers and those of the *Queen Elizabeth* type on a north-westerly to westerly course and then turned on an easterly to a southeasterly course.

With the advent of the British main fleet, whose center consisted of three squadrons of eight battleships each, with a fast division of three battle-cruisers of the *Invincible* type on the northern end, and three of the newest vessels of the *Royal Sovereign* class, armed with fifteen-inch guns, at the southern end, there began about 8 o'clock in the evening the third section of the engagement, embracing the combat be-tween the main fleets.

Vice-Admiral Scheer determined to attack the British main fleet, which he now recognized was completely assem-bled and about doubly superior. The German battleship squadrons, headed by battle-cruisers, steered first toward the extensive haze bank to the northeast, where the crippled cruiser *Wiesbaden* was still receiving a heavy fire. Around the *Wiesbaden* stubborn individual fights under quickly changing conditions now occurred.

The light enemy forces, supported by an armored cruiser squadron of five ships of the *Minatour. Achilles,* and *Duke of Edinburgh* classes coming from the northeast, were encountered and apparently surprised on account of the decreasing visibility by our battle-cruisers and leading battleship division. The squadron came under a violent and heavy fire, by which the small cruisers *Defense* and *Black Prince* were sunk. The cruiser *Warrior* regained its own line a wreck and later sank. Another small cruiser was damaged.

Two destroyers already had fallen victims to the attack of German torpedo boats against the leading British battleships and a small cruiser and two destroyers were damaged. The German battle-cruisers and leading battleship division had in these engagements come under increased fire of the enemy's battleship squadron, which, shortly after 8 o'clock, could be made out in the haze turning to the northeastward and finally to the east. Germans observed, amid the artillery combat and shelling of great intensity, signs of the effect of good shooting between 8.20 and 8.30 o'clock particularly. Several officers on German ships observed that a battleship of the *Queen Elizabeth* class blew up under conditions similar to that of the *Queen Mary*. The *Invincible* sank after being hit severely. A ship of the *Iron Duke* class had earlier received a torpedo hit, and one of the *Queen Elizabeth* class was running around in a circle, its steering apparatus apparently having been hit.

The *Lützow* was hit by at least fifteen heavy shells and. was unable to maintain its place in line. Vice-Admiral Hipper, therefore, transshipped to the *Moltke* on a torpedo boat and under a heavy fire. The *Derfflinger* meantime took the lead temporarily. Parts of the German torpedo flotilla attacked the enemy's main fleet and heard detonations. In the action the Germans lost a torpedo boat. An enemy destroyer was seen in a sinking condition, having been hit by a torpedo.

After the first violent onslaught into the mass of the superior enemy the opponents lost sight of each other in the smoke by powder clouds. After a short cessation in the artillery combat Vice-Admiral Scheer ordered a new attack by all the available forces.

German battle-cruisers, which with several light cruisers and torpedo boats again headed the line, encountered the en-

emy soon after 9 o'clock and renewed the heavy fire, which
was answered by them from the mist, and then by the leading division of the main fleet. Armored cruisers now flung
themselves in a reckless onset at extreme speed against the
enemy line in order to cover the attack of torpedo boats. They
approached the enemy line, although covered with shot from
6,000 meters distance. Several German torpedo flotillas
dashed forward to attack, delivered torpedoes, and returned,
despite the most severe counter-fire, with the loss of only one
boat. The bitter artillery fight was again interrupted, after
this second violent onslaught, by the smoke from guns and
funnels.

Several torpedo flotillas, which were ordered to attack
somewhat later, found, after penetrating the smoke cloud,
that the enemy fleet was no longer before them; nor, when
the fleet commander again brought the German squadrons
upon the southerly and southwesterly course, where the enemy was last seen, could our opponents be found. Only once
more—shortly before 10.30 o'clock—did the battle flare up.
For a short time in the late twilight German battle cruisers
sighted four enemy capital ships to seaward and opened fire
immediately. As the two German battleship squadrons attacked, the enemy turned and vanished in the darkness.
Older German light cruisers of the fourth reconnoissance
group also were engaged with the older enemy armored
cruisers in a short fight. This ended the day battle.

The German divisions, which, after losing sight of the
enemy, began a night cruise in a southerly direction, were
attacked until dawn by enemy light force in rapid succession.

The attacks were favored by the general strategic situation and the particularly dark night.

The cruiser *Frauenlob* was injured severely during the engagement of the fourth reconnoissance group with a superior
cruiser force, and was lost from sight.

One armored cruiser of the *Cressy* class suddenly appeared close to a German battleship and was shot into fire
after forty seconds, and sank in four minutes.

The names were hard to decipher in the darkness and
therefore were uncertainly established, but six destroyers

were destroyed by our fire. One destroyer was cut in two by the ram of a German battleship. Seven destroyers, including the *G-30*, were hit and severely damaged. These, including the *Tipperary* and *Turbulent,* which, after saving survivors, were left behind in a sinking condition, drifted past our line, some of them burning at the bow or stern.

The tracks of countless torpedoes were sighted by the German ships, but only the *Pommern* fell an immediate victim to a torpedo. The cruiser *Rostock* was hit, but remained afloat. The cruiser *Elbing* was damaged by a German battleship during an unavoidable maneuver. After vain endeavors to keep the ship afloat the *Elbing* was blown up, but only after her crew had embarked on torpedo boats. A post torpedo boat was struck by a mine laid by the enemy.

BY ADMIRAL SIR JOHN JELLICOE<br>Official Report to the British Admiralty

June 24, 1916.

SIR,—Be pleased to inform the Lords Commissioners of the Admiralty that the German High Sea Fleet was brought to action on May 31, 1916, to the westward of the Jutland Bank, off the coast of Denmark.

The ships of the Grand Fleet, in pursuance of the general policy of periodical sweeps through the North Sea, had left its bases on the previous day, in accordance with instructions issued by me.

In the early afternoon of Wednesday, May 31st, the 1st and 2nd Battle-cruiser Squadrons, 1st, 2nd and 3rd Light-cruiser Squadrons and destroyers from the 1st, 9th, 10th and 13th Flotillas, supported by the 5th Battle Squadron, were, in accordance with my directions, scouting to the southward of the Battle Fleet, which was accompanied by the 3rd Battle-cruiser Squadron, 1st and 2nd Cruiser Squadrons, 4th Light-cruiser Squadron, 4th, 11th and 12th Flotillas.

The junction of the Battle Fleet with the scouting force after the enemy had been sighted was delayed owing to the southerly course steered by our advanced force during the first hour after commencing their action with the enemy battle-cruisers. This was, of course, unavoidable, as had our battle-cruisers not followed the enemy to the southward the main fleets would never have been in contact.

The Battle-cruiser Fleet, gallantly led by Vice-Admiral Sir David Beatty, and admirably supported by the ships of the Fifth Battle Squadron under Rear-Admiral Hugh Evan-Thomas, fought an action under, at times, disadvantageous conditions, especially in regard to light, in a manner that was in keeping with the best traditions of the service.

On receipt of the information that the enemy had been sighted, the British Battle Fleet, with its accompanying cruiser and destroyer force, proceeded at full speed on a S.E. by S. course to close the Battle-cruiser Fleet. During the two hours that elapsed before the arrival of the Battle Fleet on the scene the steaming qualities of the older battleships were severely tested. Great credit is due to the engine-room departments for the manner in which they, as always, responded to the call, the whole Fleet maintaining a speed in excess of the trial speeds of some of the older vessels.

The Third Battle-cruiser Squadron, which was in advance of the Battle Fleet, was ordered to reënforce Sir David Beatty. At 5.30 p. m. this squadron observed flashes of gunfire and heard the sound of guns to the southwestward. Rear-Admiral Hood sent the *Chester* to investigate, and this ship engaged three or four enemy light-cruisers at about 5.45 p. m. The engagement lasted for about twenty minutes, during which period Captain Lawson handled his vessel with great skill against heavy odds, and, although the ship suffered considerably in casualties, her fighting and steaming qualities were unimpaired, and at about 6.05 p. m. she rejoined the Third Battle-cruiser Squadron.

The Third Battle-cruiser Squadron had turned to the northwestward, and at 6.10 p. m. sighted our battle-cruisers, the squadron taking station ahead of the *Lion* at 6.21 p. m. in accordance with the orders of the Vice-Admiral Commanding Battle-cruiser Fleet.

Meanwhile, at 5.45 p. m., the report of guns had become audible to me, and at 5.55 p. m. flashes were visible from ahead round to the starboard beam, although in the mist no ships could be distinguished, and the position of the enemy's battle fleet could not be determined. The difference in estimated position by "reckoning" between *Iron Duke* and *Lion,* which was inevitable under the circumstances, added to the uncertainty of the general situation.

Shortly after 5.55 p. m. some of the cruisers ahead were seen to be in action, and reports received show that *Defense,* flagship, and *Warrior,* of the First Cruiser Squadron, engaged an enemy light-cruiser at this time. She was subsequently observed to sink.

At 6 p. m. *Canterbury,* which ship was in company with the Third Battle-cruiser Squadron, had engaged enemy light-cruisers which were firing heavily on the torpedo-boat destroyers *Shark, Acasta* and *Christopher;* as a result of this engagement the *Shark* was sunk.

At 6 p. m. vessels, afterwards seen to be our battle-cruisers, were sighted by *Marlborough* bearing before the starboard beam of the battle fleet.

At the same time the Vice-Admiral Commanding Battle-cruiser Fleet, reported to me the position of the enemy battle-cruisers, and at 6.14 p. m. reported the position of the enemy battle fleet.

At this period, when the battle fleet was meeting the battle-cruisers and the Fifth Battle Squadron, great care was necessary to insure that our own ships were not mistaken for enemy vessels.

I formed the battle fleet in line of battle on receipt of Sir David Beatty's report, and during deployment the fleets became engaged. Sir David Beatty had meanwhile formed the battle-cruisers ahead of the battle fleet.

At 6.16 p. m. *Defense* and *Warrior* were observed passing down between the British and German Battle Fleets under a very heavy fire. *Defense* disappeared, and *Warrior* passed to the rear disabled.

It is probable that Sir Robert Arbuthnot, during his engagement with the enemy's light-cruisers and in his desire to complete their destruction, was not aware of the approach of the enemy's heavy ships, owing to the mist, until he found himself in close proximity to the main fleet, and before he could withdraw his ships they were caught under a heavy fire and disabled.   It is not known when *Black Prince,* of the same squadron, was sunk, but a wireless signal was received from her between 8 and 9 p. m.

The First Battle Squadron became engaged during deployment, the Vice-Admiral opening fire at 6.17 p. m. on a battleship of the *Kaiser* class.   The other Battle Squadrons, which had previously been firing at an enemy light-cruiser, opened fire at 6.30 p. m. on battleships of the *Koenig* class.

At 6.06 p. m. the Rear-Admiral Commanding Fifth Battle Squadron, then in company with the battle-cruisers, had sighted the starboard wing division of the battle fleet on the port bow of *Barham,* and the first intention of Rear-Admiral Evan-Thomas was to form ahead of the remainder of the battle fleet, but on realizing the direction of deployment he was compelled to form astern, a maneuver which was well executed by the squadron under a heavy fire from the enemy battle fleet.   An accident to *Warspite's* steering gear caused her helm to become jammed temporarily and took the ship in the direction of the enemy's line, during which time she was hit several times.   Clever handling enabled Captain Edward M. Phillpotts to extricate his ship from a somewhat awkward situation.

Owing principally to the mist, but partly to the smoke, it was possible to see only a few ships at a time in the enemy's battle line.   Towards the van only some four or five ships were ever visible at once.   More could be seen from the rear squadron, but never more than eight to twelve.

The action between the battle fleets lasted intermittently from 6.17 p. m. to 8.20 p. m. at ranges between 9,000 and 12,000 yards, during which time the British Fleet made alterations of course from S.E. by E. to W. in the endeavor to close.   The enemy constantly turned away and opened the range under cover of destroyer attacks and smoke screens as the effect of the British fire was felt, and the alterations of course had the effect of bringing the British Fleet (which commenced the action in a position of advantage on the bow of the enemy) to a quarterly bearing from the enemy battle line, but at the same time placed us between the enemy and his bases.

At 6.55 p. m. *Iron Duke* passed the wreck of *Invincible,* with *Badger* standing by.

During the somewhat brief periods that the ships of the High Sea Fleet were visible through the mist, the heavy and effective fire kept up by the battleships and battle-cruisers of the Grand Fleet caused me much satisfaction, and the enemy vessels were seen to be constantly hit, some being observed to haul out of the line and at least one to sink. The enemy's return fire at this period was not effective, and the damage caused to our ships was insignificant.

As was anticipated, the German Fleet appeared to rely very much on torpedo attacks, which were favored by the low visibility and by the fact that we had arrived in the position of a "following" or "chasing" fleet. A large number of torpedoes were apparently fired, but only one took effect (on *Marlborough*), and even in this case the ship was able to remain in the line and to continue the action. The enemy's efforts to keep out of effective gun range were aided by the weather conditions, which were ideal for the purpose. Two separate destroyer attacks were made by the enemy.

The First Battle Squadron, under Vice-Admiral Sir Cecil Burney, came into action at 6.17 p. m. with the enemy's Third Battle Squadron, at a range of about 11,000 yards, and administered severe punishment, both to the battleships and to the battle-cruisers and light-cruisers, which were also engaged. The fire of *Marlborough* (Captain George P. Ross) was particularly rapid and effective. This ship commenced at 6.17 p. m. by firing seven salvoes at a ship of the *Kaiser* class, then engaged a cruiser, and again a battleship, and at 6.54 she was hit by a torpedo and took up a considerable list to starboard, but reopened at 7.03 p. m. at a cruiser and at 7.12 p. m. fired fourteen rapid salvoes at a ship of the *Koenig* class, hitting her frequently until she turned out of the line. The manner in which this effective fire was kept up in spite of the disadvantages due to the injury caused by the torpedo was most creditable to the ship and a very fine example to the squadron.

The range decreased during the course of the action to 9,000 yards. The First Battle Squadron received more of the enemy's return fire than the remainder of the battle fleet, with the exception of the Fifth Battle Squadron. *Colossus* was hit but was not seriously damaged, and other ships were straddled with fair frequency.

In the Fourth Battle Squadron—in which squadron my flagship *Iron Duke* was placed—Vice-Admiral Sir Doveton Sturdee leading one of the divisions—the enemy engaged was the squadron consisting of *Koenig* and *Kaiser* class and some of the battle-cruisers, as well as disabled cruisers and light-cruisers. The mist rendered range-taking a difficult matter, but the fire of the squadron was effective. *Iron Duke,* having previously fired at a light-cruiser between the lines, opened fire at 6.30 p. m. on a battleship of the *Koenig* class at a range of 12,000 yards. The latter was very quickly straddled, and hitting commenced at the second salvo and only ceased when the target ship turned away. The rapidity with which hitting was established was most creditable to the excellent gunnery organization of the flagship.

The fire of other ships of the squadron was principally directed at enemy battle-cruisers and cruisers as they appeared out of the mist. Hits were observed to take effect on several ships.

The ships of the Second Battle Squadron, under Vice-Admiral Sir Thomas Jerram, were in action with vessels of the *Kaiser* or *Koenig* classes between 6.30 and 7.20 p. m., and fired also at an enemy battle-cruiser which had dropped back apparently severely damaged.

During the action between the battle fleets the Second Cruiser Squadron, ably commanded by Rear-Admiral Herbert L. Heath, with the addition of *Duke of Edinburgh* of the First Cruiser Squadron, occupied a position at the van, and acted as a connecting link between the battle fleet and the battle-cruiser fleet. This squadron, although it carried out useful work, did not have an opportunity of coming into action.

The Fourth Light-cruiser Squadron, under Commodore Charles E. Le Mesurier, occupied a position in the van until ordered to attack enemy destroyers at 7.20 p. m., and again at 8.18 p. m., when they supported the Eleventh Flotilla, which had moved out under Commodore James R. P. Hawksley, to attack.   On each occasion the Fourth Light-cruiser Squadron was very well handled by Commodore Le Mesurier, his captains giving him excellent support, and their object was attained, although with some loss in the second attack, when the ships came under the heavy fire of the enemy battle fleet at between 6,500 and 8,000 yards.   The *Calliope* was hit several times, but did not sustain serious damage, although, I regret to say, she had several casualties.   The light-cruisers attacked the enemy's battleships with torpedoes at this time, and an explosion on board a ship of the *Kaiser* class was seen at 8.40 p. m.

During these destroyer attacks four enemy torpedo-boat destroyers were sunk by the gunfire of battleships, light-cruisers and destroyers.

After the arrival of the British Battle Fleet the enemy's tactics were of a nature generally to avoid further action, in which they were favored by the conditions of visibility.

At 9 p. m. the enemy was entirely out of sight, and the threat of torpedo-boat destroyer attacks during the rapidly approaching darkness made it necessary for me to dispose the fleet for the night, with a view to its safety from such attacks, whilst providing for a renewal of action at daylight. I accordingly maneuvered to remain between the enemy and his bases, placing our flotillas in a position in which they would afford protection to the fleet from destroyer attack, and at the same time be favorably situated for attacking the enemy's heavy ships.

During the night the British heavy ships were not attacked, but the Fourth, Eleventh and Twelfth Flotillas, under Commodore Hawksley and Captains Charles J. Wintour and Anselan J. B. Stirling, delivered a series of very gallant and successful attacks on the enemy, causing him heavy losses.

It was during these attacks that severe losses in the Fourth Flotilla occurred, including that of *Tipperary,* with the gallant leader of the Flotilla, Captain Wintour.   He had brought his flotilla to a high pitch of perfection, and although suffering severely from the fire of the enemy, a heavy toll of enemy vessels was taken, and many gallant actions were performed by the flotilla.

Two torpedoes were seen to take effect on enemy vessels as the result of the attacks of the Fourth Flotilla, one being from *Spitfire,* and the other from either *Ardent, Ambuscade* or *Garland.*

The attack carried out by the Twelfth Flotilla (Captain Anselan J. B. Stirling) was admirably executed. The squadron attacked, which consisted of six large vessels, besides light-cruisers, and comprised vessels of the *Kaiser* class, was taken by surprise. A large number of torpedoes was fired, including some at the second and third ships in the line; those fired at the third ship took effect, and she was observed to blow up. A second attack made twenty minutes later by *Mænad* on the five vessels still remaining, resulted in the fourth ship in the line being also hit.

The destroyers were under a heavy fire from the light-cruisers on reaching the rear of the line, but the *Onslaught* was the only vessel which received any material injuries.

During the attack carried out by the Eleventh Flotilla, *Castor* (Commodore James R. P. Hawksley) leading the flotilla, engaged and sank an enemy torpedo-boat destroyer at point-blank range.

There were many gallant deeds performed by the destroyer flotillas; they surpassed the very highest expectations that I had formed of them.

Apart from the proceedings of the flotillas, the Second Light-cruiser Squadron in the rear of the battle fleet was in close action for about 15 minutes at 10.20 p. m. with a squadron comprising one enemy cruiser and four light-cruisers, during which period *Southampton* and *Dublin* suffered rather heavy casualties, although their steaming and fighting qualities were not impaired. The return fire of the squadron appeared to be very effective.

*Abdiel,* ably commanded by Commander Berwick Curtis, carried out her duties with the success which has always characterized her work.

At daylight, June 1st, the battle fleet, being then to the southward and westward of the Horn Reef, turned to the northward in search of enemy vessels and for the purpose of collecting our own cruisers and torpedo-boat destroyers. At 2.30 a. m. Vice-Admiral Sir Cecil Burney transferred his flag from *Marlborough* to *Revenge,* as the former ship had some difficulty in keeping up the speed of the squadron. *Marlborough* was detached by my direction to a base, successfully driving off an enemy submarine attack en route. The visibility early on June 1st (three to four miles) was less than on May 31st, and the torpedo-boat destroyers, being out of visual touch, did not rejoin until 9 a. m. The British Fleet remained in the proximity of the battlefield and near the line of approach to German ports until 11 a. m. on June 1st, in spite of the disadvantage of long distances from fleet bases and the danger incurred in waters adjacent to enemy coasts from submarines and torpedo craft. The enemy, however, made no sign, and I was reluctantly compelled to the conclusion that the High Sea Fleet had returned into port. Subsequent events proved this assumption to have been correct. Our position must have been known to the enemy, as at 4 a. m. the Fleet engaged a Zeppelin for about five minutes, during which time she had ample opportunity to note and subsequently report the position and course of the British Fleet.

The waters from the latitude of the Horn Reef to the scene of the action were thoroughly searched, and some survivors from the destroyers *Ardent, Fortune* and *Tipperary* were picked up, and the *Sparrowhawk,* which had been in collision and was no longer seaworthy, was sunk after her crew had been taken off. A large amount of wreckage was seen, but no enemy ships, and at 1.15 p. m., it being evident that the German Fleet had succeeded in returning to port, course was shaped for our bases, which were reached without further incident on Friday, June 2nd. A cruiser squadron was detached to search for *Warrior,* which vessel had been abandoned whilst in tow of *Engadine* on her way to the base owing to bad weather setting in and the vessel becoming unseaworthy, but no trace of her was discovered, and a further subsequent search by a light-cruiser squadron having failed to locate her, it is evident that she foundered.

The enemy fought with the gallantry that was expected of him. We particularly admired the conduct of those on board a disabled German light-cruiser which passed down the British line shortly after deployment, under a heavy fire, which was returned by the only gun left in action.

The conduct of officers and men throughout the day and night actions was entirely beyond praise. No words of mine could do them justice. On all sides it is reported to me that the glorious traditions of the past were most worthily upheld—whether in heavy ships, cruisers, light-cruisers, or destroyers—the same admirable spirit prevailed. Officers and men were cool and determined, with a cheeriness that would have carried them through anything. The heroism of the wounded was the admiration of all.

I cannot adequately express the pride with which the spirit of the Fleet filled me.

### NARRATIVE OF A GERMAN SAILOR ON THE LÜTZOW

Suddenly the entire ship is roughly shaken. The colossus heaves far over, and everything that is not fixed is upset. The first direct hit! The torpedo pierces the fore part of the ship. Its effects are terrible. Iron, wood, metal, parts of bodies, and smashed ships' implements are all intermixed, and the electric light, by chance spared, continues to shine upon this sight.

Two decks lower, in the Diesel dynamo room, there is still life. That compartment has not been hit, and twenty-seven men, in the prime of life, have been spared, but the chamber is shut off from all others, for the water is rushing into all sections. They are doomed to death. Several 38-centimeter shells squarely hit their mark, working terrible havoc. The first hit the wireless department. Of the twelve living men who a moment ago were seated before the apparatus, there is nothing more to be seen. Nothing is left but a smoking heap of ruins. The second shot again pierced the fore part of the ship. The entire forepart of the vessel, as far as the Diesel motor room, was past saving.

Another broadside meant for the *Lützow* fell short, but a torpedo boat close by disappeared, leaving only a few odd pieces of wood and a smashed lifeboat drifting around. It is now half-past 7, and the hostile circle grows ever smaller. The *Lützow* and the *Seydlitz* lie with their bows deep in the water; both are badly mauled. The forepart of the *Lützow* was in flames. Shells burst against the ship's side in rapid succession. A terrible sight is presented on board the *Lützow,* and it needs iron nerves to look upon it coolly. Hundreds have lost their lives, while many have lain for hours in torture, and the fight is not yet over. The bow is now crushed in and is entirely submerged. The four screws are already sticking half out of the water, so that the *Lützow* can only make eight to ten knots an hour, as against the normal thirty-two.

The Admiral decides to transfer to the *Moltke*. He gives orders to turn and get away from the scene of the fight, but the *Lützow* has not gone a mile before she receives a broadside of 38-centimeter shells. The entire ship was filled with the poisonous fumes of the shells, and any one who failed to affix his gas mask was doomed to be suffocated.

It was three-quarters of an hour before the lighting installation was restored. Then for the first time could the extent of the damage wrought by the salvo be seen. One of the shells had landed in the sick bay. Here there were only three doctors and fifteen attendants, besides 160 to 180 wounded. Of all those, only four remained alive. These four were hurled into the next compartment by the air pressure; there they lay unconscious.

The *Lützow* was now a complete wreck. Corpses drifted past. From the bows up to the first 30-centimeter gun turret the ship lay submerged. The other gun turrets were completely disabled, with the guns sticking out in all directions. On deck lay the bodies of the sailors in their torn uniforms, in the midst of the empty shell cases. From the masts fluttered torn flags, twisted signal lines, and pieces of wire of the wireless installation. Had not the lookout man and the three officers on the commander's bridge given signs of life, the *Lützow* would have truly resembled a ship of the dead. Below, on the battery deck, there still lay innumerable wounded, but there was no longer a doctor to attend to them.

Night came on and hope was entertained of getting away without a further encounter. But at 3 o'clock in the night news of the approach of two British cruisers and five destroyers was received and just at that critical time the fore and middle bulkheads gave way.

Orders were given to carry the wounded to the stern. Then the order rings out: "All hands muster in division order abaft." A tumult arises on the lower deck, for everybody is now bent on saving his life. It is impossible in that short space of time to bring up all the wounded, for they are scattered everywhere. Eighteen men had the good fortune to be carried up, but all the rest who could not walk or crawl had to be left behind.

The twenty-seven men shut up in the Diesel dynamo chamber had heard the order through the speaking tube, for many, mad with anguish, screamed through the tube for help, and it was learned that two of their number lay bound because they had become insane. Inspired by their sense of duty, these sealed-up men had continued to carry on their work in order to provide the ship with light.

The torpedo-boats now quickly took off the crew of the *Lützow*, and those left behind were doomed to death. It was resolved that no piece of the vessel should fall into the enemy's hands. An order was given and a torpedo cleft the waters. Just then seven men were to be seen running like madmen round the rear deck. Overfatigued as they were, they had apparently dropped off to sleep and only just awakened. As the torpedo exploded, the *Lützow's* bow quickly dipped, and the stern rose until she stood on end. Then she heeled over and sank, forming a great whirlpool that carried everything within it into the depths.

When the roll was called it appeared that there were 1,003 survivors of the *Lützow;* 597 men had perished in the battle.

### BY A BRITISH SUB-LIEUTENANT
#### Letter from a Lad of Nineteen to Another of Seventeen

I have been intending to write and tell you all about the 31st, but couldn't find your address and could only remember the number.

I'm so awfully sorry you weren't in it. It was rather terrible but a wonderful experience, and I wouldn't have missed it for anything, but, by Jove! it is not a thing one wants to make a habit of.

I must say it's very different from what I expected. I expected to be excited but was not a bit; it's hard to express what we did feel like, but you know the sort of feeling one has when one goes in to bat at cricket and rather a lot depends upon you doing well and you're waiting for the first ball; well, it's very much the same as that—do you know what I mean? A sort of tense feeling waiting for the unknown to happen, and not quite knowing what to expect; one does not feel the slightest bit frightened, and the idea that there's a chance of you and your ship being scuppered does not really enter one's head—there are too many other things to think about.

This ship is just about the latest thing in destroyers and we all transferred, officers and ship's company, from the *Beaver* here.

We were attached to the battle-cruisers and were with them throughout the action, so we were probably in the thick of it, as no doubt you saw in the papers that the battle-cruisers stood the brunt of the action, and we were in action for about three hours before the battleships arrived upon the scene.

To start with, it was all at such long range that the destroyers were rather out of it, except there were plenty of 15-inch falling round us, and we just watched. It really seemed rather like a battle practice on a large scale, and we could see the flashes of the German guns on the horizon.

Then they ordered us to attack, so we bustled off at full bore. Being navigator, also having control of all the guns, I was on the bridge all the time and remained there for twelve hours without leaving it at all.

When we got fairly close I sighted a good-looking Hun destroyer which I thought I'd like to strafe. You know, it's awful fun to know that you can blaze off at a real ship and do as much damage as you like. Well, I'd just got their range on the guns and we'd just fired one round when some more of our destroyers coming from the opposite direction got between us and the enemy and completely blanketed us, so we had to stop firing as the risk of hitting one of our own ships was too great—which was rather rot. Shortly afterwards they recalled us, so we bustled back again. How any destroyers got out of it is perfectly wonderful.

Literally, there were hundreds of "progs" all round us from a 15-inch to a 4-inch, and you know what a big splash a 15-inch bursting in the water does make; we got soaked through by the spray.

Just as we were getting back a whole salvo of big shells fell just in front of us and short of our big ships. The skipper and I did rapid calculations as to how long it would take them to reload, fire again, time of flight, etc., as we had to go right through the spot. We came to the conclusion that as they were short a bit they would probably go up a bit and didn't, but luckily they altered deflection and the next lot fell just astern of us. Anyhow, we managed to come out of that lot, without the ship or a soul on board being touched.

It's extraordinary the amount of knocking about the big ships can stand. One saw them hit, and they seemed to be one mass of flames and smoke and you think they're gone, but when the smoke clears away they are apparently none the worse and still firing away.

But to see a ship blow up is a terrible but wonderful sight; an enormous volume of flame and smoke about 200 feet high and great heaps of metal, etc., blown sky-high and then, when the smoke clears away, not a sign of the ship.

We saw one rather extraordinary sight. Of course, you know the N.S. is very shallow. We came across a Hun cruiser absolutely on end. His stern on the bottom and his bow sticking up about 30 feet above the water, and a little further on a destroyer in precisely the same position.

I wouldn't be certain, but I rather think I saw your old ship crashing along and blazing away, but I expect you have heard from some of your pals.

But the night was far and away the worst time of all, and an awful strain. It was pitch dark and, of course, absolutely no lights; and the firing seems so much worse at night as you could see the flashes absolutely lighting up the sky, and it seemed to make much more noise, and you would see ships on fire and blowing up. Of course, *we* showed absolutely no lights.

One expected to be surprised any minute—and eventually we were. We suddenly found ourselves within 1,000 yards of two or three big Hun cruisers. They switched on their searchlights and started firing like nothing on earth. Then they put their searchlights on us, but for some extraordinary reason did not fire on us. As, of course, we were, going full speed, we'd lost them in a moment, but I must say that I, and I think everybody else, thought that was the end; but one does not feel afraid or panicky. I think I felt rather cooler then than at any other time. I asked lots of people afterwards what they felt like and they all said the same thing. It all happens in a few seconds, one hasn't got time to think, but never in all my life have I been so thankful to see daylight again—and I don't think I ever want to see another night like that—it's such an awful strain; one does not notice it at the time, but it's the reaction afterwards. I never noticed I was tired till I got back to harbor, and then we all turned in and absolutely slept like dogs. We were 72 hours with little or no sleep. The Skipper was perfectly wonderful—he never left the bridge for a minute for 24 hours and was either on the bridge or in the chart house the whole time we were out, and I've never seen anybody so cool and unruffled. He stood there sucking his pipe as if nothing out of the ordinary were happening.

One quite forgot all about time. I was relieved at 4 a.m., and on looking at my watch found I had been up there nearly 12 hours, and then discovered I was rather hungry.

I had my camera on the bridge the whole time and took several photographs when there was a chance, but all at rather long range and the light was not good, so I doubt if they will be good—especially as the Skipper tried to take one when I wasn't there, and not knowing anything about it took the front off instead of opening the back. Luckily it was at the last film so I hope it hasn't spoilt the lot. If they do come out they should be rather interesting and I'll send you prints.

# BRUSILOFF AGAIN BREAKS THE AUSTRIAN LINE

## CAPTURE OF BUKOWINA AND THE THIRD ADVANCE INTO HUNGARY

### JUNE 4TH-AUGUST

ROBERT MACHRAY                    GENERAL BRUSILOFF
GENERAL VON CRAMON        AUSTRIAN EYE-WITNESSES

The changing War leadership, so marked in 1916, had begun in Russia, in the previous fall, with the dismissal of Grand Duke Nicholas from command against Germany and Austria. In his place General Alexieff now took control under the nominal commandership of the Czar. Alexieff placed in command along the Austrian front that extremely able leader, General Brusiloff, Russia's chief hero of the War.

Brusiloff's advance in June was certainly a most amazing evidence of Russia's power of recuperation; and if the Czar could have re-organized his Court and Cabinet as successfully as Alexieff and Brusiloff rebuilt his army, the results which the world so eagerly expected from Brusiloff's advance might have been realized. His successes were, however, to be more than neutralized by the treachery of the Czar's new Prime Minister, Sturmer.

The enthusiasm of the western Allies over Brusiloff's success is well depicted here by Machray, the noted expert on eastern Europe. What will probably never be depicted in completeness is that other side of the case, the Austrian disarray. So sure were the Austrians of the strength of their own trenches and the weakness of the foe that they seem to have been caught wholly by surprise. Their camps behind the lines contained every luxury for the officers, and gardens and grain-fields for the men. They were even, at the very moment of Brusiloff's attack, holding an official celebration on the birthday of their commander, Archduke Frederick, one of the numerous Hapsburg royal family. How the celebration was interrupted at Czernovitz, the capital of the invaded district, is here told by some of its citizens. A more official Teuton view is that of General von Cramon, the chief German "liaison" officer with the Austrians.

This third widespread Russian advance into Austrian territory penetrated a region further south than that previously occupied. The Russian troops now spread over the whole of the Bukowina, the Austrian province bordering directly on Rumania. This naturally impressed the Rumanians more deeply than the earlier successes which had been in regions beyond their vision. Moreover, the Carpathian Mountains being here less formidable than further north, the Russians found it easier to speed their Cossack cavalry across the mountains into Hungary. A picture of the terror caused by these raids is here drawn by an Hungarian.

In brief, this third breakdown of Austria seemed to offer every evidence of bringing Russia immediate and comprehensive victory. Then came its breakdown, as told in the later sections of this volume.

BY ROBERT MACHRAY

THE 4th of June, 1916, will always be one of the great dates of the War.  On that day Russia reasserted her might by opening her amazing and successful offensive under General Brusiloff against the Austro-Germans in the area lying between the Pripet and the Pruth.

It should be remembered that on that 4th of June the prospects of Germany, certainly on the European fronts if not so much so on the Asiatic, looked so rosy as to encourage her in taking a complacent view of the situation.  It could scarcely be truthfully affirmed that the Entente Powers were making genuine progress anywhere.  At Verdun, which for months had been the center of as bitter fighting as was ever witnessed, the French, in spite of the most heroic efforts, were decidedly, if slowly, losing ground.  In the Trentino the brave Italians had been compelled to withdraw for several miles into their own territory before a strong and persistent Austrian offensive.  During May, Russia, according to the experts of Petrograd, was anticipating a powerful attack by Hindenburg on the Riga-Dvinsk line, to be followed by an advance on the Russian capital; and there was a violent contest near Jakobstadt on the Dvina with indecisive results.  But if the Germans did not advance in this region, neither did the Russians, while in the district of Lake Narotch, east of Vilna, the latter were thrown back; south of the Pripet the respective combatants held the same trenches they had occupied since the preceding autumn.  On the surface, at least, things looked well enough for Germany along the whole Russian front in Europe, and she was sure they would never be worse; on the contrary, her contempt for the Russians flattered her into thinking it would be an easy matter to make them better.  In the Balkans some of the forces of the Entente had moved northward from the great entrenched camp of Salonika to the Bulgaro-Serbian frontier, but otherwise had done nothing worth speaking of; behind

them was an uncertain Greece, whose king was even then playing, with the merest pretense of concealment, into the hands
of the Germans by surrendering one of the best of the Greek
forts to the invading Bulgars. Such was the general position in Europe. In Armenia the Russians had been checked
and forced to retreat by a clever Germano-Turkish scheme
of attack, which for a while was so strongly pressed as to
threaten Erzerum, and did result in the recapture of Bitlis
and Mush later. And if the position in Egypt was unfavorable to Germany, the reverse was the case with respect to
Mesopotamia; and large Turkish forces, set free by the fall
of Kut, were marching from Bagdad and Mosul to the Persian frontier to strengthen the troops then in contact with
the Russians and drive the latter eastward again—which
was what happened. Surveying the whole field of the War,
Germany could congratulate herself. She invited the Allies
to study the "war-map," and late in the spring Bethmann-
Hollweg, her Chancellor, boasted in the Reichstag that she
would never retrace her "iron step." His speech on that
occasion was couched in terms very different from those
which he employed at the reassembling of the Reichstag on
the 28th of September, when he made another review of the
War. He had much less to say of the conquests Germany
had made, and a good deal more about the territorial changes
the Entente Powers desired to effect; he still protested that
Germany was unconquerable, but he let it be seen, whether
intentionally or not, that he was not quite so sure about the
irretractability of that iron step—he knew, as a matter of
fact, that first the Russians and then the British, French, and
Italians had demonstrated the opposite. In the first two or
three days of June no suspicion of anything of the sort had
entered the German mind.

Brusiloff's wonderful offensive came as a tremendous surprise not only to the enemy but to the vast majority of the
peoples of the Allies, who had regarded Russia as likely at
best to remain on the defensive for a long time in Europe,
because of the serious losses she had sustained in 1915 and her
tragical deficiencies in munitions. Throughout the West it
was indeed generally thought that Russia at that time was

doing nothing more than making a gallant attempt to relieve the pressure, then most formidable, on the Italians in the Trentino.  When an official Petrograd *communiqué,* issued on the 7th of June, announced that up to noon on the preceding day Brusiloff's operations had led to the capture of more than 40,000 men and nearly eighty guns, with fifty trench-mortars and above one hundred and thirty machine guns, it was perceived that the Russians were in strong force, and that this was no mere demonstration but the commencement of a powerful offensive.

When June opened the Russian armies in Europe were disposed in three groups along a front not far short of nine hundred miles in length from north to south.  The northern Russian armies, then under General Kuropatkin, composed the first group, and they held the line from Riga to Dvinsk. The central Russian armies, under General Evert, formed the second group, and they continued the line southward from Dvinsk to the Pripet.  The southern Russian armies, under General Brusiloff, were the third group, and they stood on the front from the Pripet to the Pruth.  All three groups were under the command of General Alexieff, who took orders only from the Czar himself.  Definite figures of the strength of any of these groups, or of the individual armies comprised in them, are still to seek, but it is certain that Russia had from two to three millions of armed men on or immediately behind her European front, with plenty of reserves at the depots in the near interior.  In all probability she had nearly as many men on this front in October, 1915, but not a million of them had rifles; in the great retreat, which was caused by Russia's melancholy shortage of munitions, it was frequently the case that only one soldier out of four had a rifle.  According to a German estimate, which was published shortly before the start of Brusiloff's offensive, that general had at his disposition in this area forty-one infantry and fourteen cavalry divisions, or something like a million men, if the divisions were in full strength.  Under him he had the Eighth Russian Army, commanded by General Kaledin, in Volhynia; the Eleventh Russian Army, led by General Sakharoff, in Volhynia and Galicia; the Seventh Rus-

sian Army, under General Shcherbacheff, in Galicia; and the
Ninth Russian Army, commanded by General Lechitsky, in
the Dniester-Pruth valleys. Opposed to him were five Austro-Hungarian armies, with which had been incorporated several German divisions, all under the command of the Archduke Frederick, the only member of the House of Hapsburg who was a professional soldier. The total strength
of these five armies was about forty-one divisions, with ten
divisions of cavalry; in other words, the Archduke and Brusiloff had much the same number of men, and when later
the Austrians claimed, in extenuation of their defeats, that
they were overwhelmed by the vastly superior numerical
forces of the Russians, they were talking unmitigated non-
sense. They had besides the benefit of being in strong defensive positions, and of better railway facilities. Nor were
the Russians much helped by large defections of Austrian
Slavs in this campaign, for most of the latter were in the
Trentino, and the Austrian soldiers on the Russian front were
drawn from Austrian-Poland, Hungary and Austria proper
—some of the best fighting men of the Dual Monarchy. The
truth was that the enemy was outgeneraled and outfought
in the field, first on the flanks and then in the center.

No other operations of the War have quite the same
impressive character as those which Brusiloff began on the
4th of June, inasmuch as his offensive started with a simultaneous frontal assault on a line of enemy positions over two
hundred and fifty miles in length. One of the reasons for the
success of Germany had been her ability to move her forces
quickly from one sector, where little or nothing was doing,
to another which was being heavily attacked. Knowing
this, the Russian High Command determined to deprive her
of this advantage by taking the offensive over so long a
front that it would be extremely difficult, if not impossible,
for her to employ similar tactics in this instance. Therefore
Brusiloff, through Kaledin, Sakharoff, Shcherbacheff, and
Lechitsky, attacked the Austro-Germans not at one point, or
at several points, but at every point of their two-hundred-
and-seventy-mile line. It has been stated in the Press that
Russia, in her solicitude for the hard-pressed Italians, under-

took this vast and in its way unparalleled venture earlier than she had intended. No doubt she was most desirous of helping Cadorna, and she has never hesitated to make the most gallant efforts, not without heavy sacrifices to herself, on behalf of her Allies in their need, but in this case it appears that there was nothing unpremeditated, nothing that was not in conformity precisely with her own plans. Careful and extensive preparation preceded Brusiloff's offensive, every feature of which had been studied beforehand. Staff organization had been perfected, transport and the means of communication improved almost out of knowledge, and munitions of every kind accumulated in adequate quantities. By experimental fire the Russian gunners had learned the ranges on the enemy's front with exactitude. The element of chance was eliminated, as far as it was possible. The 4th of June was, as it happened, a Sunday, and shortly after dawn the Russian guns opened the campaign with an intense bombardment of the entire Austro-German line, the shelling lasting for from twelve to thirty hours on the various parts of it according to the results obtained. An Austrian *communiqué* of that date reported that the Russian fire was especially violent in Volhynia, on the army of the Archduke Joseph Ferdinand near Olyka; in Galicia, northwest of Tarnopol, and on the Lower Strypa; and in the region of the Dniester. But the bombardment was intense everywhere; here and there, as at Okna across the Dniester, it completely flattened out the enemy's trenches, and its general effect elsewhere was to cut wide avenues through the serried rows of wire entanglements, thus providing open roads for the advance of the Russian infantry and, where practicable, cavalry. The official message of the Austrians also noted that Russian infantry attacks seemed to be imminent all along the line. Next day Petrograd announced that fighting had begun the previous morning "from the Pripet River front to the Rumanian frontier."

On the 5th and 6th of June, Brusiloff's offensive really began to develop in the most remarkable manner. On his extreme left flank his troops forced the Austrians to retire for three miles from their first lines of trenches near Okna on the former day, and gave General Lechitsky his opportunity in Bukovina. Also on that day and on the next, the Russians, on Brusiloff's right wing, having crumpled up the enemy's strongly fortified positions around Olyka, marched on rapidly towards Lutsk (Luck), and energetically beating down all opposition threw the Austro-Germans into such a panic that, abandoning their guns, they surrendered in thousands, whole regiments laying down their arms.

So great was the demoralization of the enemy, that General Kaledin, who was in command of the Russian operations in this quarter, was able to capture the fortress on the evening of the 6th of June with hardly an effort. The Archduke Joseph Ferdinand, the commander of the Fourth Austro-Hungarian Army, had fled from the place only two or three hours before the Russians entered it. In their flight the Austrians left behind them many of their heavy guns, without stopping to unload them, and vast quantities of material; they did not even try to clear the hospitals of their wounded. This was Brusiloff's first great triumph. Within sixty hours of the initiation of his offensive he was in a position to report to the Czar and Alexieff this very considerable gain, in addition to other, if less striking, successes on his whole front. Late that same night the Czar telegraphed his congratulations, and bade Brusiloff tell his troops that he was watching their bold deeds with pride and heartfelt gratitude.

Fighting all the way, Kaledin had advanced twenty-five miles in two and a half days, and he drove on without giving the defeated enemy a chance to recover. On the 7th and 8th he forced the passage of the Styr and its affluent, the Ikva, at many points. On the 8th and 9th he fought and won a fierce battle thirteen miles north of Lutsk at Rojische, a junction on the Rovno-Kovel railway, and the town at which was the chief crossing over the Styr. The day which saw the capture of the Rojische bridgehead, an action in which young, untried Russian troops gloriously distinguished themselves, also witnessed, farther south in Volhynia, the second great triumph of Brusiloff in the storming of the fortress of Dubno on the Ikva, the district in which Kaledin's army joined up and coöperated with that of General Sakharoff. Of the three fortresses known as the Volhynian Triangle Russia, in 1915, had retained only Rovno, and that she had kept it then was largely owing to the fine generalship and the characteristic aggressive resoluteness of Brusiloff, at that time one of Ivanoff's army commanders. Now the two other fortresses of the group were again in her possession. As was to be expected, there was much rejoicing in Russia over these signal victories, and the other Allies, beholding these unmistakable proofs of the renewed vigor and power of Russia, were greatly encouraged.

Nor did these successes stand alone. In Galicia, south of Burkanoff, General Shcherbacheff carried the line of the Olekhoviets by the 7th of June, captured the important town of Buczacz on the 8th, and thereafter pushed on some miles to the west of the Lower Strypa. In the region of the Dniester Lechitsky, developing his victorious assault on Okna, took by storm on the 11th, after five days of desperate fighting, the strong Austrian positions south of Dobronovtse, fourteen miles northeast of Czernovitz, and laid open the whole duchy of Bukovina.

In a week Brusiloff had gained several astounding victories. His general offensive had succeeded in four sectors —Lutsk, Dubno, Buczacz, and between the Dniester and the Pruth, and if it failed, as fail it did at the moment, in the district about Kolki on the Styr, and on the Upper Strypa, there remained a splendid balance of achievement, which came as a very unpleasant and unexpected shock to the arrogant calculations of Germany. The most disquieting result to her was the progress made by the Russians on the Styr, in the area of which Rojische and Lutsk might be regarded as centers, and on the Ikva, with Dubno as the pivotal point there. In front of these three towns respectively were three Austro-German bases, Kovel, Vladimir Volynsk, and Lemberg, the first and third being of the highest military significance, with the second not far behind in value; and all three were menaced.

In the second week of Brusiloff's offensive the menace grew much stronger. From Rojische the Russians by the end of that time had advanced to Svidnikhy on the Stokhod, and the threat to Kovel became intensified. Profoundly perturbed by the Russians' amazingly rapid and successful advance, Germany took steps to counter it by sending into the district large reënforcements of German troops, which she withdrew from Hindenburg's armies north of the Pripet and from the German Crown Prince's at Verdun. It certainly was high time for her to bestir herself. Kaledin was only a little over twenty miles from both Kovel and Vladimir Volynsk, while Sakharoff was about sixty miles from Lemberg. The Austrians transferred to this front all their reserves from the Trentino, and even brought up troops from Serbia and Albania.

It was chiefly against the Lutsk Salient that the Germans, who relegated their defeated Austrian and Hungarian friends to entirely subordinate positions of command, now proceeded to start a powerful and for a while not unsuccessful counter-offensive, under General Linsingen, about the 16th of June. Thanks to his superior railway facilities, the enemy was able to concentrate forces in strength sufficient to counter-attack Kaledin, and, with more powerful artillery than was at the latter's disposal, to check him.

On the 8th of July Kaledin broke through the Austro-German, or rather German, front, and two days afterwards was successful in a pitched battle at Svidnikhy, while he also struck a heavy blow at the enemy at Kieslin. A week later he repulsed a vigorous German attack near Sviniukhy. Then heavy rains interposed, and for a week or two operations became practically impossible, but as July came to an end Kaledin pushed Linsingen out of his heavily fortified positions at Trysten, four miles from the Stokhod, and forced him to the opposite side of the stream. A Berlin official statement admitted, for once, a serious defeat when it said that "the enemy succeeded in penetrating our lines at Trysten, and obliged us to evacuate the positions we still held in front of the Stokhod."

We now pass to review what Sakharoff achieved, far-

ther south in Galicia. In July Sakharoff's front extended
southwest of Lutsk, across to the Lipa, a western tributary
of the Upper Styr. A part of Linsingen's counter-offensive was a thrust from the southwest at Lutsk, and for it
he had concentrated strong forces, admirably gunned.
Guessing the enemy's plan, Sakharoff anticipated and absolutely defeated it by what the Russian High Command
officially characterized as a "clever maneuver." The Russians style the battle the Battle of Mikhailovka, and its chief
feature was that, forestalling the German move by a day,
Sakharoff suddenly and unexpectedly drove hard at Linsingen's flanks and crumpled them up. On the 16th of July
he broke Linsingen's left wing at Pustomity, and his right
near the mouth of the Lipa, not only foiling this counter-
offensive but completely smashing it to pieces. On the 20th
Linsingen, having somewhat recovered, thanks to reënforcements, attempted an attack, but was quickly checked by
Sakharoff, who on that same day and the following won
the great battle which the Russians have denominated the
Battle of Berestechko.

With scarcely a pause Sakharoff continued his victorious
progress. On the night of the 24th the third of the series
of his big operations was begun by his breaking through
the Austrian front on the river Slonuvka, an eastern affluent
of the Upper Styr, here flowing in Galicia. Attracting the
attention of the Austrians by a feint on Leznioff, he pressed
on with his main forces across the Slonuvka, a few miles
north of Brody, towards which town the Russians made
good progress next day. Early in the morning of the 28th
of July Sakharoff captured Brody, another heavy blow to
the enemy and an appreciable shortening of the distance of
the Russians from Lemberg.

General Lechitsky had perhaps had a harder task than
either Kaledin or Sakharoff in that he had more difficult
country to negotiate at the start. He had to break through
the fortified mountainous barrier of Eastern Bukovina, and
to get across the wide Dniester, but he did both. Only one
bridgehead on the Dniester—that at Uscieczko—was held
by the Russians on the 4th of June, but his heavy defeat of

the Austrians at Dobronovtse, previously mentioned, and his rapid movements thereafter westward, turned the nearer of the Austrian positions on the great river, as at Zalesczyki, and led to their being evacuated by the enemy after only a show of resistance. By the 11th of June one part of his forces had taken Horodenka, while another reached Sniatyn. A third column stormed the strong line of the Pruth, and on the 17th Czernovitz was captured, for the fifth time since the outbreak of the War, by the Russians.

Within the next week Lechitsky, by a fine fighting march at top speed, made himself master of Bukovina, a territory half as large as Wales. Pressing on from Sniatyn, he was the victor in a terrific battle, on the 28th of June, fought on the ground lying between the Dniester and the Pruth. Following fast on the heels of the beaten foe, he took Kolomea on the last day of the month and, steadily advancing westward as July opened, captured Delatyn on the 8th—he was now about seventy miles from his starting-point five weeks before.

Bothmer was now deeply outflanked in this southern area, but continuous heavy rains prevented Lechitsky from moving, and permitted the German general to hold his positions. Both the Dniester and the Pruth were flooded, the former rising ten and the latter sixteen feet. Not till the end of July was Lechitsky able to advance, and it was August before he got into motion on a big scale. About the 7th of the latter month, notwithstanding the most violent opposition, he stormed his way through Tlumacz to Tysmienitsa, took Niznioff, and occupied Ottynia. On the 9th he captured Chrpylin, only two miles from Stanislau, which fell into his hands next day, after an obstinate fight on the river Bystrzyca. The capture of Stanislau, a place of great strategical importance, ranks as one of the leading events of 1916. Bothmer's army on the Strypa was now effectively enveloped from the south, and two days after Lechitsky's occupation of the town Bothmer retreated from the ground he had held for nearly a year to the line of the Zlota Lipa.

On the 12th of August a statement was issued by the Russian High Command announcing the fall of the last sector of the powerfully fortified rampart which the enemy had erected from the Pripet as far as the Rumanian frontier during the preceding winter. "To-day," it said, "as the result of seven weeks of persistent effort on the part of the glorious troops of Generals Sakharoff and Shcherbacheff, under the direction of General Brusiloff, the whole line of the river Strypa fell into our hands. The entire sector of the winter base position established by the enemy in front of Tarnapol and Buczacz is in our possession."

With the retirement of Count Bothmer from the Strypa, Brusiloff's marvelous offensive reached a definite stage. In seventy days his splendid Russians had advanced on their 270-mile front from ten or twelve miles in the center to sixty and eighty miles respectively on the flanks, had fought and won a dozen great battles, and including Bukovina had reconquered several thousand square miles of territory. The capture of prisoners was simply colossal, the total figure exceeding 350,000 men, while in guns the Russians took over 400, many of them heavy pieces, as well as upwards of 1,300 machine guns.

### BY GENERAL ALEXEI BRUSILOFF

If there remain any Germans still hopeful for their cause, let them realize that to-day, when the Central Powers have lost the initiative and are finding a difficulty in refilling their ranks, Russia has not yet reached the zenith of her power, which will only be approached next year, when she will have the largest and best army since the beginning of the War. Next year we shall have material on an equality with the enemy and a superiority in human resources, which should steadily increase as long as the War endures. Our new levies which come in each year equal our best troops, and, as I believe, they are far superior to anything which the enemy can still find to send against us for next year's campaign.

To illustrate the desperate shortage of the German armies, I need only recall the well-established fact that four divisions were hurried here from France soon after June 4th, when our offensive began. These were the 19th and

20th, forming the 10th Active Corps, and the 11th Bavarian and 43rd Reserve Divisions. We were expecting the 44th Division, but it did not appear. As usual, the Germans had underrated French powers of resistance. Although 17 divisions remained before Verdun, the enemy found it impossible to move another man hither, and as soon as the British armies advanced all idea of transferring troops had to be abandoned. The units confronting us represented the maximum effort of Germany. They were moved about along the Russian front chiefly to the southward, in order to fill the gaps left by the fleeing Austrians.

### BY GENERAL A. VON CRAMON

On the 4th of June the great Russian attack began. It was stated on good authority that a decision was to be fought for in the East. Verdun, and particularly Tyrol, had forced upon the Entente the beginning of the fighting some weeks earlier than was expected.

Events crowded on events. On the northern wing the positions west of Rovno were lost. The report that Russian attacks had been repulsed followed hard on the news of the defeat. Our reserves had been used up with astonishing rapidity, but ineffectually. The ceaseless torrent poured westward. Lutsk with its notorious bridgehead fell. The Russian stood on the western bank of the Styr, and before him were only the shattered remnants of divisions.

On the southern wing a Russian attack pierced the front between the Dniester and the Pruth; whereupon one part withdrew to the west, the other crossed the Pruth.

In the center of the front the Army of the South alone maintained its ground.

Already on June 7th the Austrian Headquarters declared that the situation could not be maintained with the help of Austro-Hungarian troops alone. "After the experiences of the Fifth and the Sixth Armies, it is quite impossible to make any prediction regarding the Fourth Army." It had broken asunder west of Lutsk; the way to Vladimir-Volynsk was open. The Russian, however, did not pursue. Whether he overlooked the extent of his success—something that has happened to the attacker on every front,— whether he was anxious about his northern flank, or whether he did not have forces sufficient to continue the pursuit, these facts cannot be determined here. The point is that he missed his opportunity, wavered between taking the direction toward Lemberg or Kovel, and lost precious time.

Army hearquarters did not consider a suspension of the offensive in Italy. It invoked German aid, pointing out that the Russian attack appeared to be directed exclusively against the Austrian front, and that the German front contiguous to it on the north could spare troops. The high German command did not concur in this view. It maintained that it was engaged in waging heavy battles on the western front and, as could be shown, no Russian divisions had been removed from the German front in the East. The Austrian army headquarters should therefore relieve the situation, for which it was responsible, with its own troops.

The situation became graver, the call for aid more urgent, and the German high command, with a heavy heart and "with a temporary suspension and limitation of the aims on the Western front," was compelled to give up several divisions. On June 8th the respective chiefs of staff of the two armies met in Berlin. It was decided to relieve the situation by a counter-attack from the direction of Kovel. Germany supplied several additional divisions. From the Italian front the first troops moved to the East on June 11th. General Linsingen was put in command also of the Austrian Fourth Army. Archduke Joseph Ferdinand was replaced by General Tersztyansky.

After the surprising success of his first attack the Russian now began to bring the weight of his numerical preponderance to bear in the South. Ceaselessly his transport wagons rolled toward the Austro-Hungarian front. Several attacking groups were formed: against Kovel from the south and southeast, and against Lemberg from three concentric directions and south of the Dniester. The Austrian army headquarters still refused to believe in the necessity for the absolute termination of hostilities in Italy. The

order to this effect, indeed, was not given until June 18th.
A proud hope was thus relinquished. The Eastern front
now became a source of solicitude to all.

The counter-attack made from the direction of Kovel
succeeded, toward the end of June, in compressing somewhat the Russian offensive circle west of Lutsk, but soon
came to a standstill. The Russian again "had the floor."
In the beginning of July he penetrated the Styr circle, northwest of Rovno and forced the defender back behind the
Stokhod. The German high command had been opposed to
a voluntary evacuation. This, now enforced by the enemy,
cost many lives. The Russians were not successful in
proceeding farther, that is, across the Stokhod toward
Kovel. The front remained intact, even though it wavered
at times. It was a mistake on the part of the Russian
leaders to make their attack in the direction of Kovel directly against the point of greatest resistance. In the direction of Lemberg a success west of the Styr would have been
certain; against Kovel effective resistance would have suf-
ficed.

The attack on Lemberg was made from three directions:
west of the Styr; on both sides of the railroad via Brody;
and north of the railroad via Tarnopol.

As already stated, the territory affording the most effective direction for the thrust—that lying west of the Styr—
was not supplied with troops sufficient to secure more than
a partial success; the attack stopped at the Lipa. On both
sides of the railroad through Brody the Austro-Hungarian
First and Second Army, by the end of July, had been forced
back westwardly over Brody and beyond. North of the
Tarnopol railroad the Russian attack, at the beginning of
August, had advanced beyond the upper Sereth. German
troops had to assist in guarding Lemberg.

In the center of the front the Army of the South held
well. It bent back its wings so as not to lose touch, and
projected forward as a last bastion eastwardly into the
ranks of the onstorming Russians. Both leaders and troops
acquitted themselves admirably. Finally they also had to

give up their positions; voluntarily they withdrew behind the Zlota-Lipa.

South of the Dniester the westwardly retreating part of the Seventh Army was becoming more and more demoralized. A counter-attack by German troops on the north wing in the direction of Obertyn was indeed successful, but could not change the situation. The defense had to be transferred back west of Stanislau, because demoralized detachments, yielding to every attack, exposed the flanks and rear of bravely struggling troops. The valuable oil district of Boryslaw was seriously menaced. And now the Russian repeated his mistake of relinquishing his attack on the position offering the weakest resistance and diverting it against parts of the front more strongly defended. He transferred part of his forces northwardly across the Dniester and attacked the Army of the South.

The divisions of the Seventh Army retreating across the Pruth toward the southwest and south, had fallen back into the Carpathian Mountains. The Russian was undecided as to where he should bring the greatest pressure of his pursuit to bear. Finally the pressure which he brought to bear against the Carpathians became so strong and the danger of an invasion of Hungary with its resultant effect on Rumania so urgent, that German and Austro-Hungarian reinforcements had to be employed in counter-attacks. These troops took the passes of the Carpathians firmly in hand, compelled the Russians also to send forces into the mountains, and so relieved the Stanislau front.

The Russian massed attack, the main features of which have been described in the foregoing, did not make any further notable progress. It succeeded in reaching neither Kovel nor Lemberg. The defense, however, had been successful only because 20 German divisions in all had been brought here, notwithstanding the fact that the Battle of the Somme had been raging since July 1st on the Western front. The resources of the Central Powers had been taxed to the utmost. The Russian attack was checked just at the right moment: the Rumanians arrived too late.

NARRATIVE OF A POLISH LANDOWNER NEAR CZERNOVITZ

During the night of June 12th-13th terrific artillery fire was heard in the town. Somewhere near a battle was raging. For the third or fourth time since the beginning of the war we were passing through that experience. I went to the army-command to ask advice. A staff-captain had just arrived with news from the front. The Austrian troops were resisting. Still, after the front between the Dniester and Pruth had once been broken there was no other natural line for resistance. According to the accounts of the Austrian officers, the Russian artillery was, with magnificent bravery, driving up to new positions, thus preventing our men from entrenching and preparing a new line.

"How long can we hold out?" was my question. The old general looked at me and answered: "Only our rear-guards are now engaged; our forces are gathering a few miles from here. If our flank near Horodenka holds out overnight we shall not evacuate the town."

I returned to Sniatyn. Small groups of inhabitants were standing about the streets, commenting on the news. Artillery and ammunition were at full speed passing through the town for the front. A few regiments of infantry marched through at night. The horizon was red with the glow of fires. For the third time our poor villages were burning. Whatever had survived previous battles was now given up to the flames. Homeless refugees, evacuated from the threatened villages, were passing with their poor, worn-out horses and their cows—all their remaining wealth. In perfect silence; no one complained; it had to be. Mysterious cavalry patrols and dispatch-riders were riding through the streets. No one slept that night.

In the morning the first military transports passed through the town. The retreat had begun. Questions were asked. The Magyar soldiers quietly smoked their pipes; there was no way for us of understanding one another. Only one of them, who knew a few German words, explained, *"Russen, stark, stark, Masse"* (Russians, strong, strong, a great mass). The approaching violent fire of heavy guns was even more enlightening. Our trained ears could distinguish their voices. Like a continuous thunder was the roar of the Japanese [Russian] guns; at intervals they were answered nervously by the Austrian artillery.

Suddenly the gun-fire stopped and the expert ear could catch the rattling of machine guns. The decisive attack had begun. All a-strain, we were awaiting news. Some soldiers appeared round the corner of the road, slightly wounded. Then a panic began. Some one had come from a neighboring village reporting that he had seen Cossacks. Soon refugees from the villages outside were streaming through the town. General confusion. Children were crying, women sobbing. A mass flight began. Again cavalry and dispatch-riders. Then a drum was heard in the square. It was officially given out that the situation was extremely grave and that whoever wished to leave the town had better do so immediately.

We had to go. As I was mounting the carriage I perceived in the distance, near the wood on the hill, a few horsemen with long lances—Cossacks from Kuban. They were slowly emerging from the forest and approaching the town. "Drive ahead!" I shouted to the coachman.

### NARRATIVE OF AN AUSTRIAN CITIZEN OF CZERNOVITZ

Even the fatal day of June 4th was still meant to be at Czernovitz a day of festivities. The town was beflagged as "an Imperial Eagle in Iron" (*ein Reichsaar in Eisen*) was unveiled at the *Rathaus* "in memory of the time of Russian invasion" (*zur Erinnerung an die Russenzeit*). The wide town-square was filled with people, and General von Pflanzer-Baltin himself was expected. But then in the afternoon, whilst the artillery fire in the north, in the direction of Okna and Dobronovtse, was getting louder and louder, a dispatch-rider arrived with the following message, which was read out to the expectant crowds in the square: "His Excellency General von Pflanzer-Baltin is prevented from taking part in the festivities of to-day, and gives notice of his absence."

Six days later crowds were again filling the town square

—no longer to "commemorate" the Russian occupation of Czernovitz. On Saturday, June 10th, at 6 p. m., military transports began to traverse the main streets of the town, moving from the direction of the bridgehead of Zhuchka towards Starozhyniets. It was an interminable chain of all kinds of vehicles, from huge, heavy motor lorries down to light gigs driven by army officers. The waves of war were rolling through the city.

As if at a given sign the town square filled with people. Frightened, searching eyes were asking for an explanation. Terrifying news began to circulate, the excited imagination of the crowd was at work. Mysterious information was passed from mouth to mouth, yet no one knew anything definite. A fever got hold of the town. With bags, boxes and baskets people were hurrying to the railway station. "Is an evacuation-train leaving, and when?" they were asking with the persistence of desperation. The hours were moving slowly, and the night came over the city, full of despondency and gloom.

And still the endless military transports were traversing the streets. But no longer was any notice taken of them. The guns were playing, the excitement was growing. At 7 p. m. the civilian authorities received the order of evacuation. Everything was to be ready for the train at 6 a. m. which, besides Government property, was to carry off the railway employees and their families.

The coffee-houses were filling with people. All Government officials put on their uniforms, all Government authorities, even the police, granted leave to their employees, demanding no more than a show of the performance of official duties. The town corporation paid out to its officers two months' salaries and sent them off to Sutchava, where all the evacuated Government authorities were going. No official was, however, to leave the Bukovina without permission.[1]

[1] The fact which naturally is not mentioned in this account is that, before leaving the town, the Austrian authorities arrested a number of prominent citizens of Russian or Rumanian nationality—among them the Greek-Orthodox Archbishop, Dr. Repta—and carried them away to Dorna Vatra, and subsequently farther on to the interior.

Suddenly—no one knows how—the news spread that the army group of General Papp had evacuated its positions and was retreating. Even the hour of the event was known. The information was correct. The greatest optimists now gave up all hope. The safety of the Bukovina was closely connected with the name of General Papp.

The gray dawn found the city in full flight. The streets were filled with crowds, the tramcars were carrying wounded soldiers, as at the order of the army command the evacuation of the military hospitals had been started. The square before the railway station was closely packed with people, but the police were admitting only railway officials. The women were begging, crying, lifting up their children. They had to wait—that train was not meant for them.

At 8 a. m. the first evacuation train left the city. The next was due at noon, or at 3 p. m. Many people preferred to fly by foot, as the prices of cabs and cars had risen to an incredible height. The artillery fire was drawing closer and closer, and above the heads of the crowd appeared a Russian aviator. Their hearts were shaking with fear.

The prices of goods in the town were falling rapidly. Tobacco and cigarettes, which previously were hardly to be had anywhere, were offered at half-price without any restrictions. Women from the suburbs who, not knowing what had happened, had brought their vegetables to the market, were selling them for a third of the usual price, only to be able to return to their homes and children. For the merchants in Czernovitz the evacuation was a catastrophe. As they had been supplying the army with goods, they had gathered stores valued at millions of crowns. None of them could be carried away; only Government property was being removed.

The news that the town would soon come under fire led to a sheer panic. The crowd in front of the station was seized with frenzy. Against the resistance of the officials it forced its way into the station and invaded a half-empty military train. The same happened in the case of the next train, and to all the following ones. In the course of Sunday 6 to 8,000 people left Czernovitz.

## HUNGARIAN ACCOUNT OF THE RUSSIAN RAIDS INTO HUNGARY

In the Bukovina the fighting continues to be very stubborn, especially on the western bank of the Moldava and between the Rumanian and Hungarian frontiers. The Russian objective in fighting these battles is to establish a line which will enable them to proceed against Hungary. The Russians are only employing their Caucasian divisions, and these are divided into small reconnoitering units, sometimes three hundred and sometimes a thousand strong. The smaller ones, under N.C.O.'s, advance along the narrow mountain passes and paths, and when they encounter enemy detachments, whatever their strength, they attack them, thus drawing as many troops as possible from the other sectors to these wild regions. One of these Russian units succeeded in crossing the Hungarian frontier and in penetrating into the country for about twenty miles. They encountered, however, a superior force, and after a regular battle lasting for many hours withdrew, only to appear at another point the next day. This seemingly unimportant incursion into Hungarian territory by a small band of Russian cavalrymen set many thousands of people on the move, and the refugees are still pouring southwards. Since then similar raids have taken place every day, and now the Russians appear sometimes in three different places simultaneously. It was noticed that in these minor engagements the Cossacks put their wounded comrades on their horses and took them away with them. In some cases they even carried off their dead.

The assault on the Kapul heights in this region was conducted in a novel manner. On one side of the heights the infantry attacked in columns, and on the other the cavalry dashed up. These attacks were particularly fierce. The infantry were almost as quick in gaining the summits as the cavalry, the latter having at times to climb steep places, and offering naturally a much better target than the infantry. In fact, Russian cavalrymen have shown marvelous aptitude in the fighting in this most difficult region.

# THE CLIMAX OF THE VERDUN FIGHT

## THE BATTLES FOR LE MORT HOMME, FORT VAUX AND THIAUMONT

JUNE-JULY

GABRIEL HANOTAUX                EDWIN GREWE
NARRATIVES BY PARTICIPANTS
MARSHAL JOFFRE          GENERAL VON LUDENDORFF

Perhaps never elsewhere has man's fierce love of battle been roused to such a frenzied height as at Verdun. No outside account of the struggle could portray this as do the narratives herewith, told by the men who actually fought there. Their passions had exalted them to an ecstatic state scarce to be described as human. Germany had indeed brought into existence "supermen"—though in a fashion she had little reckoned on.

The general meaning of the stupendous battle is here explained by M. Hanotaux, France's most celebrated historian. An outline of its chief events is then given by the British historian, Edwin Grewe. Then comes the official German view. Germany's supreme chief of staff at the time was General Falkenhayn. Verdun was his last battle; for, as its failure became manifest to German eyes, he was superseded by the mighty Hindenburg.

The real story of this deadliest of all battles is, however, best told in the personal narratives that here follow. Verdun became the awesome and eternally unforgetable event it was, not because of any specific consequence or result achieved, but because of the individual intensity displayed in will and action. From whatever stimulus the sacrifice arose there was, upon either side, a most supreme concentration of effort, a complete surrender of self-interest, in devotion to the State.

In its second and most desperate stage the Verdun struggle reopened on May 20th with huge German assaults upon Le Mort Homme (Dead Man's Hill) west of the Meuse River. The next day equally tremendous fighting broke out east of the Meuse on the scene of the earlier battling around Fort Douaumont. Slowly and at enormous cost the Germans won possession of both these heights. By June they began an equally terrible series of attacks on Fort Vaux, the next neighbor to Douaumont. By July they had hammered onward a few rods further and were attacking the villages of Fleury and Thiaumont. These marked the high tide of the German advance. They were taken and retaken day after day. Thiaumont, or the hole in the earth which once was Thiaumont, is reckoned to have changed hands twenty-one times before its final recapture made it French forever.

BY GABRIEL HANOTAUX

THE persistent attack upon Verdun gave increasing proof each day of the importance the Germans attached to the enterprise. The French soldier, the "soldier of Verdun," should be told the causes of this desperation in attack; thus he will be convinced that he not only fights for the ground he holds and the honor of victory, but that he defends, at the price of his blood, the very life of France.

Each minute throughout these long months and each sod of that earth presents a unit of our national existence. By each act, each moment of suffering, our soldiers are preparing the conditions which will win for us a liberating peace. They are the creators of the future. With cannon shots, and rifles, with bayonet thrusts, and grenades, they are destroying, bit by bit, the "grand German plan." The Kaiser decided to risk his highest stakes upon this card; he entrusted to his soldiers at Verdun the supreme ambition of Germany. If this attack failed, the whole Pan-German scheme must crumble and be prostrate on the earth. The monster has no longer any hope except to prolong its death agony.

From the opening of the war the German plan has aimed chiefly at Verdun. The Crown Prince was placed at the head of its assailants, because the decisive victory was reserved for him. The movement in Belgium was to turn the flank of the adversary; but to conquer him the Germans depended—in accordance with the principles of the elder Moltke—upon the offensive in the center.

The principal force of the French Army has been in the east from the beginning, and it is still that frontier which popular instinct calls the "iron frontier." Verdun is there the apex of resistance, it is the tooth piercing the live flesh of the foe. Without Verdun the German army advancing on Paris could have no free communication with Germany. Without Verdun there could be no sure protection for Metz. Ever since that ancient treaty that divided the heritage of the sons of Charlemagne, Verdun has been the disputed point around which has pivoted the history of France and

Germany.   Verdun is the name that one finds again and again on every page of our history.

Topographically Verdun presents two incomparable advantages for the German attack.   It commands the valley of the Meuse, and thus becomes the "hinge" between the eastern and northern provinces.   We have no way of liberating our country from German servitude except to hold on until death to this central position.   There is no other line of communication between Lille and Nancy.   To allow the line of the Meuse River to be crushed would be to wipe from our history the battle of the Catalonian Fields, the battle of Valmy, our eternal defense of the Argonne, and even the battle of the Marne itself.   For this last great victory was but a repetition of its glorious predecessors.

The geographic value of Verdun is balanced, as we now know from the luminous writings of M. Engerand, by an economic value no less powerful and no less terrible to lose. Germany cannot remain mistress of the world's metal industries, unless she can keep and extend her possession of the minerals of the French province of Briey, and the neighboring regions.   German metallurgists declare that Germany could not have continued the War if she no longer controlled the iron ore of Lorraine.   German experts declare that so long as these mines are threatened by the cannon of Verdun, so long will the economic and military destiny of Germany remain at the mercy of French dominion.   We are in a position to affirm positively that one of the chief reasons for the War has been the desire to conquer the Briey basin, to seize the strategic key of that immeasurable wealth —Verdun!

The reiterated determination of the Germans to conquer at this point may be gathered from their own avowals. In the first campaign of the War the plan was to capture Verdun; and because Verdun did not fall the German Army had to substitute the war of trenches for the war of maneuvers.   We have their own statements on this subject.   One of their historians, Gottlieb Egelhaaf, wrote: "If the Crown Princes of Bavaria and Prussia had been able to take Verdun in August-September, 1914, and thus pierce the line of the

Meuse, the German armies would have broken through to Paris in that first movement. But the Princes remained nailed at Verdun; so the supreme commander had to withdraw the right wing of the German Army. The Germans retired from the Marne as far back as the Aisne. Because Verdun could not be taken, it became necessary to change the plan of the war."

Is that clear? Do we need any more striking proof? If so, let us recall the telegram addressed by the Kaiser to the parliament of Brandenburg, in which he celebrated the taking of Verdun, which he mistakingly believed to be an accomplished fact: "I rejoice greatly in the new and grand examples of Brandenburg energy and faithfulness even unto death which the sons of that province have furnished in the last few days, by their irresistible assault upon the powerful fortress of our chief enemy."

He really thought, and so did the rest of Germany, that the taking of Verdun was the closing of the war, a decisive German victory. The desperate resistance of our soldiers, "the French victory of Verdun," has been and will be for him and his followers the supreme disillusionment.

That is why our magnificent corps of leaders and our army now responding so nobly to their appeals, realize that at Verdun, as at the Marne, we must conquer or perish. Marshal Joffre voiced these unanimous sentiments in his telegram sent at the time of his famous order of the day on the Meuse: "The evening of the same day, the 25th, the Commander-in-Chief sent to General Pétain, then taking command, the following order: 'Yesterday, the 24th, I gave orders to hold the right bank of the Meuse, north of Verdun. Any commander who gives an order to retreat will be court-martialed.'"

### BY EDWIN S. GREWE

By the end of April the Germans had been pushed back from the base of the Mort Homme, and the safety of that position seemed so far assured as to justify the view that the Germans had arrived at the point of recognizing their failure.

With the beginning of May these theories were blown to fragments by the reawakening roar of the German howitzers, the prelude to a renewal on a greater scale of the fighting which had already lasted between two and three months. More guns had been brought up, old divisions had been reorganized, new divisions thrown in. There was now no idea of surprise: the German purpose was to smash in the French front by weight and determination. It might cost half a million German soldiers and run the stores of ammunition low; but the French must pay the price too; and it might be a price which they could afford the less. The German Intelligence Department knew probably quite well that they had some time to spare before this murderous game of hammer and tongs could be interrupted by an effective intervention on the British-held sectors of their line. The first blow was struck at the left bank of the Meuse again. Instead of attempting to storm the Mort Homme directly the German Staff aimed at securing Hill 304, which lies west of the Mort Homme and the Meuse. If this hill could be freed of Frenchmen and German batteries established on it, the Mort Homme position could be caught by a flanking fire, and the whole ridge of the Côte de l'Oie, on the west side of the river, would fall into German hands. Doubtless the Germans knew the enterprise would be costly. They were prepared with the price.

The plan of attack was extremely simple. The Germans themselves compared it to the strokes of a wood-cutter, who hacks alternately at each side of the trunk of a tree, and at each blow drives the ax farther in, till the tree totters. Thus on the left side of the trunk—the western side of the Meuse—each blow strove to bite through the Mort Homme position. On the eastern bank the assaults were symmetrically reversed. The blows of the ax sometimes fell between Douaumont and the river, but more often on its eastern side, towards Fort Vaux.

After three days' preparation three simultaneous attacks were made on the flanks of the main position at midday on May 7th. One was directed against Hill 287, which is a northwesterly spur of Hill 304; another against the Avocourt Wood positions (west), and a third against the defenses of the ravine between Hill 304 and the Mort Homme. A bitter fight went on all day and all night. At great expenditure the Germans made some headway towards the eastern ravine; and they claimed that they had captured the whole system of trenches on the northern slopes of Hill 304. The French certainly no longer attempted to hold that system, because, owing to the steepness of the slopes, their artillery firing over the hill from its southern side could not command them. They held the crest, and tactically the Germans had made very little headway, while the crest could be swept by French fire. The convincing testimony to a German failure is that they made no attempt at once to push their advantage, as they always did when it was a real one. The action was broken off.

The main part of their failure was on the French left, the Avocourt Wood, which the French, realizing its importance, had bought at a stiff price some time before. The next German attempt was therefore made here, with a view to easing the prospects of another flank attack on Hill 304. They made two heavy cuts at it on the evenings of May 17th and 18th, but the ax did not bite deep enough, and lost a good deal of its edge. But all the while new divisions were pouring in, and the Avocourt attack spread eastwards, and continued to spread till the whole of the battle front from the wood to the river was involved. While the attack was kept up on the Avocourt and Hill 304 defenses, the chief weight of the blows fell again on the Mort Homme. Part of the main assault aimed at the ravine between Hill 304 and the Mort Homme, through which the Esnes brook ran; the other part synchronizing with it strove to cut in behind the Mort Homme on the river side. The troops of a German division newly brought up were told off to push through the latter attack from the northeast, to carry Crow's Wood and Les Caurettes, and to join up with the thrust from the northwest.

Sixty German batteries played this double assault in. The new divisions on the Crow's Wood side had little success, though the French trenches had melted under the German bombardment. The Germans occupied the first line with some loss; to the second line they fought their way with a determination undeterred by the machine-gun fire and melinite which barred their way; but they could not hold the second line, and supports were unavailing. The contemporaneous attack made on the west of the Mort Homme got farther. It was an attack made with a resolution which was the high-water mark reached by the best German fighting material. The slight V-shaped wedge which the Germans had already made between Hill 304 and the Mort Homme they widened and deepened to a big U-shaped depression, which on its right-hand side was planted in French trenches south and southwest of the hill the enemy sought. The Germans paid a heavy bill for this advantage, which looks so small on a map, but which had nevertheless solid tactical value, for the Mort Homme was no longer a possession solely French.

For some days the battle on the west side of the Meuse paused—if such a struggle can ever be said to pause for a moment—while the Germans gathered themselves together for another effort, and the French deliberately extended the area of conflict by a great counter-attack on the other side of the river at Douaumont. This counter-attack was an episode in the history of Verdun, but it was also one of the most daring tactical strokes of the French Higher Command.

Douaumont, since the day in February when it was described, in the same German *communiqué* that prematurely reported its capture, as the northeastern pillar of the defenses of Verdun, had been a critical point of conflict. The capture by the Kaiser's Brandenburgers had proved of exaggerated value, since it no longer implied command of the ridge on which it stood, but it had the great usefulness of furnishing an observation post, and of enabling any force which could establish itself there to sweep the approaches to Vaux, the next fort to the southeast of it. On May 22nd the French made their first dash to shake it. The Crown Prince was at this moment preoccupied with the assault on the other bank of the river, where the new attack on the

Mort Homme and the neighboring ridges was eating up men. General Nivelle, who had succeeded General Pétain [given command of the central group of armies] at the beginning of May, entrusted the operation to General Mangin and to the Fifth Division. The Fifth Division had been in the Vaux-Douaumont sector when the German assault on Verdun rose to what was then believed to be its culminating pitch of violence, and had then been withdrawn to refit their sorely tried and depleted ranks. When they went on leave and to billets for this purpose General Mangin told them to prepare for further battles. "You march under the wings of Victory," said he. Five weeks later they came back to justify his confidence.

The French prepared the attack by two days' bombardment of the battered fort; and they heralded the assault with a device of deadly usefulness. It was a new bomb for the destruction of "sausage," or observation, balloons, and it was so successful that a few minutes after the aëroplanes had been launched to pepper the German observers with them, six of the German sausage balloons had exploded, and the German artillery was thus temporarily and partially blindfolded. But the significance of the act, joined to the bombardment, was not lost on the enemy, who began to pour a flood of precautionary shrapnel on the lines where the French were in waiting. The Fifth Division waited patiently till nearly midday. They had been divided into three sections for their task; the middle section were to strike directly for the ruins of the fort, the others for the trenches which flanked and protected it to right and to left. They went forward together at the appointed minute, and they moved with great swiftness from shell-hole to shell-hole. In eleven minutes the 129th Regiment in the center had reached Douaumont Fort across three lines of trenches, and had lit a Bengal flare to signal their arrival. On the left the 36th Regiment had carried out its part of the task, and held the road which led from Douaumont to Fleury. The sappers began now to come in behind the infantry, and got into the fort to block its exits, while the infantry in possession covered the 36th Infantry in its task of destroying the flanking positions.   All was going well on this side of Douaumont.   On the eastern side matters did not prosper so fast or so fully.   The 74th Regiment had been held up by a galling fire from the German communication trenches, and though German prisoners were being sent back from the fort to the French lines, in the northeast corner the enemy still held out—and the German counter-attack, as the French Command well knew, was bound to come.   So, restraining their men from pushing on, the French in possession strengthened their hold as much as they could, and all that night fought hand-to-hand combats with Germans grimly holding the passages of the uncaptured corner.

The Germans massed for their counter-attack in Haudremont Wood, and on the morning of the 23rd poured in their turn all the artillery fire at their command on the fort and the French-held trenches.   They sent their infantry forward on top of the bombardment, but repeated assaults failed. All day long the 129th Regiment held on; while fresh German troops were brought up.   They were too few to hold it; their work had been done—its hardest part began with the dawn of the 23rd—and at last orders had to be given to withdraw them.   Two Bavarian Divisions were sent up by the Germans at the close of the day, and by the 24th the ruins of Douaumont had again changed hands—for the last time but one.

The counter-thrust had served its turn, but it had not diverted the Germans from the pursuit of their other attack on the western bank.   On May 23rd they began an attack on the complementary positions of Hill 304 and the Mort Homme, such as transcended the previous one as an attack in force transcends a reconnoissance, and the violence of which may be estimated by its duration through six days. But if the German effort this week in May rose to greater heights than ever before, it met with a resistance that was less penetrable and more scientific than before.   The French had learned the lessons of Verdun, and were at this time evolving that coöperation between the artillery barrage and the infantry's rifles which, powerful though they proved it in defense, was to become a more deadly weapon when employed offensively on the Somme. The 75's, beautiful weapons though they were, could not stop the waves of German soldiers whose lives their leaders were willing to expend with such prodigality; but the melinite shells of the French heavies, when massed as Pétain and Nivelle massed them, could do so. This barrage stayed the German rushes in bloody confusion east of the Mort Homme on the first day; but between Hill 304 and the Mort Homme the residual onrush of the German waves got through the curtain of fire, and on to the first French trench lines. *Flammenwerfer* were brought up, and the Germans burnt their way in by liquid flame. A French counter-attack threw them out at nightfall: renewed German attacks continued through the night.

While the French were fully occupied with holding on to the Mort Homme and Hill 304 gap with tooth and claw, two fresh German Divisions were flung at the point east of the Mort Homme where the village of Cumières blocked the way. There was little *finesse* about the German method; a few hours' bombardment were followed by waves of infantry; when they returned broken the bombardment was resumed till it was judged time to send in new waves. By this elementary but resistless expenditure of shells and men the Germans, on May 24th, got through, and reaped the interest on their outlay. For when the line at Cumières was broken the Germans had nothing there to stop them, and they poured on through the disarrayed French defenders till they got right down to Chattancourt.

The cup seemed to be at the German lips; but once again the French counter-attack, as automatic as the recoil of a gun, dashed it away. The French infantry in reserve bore down on the Germans with a ferocity that would not be denied, and fought them back to Cumières, where they held them through the night of the 24th. The Germans could not again get up the momentum to carry the outskirts, and the French exchanged rushing for bombing, winning here a barn and there a cellar or part of a ruined street. After three days of this two assaulting columns were brought up by the French, and fought their way onward on either side of the village, taking the mill, and bringing back the line to near the point where it had bent and broken.

The Germans counter-attacked, but their counter-attack was not a recoil. It was a blow struck with all the force at the German command, and though aimed at a wider front than the village, and with a greater object, it comprised the Cumières-Mort Homme sector, and made it the chief one. The first attack began on the evening of May 28th. It did not get through the curtain fire, nor did the second attack. The task then passed to the German heavy artillery for twelve hours, as a preparation for next day; and next day five new divisions went forward on the heels of the destruction wrought by the artillery fire. But great as that destruction had been it was not enough. The first-line trenches at the French center no longer existed, for it was there that the German fire had been heaviest. Here the Germans had their greatest measure of success. But summed up this did not amount to a great deal. The French had to abandon the summit of the Mort Homme, as the wedge between it and Hill 304 was deepened, and they established themselves on the western and southern slopes. The crest of the Mort Homme remained untenable by either side. At Cumières the Germans could not materially improve their position. Consequently at the end of the week's battle the Germans had won advantages which were insignificant from a territorial point of view, and which could only be regarded as important tactically if they could be pushed home. They could not be pushed home; and at the end of May the French line, running from Avocourt Wood over Hill 304, along the south of Mort Homme to the Bois de les Caurettes and the remains of Cumières, was as capable of offering resistance to further attacks as heretofore.

On the other bank the Germans began a more piecemeal reduction, which, though less magnificent in aim, was more valuable in moral effect. Failing to place their occupation of the ridge on the west of the Meuse beyond dispute, they determined to hack at the flank of the Douaumont plateau from the east, advancing up the wooded coombes by which the plateau declines to the eastern plain. The first step was to capture Fort Vaux. Fort Vaux is situated on the edge of the ravine which lies between Vaux hill and the triple southerly bastions of the Douaumont plateau, and had to be carried before any further operations east of the Meuse were undertaken. The Germans had other reasons than these tactical ones for bringing to bear on its capture all the resources they could command. If anything was to be done at Verdun it must be done quickly, in order to anticipate or to precipitate the Franco-British push which was in preparation at some other part of the line.

On June 1st, therefore, the attack on Fort Vaux was launched, preceded by a bombardment of "extreme intensity." The assault was calculated to encircle the fort by attacks from the northeast and the northwest, as at the Mort Homme. The first of these attacks, advancing under cover of the heavy artillery, spread out from Haudremont Wood and over the Douaumont plateau down to the innermost of the triple-wooded spurs. This was the Bois de la Caillette or Caillette Wood. The Germans seized it, and on the next day (June 2nd), descending from it into the ravine, began the direct attack on Fort Vaux. At the same time they set in motion their attack from the northeast, and captured the village of Damloup, which is in the ravine on the other or southern side of Fort Vaux. The northern attacking party tried to rush the fort. They were blown back by the guns; but more and more men were brought up to the task, and late at night a brave party of them got into the fort ditch. Here these desperate men remained for four days, unable to enter the fort.

Their courage and their plight found many parallels in the defense of elements of isolated French trenches, where men held on under a pitiless bombardment day after day without water, and with the most shadowy prospect of relief. This individual heroism went on east and west of Vaux, and meanwhile the attack on the fort developed, and developed in a new way. The Germans had learned from their failure in March that it was extravagantly hopeless to try to encircle the fort with infantry; they therefore fed their flank attacks with fresh troops, and maintained so heavy an artillery barrage on the southern slopes of the fort that no troops could get up to succor it. The whole of the southern approaches were closed by this wall of bursting steel; the fort itself was beaten into a ruin. Yet in it a tiny garrison under Major Raynal continued to resist. They could not get out except at the risk of being blown to pieces at every step they took in the open; they could communicate with their own lines only by signal, and imperfectly. The heroism of Fort Vaux's defense became the symbol of all that Frenchmen did and endured there. As on the "little *Revenge*" in Sir Richard Grenville's day, the cry was to fight on, though men were dying of thirst and wounds, and every hour renewed danger and anguish and death. The Germans advanced on the higher levels of the walls, but the Frenchmen organized the débris of the fort. At every window, behind every heap of bricks, machine guns were placed, or the picked shots took refuge and shot down every enemy who set foot in the courtyard. The Germans, with renewed ingenuity, tried to blast the defenders out with grenades, letting basketfuls of them down by ropes to the level of the windows and swinging them in with a time fuse to burst inside.

The fight went on. The limit to human endurance was not reached till June 6th, when Major Raynal got out his last message: "We are near the end. Officers and soldiers have done their whole duty. *Vive la France!*" A few soldiers, among them wounded, escaped through a grating and crawled towards the French lines; others who had sought to escape with them were killed on the way. Fort Vaux fell on the same day in a renewal of the bombardment. Its defense was one of the greatest testimonies to that spirit of cold unflinching endurance which before the war we associated so little with France, but of which they showed us at Verdun an example the peer of any in our own history. Major Raynal, though a prisoner, was promoted to the rank of Commander in the Legion of Honor; the Germans gave him back his sword—one act, at any rate, to be reckoned to the credit of the Crown Prince.

The fall of Vaux came too late for the Germans. In the

exaltation of Raynal's defense the moral effect of its loss on the French was negligible. Its value to the Germans, judged by the standard of its indispensability if any further attack was to be made on the eastern Verdun lines, was considerable; on the other hand, it had not fallen soon enough to assume the character of a dangerous gap in the defenses. These defenses were now drawn anew on a line from Hill 321 (which is a mile north of the Froide Terre Ridge) through Thiaumont Redoubt, Fleury village, and the woods of Chapitre and Fumin. It then curled round through the woods of Chenois and La Laufée, which look past Damloup eastwards to the plain below. These must be turned or conquered to approach Forts Souville or Tavannes, part of the inner lines of defenses. From Verdun on this side the Germans were now less than four miles away.

There was a long pause after the fall of Fort Vaux before the Germans gathered themselves together for this new effort. Then, conscious that time was growing short and the need of a superlative effort was vital, they began an attack which retained unchanged all the old weight and violence. On June 12th they had tested the nature of the new French defenses by an attack on the lines from Thiaumont Farm to Hill 321. A road runs southwest from Douaumont Fort through Thiaumont Farm to the Côte de Froide Terre. A main German attack was bound to come along the line of this road. Fighting took place to east and west of it. The Germans made some advance on the slopes of Hill 321. Thiaumont Redoubt was unscathed. They tried again on the 15th, having found that the Thiaumont Redoubt was the key of the position. Then on the 18th and 19th their major attack developed.

It bore down in the three prescribed directions: (1) upon Ridge 321; (2) Thiaumont Redoubt; (3) Fleury village. The Thiaumont position bore the brunt of it, and over a front of just over a mile it was assailed by three divisions. But this was not till June 23rd, when the attack had fully developed, and the whole line had been hotly engaged for four days. The great attack began at eight in the morning; seven hours afterwards a slight break was made in the line, just east of Thiaumont, and into the gap the Germans flung men with promptitude and burst right through. They had got Thiaumont; but they had not then got Fleury. They reached the village, and were thrown out. It was not till the 25th that they had driven a wedge in the French positions and, widening it as before, gained the village. The gap was now wide indeed: but before they could exploit their success at Fleury the French had counter-attacked, had reached and held the outskirts, and were reorganizing their line. On June 23rd General Nivelle in an Army Order had told his soldiers that this was the supreme German assault before the enemy in their turn would be assailed, and *"Ils ne passeront pas, Camarades!"* They did not pass: the Army of Verdun kept its honor intact.

The hour was fast approaching when the beginning of the combined operations by the British and French armies on the Ancre and the Somme was to compel the Germans to put a period to their endeavor to wear the French down at Verdun. The Somme battle began on July 1st, and drew an ever-increasing number of German divisions into its furnace. Though the Germans loudly asserted that the French were mistaken if they thought the pressure on Verdun would be relaxed, guns and men were steadily if stealthily withdrawn, and ultimately it was pressure from the French side which broke through the German defenses, and compelled the relinquishment of gains which the Germans had so hardly won. Their last attempt to demonstrate their indifference to the attack on the Somme was made between July 11th and 15th, when they attacked on an extending front from Fleury to Damloup. Their chief aim was to burst out from Fleury and, striking along the southeasterly road, break up the French organization between the Thiaumont works and the defenses of Fort Souville. This raid in force progressed some distance before it was stopped; but stopped it was, and by the 15th General Nivelle was in a position to strike back. He entrusted the counter-thrust to General Mangin, who was what the British would have called a "thruster" of the General Foch school. Mangin attacked Fleury furiously, and the Germans, instead of being able to develop their success with a new assault on Fort Souville, found themselves battling to hold on to their positions. They resisted with an almost indignant determination, and Fleury and the Thiaumont work changed hands several times in the succeeding weeks. The French won Fleury on August 3rd: the Germans regained a footing there, and clung on till August 10th. Thiaumont work changed hands time after time; the ruins of Fleury were not irrevocably French till August 18th. A little more than a fortnight afterwards the German attack flickered up once more for the last time. Instead of taking the southeast road from Fleury to Fort Souville, they came along the road that runs southwest from Fort Vaux to join it. This attack of September 3rd shared the fate of its predecessors, a slight advance immediately extinguished by a counter-attack, and for six weeks there-after the Verdun front relapsed into snipings and regular-ized exchanges of artillery fire.

### BY A FRENCH VETERAN OFFICER
Account of the Attacks on Le Mort Homme from May 20th to 24th

Nothing that the manuals say, nothing that the techni-cians have foreseen, is true to-day. Even under a hail of shells troops can fight on, and beneath the most terrific bom-bardment it is still the spirit of the combatants which counts. The German bombardments outdid all previsions.

When my battalion was called up as reënforcements on May 20th, the dugouts and trenches of the first French line were already completely destroyed. The curtain fire of the Germans, which had succeeded their bombardment of the front lines, fell on the road more than two kilometers behind these. Now and then the heavy long-distance guns of the Germans lengthened their fire in an attempt to reach our bat-teries and their communications. At eight o'clock in the evening, when we arrived in auto-buses behind the second or third lines, several shells reached our wagons, and killed men. The excellent spirit of the battalion suffered not at all, and this is the more to be noted, since it is far easier to keep one's dash and spirit in the heat of actual battle than when one is just approaching it. I have read a good many stories of battle, and some of their embroideries appear to me rather exaggerated; the truth is quite good enough by itself. Although they were bombarded beforehand, my men went very firmly into action. The cannonade worked on the ears and the nerves, getting louder with every step nearer the front, till the very earth shook, and our hearts jumped in our breasts.

Where we were there were hardly any trenches or communication trenches left. Every half-hour the appearance of the earth was changed by the unflagging shell fire. It was a perfect cataract of fire. We went forward by fits and starts, taking cover in shell-holes, and sometimes we saw a shell drop in the very hole we had chosen for our next leap forwards. A hundred men of the battalion were half buried, and we had scarcely the time to stop and help them to get themselves out. Suddenly we arrived at what remained of our first-line trenches, just as the Boches arrived at our barbed wire entanglements—or, rather, at the caterpillar-like remains of our barbed wire.

At this moment the German curtain fire lengthened, and most of our men buried in shell-holes were able to get out and rejoin us. The Germans attacked in massed formation, by big columns of five or six hundred men, preceded by two waves of sharpshooters. We had only our rifles and our machine guns, because the 75's could not get to work.

Fortunately the flank batteries succeeded in catching the Boches on the right. It is absolutely impossible to convey what losses the Germans must suffer in these attacks. Nothing can give an idea of it. Whole ranks are mowed down, and those that follow them suffer the same fate. Under the storm of machine gun, rifle and 75 fire, the German columns were plowed into furrows of death. Imagine if you can what it would be like to rake water. Those gaps filled up again at once. That is enough to show with what disdain of human life the German attacks are planned and carried out.

In these circumstances German advances are sure. They startle the public, but at the front nobody attaches any importance to them. As a matter of fact, our trenches are

so near those of the Germans that once the barbed wire is
destroyed the distance between them can be covered in a few
minutes.   Thus, if one is willing to suffer a loss of life cor-
responding to the number of men necessary to cover the
space between the lines, the other trench can always be
reached.   By sacrificing thousands of men, after a formidable bombardment, an enemy trench can always be taken.

There are slopes on Hill 304 where the level of the ground
is raised several meters by mounds of German corpses.
Sometimes it happens that the third German wave uses the
dead of the second wave as ramparts and shelters.   It was
behind ramparts of the dead left by the first five attacks, on
May 24th, that we saw the Boches take shelter while they
organized their next rush.

We make prisoners among these dead during our counter-
attacks.   They are men who have received no hurt, but have
been knocked down by the falling of the human wall of their
killed and wounded neighbors.   They say very little.   They
are for the most part dazed with fear and alcohol, and it is
several days before they recover.

### BY A FRENCH STAFF OFFICER
#### Account of the Struggle for Fort Douaumont on May 20th-23rd

Verdun has become a battle of madmen in the midst of
a volcano.   Whole regiments melt in a few minutes, and
others take their places only to perish in the same way.   Between Saturday morning [May 20th] and noon Tuesday
[May 23rd] we estimate that the Germans used up 100,000
men on the west Meuse front alone.   That is the price they
paid for the recapture of our recent gains and the seizure
of our outlying positions.   The valley separating Le Mort
Homme from Hill 287 is choked with bodies.   A full brigade
was mowed down in a quarter hour's holocaust by our machine guns.   Le Mort Homme itself passed from our possession, but the crescent Bourrus position to the south pre-
vents the enemy from utilizing it.

The scene there is appalling, but is dwarfed in comparison with fighting around Douaumont.   West of the Meuse,
at least, one dies in the open air, but at Douaumont is the

horror of darkness, where the men fight in tunnels, screaming with the lust of butchery, deafened by shells and grenades, stifled by smoke.

Even the wounded refuse to abandon the struggle. As
though possessed by devils, they fight on until they fall senseless from loss of blood. A surgeon in a front-line post told
me that, in a redoubt at the south part of the fort, of 200
French dead, fully half had more than two wounds. Those
he was able to treat seemed utterly insane. They kept shouting war cries and their eyes blazed, and, strangest of all,
they appeared indifferent to pain. At one moment anes-
thetics ran out owing to the impossibility of bringing forward fresh supplies through the bombardment. Arms, even
legs, were amputated without a groan, and even afterward
the men seemed not to have felt the shock. They asked for
a cigarette or inquired how the battle was going.

Our losses in retaking the fort were less heavy than
was expected, as the enemy was demoralized by the cannonade—by far the most furious I have ever seen from French
guns—and also was taken by surprise. But the subsequent
action took a terrible toll. Cover was all blown to pieces.
Every German rush was preceded by two or three hours of
hell-storm, and then wave after wave of attack in numbers
that seemed unceasing. Again and again the defenders'
ranks were renewed.

Never have attacks been pushed home so continuously.
The fight for Cemetery Hill at Gettysburg was no child's
play, nor for Hougoumont at Waterloo, but here men have
been flung 5,000 at a time at brief intervals for the last
forty-eight hours. Practically the whole sector has been
covered by a cannonade, compared to which Gettysburg
was a hailstorm and Waterloo mere fireworks. Some shell-
holes were thirty feet across, the explosion killing fifty men
simultaneously.

Before our lines the German dead lie heaped in long
rows. I am told one observer calculated there were 7,000
in a distance of 700 yards. Besides they cannot succor
their wounded, whereas of ours one at least in three is removed safely to the rear. Despite the bombardment sup-

plies keep coming. Even the chloroform I spoke of arrived after an hour's delay when two sets of bearers had been killed.

The dogged tenacity needed to continue the resistance far surpasses the furious élan of the attack. We know, too, the Germans cannot long maintain their present sacrifices. Since Saturday the enemy has lost two, if not three, for each one of us. Every bombardment withstood, every rush checked brings nearer the moment of inevitable exhaustion. Then will come our recompense for these days of horror.

## BY A FRENCH LIEUTENANT
### Account of the Assaults upon Fort Vaux in June

We had scarcely arrived at the right of Fort de Vaux, on the slope of the ravine, when there came an unprecedented bombardment of twelve hours. Alone, in a sort of dugout without walls, I pass twelve hours of agony, believing that it is the end. The soil is torn up, covered with fresh earth by enormous explosions. In front of us are not less than 1,200 guns of 240, 305, 380, and 420 caliber, which spit ceaselessly and all together, in these days of preparation for attack. These explosions stupefy the brain; you feel as if your entrails were being torn out, your heart twisted and wrenched; the shock seems to dismember your whole body. And then the wounded, the corpses!

Never had I seen such horror, such hell. I felt that I would give everything if only this would stop long enough to clear my brain. Twelve hours alone, motionless, exposed, and no chance to risk a leap to another place, so closely did the fragments of shell and rock fall in hail all day long. At last, with night, this diminished a little. I can go on into the woods! The shells still burst all around us, but their infernal din no longer makes any impression on me—a queer trait of the human temperament. After that we are lodged in fortified caves where we pass five days in seclusion, piled on top of each other, without being able to lie down.

I bury three comrades in a shell-hole. We are without water, and, with hands that have just touched the poor mangled limbs, we eat as if nothing were wrong.

We are taken back for two days into a tunnel where the lacrymal shells make us weep. Swiftly we put on our masks. The next day, at the moment of taking supper and retiring to rest, we are hastily called into rank; that's it—we are going to the motion-picture show. We pass through an infernal barrage fire that cracks red all around in the dark. We run with all speed, in spite of our knapsacks, into the smother of broken branches that used to be a forest. Scarcely have we left a hole or a ditch when shells as big as a frying pan fall on the spot. We are laid flat by one that bursts a few yards away. So many of them fall at one time that we no longer pay any attention to them. We tumble into a ravine which we have named Death Ravine. That race over shell-swept, open country, without trenches, we shall long remember.

At last we enter the village—without suspecting that the Germans are there! The commanding officer scatters us along the steep hill to the left and says: "Dig holes, quickly; the Boches are forty yards away!" We laugh and do not believe him; immediately, cries, rifle shots in the village; our men are freeing our Colonel and Captain, who were already prisoners. Impossible! Then there are no more Frenchmen there? In two minutes the village is surrounded, while the German batteries get a rude jolt. It was time! All night long you hear tools digging from one end to the other; trenches are being made in haste, but secretly. After that there is a wall, and the Germans will advance no further.

The next morning a formidable rumor—the Boches are coming up to assault Fort de Vaux. The newspapers have told the facts; our 75's firing for six hours, the German bodies piling up in heaps. Horrible! but we applauded. Everybody went out of the trenches to look. The Yser, said the veterans, was nothing beside this massacre.

That time I saw Germans fleeing like madmen. The next day, the same thing over again; they have the cynicism to mount a battery on the slope; the German chiefs must be hangmen to hurl their troops to death that way in masses and in broad daylight. All afternoon, a maximum bombardment; a wood is razed, a hill ravaged with shell-holes.

It is maddening; continuous salvos of "big chariots"; one sees the 380's and 420's falling; a continuous cloud of smoke everywhere. Trees leap into air like wisps of straw; it is an unheard-of spectacle. It is enough to make you lose your head, yet we patiently wait for the outcome.

The barrage fire cuts our communication with the rear, literally barring off the isthmus of Death Ravine. If the attacks on our wings succeed, our two regiments are prisoners, hemmed in, but the veterans (fathers of families) declare that we shall not be taken alive, that we will all fight till we die. It is sublime.

"Keep up your courage, coolness, and morale, boys, and we will drive them back in good time."

It is magnificent to see that our last recourse is a matter of sheer will; despite this monstrous machinery of modern war, a little moral effort, a will twenty years old that refuses to weaken, suffices to frustrate the offensive! The rifles do not shoot enough, but we have machine guns, the bayonet, and we have vowed that they shall not pass. Twenty times the alarm is given; along the hillside one sees the hands gripping the rifles; the eyes are a little wild, but show an energy that refuses to give way.

Suddenly it is already night. A sentinel runs up to the outposts: "There they are! Shoot!"

A whole section shoots. But are the outposts driven in? Nobody knows. I take my rifle to go and see. I do not catch a ball. I find the sentinels flat on their faces in their holes, and run to the rear gesticulating and crying out orders to cease firing. The men obey. I return to the front, and soon, a hundred yards away, I see a bush scintillate with a rapid line of fire. This time it is they. Ta-ca-ta-ca, bzzi— bzzi. I hold my fire until they approach, but the welcome evidently does not please them, for they tumble back over the ridge, leaving some men behind. One wounded cries, "Frantchmen!"

I am drunk, mad. Something moves in the bushes to the right; I bound forward with set bayonet. It is my brave sergeant, who has been out to see whether the Boches have all run away. These are truly the most interesting moments of war; no longer the waiting, the anguish of bombardment, but the thrill of a free march into a glorious unknown —oh, that intoxication! I sing the "Marseillaise," the boys jubilate, all the successive attacks have failed. After this evening the offensive is going to slacken for several days.

The next day we are relieved at last. Another race with death, this time with broad daylight shining upon the horrible chaos, the innumerable dead, and a few wounded here and there. Oh! those mangled bodies, still unburied, abandoned for the moment. The danger excites us. A shell falls squarely among us, jarring us and bathing us in flame. My knapsack gets a sliver of shell; I am not touched; it is a miracle. In the evening we arrive at the river ford, and have another race. The next day, at Verdun, the Germans are still shelling us at the moment when we mount the auto trucks. In the course of all these actions our losses certainly have been high, but they are nothing compared with the frightful and unimaginable hecatomb of Germans I have witnessed.

### BY GENERAL MILLERAND
#### Official French Reports of the Struggle for Thiaumont in July

July 1st.—On the east bank the fighting has been desperate all day in the region of Thiaumont. This morning, towards ten o'clock, in the course of a very brilliant attack, our troops carried the Thiaumont work in spite of an extremely violent curtain fire delivered by the enemy.

This afternoon the Germans redoubled their efforts to drive us out again, and sustained considerable losses. In the course of these attempts an enemy attack succeeded in re-entering at about three o'clock, but a vigorous counter-attack gave us complete possession of the work once more. (Second capture and recapture.)

July 2nd (afternoon).—On the east bank the fighting begun yesterday in the Thiaumont sector was continued in a desperate struggle for the possession of the work of that name. After a series of furious assaults preceded by bombardments the Germans succeeded in once more penetrating the redoubt, which was completely wrecked, while we ourselves are established in its immediate approaches. (Third German capture.)

(Evening).—About ten in the morning our infantry dashed to the assault of the Thiaumont work, which we again captured. The afternoon was marked by a recrudescence of the bombardment in this region, as well as in the sectors of the Fumin and Chênois Woods. (Third French recapture.)

July 3rd.—On the east bank several enemy attempts against the Thiaumont work in which we are established were easily repelled.

July 5th.—About 2 p. m., after several attempts which were repulsed, an enemy attack against the Thiaumont work succeeded in capturing it for the fourth time. The Germans, who had been repulsed six times during the night in front of the Thiaumont work, smothered it under an appalling bombardment, and finally succeeded in taking it in the afternoon. (Fourth German capture.)

July 8th.—On the east bank of the Meuse there was rather fierce fighting during the day in the region of Thiaumont work. The Germans successively launched several attacks preceded by bombardment against our positions. One of these succeeded in getting a foothold in our advanced elements, but our counter-attack, developed about 2 p. m., enabled us to reëstablish entirely our line, which is maintained at the immediate approaches to this work. All the other enemy attempts were repulsed by our machine-gun fire, and occasioned him serious losses.

August 4th.—On the east bank of the Meuse our infantry, pursuing its offensive action on the Thiaumont-Fleury front, captured during the day by a series of successive attacks all the trenches between these two points as far as the southeast of Thiaumont work and the approaches of Hill 320.

Several counter-attacks with large effectives made on our positions in the neighborhood of Thiaumont were repulsed with heavy losses to the enemy. Our troops in the course of the fighting even succeeded in capturing the work, which we subsequently evacuated under the force of the bombardment, whilst bringing back ninety prisoners in this action. (Fourth French recapture and fifth German capture.)

August 5th.—On the east bank of the Meuse fighting continued all day in the Thiaumont-Fleury region. To the northwest and to the south of the Thiaumont work all enemy attacks undertaken to dislodge us from the positions captured were vain. Not only did we break the enemy's efforts and inflict on him heavy losses, but by means of a second return offensive our troops succeeded in capturing for the second time in twelve hours the Thiaumont work, which remains in our power in spite of several counter-attacks made by the enemy. (Fifth French recapture.)

August 6th.—On the east bank of the Meuse the Germans attempted by furious counter-attacks to drive us from the Thiaumont work, which we are strongly occupying. The struggle lasted from 9 p. m. yesterday till this morning, causing heavy losses for the enemy, who was repulsed at each of his attacks without succeeding in obtaining the least advantage.

August 9th (afternoon).—The Germans succeeded in obtaining a footing in the Thiaumont work after a desperate struggle, which still continues. (Sixth German capture.)

(Night).—On the east bank of the Meuse stubborn fighting continues on the whole of the front of Thiaumont-Fleury. With remarkable tenacity our troops checked and repulsed the enemy, who attempted by his counter-attacks to drive us from the ground captured by us during the last few days to the northwest and to the south of the Thiaumont work. Then passing in their turn to the offensive, our troops reoccupied all the trench elements where the enemy had obtained a foothold in the course of the battle, and again entered the Thiaumont work. (Sixth French recapture.)

August 10th.—On the east bank of the Meuse the combat round the Thiaumont work lasted a portion of the night. The enemy again obtained a footing there after numerous attacks repulsed by us. (Seventh German capture.)

August 19th.—We followed up our offensive by driving the enemy out of two fortified redoubts to the northwest of the fort. (Seventh French partial recapture.)

BY MARSHAL JOFFRE

Official Announcement of August 3rd upon the Verdun Position

The great sacrifices which France has supported at Verdun have given our Allies time to build up their resources, have enabled us to mature our plans and carry them out with perfect appreciation of the necessities of all fronts. We are now able to employ all our resources simultaneously in a thoroughgoing way. I desire to pay homage to the manner wherein all the Allies are fulfilling their part.

Drawing on her inexhaustible resources Russia has been afforded time to bring forward men in ever-increasing numbers, and is now deploying her huge armies with telling effect in Galicia, Volhynia, and Armenia. Great Britain, too, has had time in the past two years to show the world the extent of her varied resources. Her troops are proving their splendid valor on the Somme, showing what a determined nation can do in such times as these. No doubt Italy has a difficult and limited part to play in a more restricted sphere of action, but her troops are fulfilling their rôle splendidly. The Serbian army is beginning at this moment to enter the firing-line anew.

We know positively that our enemies, although fighting as desperately as ever, are drawing on their last reserves. Up to now they have followed the policy of transferring their reserves from one place to another, but in face of the Allies' united effort they now find it impossible, and will find it increasingly impossible in future, to pursue such methods. All our sources of information confirm that.

It is not for me to say how long this struggle is going to last, but the question matters little. We know that the rupture is coming. You, no doubt, feel as well as we do, that we have reached the turning point. The five months' resistance of the French troops at Verdun has shattered the plans of the German Staff, and brought us round the corner, heading for victory. Don't, however, imagine that there is yet a marked weakening of the German effort on the western front. Two-thirds of their finest troops are still opposed to us on this side. The English and French face 122 of their best divisions.   On the Russian front the Germans have 50 divisions to which must, of course, be added the Austrian armies.

I won't go into details on the condition and temper of the French army.   You cannot do better than avail yourself of the facilities to see our troops in the field with your own eyes.   You will see the army as it is after two years of the hardest fighting.   You will see an army of which the spirit and energy have been vastly increased by this bitter struggle.   To that I can add that the number of our troops at the front is greater now than at the beginning of the war.   I can think of no more eloquent fact than that as illustrating France's capacity for waging a just war.   The country is determined to see the war to a victorious conclusion.   The Allies are fighting not merely for the respective interests of their countries, but for the liberty of the world, and will not stop till the world's liberty is definitely assured.

### BY GENERAL VON LUDENDORFF
#### His Summary of the Entire Verdun Battle

Verdun had exacted a very great price in blood.   The position of our attacking troops grew more and more unfavorable.   The more ground they gained, the deeper they plunged into the wilderness of shell-holes, and apart from actual losses in action, they suffered heavy wastage merely through having to stay in such a spot, not to mention the difficulty of getting up supplies over a wide, desolate area. The French enjoyed a great advantage here, as the proximity of the fortress gave them a certain amount of support.

Our attacks dragged on, sapping our strength.   The very men who had first fought so heroically at Verdun were now terrified of this shell-ravaged region.   The command had not their hearts in their work.   The Crown Prince had very early declared himself in favor of breaking off the attack. That offensive should have been broken off immediately it assumed the character of a battle of attrition.   The gain no longer justified the losses.

# ARAB INDEPENDENCE PROCLAIMED

## THE MOHAMMEDAN RELIGIOUS LEADERSHIP LOST TO TURKEY

### JUNE 27TH

KING HUSSEIN                                        THE ULEMA

Mohammedanism ranks with Christianity and Buddhism as one of the three most widely spread religions in the world. Moreover, it is of all religions the most militant and the one most given to fanatical outbreaks of frenzy. Hence the question as to whom the Mohammedans shall reverence and follow as the leader of their faith is one of the utmost importance to the world.

For centuries Turkey has been the dominant Mohammedan power, and the high-priest at Constantinople had been looked to as the religious successor of Mohammed; while the Prophet's spiritual lordship was assumed to have descended to the Beni Osman, or sons of Osman, the royal house of the Turkish sultans. But the vast mass of Mohammedans beyond Turkish territory were deeply dissatisfied with the course of the ruling Turkish party, the "Young Turks" who had in 1909 declared all faiths equal within their empire, and had then in 1914 accepted the leadership of "Christian" Germany.

Hence the movement toward both religious and political independence in Arabia was from the start a popular one. The Hedjaz is the western coast land of Arabia between the central desert and the Red Sea, and it contains the "holy cities" Mecca, the Prophet Mohammed's birthplace, and Medina, the seat of his first kingdom. Hence the high-priest or Sherif of the Hedjaz has always been a personage of high religious importance; and Hussein, the Sherif in 1916, claimed direct descent from the family of Mohammed. He was thus of all men the most fitted to claim the right to replace the impotent high-priest at Constantinople, as the true leader of the Mohammedan faith.

Hussein's official account is that he sent his son into Syria to protest against the cruelties there being inflicted upon the native Arabs by the Turkish governor Djemal. The envoy was not only defied, but an attempt was made to imprison him. Thereon the chief men of all the Hedjaz gathered in council and decided that to escape from miseries such as Syria was enduring they must break from Turkey altogether. This they did, and made Hussein their chief, as "Hussein the First, King of Hedjaz and Hereditary Custodian of the Holy Cities." On June 9th the new king sent out three armies under his three sons; and these, traversing the Hedjaz from end to end, deposed Turkish officials everywhere, and defeated the feeble Turkish forces in the land. The Turks' final resistance was at Medina, which they only surrendered after a considerable siege.

The news of Hussein's assumption of leadership of the Mohammedan faith was celebrated with enthusiasm in the Mohammedan lands not under Turkey's control, especially in India and Morocco.

### BY KING HUSSEIN

## Proclamation of the Sherif of Mecca

In the Name of God, the Merciful, the Compassionate

---

This is our general circular to all our Brother Moslems

---

"O Lord, do thou judge between us and our nation with truth; for Thou art the best Judge"

---

IT is well known that of all the Moslem Rulers and Emirs, the Emirs of Mecca, the Favored City, were the first to recognize the Turkish Government. This they did in order to unite Moslem opinion and firmly establish their community, knowing that the great Ottoman Sultans (may the dust of their tombs be blessed and may Paradise be their abode) were acting in accordance with the Book of God and the Sunna of his Prophet (prayers be unto him) and were zealous to enforce the ordinances of both these authorities. With this noble end in view the Emirs before mentioned observe those ordinances unceasingly. I myself, protecting the honor of the State, caused Arabs to rise against their fellow Arabs in the year 1327 [1909 of the Christian era] in order to raise the siege of Abha, and in the following year a similar movement was carried out under the leadership of one of my sons, as is well known. The Emirs continued to support the Ottoman State until the Society of Union and Progress appeared in the State and proceeded to take over the administration thereof and all its affairs.

The result of this new administration was that the State suffered a loss of territory which quite destroyed its prestige, as the whole world knows, was plunged into the horrors of war and brought to its present perilous position, as is patent to all. This was all done for certain well-known ends, which our feelings forbid to dilate upon. They caused Moslem hearts to ache with grief for the Empire of Islam, for the destruction of the remaining inhabitants of her provinces —Moslem as well as non-Moslem—some of them hanged or otherwise done to death, others driven into exile. Add to this the losses they have sustained through the war in their persons and property, the latter especially in the Holy Land as is briefly demonstrated by the fact that in that quarter the general stress compelled even the middle classes to sell the doors of their houses, their cupboards and the wood from their ceilings, after selling all their belongings to keep life in their bodies. All this evidently did not fulfill the designs of the Society of Union and Progress.

They proceeded next to sever the essential bond between the Ottoman Sultanate and the whole Moslem community, to wit, adherence to the Koran and the Sunna. One of the Constantinople newspapers, called *Al-Ijtihad,* actually published an article maligning (God forgive us) the life of the Prophet (on whom be the prayer and peace of God), and this under the eye of the Grand Vizier of the Ottoman Empire and its Sheikh of Islam, and all the Ulema, ministers and nobles. It adds to this impiety by denying the word of God, "The male shall receive two portions," and decides that they shall share equally under the law of inheritance. Then it proceeds to the crowning atrocity of destroying one of the five vital precepts of Islam, the Fast of Ramadan, ordering that the troops stationed at Medina, Mecca or Damascus may break the fast in the same way as troops fighting on the Russian frontier, thereby falsifying the clear Koranic injunction, "Those of you who are sick or on a journey." It has put forth other innovations touching the fundamental laws of Islam (of which the penalties for infringement are well known) after destroying the Sultan's power, robbing him even of the right to choose the chief of his Imperial Cabinet or the private minister of his august person, and breaking the constitution of the Caliphate of which Moslems demand the observance.

In spite of all, we have accepted these innovations in order to give no cause for dissension and schism. But at last the veil was removed and it became apparent that the Empire was in the hands of Enver Pasha, Djemal Pasha and

Talaat Bey, who were administering it just as they liked and
treating it according to their own sweet will.  The most
striking proof of this is the notice lately sent to the Kadi
of the Tribunal at Mecca, to the effect that he must deliver
judgment solely on evidence written down in his presence in
court and must not consider any evidence written down by
Moslems among themselves, thus ignoring the verse in the
Surat-al-Baqara.  Another proof is that they caused to be
hanged at one time 21 eminent and cultured Moslems and
Arabs of distinction, in addition to those they had previously put to death—the Emir Omar el-Jazairi, the Emir
Arif esh-Shihabi, Shefik Bey el-Moayyad, Shukri Bey el-
Asali, Abd el-Wahab, Taufik Bey el-Baset, Abd el-Hamid el-
Zahrawi, Abd el-Ghani el-Arisi, and their companions, who
are well-known men.  Cruel-hearted men could not easily
bring themselves to destroy so many lives at one blow, even
if they were as beasts of the field.  We might hear their excuse and grant them pardon for killing those worthy men,
but how can we excuse them for banishing under such pitiful and heart-breaking circumstances the innocent families
of their victims—infants, delicate women and aged men—
and inflicting on them other forms of suffering in addition
to the agonies they had already endured in the death of those
who were the support of their homes?

God says, "No burdened soul shall bear the burden of another."  Even if we could let all this pass, how is it possible
we can forgive them confiscating the property and money
of those people after bereaving them of their dear ones?
Try to suppose we closed our eyes to this, also feeling that
they might have some excuse on their side; could we ever
forgive them desecrating the grave of that pious, zealous and
godly man the Sherif Abd el-Kadir el-Jazairi el-Hasani?
The above is a brief account of their doings, and we leave
humanity at large and Moslems in particular to give their
verdict.

We have sufficient proof of how they regard the religion
and the Arab people in the fact that they shelled the Ancient
House, the Temple of the Divine Unity, of which it is said
in the word of God, "Purify my House for those that pass

round it," the Kibla of Mohammedans, the Kaaba of believers in the Unity, firing two shells at it from their big guns when the country rose to demand its independence. One fell about a yard and a half above the Black Stone and the other three yards from it. The covering of the Kaaba was set in a blaze. Thousands of Moslems rushed up with shouts of alarm and despair to extinguish the flames. To reach the fire they were compelled to open the door of the building and climb on to the roof. The enemy fired a third shell at the Makam Ibrahim in addition to the projectiles and bullets aimed at the rest of the building. Every day three or four people in the building itself were killed, and at last it became difficult for the Moslems to approach the Kaaba at all. We leave the whole Mohammedan world from East to West to pass judgment on this contempt and profanation of the Sacred House. But we are determined not to leave our religious and national rights as a plaything in the hands of the Union and Progress Party.

God (blessed and exalted be He) has vouchsafed the land an opportunity to rise in revolt, has enabled her by His power and might to seize her independence and crown her efforts with prosperity and victory, even after she was crushed by the maladministration of the Turkish civil and military officials. She stands quite apart and distinct from countries that still groan under the yoke of the Union and Progress Government. She is independent in the fullest sense of the word, freed from the rule of strangers and purged of every foreign influence. Her principles are to defend the faith of Islam, to elevate the Moslem people, to found their conduct on Holy Law, to build up the code of justice on the same foundation in harmony with the principles of religion, to practice its ceremonies in accordance with modern progress, and make a genuine revolution by sparing no pains in spreading education among all classes according to their station and their needs.

This is the policy we have undertaken in order to fulfill our religious duty, trusting that all our brother Moslems in the East and West will pursue the same in fulfillment of their duty to us, and so strengthen the bands of the Islamic brotherhood.

We raise our hands humbly to the Lord of Lords for the sake of the Prophet of the All-Bountiful King that we may be granted success and guidance in whatsoever is for the good of Islam and the Moslems. We rely upon Almighty God, who is our Sufficiency and the best Defender.

The Sherif and Emir of Mecca,

EL HUSSEIN IBN ALI.

25 Sha'ban 1334.
(June 27, 1916.)

### PROCLAMATION OF MARCH, 1917, BY THE ULEMA OR BODY OF PRIESTS OF MECCA

In the name of Allah the Merciful.

Proclamation to the Faithful.

We, the elders and lawyers of the House of God, are among those whom God has permitted to serve the faith and defend its truths. The world and its treasures, in comparison with truth, are not worth the wing of an insect, for there is no other purpose for man in this life except to prepare for eternity.

The Moslem soul rejoices in beholding the Grand "Kaaba" in the first streak of dawn and in the shadow of evening, and he is sanctified by dwelling in the land blessed by the Prophet of God. The peace of God be upon him! Can such a man allow his faith to be scorned or see evil befall the things that are holy? Even so it is with us who dwell in this holy place.

We have discerned the hearts of the usurpers of Osman's empire. We have learned their evil purpose with regard to our faith, we have beheld their crimes and wickedness in this our holy land, and our faith has shown us the path of salvation, and in its name we have acted according to our duty to ourselves and the Moslems of the world.

Every Moslem who would consider this matter should seek its cause and ascertain the nature of evil against which we rose in arms, when we found words were of no avail.

As for us, we are absolutely certain that the secret com-

mittee of the Young Turk Party has notoriously disobeyed
God.  No words stayed their hand from crime, and no opposition prevented the evil consequences of their actions.  Let
no one think that we speak vain things.  There stand the
facts and events which every man by inquiry can ascertain
for himself.  We shall bring forth these facts and lay them
before the Mohammedan world when necessity demands.
Now we content ourselves with begging those of our brethren
who oppose us to send some reliable person or persons to
Constantinople, the capital of the Unionists, and there witness personally, as we have ourselves witnessed, Moslem
women employed by the Government and exposed in public
places unveiled before men of strange nations.  What do
our true Moslem brethren who oppose us in haste think of
this matter, an example of an evil that will greatly injure
us if it increases and of which we publicly complain?

Would the obedience of people who do such a thing (and
it is the least of their crimes against Islam and Moslems)
be a true obedience or would it be disobedience to God?
Never, by the God of the "Kaaba," never.  To obey them
is to disobey God.  Far from it that any of the faithful
should consent to this.

We endeavored to please God and avoid a rebellion so
long as it was possible.  We rebelled in order to please
God, and He gave us victory and stood by us in support of
His law and religion, and in accordance with a wisdom
known to Him which would lead to the uplifting of this people.  Every Moslem heart in the Ottoman Empire, even
among the Turks in Anatolia and among the members of
the Turkish royal family in the palaces, prays God for our
success, and God always answers the prayers of the oppressed and the righteous.  There is no doubt about it, that
if the inhabitants of those countries which the Unionists
have lost through their alliance with Germany in this war
had revolted against those oppressors, just as we did, they
would have no more been regarded as belligerents and would
thus have saved their countries for themselves.  But if
things should continue as they are, no territory will remain
for this empire.

If you keep this in mind and remember what the Indian paper *Mashrek* wrote on September 12th and 19th on the subject of the disqualification of the Beni Osman to be the Caliphs of Islam, you will understand that we have risen in order to avert these dangers and to put the Islamic rule on a firm foundation of true civilization according to the noble dictates of our religion. If our revolution were only to preserve the integrity of our country and to save it from what has befallen other Islamic countries, it is enough, and we are amply justified.

We call the attention of those who oppose us to the necessity of saving the other countries from the calamities into which their inhabitants have fallen and to deliver them from the destruction and ruin into which those criminal hands are dragging them, if any true religious enthusiasm is left at all. We have done what we ought to do. We have cleansed our country from the germs of atheism and evil. The best course for those Moslems who still side with and defend this notorious gang of Unionists, is to submit to the will of God before their tongues, hands, and feet give witness against them.

It is a great mistake to suppose that in rising against this party we are rising against a legitimate Caliph possessing all the legal or, at least, some of the conditions qualifying him to be such.

What does the Mohammedan world say of the Beni Osman who pretend to be Caliphs of Islam, while for many years they were like puppets in the hands of the Janissaries; tossed about, dethroned, and killed by them, in a manner contrary to the laws and doctrines established in the books of religion on the accession and dethronement of Caliphs—which facts are recorded in their history? History is now repeating itself. To those Janissaries, grandsons have appeared in these days who are repeating the acts enacted in the days of Abdul Aziz, Murad, and Abdul Hamid. The murder of Yussuf Izzedin, the Turkish heir apparent, is too recent to be forgotten.

Those who oppose us and side with the Beni Osman should do one of two things: (1) Consider the Janissaries and their grandsons as the final authority on the question of the Caliphate, which we do not think any reasonable man would do, because it is against the laws of religion; or (2) consider those Janissaries and their grandsons as void of authority on the Caliphate question, in which case we should ask them, "What is the Caliphate and what are its conditions?"

Therefore, it remains for those who oppose us to repent, to come to their senses and unite with us in appealing to the Moslem world to use all effective measures for the strengthening of Islam and the restoring of its glory.

We want those who are present here to tell you who are far away that we shall confess before Almighty God, on the last day, that to-day we do not know of any Moslem ruler more righteous and fearing God than the son of His Prophet who is now on the throne of the Arab country. We do not know any one more zealous than he in religion, more observant of the law of God in words and deeds, and more capable of managing our affairs in such a way as would please God. The people of the Holy Land have proclaimed him their King simply because, in so doing, they would be serving their religion and country.

As to the question of the Caliphate, in spite of all that is known of the deplorable condition in which it is situated at the present moment, we have not interfered with it at all and it will remain as it is pending the final decision of the whole Mohammedan world.

Salams to all who hear what is said and believe the good in it. May God lead us all into the path of right.

# THE BATTLE OF THE SOMME

## BRITAIN'S MIGHTIEST EFFORT OF THE WAR

### JULY IST–NOVEMBER

PHILIP GIBBS          PRINCE RUPPRECHT OF BAVARIA
LIEUTENANT ALFRED DAMBITSCH
GENERAL STEINACKER

The Somme is the largest of a series of small rivers which, rising in the low hills of northern France, take a sluggish northwestward course over the flat coastland in their short journey to the English Channel. The British troops had at first guarded only a small section of the great French trench line, their forces centering around Ypres near the northern end of the line and close to the "Channel ports." By degrees, as their numbers increased, they extended their lines southward almost to the Somme River, which here, about sixty miles from its mouth, cut directly across the great trench line and flowed westward from Peronne, where the Germans had their headquarters, to Amiens, which the British held.

It was up the valley of the Somme, and over the low hills to the north of it that the French and British commanders now agreed to make their great counter-attack which was to relieve Verdun. They began on July 1st, the French fighting their way toward Peronne directly, along the banks of the Somme, while the British attacked the German lines in the hilly region north of the river. The battle soon developed into a mighty duplicate of Verdun, only with the rôles reversed, the Allies making the tremendous attacks and the Germans holding the defense. There was the same endless slaughter, the same unbounded heroism, the same lack of decisive result.

The Britons had accumulated enormous quantities of ammunition, so that their bombardments exceeded even those of the Germans at Verdun. Lieutenant Dambitsch, a German wounded at the Somme, gave his countrymen at home the narrative here retold of the effects of this awful bombardment upon the German troops. The endurance upon one side was as stupendous as the splendid resoluteness on the other. God grant that men may never again be plunged into such a frenzy of desolation.

Philip Gibbs, the most noted of British observers at the front, tells of the battle as it looked to British eyes; and the German chief commander on the spot, Prince Rupprecht, voices the German view. France bore her equal share in the battle, though, fighting over easier ground her losses were less, nor did she have at her disposal such a mass of artillery as did the British. The German view after the War, including also the French part in the struggle, is well summarized by the official German historian, General Freiherr von Steinacker.

Only the winter weather of November at last checked the unending assault. By that time the British reported a capture of 38,000 prisoners and an advance over about fifty square miles of ground. The French reported an equal advance and the capture of over 42,000 prisoners. Peronne, however, still remained in German hands.

# EXPENDITURE OF ARTILLERY AMMUNITION IN MODERN BATTLES

One of the most striking developments of the World War was the great increase in the use of artillery to precede infantry action in battle. This is illustrated by a comparison of the expenditure of artillery ammunition in characteristic battles of recent wars with that in important battles of the World War. The special features of the several battles should be kept in mind. Chickamauga was fought in a heavily wooded region; Gettysburg and St. Privat over open farm land. The latter battles, together with Nan Shan, and all the battles of the World War considered below, involved artillery preparation for assault upon armies in defensive position. The expenditures, therefore, are roughly comparable.

The high mark of the use of artillery in offensive battle was reached at the Somme and Messines Ridge, before the effective use of tanks was developed.

Source of information:   Ordnance Department.

| Year | Battle | Days' duration | Army | Rounds of artillery ammunition expended |
|------|--------|------|------|-----------|
| 1863 | Chickamauga | 2 | Union | 7,325 |
| 1863 | Gettysburg | 3 | Union | 32,781 |
| 1870 | St. Privat | 1 | German | 39,000 |
| 1904 | Nan Shan | 1 | Japanese | 34,047 |
| 1904 | Liao Yang | 9 | Russian | 134,400 |
| 1904 | Sha Ho | 9 | Russian | 274,360 |
| 1915 | Neuve Chapelle | 3 a | British | 197,000 |
| 1915 | Souchez | 1 b | French | 300,000 |
| 1916 | Somme | 7 c | British | 4,000,000 |
| 1917 | Messines Ridge | 7 c | British | 2,753,000 |
| 1918 | St. Mihiel | 4 b | U. S. | 1,093,217 |

Artillery preparation lasted:
  a 35 minutes.
  b 4 hours.
  c Intermittent 7 days.

# IMPROVEMENT OF FIELD GUNS SINCE THE NAPOLEONIC WARS

The limiting factor in the development of light field guns has always been the continuous hauling power of 6 horses, which is about 4,000 pounds. The gun has been as powerful as possible within the limits of this weight, which includes the carriage and limber as well as the cannon itself. Improved technique and materials have reduced the necessary weight of the cannon from 1,650 pounds in 1815 to about 800 pounds today, permitting the use of weight for recoil mechanism and shield of armor plate without exceeding the limit.

The 800 pound nickel steel gun of 1918 fires as heavy a projectile (12–15 pounds) as the 1,650 pound bronze gun of the Napoleonic wars. The improved material permits a more powerful propellant charge, which results in greater muzzle velocity, a flatter trajectory, and longer maximum range. The latter is due in part also to improved shapes of projectiles and the introduction of rifling. The efficiency of artillery is further increased by the introduction of high explosive bursting charge. The modern 75 mm shell contains about 1.76 pounds of high explosive as against about .5 pound of black powder in shell prior to 1893.

Source of information:   Ordnance Department.

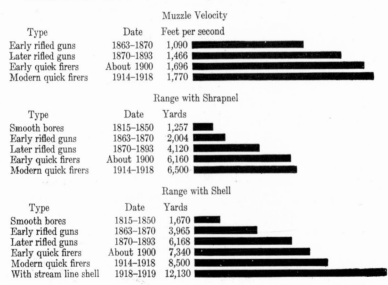

Muzzle Velocity

| Type | Date | Feet per second | |
|---|---|---|---|
| Early rifled guns | 1863–1870 | 1,090 | |
| Later rifled guns | 1870–1893 | 1,466 | |
| Early quick firers | About 1900 | 1,696 | |
| Modern quick firers | 1914–1918 | 1,770 | |

Range with Shrapnel

| Type | Date | Yards | |
|---|---|---|---|
| Smooth bores | 1815–1850 | 1,257 | |
| Early rifled guns | 1863–1870 | 2,004 | |
| Later rifled guns | 1870–1893 | 4,120 | |
| Early quick firers | About 1900 | 6,160 | |
| Modern quick firers | 1914–1918 | 6,500 | |

Range with Shell

| Type | Date | Yards | |
|---|---|---|---|
| Smooth bores | 1815–1850 | 1,670 | |
| Early rifled guns | 1863–1870 | 3,965 | |
| Later rifled guns | 1870–1893 | 6,168 | |
| Early quick firers | About 1900 | 7,340 | |
| Modern quick firers | 1914–1918 | 8,500 | |
| With stream line shell | 1918–1919 | 12,130 | |

STATISTICS BRANCH  -  GENERAL STAFF
WAR DEPARTMENT

7 - 17 - 20

### BY PHILIP GIBBS

FROM January to May of this year the German Command on the Western front was concentrating all its energy and all its available strength in man power and gun power upon the attack of Verdun. The Crown Prince had staked all his reputation upon this adventure, which he believed would end in the capture of the strongest French fortress and the destruction of the French armies.

He demanded men and more men until every unit that could be spared from other fronts of the line had been thrown into this furnace. Divisions were called in from other theaters of war, and increased the strength on the Western front to a total of about 130 divisions.

But the months passed, and Verdun still held out above piles of German corpses on its slopes, and in June Germany looked East and saw a great menace. The Russian offensive was becoming violent. German generals on the Russian fronts sent desperate messages for help. "Send us more men" they said; and from the Western front four divisions containing 39 battalions were sent to them.

They must have been sent grudgingly, for now another menace threatened the enemy, and it was on the Western side. The British armies were getting ready to strike. In spite of Verdun, France still had men enough—withdrawn from a part of the line in which they had been relieved by the British—to coöperate in a new attack.

It was our offensive that the German Command feared most, for they had no exact knowledge of our strength or of the quality of our new troops. They knew that our army had grown prodigiously since the assault on Loos, nearly a year before.

They had heard of the Canadian reënforcements, and the coming of the Australians, and the steady increase of recruiting in England, and month by month they had heard the louder roar of our guns along the line, and had seen their destructive effect spreading and becoming more terrible. They knew of the steady, quiet concentration of batteries and divisions on the north and south of the Ancre.

The German Command expected a heavy blow, and prepared for it, but as yet had no knowledge of the driving force behind it. What confidence they had of being able to resist the British attack was based upon the wonderful strength of the lines which they had been digging and fortifying since the autumn of the first year of war—"impregnable positions" they had called them—the inexperience of our troops, their own immense quantity of machine guns, the courage and skill of their gunners, and their profound belief in the superiority of German generalship.

In order to prevent espionage during the coming struggle, and to conceal the movement of troops and guns, they ordered the civil populations to be removed from villages close behind their positions, drew cordons of military police across the country, picketed cross-roads, and established a network of counter espionage to prevent any leakage of information.

To inspire the German troops with a spirit of martial fervor (not easily aroused to fever-pitch after the bloody losses before Verdun) Orders of the Day were issued to the battalions counseling them to hold fast against the hated English, who stood foremost in the way of peace (that was the gist of a manifesto by Prince Rupprecht of Bavaria, which I found in a dugout at Montauban), and promising them a speedy ending to the war.

Great stores of material and munitions were concentrated at railheads and dumps ready to be sent up to the firing lines, and the perfection of German organization may well have seemed flawless—before the attack began.

The British attack began with the great bombardment several days before July 1st and was a revelation, to the German Command and to the soldiers who had to endure it, of the new and enormous power of our artillery. A number of batteries were unmasked for the first time, and the German gunners found that in "heavies" and in expenditure of high explosives they were outclassed.

They were startled, too, by the skill and accuracy of the British gunners whom they had scorned as "amateurs" and by the daring of our airmen who flew over their lines with the utmost audacity "spotting" for the guns, and registering on batteries, communication trenches, cross-roads, railheads, and every vital point of organization in the German war-machine working opposite the British lines north and south of the Ancre.

Even before the British infantry had left their trenches at dawn on July 1st German officers behind the firing lines saw with anxiety that all the organization which had worked so smoothly in times of ordinary trench-warfare was now working only in a hazardous way under a deadly storm of shells.

Food and supplies of all kinds could not be sent up to front line trenches without many casualties, and sometimes could not be sent up at all. Telephone wires were cut, and communications broken between the front and head-quarter staffs. Staff officers sent up to report were killed on the way to the lines. Troops moving forward from reserve areas came under heavy fire and lost many men before arriving in the support trenches.

Prince Rupprecht of Bavaria, sitting aloof from all this in personal safety, must have known before July 1st that his resources in men and material would be strained to the uttermost by the British attack, but he could take a broader view than men closer to the scene of battle, and taking into account the courage of his troops (he had no need to doubt that), the immense strength of their positions, dug and tunneled beyond the power of high explosives, the number of his machine guns, the concentration of his artillery and the rawness of the British troops, he could count up the possible cost and believe that in spite of a heavy price to pay there would be no great break in his lines.

At 7.30 a. m. on July 1st the British infantry left their trenches and attacked on the right angle southwards from Gommecourt, Beaumont Hamel, Thiepval, Ovillers, and La Boiselle, and eastwards from Fricourt, below Mametz and Montauban. For a week the German troops—Bavarians and Prussians—had been crouching in their dugouts, listening to the ceaseless crashing of the British "drum-fire."

In places like Beaumont Hamel the men down in the deep

tunnels—some of them large enough to hold a battalion and a half—were safe as long as they stayed there. But to get in or out was death. Trenches disappeared into a sea of shell-craters, and the men holding them—for some men had to stay on duty there—were blown to fragments of flesh.

Many of the shallower dugouts were smashed in by heavy shells, and officers and men lay dead there as I saw them lying on the first days of July, in Fricourt and Mametz and Montauban.

The living men kept their courage, but below ground, under that tumult of bursting shells, wrote pitiful letters to their people at home describing the horror of those hours. "We are quite shut off from the rest of the world," wrote one of them. "Nothing comes to us. No letters. The English keep such a barrage on our approaches it is terrible. To-morrow evening it will be seven days since this bombardment began. We cannot hold out much longer. Everything is shot to pieces."

As far as the German troops were concerned there were no signs of cowardice, or "low morale," as we call it more kindly, in those early days of the struggle. They fought with a desperate courage, holding on to positions in rearguard actions when our guns were slashing them, and when our men were getting near to them making us pay a heavy price for every little copse or gully or section of trench, and above all serving their machine guns at La Boiselle, Ovillers, above Fricourt, round Contalmaison, and at all points of their gradual retreat, with a splendid obstinacy until they were killed or captured. But they could not check our men or stop their progress.

After the first week of battle the German General Staff had learnt the truth about the qualities of those British "New Armies" which had been mocked and caricatured in German comic papers. They learnt that these "amateur soldiers" had the qualities of the finest troops in the world—not only extreme valor but skill and cunning, not only a great power of endurance under the heaviest fire, but a spirit of attack which was terrible in its effect.

They were great bayonet fighters.  Once having gained a bit of earth or a ruined village nothing would budge them unless they could be blasted out by gunfire.  General Sixt von Arnim put down some candid notes in his report to Prince Rupprecht.

"The English infantry shows great dash in attack, a factor to which immense confidence in its overwhelming artillery greatly contributes.  It has shown great tenacity in defense.  This was especially noticeable in the case of small parties which when once established with machine guns in the corner of a wood or a group of houses were very difficult to drive out."

The German losses were piling up.  The great agony of the German troops under our shell fire was reaching unnatural limits of torture.  The early prisoners I saw—Prussians and Bavarians of the 14th Reserve Corps—were nerve-broken, and told frightful stories of the way in which their regiments had been cut to pieces.  The German Generals had to fill up the gaps, to put new barriers of men against the waves of British infantry.  They flung new troops into the line, called up hurriedly from reserve depots.

But now, for the first time, their staff work showed signs of disorder and demoralization.  When the Prussian Guards reserves were brought up from Valenciennes to counter-attack at Contalmaison they were sent on to the battlefield without maps or local guides, and walked straight into our barrage.  A whole battalion was cut to pieces, and many others suffered frightful things.  Some of the prisoners told me that they had lost three-quarters of their number in casualties and our troops advanced over heaps of killed and wounded.

The 122nd Bavarian Regiment in Contalmaison was among those which suffered horribly.  Owing to our ceaseless gunfire they could get no food supplies and no water.  The dugouts were crowded, so that they had to take turns to get into these shelters, and outside our shells were bursting over every yard of ground.

"Those who went outside," a prisoner told me, "were killed or wounded.  Some of them had their heads blown off, and some of them had both their legs torn off, and some of them their arms. But we went on taking turns in the hole, although those who went outside knew that it was their turn to die, most likely. At last most of those who came into the hole were wounded, some of them badly, so that we lay in blood." It is one little picture in a great panorama of bloodshed.

The German Command was not thinking much about the human suffering of its troops. It was thinking, necessarily, of the next defensive line upon which they would have to fall back if the pressure of the British offensive could be maintained—the Longueval-Bazentin-Pozières line. It was getting nervous. Owing to the enormous efforts made in the Verdun offensive the supplies of ammunition were not adequate to the enormous demand.

The German gunners were trying to compete with the British in continuity of bombardments and the shells were running short. Guns were wearing out under this incessant strain, and it was difficult to replace them. General von Gallwitz received reports of "an alarmingly large number of bursts in the bore, particularly in field guns."

General von Arnim complained that "reserve supplies of ammunition were only available in very small quantities." The German telephone system proved "totally inadequate in consequence of the development which the fighting took." The German air service was surprisingly weak, and the British airmen had established a complete mastery.

"The numerical superiority of the enemy's airmen," noted General von Arnim, "and the fact that their machines were better made, became disagreeably apparent to us, particularly in their direction of the enemy's artillery fire and in bomb-dropping."

On July 15th, one of the greatest days in the history of the Somme battles, the British troops broke the German second line at Longueval and the Bazentins, and inflicted great losses upon the enemy, who fought with their usual courage until the British bayonets were among them.

A day or two later the fortress of Ovillers fell, and the remnants of the garrison—150 strong—after a desperate and gallant resistance in ditches and tunnels where they had fought to the last, surrendered with honor.

Then began the long battle of the woods—Devil's Wood, High Wood, Trones Wood—continued through August with most fierce and bloody fighting, which ended in our favor and forced the enemy back, gradually but steadily, in spite of the terrific bombardments which filled those woods with hell-fire, and the constant counter-attacks delivered by the Germans.

"Counter-attack!" came the order from the German Staff —and battalions of men marched out obediently to certain death, sometimes with incredible folly on the part of their commanding officers, who ordered these attacks to be made without the slightest chance of success.

In all the letters written during those weeks of fighting and captured by us from dead or living men there is one great cry of agony and horror.

"I stood on the brink of the most terrible days of my life," wrote one of them. "They were those of the battle of the Somme. It began with a night attack on August 13th-14th. The attack lasted till the evening of the 18th, when the English wrote on our bodies in letters of blood: 'It is all over with you.' A handful of half-mad, wretched creatures, worn out in body and mind, were all that was left of a whole battalion. We were that handful."

"We entrained at Savigny," wrote a man of one of these regiments, "and at once knew our destination. It was our old Blood-bath—the Somme."

In many letters this phrase was used. The Somme was called the "Bath of Blood" by the German troops who waded across its shell-craters, and in the ditches which were heaped with their dead. But what I have described is only the beginning of the battle, and the bath was to be filled deeper in the months that followed.

The tale of defeat, of great losses, of grave and increasing anxiety, was told clearly enough—as I have read in captured letters—by the faces of German officers who went about in these towns behind the lines with gloomy looks, and whose tempers, never of the sweetest, became irritable and unbearable so that the soldiers hated them for all this cursing and bullying. A certain battalion commander has a nervous breakdown because he has to meet his colonel in the morning.

"He is dying with fear and anxiety," writes one of his comrades. Other men, not battalion commanders, are even more afraid of their superior officers, upon whom this bad news from the Somme has an evil effect.

The bad news was spread by divisions taken out of the line and sent back to rest. The men reported that their battalions had been cut to pieces. Some of their regiments had lost three-quarters of their strength. They described the frightful effect of the British artillery—the smashed trenches, the shell-craters, the great horror.

It is not good for the morale of men who are just going up there to take their turn.

The man who was afraid of his colonel "sits all day long writing home with the picture of his wife and children before his eyes." He is afraid of other things.

Bavarian soldiers quarreled with Prussians, accused them (unjustly) of shirking the Somme battlefields and leaving the Bavarians to go to the blood-bath.

"All the Bavarian troops are being sent to the Somme (this much is certain, you can see no Prussians there), and this in spite of the losses the 1st Bavarian Corps suffered recently at Verdun! And how we did suffer! . . . It appears that we are in for another turn, at least the 5th Bavarian Division. Everybody has been talking about it for a long time. To the devil with it! Every Bavarian regiment is being sent into it, and it's a swindle."

It was in no cheerful mood that men went away to the Somme battlefields. Those battalions of gray-clad men entrained without any of the old enthusiasm with which they had gone to earlier battles. Their gloom was noticed by the officers.

"Sing, you sheep's heads, sing!" they shouted.

They were compelled to sing, by order.

"In the afternoon," wrote a man of the 18th Reserve Division, "we had to go out again: we were to learn to sing. The greater part did not join in, and the song went feebly.

Then we had to march round in a circle and sing, and that went no better.

"After that we had an hour off, and on the way back to billets we were to sing '*Deutschland über Alles,*' but this broke down completely. One never hears songs of the Fatherland any more."

They were silent, grave-eyed men who marched through the streets of French and Belgian towns to be entrained for the Somme front, for they had forebodings of the fate before them. Yet none of their forebodings were equal in intensity of fear to the frightful reality into which they were flung.

### BY PRINCE RUPPRECHT OF BAVARIA

Since the beginning of the Anglo-French offensive on the Somme sector—called in England "The Great Sweep"—a month has now elapsed, during which, according to earlier announcements by our enemies, an encircling movement was to be completed at all costs. It will now be useful to examine briefly what has been achieved.

Though on a front of about 28 kilometers [15½ miles] they have driven a wedge of about four kilometers [2½ miles] depth, they themselves will not assert, after their experiences of July 20th, 22nd, 24th, and 30th that the German line has been shaken at any point.

This success cost the English, according to careful estimates, a loss of at least 230,000 men.

For an estimate of the French losses in this fighting no definite basis is at our disposal, but, as they had to bear the brunt of the battle, their losses must also be heavy, in spite of their greater military skill.

The total losses of our enemies must, therefore, amount to about 350,000, while ours, though regrettable, cannot be compared with theirs so far as numbers are concerned.

### A Later Statement, September 15th

Sunday, Monday, and Tuesday, September 9th, 10th, and 11th marked the culmination thus far of the first desperate effort of the Entente to force our positions. My officers will tell you the result as we on this side see it. Our losses in territory may be seen on the map with a microscope. Their losses in that far more precious thing—human life—are simply prodigious.

Amply and in full coin have they paid for every foot of ground we sold them. They can have all they want at the same price. We have a reserve, constituted of trained officers and trained men, which has not yet been drawn upon. We are not, like the Entente Generals, forced to throw raw, untrained recruits into the very front of the fighting.

Whether this will be the last effort we cannot know. We have taken measure of their strength at its maximum tide and are prepared for anything they can deliver. For the sake of the thousands whom new attacks will slay in vain we hope they have learned a lesson. So far as the interests of the Fatherland are concerned, we are indifferent; indeed, inclined to welcome any further folly they may indulge in.

It saddens us to exact the dreadful toll of suffering and death that is being marked up on the ledger of history, but if the enemy is still minded to possess a few more hectares of blood-sodden soil, I fear they must pay a bitter price.

### Prince Rupprecht's Statement of September 28th

This Somme offensive brings an attack of unusual violence every six days on the average. I know this country well from the fighting of 1914. At that time we had moving warfare, while we are now in a position of siege.

In his attacks, beginning in July, the enemy has gained some ground, but a decision of the situation is not to be thought of. One cannot prophesy how things will go here, but one thing is certain: Everything has now been so well provided for by us that one can quietly await coming events, be they what they may.

The offensive will certainly not be at an end very soon. One may well look forward to an offensive of great endurance, with very violent attacks, prepared for by a colossal expenditure of ammunition. We have, however, taken all necessary measures.

Our artillery has been strengthened and our flyers also.

In the last few days our flyers have again had some good successes after their hard fight against the enemy flyers. The fact that our flyers are getting the upper hand is of prime advantage to our artillery.

Our troops have given their all and the nut was too hard for the enemy to crack. I am of the opinion that the enemy is seeking a decision here and this year, and in this he has failed.

BY ALFRED DAMBITSCH

In respect to new methods and machines, the present French and British offensive is the last word. The aim of any offensive in modern warfare is the destruction of the enemy. This is the object of the present offensive, the idea being to enclose us in a tactical ring by simultaneous bombardment with long-range guns from the front and the rear. Accordingly the greedy beast began eating at the back lines of the German front. First of all our third and second trenches were incessantly bombarded, mostly by heavy artillery, of which the enemy had concentrated unprecedented masses in the sector of attack. It was dugouts which had to be battered down, so that at the moment of assault all the defenders, except a few survivors, and all the machine guns might be buried. Our second and third trenches were bombarded in order to prevent our bringing up reserves. For the same reason all the communication trenches leading from the rear to the front position were kept under incessant fire. On the Somme every one of our columns had a good communication trench which led from the headquarters of the battalion to the front trench.

But the attack against our front from the rear extended still further. All the main and side roads and all the cross-roads were kept under fire so that approaching troops, munitions, supplies, and provisions had to pass through several lines of fire. Bombarding villages and places behind the front where the various reserves are supposed to be quartered is an old trick of the British and French, but this time the principle was carried out more consistently and recklessly than ever. All places up to a distance of 10 miles behind the front were brought under incessant heavy artillery bombardment, which often started actual fires, thanks to the incendiary shells used by the enemy.

The battering down of our advanced trenches was almost exclusively left to the heavy artillery and trench mortars, especially the latter. The French have made great improvements in this weapon lately. For the destruction of our trenches they exclusively employed those of the heaviest caliber, and they now throw their mines with greater accuracy and over longer ranges than formerly. Opposite my company no fewer than six mortars were placed. They were worked uninterruptedly, throwing hundreds of aërial torpedoes on our position from the first to the third trenches. They tore up our wire obstacles from the ground, poles and all, and threw them all over the place, crushing the dugouts if they fell on them, and damaging the trenches. In a very short time great portions of our trenches had been flattened out, partly burying their occupants. This fire lasted for seven days, and finally there came a gas attack, also of an improved kind.

The deepest impression left on me was not a feeling of horror and terror in face of these gigantic forces of destruction, but an unceasing admiration for my own men. Young recruits who had just come into the field from home, fresh twenty-year-old boys, behaved in this catastrophic plowing and thundering as if they had spent all their life in such surroundings, and it is partly thanks to them that the older married men also stood the test so well.

### BY GENERAL VON STEINACKER

The failure of the English-French attempts to break through in Champagne and Artois in the fall of 1915—an offensive planned upon a large scale—did not dishearten the enemy. Immediately on the termination of these battles—exceptionally costly in human lives—the preparations began anew. The English command was particularly active and displayed the utmost celerity in getting the new armies ready for the field. Simultaneously the accumulation of war material of every description went on apace, in order that the enemy might be outstripped in this regard. The new offensive was planned for June. Although the drilling of the Englishmen had not been quite completed, the condition brought about at the beginning of the year by the attacks of the Germans on the positions at Verdun made it imperative for Sir Douglas Haig and General Joffre to choose the above period as the latest feasible one. The attack launched on July 1 was regarded by the German high command as one fraught with great significance as determining the outcome on the Western front. They believed, indeed, that it was designed to bring about a decisive change, not only on the Western front, but also on every other scene of action, by which the Central Powers would be irrevocably forced to assume the defensive. This end was to be achieved by piercing the Western front, which thereupon would crumble throughout its entire length and breadth. The intention of the enemy was correctly deduced from the magnitude of the preparations made. Above all, however, it is necessary to point to the fact that both Frenchmen and Englishmen had stationed tremendous masses of cavalry behind the battlefront, designed, after a successful penetration of the German lines, to fall into the rear of the enemy, annihilating such bodies as had not been directly affected in the first onset. The British command, deviating from the statement, but only after the conflict had terminated, gave out the following as the reasons for the battle: (1) Relieving the pressure on Verdun; (2) preventing further levies of troops from the Western to the Eastern front; (3) attrition of the German forces.

The front which the enemy had selected as his point of attack, extended in an airline over about 40 km. It lay in Picardy, between the villages of Sommecourt and Vermandovillers. This territory easily resolves itself into three divisions, the northern of these being Sommecourt-Hamel, the central Thiepval-Curlu, and the southern Frise-Vermandovillers. The position of our army had been admirably strengthened since its occupation a year and a half before. Many villages lay along the first line and these villages, generally built of stone and containing cellars, served as valuable *points d'appui*. Though the second line also passed through as many as ten villages, the first line was the stronger of the two, and here the greatest resistance was to be made. For this reason the second position had from one to two lines only protected by extensive wire defenses. It was so situated that it could not be affected by the fire directed against the first position. Although the enemy spared no effort to conceal his purpose, his in every respect well considered preparations did not escape the observation of Crown Prince Rupprecht of Bavaria, who was here in command.

On June 22nd the enemy prepared his attack by especially vigorous artillery fire. By June 30th all the German positions had already suffered greatly by reason of the increasingly vigorous and effective drumfire. The battle, which began on July 1st with infantry charges, lasted in all four and a half months; that is, until November 18th. It may chronologically be divided into several parts. The first comprised the period July 1st-5th. The attack was begun by one and a half French corps under General Michelet, advancing south of the Somme; by one corps north of the river commanded by General Fayolle; at Maricourt and in touch with the French stood the right wing of the English, the fourth army (consisting of five corps) here moving forward to the attack under General Rawlinson.

While on July 1st the first German line was taken south of the Somme by the French, who also advanced north of that river as far as Hardecourt-Curlu, the attack of the English on both sides of the Ancre did not go forward very well. Already by July 2nd the combined attack of the enemy forces resolved itself into single engagements, which resulted more favorably for the French south of the Somme. After uninterrupted attacks lasting five days, a pause ensued. According to the enemy's own reports, new grouping and relief troops had become necessary, and the heavy artillery had to be brought up.

The second period, July 7th-19th, presented a varying picture, but resulted in important advantages to the attacker.

The third period, July 20th-31st, was a fierce struggle intensified by the entry into the fight of German reserves, especially of the artillery division. The great united forward movement of the English-French army, consisting of seventeen divisions with 200,000 men, continued to the 30th, the day of the hottest fighting. The only result of these conflicts was the seizure of the ruins of the village of Pozières by the English.

The further development of the battle; that is, during the fourth period, which included the month of August, was characterized by varying attacks along the entire front and by efforts to gain important points of vantage and *points d'appui,* such as villages or strips of forest, the initiative being with the enemy. Here and there a slight advance was made.

On September 3rd began the fifth period of this battle, characterized by an attack north of the Somme, to be followed on the next day by one south of it. Yet, although conceived as a unity, this general attack, owing to the conditions of the ground and the direction of the advances, resulted in two distinct operations. First, as to the movement north of the Somme. Whereas the right wing, that is, the French, made a considerable advance; the left wing, that is, the English, made no headway. On the 23rd the artillery ushered in another combined attack, the infantry charges of the French resulting in their advance northwardly to the stretch Bouchavesnes-Combles, the latter city being evacuated. The English advanced to Thiepval, and at the end of the month stood before Le Sars and Eaucourt-l'Abbaye. To the south of the Somme the attack, made in a southeasterly direction on a front of 20 km., also resulted in the capture of strategical points.

In spite of all the efforts of the Germans it appeared as if the enemy in those days would succeed in his object. The measures taken for defense could not keep pace with the force of the attacks launched by the enemy. Only on September 25th had it become possible to so strengthen and increase the artillery support of the German positions that a systematic and effectual opposition to the enemy's forces might be organized—as the General German Headquarters put it, "A harmonious coöperation of the artillery of all divisions toward the suppression of any desire for attack on the part of the enemy."

Consequently the conflicts of October, which constituted the sixth period in the series of battles, presented an essentially different picture from those of the preceding months. True, the enemy attacks did not immediately diminish in vigor. On the 1st and 2nd of October, as on the 7th, the attacker succeeded in advancing, Eaucourt-l'Abbaye and Le Sars falling into his hands. Nevertheless, the result of the English-French attacks from October 9th to the 15th, which were directed under unified command against the whole German front from Courcelette southeasterly to Bouchavesnes and which belonged to the most important combats fought here, demonstrated that their goal would not be attained. The German Tenth Army successfully repelled the attack made on the 12th, the day of the hottest fighting. The day of the last great battle, October 18th, resulted in gaining for the Allies a little ground near Sailly and north of Eaucourt-l'Abbaye. After another great combined attack on the 21st had been shattered with sanguinary results, the struggle gradually diminished in vigor.

The great Battle of the Somme was ended without bringing about a decision. The result was limited to a "bulging in" of the German position, so to speak, a result achieved at a cost of approximately three quarters of a million lives. The losses of the defender were well below half a million, which is the more remarkable in view of the fact that, according to official reports, about 76 per cent. of all the wounded were able within a relatively short time to return to the front in fighting condition. A utilization of the successful defense made was impossible for the German command owing to the relative strength of the two armies. There was no decision reached on this theater of war. The failure of the attempt to break through resulted in a change in the French high command, General Joffre being replaced by General Nivelle, the commander of the Army of Verdun.

# THE FIRST AMERICANS TO "PAY THE DEBT"

## THE THRONGING OF U. S. VOLUNTEERS TO AID IN DEFENDING CIVILIZATION

### JULY 4TH

PAUL HERVIER                         E. A. McKENZIE

Many United States citizens did not wait for their country's formal entry into the Great War. Recognizing it at some earlier period as a war upon the whole human race, they felt the call of duty urging them to join the Allies. What the total number was of these knights of humanity can never be known. Many went secretly; many called themselves Britons or Frenchmen; for at first the Allies were not expecting such aid and had made no arrangement for receiving them. Except for the well-known French "foreign legion," there was no corps they could regularly enter as Americans. Forty thousand might be stated as a rough estimate of the sum of these young war heroes who were too eager to wait.

Among those who sealed such service with their death was the poet Alan Seeger. The universal acclaim of his home land and of France and Britain has declared him a genius. To many a comrade soldier and to many a woman's heart at home his poems have seemed the highest and the most inspiring of the War. To many a critic also the poem, "I Have a Rendezvous with Death," has seemed a climax in war poetry. Its sincerity was proven in the poet's death. Its closing lines, after repeating the young man's joy of living, cry in courageous repetition:

> "But I've a rendezvous with Death
> At midnight in some flaming town,
> When Spring trips north again this year,
> And I to my pledged word am true,
> I shall not fail that rendezvous."

Read Mr. McKenzie's account of his death, which follows, and you will see how close was his poetic fore-vision and how splendidly he kept his word in the French advance near the Somme.

Hence the date of his death—and by a generous coincidence it was on July 4th that he fell—has here been taken as the typical commemoration date for all the United States volunteers. Which of them all was the first to be slain in battle no man can know, but no death upon the field was more costly to the world than that of Alan Seeger, the New York youth who at the age of twenty-eight was shot down in a French uniform in the French village of Belloy while charging on the German machine guns

C. F. H.

## BY PAUL LOUIS HERVIER

THE Americans who entered the service of France after the outbreak of the War were volunteers recruited from all classes of society: Millionaires, writers, lawyers, engineers, soldiers, boxers, butchers, explorers, and especially university students. I have brought together the data regarding these gallant volunteers, and again and again I have been thrilled by their simple anecdotes as by those deeds of ancient history which we love to repeat in all our books for the lessons they teach.

Take the case of Norman Prince. After serving in the Foreign Legion, he became an aviator, achieved remarkable exploits, and was killed in action. Did his place remain vacant? No! His brother filled it.

Then there came Dr. David D. Wheeler. He left his assured practice in Buffalo to come and care for our wounded. The stories told by the injured men so impressed him that he wished to share their dangers. Abandoning his surgical instruments, he took up arms. He was wounded by a dumdum bullet, and, though exhausted by the loss of blood, dragged himself over the battlefield and used his waning strength in comforting other wounded men who lay without aid.

These anecdotes and many others will later be treasured in American history. At this moment they are the sacred heritage of all civilization fighting against aggressive barbarism.

The American volunteers, who wished, in August, 1914, to join their French brothers in defending the ideal represented by the word "liberty," almost all entered the Foreign Legion. One of them, Paul Rockwell, grievously wounded in Champagne, sent to a New York editor this response, which is sweet to our hearts:

"In the Foreign Legion about 200 Americans are serving or have served. The bitterest regret of my life is that so few Americans have come to aid France. When we Americans were in need of aid, Lafayette and his followers were a hundred times more numerous than we are in this war, and they came from a total French population scarcely larger than that of two cities in America to-day. But we have one reason to feel a little pride. With the exception of, say, six or eight, all the men who came to pay our debt to France have proved to be good fighters. None came for money. Some came for the simple love of adventure, but I believe that the motive of most of them was an ideal."

A dangerous but attractive arm, that of aviation, especially appealed to the daring of these young Americans, anxious as they were to prove their courage and devotion. Men will long continue to speak of the services rendered to the French army by the American Escadrille; they will long recount the exploits of Norman Prince, who died for. France on October 15, 1916; of Victor Chapman, who died for France in June, 1916; of Kiffin Rockwell, who died for France on September 23, 1916; of Denis Dowd, the skilled pilot, who died in an airplane accident at the Buc airdrome in the beginning of August, 1916; of William Thaw, the Pittsburgh millionaire; of Elliott Christopher Cowdin, of Lufbery, of Bert Hall, of Paul Pavelka, James R. MacConnell, and all the rest.

A brief article such as this cannot give the names of all the brave men who have come to fight for us, but must be devoted rather to the significance of their generous and fruitful service. This is what has stirred and touched us. Young Americans who had careers awaiting them in their own country, who in many cases possessed fortunes that would have given them all the material joys of life, and in other cases felt within themselves the rare forces of talent or creative genius, have by their coming proclaimed the justice of our cause to all the world. It is not a matter, then, of giving here a list of these who have achieved the supreme heights of the moral task which they voluntarily took up; the eulogy deserved by each is swallowed up in one great common glory.

Nevertheless, let us glance at the golden book of American volunteers. We shall find there the names of Edward Mandell Stone, a graduate of Harvard, the first American volunteer killed; of Henry W. Farnsworth, killed in Champagne; of the poet, Alan Seeger, an idealist, dead for France; of John Earle Fike, a former American soldier, killed June 16, 1915; of Russell A. Kelly, killed the same way; of Nelson Larson, a former American sailor, killed on the anniversary day of American independence, 1916; of Frank Clair of Columbus, dead of wounds; of René Phelizot of Chicago, a daring hunter of big game, killed in February, 1915; of Harman Edwin Hall of Chicago, killed June 16, 1916, etc. We shall not forget their acts of devotion.

Here we find also the names of Frank Musgrave of San Antonio, lawyer, made a prisoner by Germany; of John Bowe of Minneapolis, wounded and cited in the Order of the Day; of Charles Sweeney, decorated with the Legion of Honor and promoted Lieutenant; of Edgar Bouligny of New Orleans, four times wounded; of Brook B. Bonnell of Brooklyn, decorated with the War Cross and the Military Medal; of Andrew Walbron of Peterson, wounded three times; of his brother, Ernest Walbron, who had a leg carried away by a shell on the Somme; of George Delpeuche, decorated with the War Cross for having taken five prisoners alone and unaided; of Frederick Capdeville of New York, Charlie Christopher Charles of Brooklyn, Charles Trinkard, Jack Janz of Kentucky, David King of Providence, Jack Cordonnier, Frederick Mulhauser (three citations), Michael Steinfels of Chicago, Eugene Jacobs, Bob Scanlon, the negro boxer; Achille Clinger, Jack Moyet, and the rest.

This is only a short summary of the heroic chapter. A great number of Americans enlisted in the English army, others in the Canadian army, and still others came to France to serve in automobile ambulances. They have saved and cared for our wounded with ceaseless zeal, risking their lives, and often losing them. At the end of January, 1917, seventy citations in official orders had been merited and bestowed upon these brave men. A beautiful history!

### BY E. A. MC KENZIE

What have the Americans done? Many of them, the very pick of the nation, gave themselves as volunteers. The great Universities, headed by Harvard, have sent doctors and hospital staffs to nurse the sick and wounded. Groups of rich young men crossed the Atlantic when war broke out, bringing their own automobiles with them, and formed the nucleus of the splendid ambulance services that have been of incalculable service to France. In Belgium a group of Americans, Rhodes scholars, engineers and industrial leaders, headed by a supreme business organizer, saved a nation from starvation. In Serbia a brave American doctor fought almost single-handed against the brutalities of the Austrian troops when they swept over the land after the great retreat.

Americans were so eager to join the ranks of the French Army that military laws were relaxed for their benefit. The record of the American Flying Squadron in the French service is one of great brilliancy, even in that corps d'élite of France. The British roll of honor gives frequently the names of American born soldiers who have laid down their lives for the Allies.

Look at the record of Americans who have died for Britain and France. It is a very remarkable list, more especially for the quality of the men enrolled. There are Harold Chapin, born in Brooklyn, at the beginning of a brilliant career as a dramatist, and Alan Seeger, of old New England stock, whom three nations to-day hail as poet and hero. Kenneth Weeks, who died at Givenchy, twenty-four years old, had already done notable work in letters. Dilwyn Starr, of Philadelphia, a Harvard man, took his place in the ranks of the British Expeditionary Force, won his commission, and died on the Somme. Officers in the United States Army like Major Stewart and Captain Wood, on the staff of General Leonard Wood, resigned their commissions to join us, and fell for us. American students from the Latin Quarter, University men galore, sturdy plainsmen and men from the West, have died side by side with the sons of Britain fighting for justice and liberty. Many others, happily, are still alive, wearing on their breasts the ribbons of the medals they have won for gallant conduct in the field.

What drew them to us? Some came because of the instinct of race and blood. "The army of my race and tongue," said Frederick Palmer, the distinguished war correspondent, when he found himself with the British Forces. Some came because of historic memories. "I am paying for Lafayette and Rochambeau," said Kiffin Rockwell, the steel-nerved airman, shortly before his death. Others were forced to join us because of what they saw of the enemy's methods of war. Among the most active American soldiers in the Allied ranks are men who began as ambulance workers or relief agents, and who were so aroused by the cruelties they witnessed that they took up the sword to fight a foe whom they recognized as the common enemy of all who love justice and freedom.

Alan Seeger, shortly before he died, gave another reason:

"Can sneerers triumph in the charge they made,
That from a war where Freedom was at stake,
America withheld and, daunted, stood aside.
Now heaven be thanked, we gave a few brave drops;
Now heaven be thanked, a few brave drops were ours."

The Americans in the fighting ranks were only representatives of a vastly greater mass of their countrymen supporting us in their own land. The women of the United States banded themselves into five thousand groups and circles to raise money or prepare comforts for the Allies, mainly for the destitute in France and Belgium. A noted organization on the Rocky Mountains raised a fund of a million dollars for a new club house. It was to be the finest of its kind in the world. Then an eye-witness told the members what was happening in Belgium. They resolved to make their old club house do, and donated the million dollars as a gift for King Albert's needy subjects. There is a systematized movement throughout the elementary schools of America by which the boys and girls of each district adopt a certain number of Belgian children, and make themselves responsible for finding three cents a day for the feeding of each child.

As the Allied Armies moved ahead on the Western front there came on behind a group of Californian women, working out plans for rebuilding ruined French towns and villages. America aided France to grapple the most dreaded secondary result of the war—tuberculosis. American hospitals from Devonshire to Salonika helped to nurse the victims of war. To mention all the forms that active American aid has taken would be to transform this account into a mere catalogue of names.

Various attempts have been made to number the Americans in the Allied ranks. Those like myself whose affairs took them into the Allied lines were constantly surprised to find Americans in the most unlikely places. Their speech betrayed them, whatever declarations they made when joining up. "If you take a map of the United States and go up and down the American lines in France, you will find no city, great or small, which has not sent a flying man, a bomber, an artilleryman, a sniper or dispatch rider to help to destroy Prussian despotism," wrote Lord Northcliffe, after a visit to the front. "When I said in something I wrote lately that the American soldiers in France numbered 50,000, I rather underestimated their strength. I made that calculation on statements supplied by French as well as by British authorities. The great fact is that more than 50,000 young Crusaders have crossed the Atlantic to join an Army in which they are fighting not for King or country, but against what they realize to be the curse of the world at this moment—the attempt of the Germans to dominate Europe and then America."

The most spectacular and thrilling side of the work of the war is found among the Army flyers.

The American squadron of the French Aviation Corps owes its existence to three young men—William Thaw, of Pittsburgh, Norman Prince, of Boston, and Elliott Cowdin, the Long Island polo player. Thaw, a well-known American flyer, volunteered his services at the outbreak of the war. At that time the solitary French corps open to non-Frenchmen was the Foreign Legion. He joined it in August, 1914, and it was only with considerable difficulty that he was later transferred to the aviation service. Prince and Cowdin, fresh from America, came a little later, and the way was now open for them to join the aviation corps direct. A fourth American, Bert Hall, a Texan cowboy who had also joined the Foreign Legion, was transferred to the air service.

Air Corps are to modern armies what the King's Guards were in the days of the Stuarts and the Louis—the corps d'élite. In France, the army airmen rank specially high, and any one who has witnessed their marvelous work admits that they have earned their place. For foreigners to come into this picked service was a severe test. Happily the Americans were tried and experienced flyers, and their records soon made them marked men. They themselves would be the last to deny any claim to special honor. "Why write about us," demanded Kiffin Rockwell shortly before his death, "when we are doing only what our French comrades are doing every day as well as we are."

The Americans urged the idea of a separate American squadron of the French flying service. Other men were coming to join them. Soon there were six American pilots who had passed their tests, the two others being Didier Masson, a well-known American exhibition flyer, and James Bach, who came from the Foreign Legion. Thaw was promoted to lieutenant, and the American Escadrille came into being.

Among others who soon joined up were two more from the Foreign Legion, Kiffin Rockwell, of Atlanta, Ga., and Victor E. Chapman, of New York, son of the eminent writer, John Jay Chapman. James McConnell, born in Chicago, a graduate of the University of Virginia, and one of the staff of a small railroad in North Carolina, came from the American Ambulance Corps with a high record. He had left his railway work, to serve as an ambulance driver at the front, where he had been mentioned in orders of the day for conspicuous bravery in attending the wounded under fire, and decorated with the Croix de Guerre. Convinced that the cause of the Allies was the cause of freedom, he entered the active fighting ranks. He secured his license a month and a day after he entered the flying school, and soon earned fresh honor.

"All along," said Mr. McConnell, "I had been convinced that the United States ought to aid in the struggle against Germany. With that conviction, it was plainly up to me to do more than drive an ambulance. The more I saw the splendor of the fight the French were fighting, the more I began to feel like an *embusqué*—what the British call a 'shirker.' So I made up my mind to go into aviation.''

The original six had grown by the middle of 1916 to about fifty pilots and men in training. One of the first group, Bach, was captured by the Germans when going to the rescue of a comrade, and was for a time in danger of death by court-martial as a *franc-tireur*. The Germans did the American aviators the honor of ranking them with the English soldiers, as objects for their special hatred. Elliott Cowdin won the *Medaille Militaire* before the American squadron was formed, by bringing down a German machine on the Verdun front.

The first member of the squadron to lose his life was Victor Chapman. He was a student in the Latin Quarter when the war broke out, and at once joined the Foreign Legion. Soon wounded in action, he was on recovery transferred to the air service as an aërial bomb dropper, and later qualified as pilot. Chapman was a superman. He took every opportunity to fly straight for the enemy's country and to attack any enemy craft within reach. If there were several enemy planes together, so much the better. "He flew more than any of us," wrote one of his comrades. "Never missing an opportunity to go up, and never coming down until his gasoline was giving out. He was a sieve of patched-up bullet holes. His nerve was almost superhuman, and his devotion to the cause for which he fought sublime."

Soon he had the destruction of seven German planes to his credit. On one occasion he attacked four enemy planes. One of them getting behind him, swept his machine with bullets, smashing the rod of the stability control and wounding him in the head. Chapman grasped the rod with one hand, and steered himself to safety with the other. As soon as his wound was dressed, he mounted again in a fresh plane, looking out for some one else to fight.

Chapman's death was worthy of the man. He knew that a wounded comrade in hospital wanted oranges, and he started out in his warplane with a basket of fruit for him. On the way he saw an air fight far over the German lines.

Four Germans were attacking three French. He swooped down on them, destroying one of the Germans by machine gun fire, and driving the others off. What followed is not quite clear, but apparently as he passed, the bullets of one plane caught and killed him.

The French official army order telling of his death recorded his glory. "In memory of this citizen of the United States who, inspired by sentiments of lofty idealism, gave his life for the cause of the Allies." When news was brought to his father of his death, he declared, "If Victor is killed in battle, I am resigned. I am proud that he joined the French Army, and I think that every American boy ought to do the same."

The reputation of Kiffin Rockwell equaled that of Chapman. To him this war was the war for world freedom, and France was the champion of universal liberty. "If France were conquered, I should prefer to die," he wrote. "The cause of France is the cause of all mankind." His fearlessness was famous, even in this corps of fearless men. Taking great risks, ever ready for a fight, he was twice wounded, but immediately he recovered he was back again. On September 23, 1916, he attacked single-handed four German aëroplanes. An explosive ball hit him, four thousand meters high, and killed him. "More than ever I want to live," he had written shortly before, when recovering from a wound. "But not from an egotistic point of view." "This war has taught me many things. I want to live to do all the good I can. But if I must be killed in the war, I have no fear of dying, and I feel there can be no better end." "The bravest and best of us is no more," the chief of the squadrilla declared when news of his death came.

Norman Prince, of Boston (nephew of the famous psychiatrist, Dr. Morton Prince), one of the pioneers of the squadron, and himself a brilliant flyer, was mentioned five times in dispatches for conspicuous gallantry and decorated with the Medaille Militaire and the Croix de Guerre. Late in 1916, he was seriously wounded in a raid on the Mauser Rifle Factory at Oberndorf. Despite his wounds, he succeeded in flying back to French territory, where he died.

On the many decorations bestowed on the American airmen, from the Cross of the Legion of Honor for Lieutenant Thaw to other coveted decorations for his men, I do not dwell. The many deaths, many for so small a group, tell their own tale of danger and daring. Two Bostonians, Kenneth Weeks and Henry Harnsworth, died within a very short time of one another. "I want to fight, not merely to look on," said Harnsworth. "I want to fight for France, as the French once fought for us." He had his opportunity, and fought to the end. Weeks, a student in the Beaux Arts, responded to the call of France when war began. From the Foreign Legion he graduated into the air service, and from the air service to a hero's death.

The story of the American Ambulance Corps will not soon be forgotten. The two main groups were the American Volunteer Motor Ambulance Corps and the American Ambulance Field Service, the latter much the larger. The American Volunteer Motor Ambulance Corps owed its existence to a group of wealthy young Americans, headed by Mr. Richard Norton, who came over to France at the beginning of the war to offer their services. There were many difficulties in their way. The need of ambulances was tremendous, for the military cars then available were few, and anything but modern. For a time the Americans worked with a British group. Then for better organization the two worked separately. Soon the American Motor Ambulance Corps consisted of three convoys, each of twenty-five cars. Its staff numbered about 150 Americans, all of them volunteers, most unpaid and many helping to support with their money the work they were doing. It has been in every "big push." It has been twice cited before the Corps d'Armée —a very great honor, indeed; it has been repeatedly cited before Brigades; honors of every kind have been earned by its workers, and it has never failed to respond to the call for its service. A number of members of this Corps volunteered for active service, both in the British and French armies, and several of them died in the fighting ranks. Some joined the French Flying Corps. The case of Mr. Dilwyn Starr is typical of others. The son of Dr. Starr, of Philadelphia, he was conspicuous at Harvard as an athlete, playing for four years in the University football team. At the outbreak of the war he volunteered for service with this Corps, and for several months drove an ambulance for it. In December, 1914, he enlisted as a petty officer in the Armored Motor Car Section, R.N.A.S., and served with the Duke of Westminster's Squadron in France, taking part in the battle of Neuve Chapelle. Recommended for a commission, he was gazetted second lieutenant in May, 1915. At Gallipoli, he served with distinction as a machine gun officer in the trenches at Suvla Bay. Returning to England, he was given a commission in the Coldstream Guards, joined the Expeditionary Force in July, 1916, and was killed in the great mid-September fight on the Somme.

The work of the Ambulance gave its members full experience of actual war. "One of the posts which we served from the Somme Suippes was in front of and open to the German lines at Tahure," a report stated. "We had been frequently shelled there, but nothing serious had happened, though the hospital tents had been torn to ribbons, and the cars had been hit." The Americans do not trouble about trifles.

The crowning experience of the Corps came at Verdun. It was sent to the Douaumont sector, where the work was naturally very severe. The one road to the trenches and the *poste de secours* (the advanced dressing station) was entirely open to the Germans' fire, and could only be traversed at night time, when ammunition, guns and reliefs had to go up, and the wounded brought down.

Owing to the blunder of a doctor at the front, the corps was ordered to send five large ambulances in daylight to the advanced post, close to the front trenches. The Americans, knowing what was before them, started out. Immediately the cars were sighted, the Germans opened up a very heavy fire. Fortunately their range was defective, so that most got through safely. Two, however, Wendell and Hollinshead, were wounded. It was now impossible to send another car to bring them back, so two others, who had just gone through the raging fire, begged permission to return on foot, and to bring their comrades back in their own cars. The journey up to the front, exposed as they were to the shells of an alarmed and anxious enemy, may be imagined. The two wounded men refused to be helped until other wounded at the advanced post had been aided. When darkness came, all were got back. The four Americans engaged, Wendell and Hollinshead, McCreery and Harden, were all decorated with the Croix de Guerre, on the representations of the French authorities who witnessed what they had done.

For two weeks the work at Verdun went on night and day. There was active fighting at the front, and the wounded, carried by stretcher bearers to the dressing station, must be brought along to the bigger post at Verdun. The dressing station, the Sappe de Belfort, was an underground shelter, situated partly under the roadway itself in a very exposed part and fairly close up to the German line. It could only be approached at night time in absolute darkness. Even a cigarette light would have drawn fire.

A shell struck two of the doctors they were helping, and one was killed and the other wounded. Several of the ambulance cars were hit, and one of them pretty well pounded to pieces. The journey to the post was highly exciting. "On my first three trips," wrote Mr. Norton to his brother, "an artillery wagon with its horses and men was knocked out immediately in front of me. Night after night this went on—past the ruined and silent railway station, over the wooden bridge, round Dead Man's Corner, past Shell Street, and down Red Pepper Alley to the post, beyond which flashed the French guns on the hill forts and over which burst the Boche shells day and night. By dawn we never failed to have emptied all the advanced posts and to have brought back those doctors and brancardiers who did not have to stay out during the day on twenty-four-hour duty. Having got them all to Verdun, I then kept all the cars steadily at work until in two or three hours every case was out of Verdun and in the hospital. After that three or four cars stayed on all day at the Verdun post to handle the casualties which streamed into that spot, not only from our division but from all around, while the others went home for a short rest or to do the daily duty at the hospital and at the evacuation train. You can see that this kept us pretty fully occupied, but everything went well, and I can fairly say that the friends of the Corps can well be proud of the steadiness and vigor with which the men worked. Considering the fact that for many hours out of the twenty-four most of the men were under fire, it speaks well for their nerve and character that they were able to continue so long without breaking down."

There came the night when the Norton Ambulance was to be relieved by the American Field Ambulance. The leaders of both groups went up together that the newcomers might learn the lay of the land. On the previous evening, every one had suffered from the effects of an attack by "tear shells." On this last night, a very heavy gas attack was made. The sight was extraordinary. "Beside the gas," wrote Mr. Norton, "which was so thick that men and horses were dropping round about, the Boches were throwing incendiary shells along the road which our cars had to follow. Houses were burning and falling in the roadway, so that all traffic up and down was stopped. There was an absolute block. The conduct of the French during this time was very striking; not one seemed to be excited, not one raised his voice. Men on foot marched steadily on, while the drivers sat calming their horses and waiting quietly for the moment when they could hasten to their destination."

The cars returned to a sorely needed rest. There were well-earned decorations waiting for them, but there was something they prized even more. The convoy was cited before the corps d'armée. This was equivalent to giving an individual the Croix de Guerre, and gave it the right to paint the Cross on its wagons.

There were Americans in other branches of the French service besides the Flying Corps. At the beginning, most of the American volunteers—forty or fifty in all—went to the Foreign Legion. There was a memorable scene when hundreds of young Englishmen and Americans living in Paris marched in procession through the streets to offer themselves to France. Gradually they were removed from the Legion to other branches. Among them was one young poet, already stepping into recognition, Alan Seeger by name. An artist by temperament, he passed from Harvard to New York, and from there to Paris, where, still a lad in the mid-twenties, he settled in the Latin Quarter, developing his poetic soul. Then came the war. The Paris of his dreams was shattered; the stark reality remained. He faced the situation, and enlisted.

"Why did you enlist?" He sought to answer the question. "I have talked with so many of the young volunteers here. Their case is little known, even by the French, yet altogether interesting and appealing." He told how Paris had thrown her charm over them. Without renouncing their nationality, they had yet chosen to make their homes there, beyond any other city in the world. Were they not under a moral obligation to put their breasts between her and destruction?

They thought they were. The young poet found himself hard at drill, attempting to learn in six weeks what the ordinary recruit in times of peace learns in two years. Less than two months after enlistment, he and his comrades were moved up to the front. Then followed a monotonous winter of hardships of trench warfare and the spring and summer campaign of 1915. In the autumn they took part in the great Champagne attacks, a splendid and costly effort.

One can read in the letters of this young man that have been published with his poems, the development of his manhood. He had broadened, deepened, and his admiration for France, ever intense, was now taking a deeper tone. He had come to actualities. In the hour of disappointment his affection for France was stronger than ever. "We failed," he wrote, after one fight. "This affair only deepened my admiration for, my loyalty to, the French. He is a better man, man for man, than the German. Any one who had seen the charge of the Marsouins at Souain would acknowledge it. Never was anything more magnificent. I remember a captain, badly wounded in the leg, as he passed us, borne back on a litter by four German prisoners. He asked us what regiment we were, and when we told him, he cried, 'Vive la

*Legion,'* and kept repeating, *'Nous les avons. Nous les avons.'* He was suffering, but oblivious of his wound, was still fired with the enthusiasm of the assault and all radiant with victory. What a contrast with the German wounded, on whose faces was nothing but terror and despair."

Then came a long spell in the rear, which gave an opportunity to resume some of his literary activities. Back to the trenches in May, 1916, he proved his American strain by going on voluntary scouting expeditions. On one occasion he came clear up to the German barbed wire in No Man's Land and left a card with his name. "It was very thrilling work, 'courting destruction with taunts and invitations,' as Whitman would say." It was arranged that he was to return to Paris on Decoration Day, May 30th, to read before the statue of Lafayette and Washington an Ode in memory of the American volunteers fallen for France which he had written at the request of American residents. But his permission did not arrive in time. The days of the great July advance came, and Seeger was in the first rush of the Legion that stormed the village of Belloy-en-Santerre. Six German machine guns caught them with cruel, enfilading fire. Most of the storming party fell, Alan Seeger among them. Reënforcements followed and swept the enemy on one side. The young American cheered them on. As they left him behind the men heard him singing a marching song in English. All night long the wounded lay untended, and in the morning Alan Seeger was dead. "One day," wrote Mr. William Archer, the famous critic, "France will know that this unassuming soldier of the Legion,

> Who, not mindful of the antique debt,
> Came back the generous path of Lafayette,

was one whom even she may be proud to have reckoned among her defenders."

Little has been written about the Americans in the ranks of the British army. It is not that the British people have not warmly appreciated the help of the American men, but there was a desire to do nothing which should seem in any way to run counter to the American official declaration of neutrality. America is the guardian of her own honor.

The majority of Americans in the British ranks naturally enlisted in the Canadian army. At the beginning of the war a large number of Americans resident in Canada joined the ranks, and many others crossed the frontier for the same purpose.

Among the American officers, one of the best known was Major Stewart, who, although Montreal born, had served for twelve years as an officer in the United States Cavalry. He won the affection of every man under him, and it is told how, in his last gallant charge around Maple Copse, he cheered his boys on even as he fell. Lieutenant Stanley Wood, of Kansas City, fell in the same fight. Major John Lewis, an American who had become a British subject, fell gallantly when holding a small detachment together against overwhelmingly superior forces on the Somme. Major Houghton, once of the United States Navy, headed a machine gun section and went through many fights. Americans in the Canadian ranks earned many Distinguished Conduct Medals, Military Crosses and Military Medals.

Lord Northcliffe, in an article already quoted, has described his impressions of the American soldiers in the Canadian ranks in France. "When I saw them march back from the trenches to the tunes of 'My Country, 'tis of Thee,' 'The Star-Spangled Banner,' and the less classical and more modern ragtime, I wondered what the small American boys, who have so often teased me on Independence Day celebrations in your country, would have thought of a factor in the war that is not sufficiently known."

"I put one question to a score of those whose mothers were not ashamed to raise them to be soldiers. I asked them why they had come. The reply of the American in France is the same every time, whether you meet him with the Canadian army, the British army, or the French army. They all say words to this effect: 'The sort of thing that has been going on in Europe as the result of the horrible organized savagery of the Prussians has got to be stopped. We want to stop it before it reaches our own country.' "

# THE FIRST SUBMARINE TO CROSS THE ATLANTIC

## THE *DEUTSCHLAND* APPEARS IN NORFOLK HARBOR

### JULY 9TH

CAPTAIN PAUL KOENIG  ROBERT LANSING

The *Deutschland* was the first merchant submarine, the first under-seas boat capable of making a long voyage while carrying not only her own fuel and provisions but also a cargo of other goods. She was much larger than the submarines of 1914 and much more power-ful in every way. Thus her building marked an important scien-tific achievement, as well as an important addition to Germany's war strength.

Germany needed a great many commodities, such as rubber, nickel and the rarer elements used in making explosives, which the still neutral merchants of the United States could legitimately supply, if only these could escape the British blockade and so reach Germany. The *Deutschland* furnished the means of transporting them.

She appeared quite unexpectedly on July 9th in the broad harbor of Chesapeake Bay, docked at Norfolk, Virginia, and returned to Germany in August with an inestimably valuable cargo. On No-vember 1st she rose out of the waters again in Long Island Sound, docked at New London, Connecticut, and returned again to Germany. A second similar boat, the *Bremen,* also undertook the voyage. The British "destroyers," however, managed to block the sea road for both the big submarines. The *Deutschland* lay idle in a German harbor. Just what fate overtook the *Bremen* we do not know. She simply disappeared, and thus became a mystery of the sea.

Naturally the first voyage of the *Deutschland* raised new questions of International Law. The Allies united in presenting to the United States a note of protest. They urged that the *Deutschland* was really a warship, not a peaceful and unarmed merchant ship, and that therefore she could not be allowed to rest and provision herself in an American port. Having stopped there, she must be interned as a warship until the end of the War. In this discussion, however, the United States Government upheld the German viewpoint, that the *Deutschland* was really a merchant ship and entitled to harborage as such. Doubtless the United States Government was glad to demonstrate to the Ger-mans that it would still be fair to them in any case where they had any real justice on their side.

## BY CAPTAIN PAUL KOENIG

THE submarine *Deutschland,* which I have the honor to command, is the first of several submarines built to the order of the Deutsche Ozean Rhederei G.M.B.H., Bremen. She will be followed by the *Bremen* shortly.

The idea of the building of this submarine emanated from Alfred Lohmann, then President of the Bremen Chamber of Commerce. He brought his idea in the fall of last year confidentially before a small circle of friends, and the idea was taken up at once. A company was formed under the name of *"Deutsche Ozean Rhederei* G. M: B. H.," and the Germaniawerft, Kiel, was intrusted with the building of the submarines.

The Board of Directors is composed of Alfred Lohmann, President of the Board; Philipp Heineken, General Manager of the Nord Lloyd, and Kommerzienrat P. M. Herrman, Manager of the Deutsche Bank. Carl Stapelfeldt, Manager of the Nord Lloyd, has taken over the management of the company.

We have brought a most valuable cargo of dyestuffs to our American friends, dyestuffs which have been so much needed for months in America and which the ruler of the seas has not allowed the great American Republic to import. While England will not allow anybody the same right on the ocean because she rules the waves, we have, by means of the submarine, commenced to break this rule.

Great Britain cannot hinder boats such as ours to go and come as we please. Our trip passing Dover across the ocean was an uneventful one. When danger approached we went below the surface, and here we are, safely in an American port, ready to return in due course.

I am not in a position to give you full details regarding our trip across the ocean, in view of our enemies. Our boat has a displacement of about 2,000 tons and a speed of more than fourteen knots. Needless to say that we are quite unarmed and only a peaceful merchantman.

Our boats will carry across the Atlantic the mails and save them from British interruption. We trust that the old friendly relationship with the United States, going back to the days of Washington, when it was Prussia who was the first to help America in its fight for freedom from British rule, will awake afresh in your beautiful and powerful country.

The house flag of the *Deutsche Ozean Rhederei* is the old Bremen flag—red and white stripes, with the coat of arms of the town, the key in the corner. This key is the sign that we have opened the gates which Great Britain tried to shut up on us and the trade of the world. The gates which we opened with this key will not be shut again. Open door to the trade of the world and freedom of the oceans and equal rights to all nations on the oceans will be guaranteed by Germany's victory in this struggle for our existence.

*Official Joint Protest Sent by the Allied Governments to the U. S. Government Against Treating Any Submarine as Other Than a Ship of War*

In view of the development of submarine navigation and by reason of acts which in the present circumstances may be unfortunately expected from enemy submarines, the allied Governments consider it necessary, in order not only to safeguard their belligerent rights and liberty of commercial navigation, but to avoid risks of dispute, to urge neutral Governments to take effective measures, if they have not already done so, with a view to preventing belligerent submarine vessels, whatever the purpose to which they are put, from making use of neutral waters, roadsteads, and ports.

In the case of submarine vessels, the application of the principles of the law of nations is affected by special and novel conditions: First, by the fact that these vessels can navigate and remain at sea submerged, and can thus escape all control and observation; second, by the fact that it is impossible to identify them and establish their national character, whether neutral or belligerent, combatant or noncombatant, and to remove the capacity for harm inherent in the nature of such vessels.

It may further be said that any place which provides a submarine warship far from its base with an opportunity for rest and replenishment of its supplies thereby furnishes such addition to its powers that the place becomes in fact, through the advantages which it gives, a base of naval operations.

In view of the state of affairs thus existing, the Allied Governments are of the opinion that submarine vessels should be excluded from the benefit of the rules hitherto recognized by the law of nations regarding the admission of vessels of war or merchant vessels into neutral waters, roadsteads, or ports, and their sojourn in them.  Any belligerent submarine entering a neutral port should be detained there.

The allied Governments take this opportunity to point out to the neutral powers the grave danger incurred by neutral submarines in the navigation of regions frequented by belligerent submarines.

BY ROBERT LANSING

Official U. S. Response to the Above Protest

WASHINGTON, August 31, 1916.

The Government of the United States has received the identic memoranda of the Governments of France, Great Britain, Russia, and Japan in which neutral Governments are exhorted "to take efficacious measures tending to prevent belligerent submarines, regardless of their use, to avail themselves of neutral waters, roadsteads, and harbors." These Governments point out the facility possessed by such craft to avoid supervision or surveillance or determination of their national character and their power "to do injury that is inherent in their very nature" as well as the "additional facilities" afforded by having at their disposal places where they can rest and replenish their supplies.  Apparently on these grounds the allied Governments hold that "submarine vessels must be excluded from the benefit of the rules heretofore accepted under international law regarding the admission and sojourn of war and merchant vessels in neutral waters, roadsteads, or harbors; any submarine of a belligerent that once enters a neutral harbor must be held there," and therefore the allied Governments "warn neutral powers of the great danger to neutral submarines attending the navigation of waters visited by the submarines of belligerents."

In reply the Government of the United States must express its surprise that there appears to be an endeavor of the allied powers to determine the rule of action governing what they regard as a "novel situation" in respect to the use of submarines in time of war, and to enforce a compliance of that rule, at least in part, by warning neutral powers of the great danger to their submarines in waters that may be visited by belligerent submarines. In the opinion of the Government of the United States, the allied powers have not set forth any circumstance, nor is the Government of the United States at present aware of any circumstances, concerning the use of war or merchant submarines which would render the existing rules of international law inapplicable to them. In view of this fact and of the notice and warning of the allied powers announced in their memoranda under acknowledgment, it is incumbent upon the Government of the United States to notify the Governments of France, Great Britain, Russia, and Japan that, so far as the treatment of either war or merchant submarines in American waters is concerned, the Government of the United States reserves its liberty of action in all respects, and will treat such vessels as, in its opinion, becomes the action of a power which may be said to have taken the first steps toward establishing the principles of neutrality and which for over a century has maintained those principles in the traditional spirit and with the high sense of impartiality in which they were conceived.

In order, however, that there should be no misunderstanding as to the attitude of the United States, the Government of the United States announces to the allied powers that it holds it to be the duty of belligerent powers to distinguish between submarines of neutral and belligerent nationality, and that responsibility for any conflict that may arise between belligerent warships and neutral submarines on account of the neglect of a belligerent to so distinguish between these classes of submarines must rest entirely upon the negligent power.

# EXECUTION OF CAPTAIN FRYATT

## GERMANY ROUSES BRITISH SEAMEN TO VENGEANCE

### JULY 27TH

### GERMAN GOVERNMENT STATEMENT
### ARTHUR BALFOUR

The so-called "execution" of Captain Charles Fryatt roused the British people as no other event of the War had roused them. In the outer world, the execution of Edith Cavell, or even that of Sir Roger Casement in connection with the Sinn Fein uprising, had caused wider comment. That of Edith Cavell was lamented because she was a woman and a very noble one, done to death amid falsehood and callous severity. That of Sir Roger Casement was regretted because however mistaken in his methods, he was yet struggling for the freedom of his people. But in the Cavell case there had been some legal justification for the sentence; and in Casement's case there had been no question whatever that he had broken the long established law under which he was condemned, and in breaking it he had directly caused hundreds of deaths. In the Fryatt case, however, Germany officially broke every existing form of law, made a new law of her own and then condemned Captain Fryatt for not having followed this law before it had existed.

What Captain Fryatt did was to ram a German U-boat with a British merchant ship. And the world in general hailed him as a hero. What Germany did was to wait her chance, capture the captain on a later voyage, and condemn him as a *"franc-tireur,"* which means a disguised and secret foe who under pretense of being a noncombatant tricks the military into sparing him and then attacks them.

The German pretense was too shallow for argument. Captain Fryatt was absolutely within his rights; and the real German purpose was manifestly so to terrify merchant captains that they should not dare to resist.

The effect upon Britain of this murderous threat was extraordinary. The British people are really a great sea-faring company, and to interfere with their long established sea-law is to touch them in their tenderest spot. The Fryatt murder was thus far indeed from breaking the courage of British sea captains. Instead it hardened the resolution of all Britain to fight Germany to the bitter end. Mr. Asquith, then Prime Minister, the leader of the nation, solemnly announced in Parliament, "His Majesty's Government desire to repeat emphatically that they are resolved that such crimes shall not, if they can help it, go unpunished. When the time arrives they are determined to bring to justice the criminals, whoever they may be and whatever their station." And after later thought he added, "This country will not tolerate a resumption of diplomatic relations with Germany after the war until reparation is made for the murder of Captain Fryatt." Britain meant exactly what she said. The War thereafter was to be fought to a finish.                                    C. F. H.

## GERMAN GOVERNMENT STATEMENT OF JULY 28TH

THE accused was condemned to death because, although he was not a member of a combatant force, he made an attempt on the afternoon of March 20, 1915, to ram the German submarine *U-33* near the Maas lightship. The accused, as well as the first officer and the chief engineer of the steamer, received at the time from the British Admiralty a gold watch as a reward of his brave conduct on that occasion, and his action was mentioned with praise in the House of Commons.

On the occasion in question, disregarding the U-boat's signal to stop and show his national flag, he turned at a critical moment at high speed on the submarine, which escaped the steamer by a few meters only by immediately diving. He confessed that in so doing he had acted in accordance with the instructions of the Admiralty.

One of the many nefarious *franc-tireur* proceedings of the British merchant marine against our war vessels has thus found a belated but merited expiation.

### Supplementary Statement of August 10th

It is only too intelligible that the English Government attempts to justify Captain Fryatt's action, for it is itself in a high degree a fellow-culprit. Captain Fryatt, acting as he did, acted only on the advice of his Government.

The British Government's statement intentionally misleads the public. Captain Fryatt did not attempt to forestall an under-water attack, without warning, by the submarine. The U-boat was above water, and signaled to him when above water to stop, according to the international code of naval warfare. Therefore, he did not merely attempt to save the lives of his crew, because they were not endangered. Moreover, on March 28, 1915, Captain Fryatt allowed the submarine, which was approaching his ship for the purposes of examination, to draw up close, so as to ram her suddenly and unexpectedly, his object being to destroy her, and so gain the reward offered by the British Government. This act was not an act of self-defense, but a cunning attack by hired assassins. Captain Fryatt boasted of his action, though happily he failed to attain his object. This was brought home to him during the trial by witnesses from the crew of the submarine in question, whose evidence was against him. The British Parliament believed he had succeeded and praised his conduct, and the British Government rewarded him.

The German War Tribunal sentenced him to death because he had performed an act of war against the German sea forces, although he did not belong to the armed forces of his country. He was not deliberately shot in cold blood without due consideration, as the British Government asserts, but he was shot as a *franc-tireur,* after calm consideration and thorough investigation. As martial law on land protects the soldiery against assassination, by threatening the offender with the penalty of death, so it protects the members of the sea forces against assassination at sea. Germany will continue to use this law of warfare in order to save her submarine crews from becoming the victims of *francs-tireurs* at sea.

### BY ARTHUR BALFOUR

If any desire yet further proof of the value which the Germans really attach to their "victorious" fleet I advise them to study the German policy of submarine warfare. The advantage of submarine attacks on commerce is that they cannot be controlled by superior fleet power in the same way as attacks by cruisers. The disadvantage is that they cannot be carried out on a large scale consistently with the laws of war or the requirements of humanity. They make, therefore, a double appeal to German militarism; an appeal to its prudence and an appeal to its brutality. The Germans knew their "victorious" fleet was useless; it could be kept safe in harbor while submarine warfare went on merrily outside. They knew that submarines cannot be brought to action by battleships or battle cruisers. They thought, therefore, that to these new commerce destroyers our merchant ships must fall an easy prey, unprotected by our ships of war and unable to protect themselves.

They are wrong in both respects; and doubtless it is their wrath at the skill and energy with which Britsh merchant captains and British crews have defended the lives and property under their charge that has driven the German Admiralty into their latest and stupidest act of calculated ferocity—the judicial murder of Captain Fryatt.

I do not propose to argue this case; it is not worth arguing. Why should we do the German military authorities the injustice of supposing that they were animated by any solicitude for the principles of international law, and blundered into illegality by some unhappy accident? Their folly was of a different kind, and flowed from a different course. They knew quite well that when Captain Fryatt's gallantry saved his ship, the Germans had sunk without warning 22 British merchant ships, and had attempted to sink many others. They knew that in refusing tamely to submit himself to such a fate he was doing his duty as a man of courage and of honor. They were resolved at all costs to discourage imitation!

What blunderers they are! I doubt not their ability to manipulate machines. But of managing men, unless it be German men, they know less than nothing. They are always wrong; and they are wrong because they always suppose that if they behave like brutes they can cow their enemies into behaving like cowards. Small is their knowledge of our merchant seamen. Their trade, indeed, is not war —they live by the arts of peace. But in no class does patriotism burn with a purer flame, or show itself in deeds of higher courage and self-devotion. I doubt whether there is one of them to be found who is not resolved to defend himself to the last against piratical attack; but if such a one there be, depend upon it he will be cured by the last exhibition of German civilization.

And what must the neutrals think of all this? They are constantly assured by German advocates that the Central

Powers are fighting for the "freedom of the seas." It is a phrase with different meanings in different mouths; but we have now had ample opportunities of judging what it means to the Germans. It means that the German Navy is to behave at sea as the German Army behave on land. It means that neither enemy civilians nor neutrals are to possess rights against militant Germany; that those who do not resist will be drowned, and those who do will be shot.

### OFFICIAL BRITISH STATEMENT

On March 28, 1915, a German submarine sank the *Falaba*. It is well known that the *Falaba* stopped when ordered to do so by the German aggressor. Nevertheless, the German captain of the submarine did not give time for the passengers to be put into boats, and torpedoed this great liner while non-combatants were still on board. One of those who were on the deck describes the scene as follows: "The Commander of the submarine ordered our Captain to get every passenger into the boats at once, saying in good English: 'I am going to sink your ship.' Then followed a terrible scene. Some of the boats were swamped and their occupants thrown into the sea, several being drowned almost immediately. Barely ten minutes after we received the order to leave the ship, and before the last boat had been lowered, I heard a report, and saw our vessel heel over. The pirates had actually fired a torpedo at her at a range of 100 yards, when they could distinctly see a large number of passengers and crew on board. It was a dastardly thing to do;—nothing but murder in cold blood." One hundred and four men and women lost their lives.

It was on this same Sunday, March 28th, that Captain Fryatt met the *U-33* in the North Sea. In the afternoon, when on a voyage from Parkeston to Rotterdam, the *Brussels* sighted a German submarine, at least three hundred feet long, with a very high bow, a very large circular conning tower, and without distinguishing marks, on her starboard bow. Captain Fryatt soon realized that the speed of the submarine was far greater than his own, and that if he attempted to turn away, he could easily be torpedoed. **The** submarine signaled him to stop, but his British courage revolted at the thought of surrender, and the experience of German methods of warfare warned him that surrender would be no guarantee that the lives of his crew would be spared. He determined therefore to take the best chance of saving his ship, and to steer for the submarine in order to force her to dive, and, if she were not quick enough in diving, to ram her.

This was his undoubted right under international law—to disregard her summons and resist her attack to the best of his power. It was a contest of skill and courage in which each side took their chance. Captain Fryatt, therefore, starboarded his helm, and gave orders to his engineers to make all possible speed. He sent all the crew aft to a place of safety, in case the submarine should fire upon him, and steered straight for the conning tower. The latter, when she saw that the *Brussels* would not surrender, but was bent upon exercising her undoubted right of resistance, immediately submerged. The *Brussels* saw her disappear about twenty yards ahead, and steered for the place where she had been. Almost immediately her periscope came up abreast of the *Brussels,* two feet out of the water. Captain Fryatt did not feel his ship strike the submarine, but one of the firemen felt a bumping sensation. The submarine reappeared with a decided list, and afterwards vanished from view. Captain Fryatt held his course at top speed until he was safely within the territorial waters of Holland.

The claim of the Wolff Bureau that Captain Fryatt allowed the submarine to approach for examination is utterly false, and the pretense of some German papers that he surrendered, and afterwards attacked the *U*-33, or that he was guilty of any deception or any underhand dealing, is equally untrue. These false pleas can only be attributed to their desire to conceal a foul crime under a cloak of lies.

Let us not be deceived into thinking that the request to stop was any evidence of humane intention. The *Falaba* stopped, and her list of dead is eloquent. Captain Fryatt, already familiar with the designs of German submarines from his previous adventure, sought to save his ship's company from a similar fate. Did he do it, as the *Weser Zeitung* of Germany pretends, "from ambition and lust of gain?"

No; though he is dead, his comrades live, and through his courage and resource they have been saved the fate of the women and children on the *Lusitania* and many other ships which stopped and surrendered, and whose passengers, through the inhuman conduct of a German submarine, were drowned at sea.

By his action Captain Fryatt undoubtedly saved the lives of those under his charge. At the date of this gallant act the Germans had already sunk without warning twenty-two British merchant ships, and had attempted to sink many others. The German Proclamation of February 4th was an offer of attack without further notice to any merchant vessel flying the British flag in those waters; and the Captain, in acting as he did, did no more than defend himself against the illegally proffered violence of the enemy.

The British Admiralty presented Captain Fryatt with a gold watch, suitably inscribed, in recognition of his services. This watch, and the watch awarded by the Great Eastern Railway Company for his previous exploit, did not fall into the hands of a pirate submarine, but are in the safe keeping of his widow, to be an heirloom in his family. The award of the watch by the Admiralty was announced in the British House of Commons on April 28, 1915, by Dr. Macnamara, Secretary to the Admiralty, who mentioned, amongst other merchant captains, the name of Captain Fryatt, as one who had baffled a German submarine by his bravery and resource, and had been selected by the Admiralty "as deserving of reward for specially meritorious services."

His Majesty, King George, in a letter addressed to Mrs. Fryatt from Buckingham Palace, lately expressed what will be the feeling of the whole world when he said: "The action of Captain Fryatt in defending his ship against the attack of an enemy submarine was a noble instance of the resource and self-reliance so characteristic of his profession."

Captain Fryatt sailed from the Hook of Holland on the evening of June 22, 1916, more than a year after his last recorded encounter with a submarine. A friend who shook his hand as he went on the bridge found him calm and cheerful as ever. The *Brussels* had a cargo of foodstuffs and some Belgian refugees on board. But when well on her voyage to Tilbury she was captured by a flotilla of German torpedo boats, and she was taken as a prize to Zeebrugge. It was reported at the time that there was a suspicious character on board the *Brussels,* who spoke German fluently, and was afterwards treated with the utmost consideration by the Germans. The Amsterdam *Telegraaf* bears testimony to the quiet and dignified conduct of the crew and its Captain after capture. It speaks of Captain Fryatt himself as standing in the midst of his officers, his face as calm as if he were on the bridge, comforting the weeping Belgian women with a kindly word, and thinking only of others.

On the 1st of July, the American Ambassador, in reply to an inquiry from the British Foreign Office, assured Sir Edward Grey that the officers and crew of the *Brussels* were safe and well, and that the Master of the vessel "desired that his wife might be informed." Nobody suspected at that time the import and terrible significance of those pathetic words.

It was not until the 16th of July that the Government and public of Great Britain first learned, in the columns of the Amsterdam *Telegraaf,* that Captain Fryatt was to be tried by court-martial on a charge of ramming a German submarine. The British Foreign Office immediately made inquiries of the American Ambassador, and requested that proper steps might be taken for the Captain's defense. The report in the *Telegraaf* was only too true.

We have no particulars of the court-martial which was held at Bruges. It is not certain whether any independent witnesses were present, and it is unlikely that the Germans will ever disclose what took place there. Everything appears to have been done in the dark and in haste, as by those who shunned the light of publicity in the performance of their sinister work. We can only quote the bald outlines of the German official telegram, which stated that:

"On Thursday, at Bruges, before the Court-Martial of

the Marine Corps, the trial took place of Captain Charles Fryatt, of the British steamer *Brussels,* which was brought in as a prize."

A postponement of the trial had been asked for; but this was refused, on the ground that "German submarine witnesses could not be further detained"! Upon such an outrageous pretext, the trial was immediately held, and Captain Fryatt was "defended" by Major Neumann, "in civil life an attorney and Justizrat." Under what principle of international law was he tried? What was the nature of the impeachment? What are the names of the judges who condemned him?

According to the German official pronouncement, Captain Fryatt was condemned because: "Although he was not a member of a combatant force, he made an attempt on the afternoon of March 28, 1915, to ram the German submarine, *U*-33, near the Maas Lightship."

That resistance to such an attack is legitimate, is clear from the prize law of all the great states; of the British Empire, the United States, Italy, Spain, and others. It is even admitted by the German prize regulations; for in an appendix to these, dated June 22, 1914, may be found the following clause: "If an armed enemy merchant vessel offers armed resistance to the right of visit, search and capture . . . the crew are to be treated as prisoners of war."

It is true that the German regulation speaks of armed merchant vessels; but that can make no difference. A merchant vessel is none the less a merchant vessel because she is armed; her officers and crew do not become members of a combatant force because the vessel carries guns for defense; a merchantman is permitted to resist an enemy warship, not because she has any combatant quality, but because she will be captured at the best, or if she meets a German submarine, probably sunk without warning; and even capture is an act of hostility to which a merchantman need not submit.

The justice of these contentions has been admitted by an eminent German international lawyer, Dr. Hans Wehberg, in his book, *"Das Seekriegsrecht,"* published since the outbreak of the present war. He writes: "In truth no single example can be produced from international precedents in which the States have held that resistance is not permissible. On the contrary, in the celebrated decision of Lord Stowell in the case of the *Catharina Elizabeth* resistance was declared permissible, and Article 10 of the American Naval War Code takes up the same standpoint. By far the greater number of authors and the Institute of International Law share this view. . . . The enemy merchant ship has then the right of defense against an enemy attack, and this right she can exercise against visit, for this is indeed the first act of capture."

The opinion that such resistance is illegal is scarcely held outside Germany; it is of recent growth; and its chief exponent is Dr. Schramm, who is legal adviser to the German Admiralty. It is not difficult to conjecture that his opinion, and the opinion of his friends, was first conceived at the time when Germany was making her final preparations for an assault upon civilization.

Moreover, the German Government, in a memorandum which it handed to neutral Powers on February 10, 1916, while maintaining that, in the view of Germany, merchant vessels were not entitled to defend themselves, stated that: "It takes into consideration also the contrary conception by treating their crews as belligerents."

In the face of the horror and incredulity of the whole world, which, despite a surfeit of German barbarity, could scarcely comprehend this latest crime, the Germans have made frantic efforts to justify this judicial murder. They have justified it under a German prize rule relating to *neutral* ships! They have argued that the good of their cause demanded it—a wicked argument which can weigh with nobody outside Germany. They have argued further that Captain Fryatt was a *franc-tireur*.

"One of the many nefarious *franc-tireur* proceedings of the British Merchant Marine against our war vessels," states the German official telegram, "has thus found a belated but merited expiation."

During the Franco-German War of 1870, various French irregular forces carried on an intermittent warfare

The Austrian Defense of Gorizia

The river and the cliffs which formed the chief barrier to the Italian advance

Painting by the Austrian artist Prof. Hans W. Schmid.

The Austrian Defense of Gorizia
The river and the cliffs which
formed the chief barrier to the
Italian advance

Painting by the Austrian artist,
Prof. Hans W. Schmidt

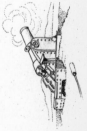

against the German army.  Throughout the war the Germans shot every such irregular soldier that fell into their hands.  This brutal conduct aroused the indignation of many peoples in many lands, and now, by an article of the Hague regulations for the conduct of warfare on land, such irregulars are entitled to be treated on the same footing as regular forces when they are under a responsible commander, wear a distinctive badge, carry arms openly, and conform with the laws of war.  Further, even the requirements of a responsible commander and a distinctive badge are dispensed with, where the population rises spontaneously to resist an invader, and in this case unauthorized bodies of men, armed and obeying the laws of war, are entitled, if captured, to be treated as prisoners of war.

Here then is an exception to the general rule that a fighter must be a member of the authorized armed forces in order to make good his claim to be treated as a prisoner. A similar exception has existed from time immemorial at sea.  And indeed the difficulty felt by the Hague Conference in granting to irregulars on land the right to be treated as prisoners does not exist in the case of a merchant seaman.  He and his ship are on the open sea, and in full view; he cannot change his clothes, and lose his identity amid a crowd of civilians; he cannot take his enemy unawares. From the moment when he is attacked, he is permitted to defend himself, and his attacker is at no disadvantage.

Every German submarine in the war area may be assumed by a British merchant captain to be engaged in carrying out the orders of the German "Higher Command."  The presence of such a submarine in the neighborhood of a British merchant ship is an offer to strike coupled with the capacity to fulfill the threat.  It is, in other words, an offensive act, for visit is, as Dr. Wehberg says, the first act of capture.  Under these circumstances the captain of a merchant ship may defend his ship, and is not a *franc-tireur* if he does so; when captured, he must be treated as a prisoner of war.  Captain Fryatt defended his ship; he was not captured; at a later date he fell into the enemy's hands, and has been shot because he dared to exercise his undoubted

legal right.  We say "undoubted," because no doubt arose
until the apostles of German militarism and of the "freedom
of the seas" were perfecting their final plans.

But what need is there to pay the German Government
the compliment of supposing that it has acted under any mistaken view of law?  Consistently with itself, it has but
complied with its own military needs.  It has now become
a habit in Germany to reckon as a *franc-tireur* any class of
persons who are particularly obnoxious to the advancement
of German militarism.  For instance, the *Rheinisch West-
fälische Zeitung* of August 1, 1916, published an article
calling upon the German Government to treat American
volunteers fighting with Allied troops against Germany as
*francs-tireurs* and, when captured, to shoot or, preferably, to
hang them.

On the 30th of July the *Telegraaf* learned that Captain
Fryatt had been shot towards the evening of the Thursday
before, on an enclosed part of the harbor grounds at Bruges,
and that an Alderman of the town had attended as witness.
The news of his death was officially confirmed by a telegram from the American Ambassador.  No further details
are known; nor probably will they ever be known.  The
German Government had learnt enough wisdom from its execution of Edith Cavell to know that such things are better
done in secret, though they had not learned sufficient humanity, nor won enough sense of justice nor common sense,
to feel that such things cannot be done at all, without outrage
to the feelings of the civilized world.

The Germans well knew that this latest judicial murder
would arouse the indignation of the whole world; but they
were resolved, if possible, to discourage imitation of Captain Fryatt's gallantry at all costs.  "Doubtless there will be
among England's sympathizers all the world over a storm
of indignation against German barbarism similar to that
roused by the case of Miss Cavell.  That must not disturb
us," wrote the German *Kölnische Volkszeitung* of July 29,
1916.

The *Volkszeitung* was not disappointed.  A shudder of
loathing and detestation, of horror and incredulity ran

through every neutral country, the British Empire, and the countries of our Allies. The universal verdict was that the barbarities of the world's past, even of the German past, were outdone. The voice of the New York *Herald* was raised in protest against a "CROWNING GERMAN ATROCITY." The New York *Times* saw in the shooting of Captain Fryatt "a deliberate murder—a trifle to the Government that has so many thousands to answer for."

In Holland, the *Nieuwe Rotterdamsche Courant* of July 29th condemned the outrage, and said: "At the time that the Captain of the *Brussels* made his unsuccessful attempt, the submarine war was being carried on in the most brutal manner in contempt of all rules of humanity. The mere sighting of a German submarine meant death for hundreds who are now called '*francs-tireurs*' in the German communiqué. To claim for oneself the right to kill hundreds of civilians out of hand, but to brand as a *franc-tireur* the civilian who does not willingly submit to execution, amounts, in our opinion, to measuring justice with a different scale, according to whether it is to be applied to oneself or to another. This is, in our view, *arbitrariness* and *injustice*. And that touches us even in the midst of all the horrors of the war. It shocks the neutrals, and arouses fresh bitterness and hatred in the enemy."

A Swiss paper, the *Journal de Genève*, denounces the German crime and says: "It is monstrous to maintain that armed forces have a right to murder civilians but that civilians are guilty of a crime in defending themselves."

# THE STORMING OF GORIZIA

## ITALY'S CHIEF AGGRESSIVE CAMPAIGN

### AUGUST 9TH

GENERAL CADORNA                      EDWIN GREWE
WALTER OERTEL

The Italian forces having, as depicted in the previous pages, repulsed the huge Austrian assault from the Alps, were now ready to resume their own aggressive campaign. General Cadorna had been long preparing a main attack to sweep across the northeastern frontiers of Italy and drive the Austrians from their strong positions among the mountains bordering on the Isonzo River. Here for over a year the Italian armies had been held in check by lesser Austrian forces secure in their almost impregnable defenses.

Cadorna's great attack was launched on August 6th, and was carried forward by the eager Italian soldiers with such dash and energy that in three days they swept aside the Austrian defenses and captured Gorizia, the chief city of the Isonzo valley. The success was brilliant and spectacular.

Unfortunately, however, Gorizia was but a single forward step. Beyond it towered one mountain range after another. Trieste, the great Austro-Italian city which was Cadorna's ultimate goal was only some score of miles beyond his outposts. But almost every foot of the way would require a costly battle against great natural disadvantages. So the Italians fought on all summer without ever getting much beyond Gorizia. They compelled the Austrians to transfer many troops from the Russian front to hold back the Italian advance; but that was all.

Thus the Isonzo battle, like the even greater struggles of Verdun and the Somme, was indecisive, a vast hecatomb of human victims, another long stride toward the utter exhaustion of humanity.

### BY GENERAL CADORNA

Official Report of December 26, 1916

IN the spring we sustained in the Trentino the powerful, long-prepared Austrian offensive, which the enemy with insolent effrontery styled a punitive expedition against our country. But after the first successes, which were due to the preponderance of material means collected, above all in artillery, the proposed invasion was quickly stopped and the enemy was counter-attacked and forced to retire in haste into the mountains, leaving on the Alpine slopes the flower of his army and paying bitterly the price for his fallacious enterprise not only here but also on the plains of Galicia.

Our army did not rest after its wonderful effort. While maintaining a vigorous pressure on the Trentino front, in order to gain better positions and to deceive the enemy as to our intentions, a rapid retransfer of strong forces to the Julian front was made. In the first days of August began that irresistible offensive which, in two days only, caused the fall of the very strong fortress of Gorizia and of the formidable system of defenses on the Carso to the west of the Vallone. Doberdò, San Michele, Sabotino—names recalling sanguinary struggles and slaughter—ceased to be for the Austro-Hungarian Army the symbols of a resistance vaunted insuperable, and became the emblems of brilliant Italian victories. The enemy's boastful assertions of having inexorably arrested our invasion on the front selected and desired by himself were refuted at one stroke.

From that day our advance on the Carso was developed constantly and irresistibly. It was interrupted by pauses indispensable for the preparation of the mechanical means of destruction without which the bravest attacks would lead only to the vain sacrifice of precious human lives.

Our constant and full success on the Julian front is witnessed by 42,000 prisoners, 60 guns, 200 machine guns, and the rich booty taken between the beginning of August and December.

Also on the rest of the front our indefatigable troops roused the admiration of all who saw them for their extraordinary efforts to overcome not only the forces of the enemy but also the difficulties of nature. Our soldiers are supported by the unanimous approval of the nation, by faith in themselves and in the justice of their cause. They face willingly their hard and perilous life, under the guidance of their beloved sovereign, who from the first day of the war with a rare constancy has shared their fortunes. Our army is waiting in perfect readiness to renew the effort which will carry it to the fulfillment of the unfailing destiny of our people.

BY EDWIN GREWE

The expectations of distant onlookers may have been disappointed when, during the latter half of June and in the month of July, the Italians, though apparently pressing on a rebuffed Austrian army, had little to show in the way of captures of men or guns, and showed no great persistence in pushing for positions in Trentino. What was in fact happening was that General Cadorna, though making a great display of activity there, was quietly withdrawing men and guns to supplement the effort which he had from the first projected on the Isonzo. By the first week in August, 1916, he was ready to strike here.

The capture of the bridgehead of Gorizia was an essential preliminary to any attack on Austrian territory, or on the Austrian forces, which could be undertaken at anything like a cost commensurate with the advantages to be obtained. It was deeply wedged in behind mountain positions which had been strengthened by every device of rock trenching and tunneling, and by every caliber of fortress gun which the Austrians had at their command. The buttresses of its defense were Mt. Sabotino on the hither side of the Isonzo River, with ridges running south from Mt. Sabotino to Oslavia and the Podgora plateau; on the farther side of the river was the rock position of San Marco, and farther south the great bastion of the Carso, jutting out into Mt. San Michele and cleft by the long ravine of the Vallone.

The Austrian front was defended by the Fifth Austrian Army under General Boroviec, whose command extended from the sea up to Tolmino, 25 miles north of Gorizia, where he was joined by the Tenth Austrian Army under General Rohr. It was on General Boroviec's front that Cadorna's attack, supported by 100,000 men in line, was launched. The first assault made by the Italians was not the principal one, but was a feint attack delivered ten miles south of Gorizia on those Austrian positions at Monfalcone which lie in front of one of the southern buttresses of Carso. The inference which Cadorna wished the enemy to draw was that here he proposed to undertake a movement to turn the great mountain-block which lies on this side of the Carso and is separated from it by the Vallone. Plenty of fire was put into this subsidiary assault, and about 150 Austrian prisoners were taken. The attack fulfilled its object of drawing Austrian forces to the threatened point and of provoking a strong counter-attack. August 5th was an artillery day only. On August 6th the Italian batteries began in earnest, and this time neglected the Monfalcone sector for the points selected for the real attack—the Sabotino block and the San Michele height which forms the northern boundary of the Gorizian Carso.

The work of the batteries and trench howitzers was a classic example of the concentration of fire against fortified lines. It had long been carefully prepared; the ground carefully examined by patrols, photographed by aviators, and the ranges marked to the yard. The tempest of fire wrecked the Austrian first lines, demolishing the shelters, destroying the observation posts, cutting the communications. Then the infantry advanced on the model taught by the experience of the Western fronts, one artillery curtain going in front of the infantry advancing in column, and spreading fanwise; another curtain barring the way against enemy reënforcements. The infantry went forward with Italian fire. They flowed over every obstacle on the rampart between Sabotino and the Gorizia bridgehead. On the heights which protected the town from the west a column under Colonel Badoglio took by assault the defenses of Oslavia, and the whole position of the Sabotino followed. In the open country below Oslavia the infantry broke through the entanglements and the trench network constructed by the enemy between the southern spurs of Podgora and the Isonzo, and got well down to the bank of the river. On the Gorizian Carso the strong lines of Mt. San Michele which had broken so many Italian assaults in the past were in their turn broken, and a long line of trenches was carried thence southwards to San Martino. Finally, towards Monfalcone the attack begun two days before was renewed by a battalion of Bersaglieri cyclists, who, after a desperate fight, took one of the key positions and held it.

With Sabotino and San Michele in their hands the Italians had now to turn the keys in the lock, and to sweep the ridge which lay between them immediately west of the town. Three days of bloody clearance followed among the deep-sunk trenches, the fortified and armored parts, the mutually supporting lesser heights which formed the last defenses of Gorizia. But with the help of the artillery, and the confidence born of success, the work was done. On August 8th all the heights on the west bank of the Isonzo were Italian, and on the 10th the Duke of Aosta entered Gorizia at the head of the 3rd Army, which he commanded. The fighting had been too close and continuous for the capture of many Austrian guns, but 10,000 prisoners testified to the completeness of the victory.

The taking of Gorizia was one of the great feats of the war; it was one of the greatest in Italian military history. To Italy it was the turning of the tide, the assurance that, after what at one time seemed like the threat of disaster in the Trentino, their feet were now set on the steps to victory and on the pathway to Trieste. General Cadorna deserved the congratulations showered on him. From the beginning of the war he had played a waiting game, often hampered by the malign influences which in every country are due to underground German intrigue, but watching always for every opportunity, missing none that was offered, and husbanding the precious lives of his men for the moment that was bound to come.

He lost no time in following up his success. During the days between August 6th and 10th the Austrians had made frantic efforts to recover Monte San Michele. They did not succeed, and they also lost Baschini. Cadorna, as soon as his engineers had repaired the bridges, sent his cavalry into the wedge of the plain, and forced the Austrians back to their positions on the hills east of the Isonzo. Here, however, they had strong positions long prepared, stretching from Monte Gabriele, which is *vis-à-vis* to Monte Sabotino, across the river, down to the bulk of San Marco, which is

east and south of Gorizia. This position was protected by
flanking batteries on the Bainsizza plateau, and the plateau
itself was very strongly fortified, as the Italians had found
when they had tried months before to push their advantage
from Plava. Simultaneously with the movement in the plain
the Italians began to work their way across the Carso. It
was a task for supermen. The surface is undulating, and
honeycombed with holes and caves of which the Austrians
had made the fullest use for purposes of defense, linking
them up with concrete and steel-lined trenches, and con-
verting the natural features into modern fortifications. They
thought it impregnable; it might have been, had the Italian
attack been less scientifically furious or the surprise less effective. On August 10th Rubbini followed Boschini, and the
whole of the Gorizian plateau at its northern end was secured as far as the deep gash of the Vallone. On the 11th
the Italians crossed the Vallone and occupied the village of
Oppacchiasella. Next day, irresistibly pressing on, they
carried further heights, and stormed the position of Nad
Logem, where they took 1,600 prisoners. On the subsequent
days, down to the 15th, they prosecuted their success with the
same vigor, carrying their lines past Debeli and Nad Logem
up to Monte Pecinka. Then they settled down to reorganize their lines and positions for the next push. In the
course of their operations from August 4th to 15th they took
18,758 prisoners, of whom 393 were officers, 30 big guns,
63 bomb throwers, 92 machine guns, 12,225 rifles, 5,000,000
cartridges, 3,000 shells, 60,000 bombs, and other war material.

During the next two months the Italians steadily con-
solidated their gains. Much that had fallen to them had
been the fruits of surprise and of swiftly-seized opportunity.
The Austrians still had numerous valuable and patiently
fortified positions and had every incentive to prevent the
Italians from debouching from these that had fallen to them.
Between mid-August and mid-September, nevertheless, the
Italians took the San Grado position northeast of Nad
Logem, so securing the northern angle of the Carso com-
pletely, and removing the damaging effect of the Austrian

fire based on that point. Progress was necessarily slow on the Carso, the difficulties of supply were very great, and on that parched, desert-like plateau water was lacking. But the capture of the San Grado position enabled the Italians to steal down in the plain along the Vipacco River, and so to turn some of the Austrian lines so obstinately held on the higher ground. On October 10th a surprise attack was successfully driven into the Austrian positions north and south of the Vipacco River, and conformably with this success the Italian line on the Carso pushed forward by about a mile. In the two days' fighting, 7,000 Austrian prisoners were taken.

This was the prelude to a still more important advance on the northern Carso at the beginning of November. It was made along the northernmost ridge, which commands the Vipacco valley, as well as on the mid-Carso, and on the Carso's chief road, which cuts across it from Doberdo to Comen. From the Vallone ravine (November 2nd) the assault began by scaling the rocky ascent which rises in successive terraces towards the east, and from there was pressed over a 3½-mile front till it had won a depth of over 2 miles from the Vallone. It captured the two Austrian defensive lines of Nad Logem-Oppacchiasella, and the line running through the village of Lokvica, with the roads radiating from Castagnevizza. Two days of incessant fighting did not exhaust the momentum of the advance. The 11th Italian Army Corps succeeded on November 3rd in driving a wedge through the two Austrian lines until Monte Faiti was reached and occupied. On November 3rd, pivoting on that height, the Army Corps moved in echelon southwards and eastwards till the whole enemy salient was cleared, and the new Italian line ran from Monte Faiti to Castagnevizza. Farther north all the minor heights, where the northern brow of the Carso slopes down to the Vipacco River, were carried by assault. The whole advance covered a tract of ground more than 2 miles deep, and the total number of prisoners taken in three days amounted to 9,000 men. It was another step on the way to Trieste; but the last step to be accomplished before the winter storms.

BY WALTER OERTEL

Gorizia has fallen. After a long and stubborn resistance the city of violets has surrendered to the Italians. Once a beautiful and flourishing city, it is now but a heap of ruins, a sacrifice to the great general offensive instituted by the Entente on all three fronts.

In preparation for the Italian offensive Cadorna had sent large bodies of troops to the Isonzo front. Out of these, strengthened by reserves and new formations, he built up a new army, which he collected at Livorno and placed under the command of the Duke of Aosta. The appointed task of the new army was to capture the positions on the plateau of Doberdo, which had been long and hotly contested, and to break through to Gorizia. In the latter half of July the greatly increased activity of the Italian artillery was noticeable on the left wing of the Austro-Hungarian Isonzo front. Many new batteries, among which were numerous guns of heavy caliber, including, indeed, some of the heaviest, joined in the bombardment. At the same time the infantry showed increased initiative and made some local attacks, which were in each case sharply repulsed.

The 5th of August drew near, the day on which the great offensive was to open. At five o'clock in the afternoon of that day the Italian artillery began to pour a hail of shot into the Austro-Hungarian lines from Monte Sabotino down to Monte San Michele. The bursting of the heavy shells one after another soon enveloped the defenders' positions in a thick pall of smoke, which was lighted up only by the flames from new explosions. Nor was the Italian infantry idle. Mine throwers worked by compressed air, of which a great quantity had been collected before the beginning of the offensive and set up in the Italian trenches, discharged heavy aërial mines unceasingly; winged torpedoes sang overhead; while underground the Italian sappers burrowed feverishly in the effort to push out their long galleries far enough to blow up the Austro-Hungarian trenches from below. Under the terrible hail of iron, trench walls collapsed and dugouts were blown to pieces, but the men—Hungarians, Dalmatians,

and Bosnians—held out stubbornly, resolved to die gloriously rather than to give up the positions entrusted to them.
Whenever the Italians attempted to carry forward their long
bombs made of gas pipe, from five to eight meters in length,
filled with ekrasite—similar to those which the Japanese
made use of in their Manchurian campaign—a well-aimed
Austrian shot whistled over the spot, and whenever an Italian
cap showed over the breastworks, it quickly dropped back
again, pierced by a bullet.  Bold volunteers even came to
grips with the Italians, and literally tore from their hands
the destructive instruments with which they intended to blow
up the remaining defenses and make a breach for the attack.

Protected by the furious drum fire, the Italians went
forward to the assault.  Having in previous battles received
disheartening proof of the strength of our positions west of
the Isonzo, and especially of the Podgora position, the army
commander decided this time to direct the main weight of
the attack against the two wings, so as to be able to approach
the Podgora from the rear.  The first attack on Monte
Sabotino was a bloody repulse.  Elsewhere the Italians
stormed forward in furious rushes.  They fought desperately, for they knew that machine guns had been set up
behind them with orders to fire on any company that gave
ground.  According to the accounts of prisoners, these orders had been communicated even to the picked storm troops.[1]

The defenders bore themselves magnificently.  In front
of their wrecked trenches the bodies of the enemy were piled
high, but new Italian battalions were continually thrown into
the battle, and the final result was what must be expected
when the odds are ten to one.

The next phase of the attack was against the communication trenches.  These molehills turned into volcanoes belching fire.  Machine guns in shell holes spit death and destruction; rifles cracked incessantly; hand grenades were rained
upon the Italians.  But however many fell dead or dying,
new waves came on over their bodies, until at last the trenches
were entered.  Bitter hand-to-hand fighting then developed.

[1] No evidence supports either this charge or the imaginative numbers in the next paragraph.

The Podgora was opened to attack from the south. Let us see how the battle had been going at Podgora itself. A frontal assault by the Italians had been completely repulsed and a number of prisoners taken. The Podgora stood like a rock against which the surf dashes in vain. Then from north and south the Italian flood surged around it. Flanking defenses were hastily built and the Podgora was held, although the first Italian divisions were already wading the shallows of the Isonzo in order to advance against Gorizia from the west. Something had to be done, and a decision was quickly reached. After the Podgora had been isolated by the fall of Monte Sabotino and the break through at Lucinico, it could not possibly be retained; evacuation of the position was inevitable. The garrison in good order abandoned the heights which they had defended so long and gloriously, taking with them their wounded and also numerous prisoners. In the meanwhile a counter-attack by fresh reserves from the city had driven back across the river the Italian patrols who were attempting to enter the southern railway station. As the last man of the Podgora garrison reached the Gorizia side of the Isonzo, all bridges were blown up.

It was Sunday afternoon. But no church bells were ringing in Gorizia, which was now under heavy fire from the Italian artillery. Instead, the deserted streets resounded to the crash of bursting shells, the sharp rattle of shrapnel, the roar of falling walls. Reserves were being hurried to the front; wounded were being brought back. Through all the bombardment the evacuation of the city went on calmly. Only six guns, on fixed emplacements, had to be destroyed and left behind. All other material was saved, and even the hospitals were evacuated.

The battle raged on the western edge of the town. After the west bank of the Isonzo was given up to them, the Italians, favored by the low water, threw across heavy infantry forces to make an assault upon the city. But the Austro-Hungarians still held out, fighting stubbornly on the western outskirts and then in the city streets until the evacuation of the city was complete.

The city of violets belonged to the Italians.

After a short breathing space the Italian commander struck out vigorously from Gorizia against the Austro-Hungarian key position, but was repulsed with heavy losses.

The loss of Gorizia entailed, of course, a readjustment of the Austro-Hungarian front. To straighten the line and link it up with the new positions east of Gorizia, the plateau of Doberdo west of the valley of Vallone was subsequently evacuated. In this last great battle of the Isonzo, Cadorna has to his credit the occupation of Gorizia and the gain of territory on the plateau of Doberdo; but he is still far from achieving the strategic object of his great offensive, namely, the opening of the road to Trieste. A chain of steel, tough yet elastic, which he has not yet succeeded in breaking at any point, is stretched across his path.

# THE BLACK BETRAYAL

## RUSSIA'S COURT INTRIGUERS BETRAY BOTH RUSSIA AND RUMANIA

### AUGUST-SEPTEMBER

J. Y. SIMPSON
L. J. MAXSE

PAUL MILYUKOF
RAYMOND RECOULY

When the Russian Revolution broke out in 1917, its chief cause was the widespread belief among the Russians that their governmental officials were betraying them to Germany. Evidences of this were found on every hand; and the new leaders promised that as soon as they were in power the secret documents of state should be ransacked and every traitor exposed. This promise, however, brought very little result. Either treason was less rampant than the revolutionists believed, or the evidence of it had been destroyed. Only one important public trial was held, that of the former Minister of War, Sukhumiloff; and while proofs of his mismanagement were many, the evidence of treachery was vague and indecisive. Of other leaders not brought to public trial, the suspicion of actual treason was strongest against three, Prime Minister Sturmer, General Rennenkampf, and the Czarina. The latter has repeatedly been accused of conveying all possible information to the Germans, and specifically of betraying to them the secret code of the Russian army, so that Germany knew of every move the Russians planned. But no legally convincing evidence of this hideous charge has ever been produced. The charges against Rennenkampf have been already told in our account of the Tannenburg disaster of 1914.

There remains as the dastardly betrayer of his fellowmen against whom the charges are most clear, Boris Sturmer. He was afterward executed by the Bolsheviki, who did not bother much about the legal proofs of his guilt; but all the charges made against him in the following articles seem fully established. He betrayed Russia, and he betrayed Rumania. Milyukof, leader of the conservative wing of the revolutionists, gave in the following address the first clear voice to the suspicions against Sturmer. Maxse, a noted British editor, sums up the tale as it later became clear to all the world. General Brusiloff's victorious advance against the Austrians was blocked; and Rumania was entrapped and handed over to the Germans helpless, for their devouring. The nearest the world is ever likely to get to an official statement of Russia's treatment of Rumania is the account here given "from unpublished French and Russian documents," by Recouly, the renowned editor of the Paris *Figaro*.

C. F. H.

## BY J. Y. SIMPSON

THE patriotic work of the "Zemstvos" or local councils of Russia during the War had been enormous. This united work had been most developed in the case of the con-

305

joint Department for Army Supply, which was composed of five members from each of the Unions with the Mayor of Moscow (M. Tchelnakoff) and Prince Lvoff at the head. Amongst these is distributed the supervision of its five main departments, one for distributing orders to the factories; another for materials—concerned with coal, iron, leather, wood; a chemical department dealing with sulphuric acid, nitric acid, gases, masks, etc.; a Transport Department, and a Commercial Department. This Council, which met three times a week, had also a member in America, and another in Petrograd. Its greatest advance was in the increase of factories, particularly for making explosives and shells, but also other necessities such as saddles, carts, horseshoes, articles of wood and army clothing. Hitherto the Orders Department had been buying in bulk, but difficulty arose as the railways were no longer allowed to handle in bulk. Again, it fixes the prices for goods where it has been given the monopoly in a commodity, as, for instance, leather; no private individual can give or take orders for leather goods. This Department of Army Supply was directly under the War Office, through which came all the orders, but working at its own hand it effected some very remarkable savings. Thus on a 9-million ruble order to three firms, the Department got the work done for 238,000 rubles less than the Government allowance. From June, 1915, to June, 1916, the Department was given orders to the extent of 75 million rubles by the Government, and arranged the contracts for the work for 62 millions, thus saving some 13 millions to the country; 63 per cent. of the contracts had been completed by September. A second order from June, 1916, to June, 1917, for 91 millions had been placed to the extent of 74 millions up to October, 1916, and on these contracts 8½ millions had been saved. The contracts were largely given to young firms and organizations.

It is apparent that activities on such a scale and conducted in such a spirit of genuine patriotism, contrasting in every respect with the administrative work of the Government, could not fail to appeal to the imagination of the people, to whom and to the army the synthetic word "Zem-

gor" [1] means as much as the word "Anzac" does to us. Yet
when the Union of Towns proposed in November to convoke
a Conference to deal with the question of the food and fuel
supply, which was rapidly becoming acute, Protopopoff
vetoed the project. The stupidity which forbade grain to
be sold between adjacent districts, so that while one might
have plenty it could do nothing to assist its beleaguered
neighbor, and which enveloped every attempt to bring food
into the towns, was too colossal to be normal, and the impression rapidly grew that it was all part of a scheme to
foment popular discontent that might give the Government
an opportunity to arrange a separate peace and at the same
time crush the people. Simultaneously measures were introduced, *e.g.,* to make violent requisitions of grain from the
peasants, to compel them to work for normal wages with
every other price abnormal, to call up old classes of re-
servists for the army from useful work while it was not
possible to employ them in the army owing to the lack of
arms and munitions—all of which tended to disorganization.

But most amazing of all were the strikes which broke out
with systematic regularity in the different "munition" factories—one day in the Baranovsky Factory on the Viborg
side of Petrograd, next day in another on the Vasili Ostrov
side. A friend of the writer made a private investigation
of some of these strikes. In one case his emissary received
the following reply to a question addressed to one of the
strikers as to the reason for their coming out. "We are
doing nothing, out here on strike. Comrades arrived and
said that there were traitors in the Government and that
it was necessary to make a demonstration and so go on
strike. At 6 o'clock the night shift arrived and found the
factory closed. We arrived at seven in the morning and
found the place still shut, but I don't know why." In another case the strikers came out in answer to a leaflet supposedly issued by one of the smaller Socialist parties. It

[1] It is compounded from the first syllables of the words Zemstvo
(County Council) and Gorod (Town), and is used with reference to
the Unions or any of their activities.

ran as follows: "We invite our comrades to follow the example of our comrades in Europe, and above all, of our comrades in Germany, who are all united and who fight against the War." So manifest a falsehood could not have been signed, in the investigator's opinion, by any genuine party Socialist. His first probings elicited an admission from one of the signatories that the statement was not true, but that it was necessary to exaggerate to make an impression on the people. His further examination left him convinced that a majority of the signatories were police agents in disguise.

In such an atmosphere, amidst the mutterings of the coming storm, the Duma met in November. So far M. Protopopoff's sole piece of constructive policy was an attempt (which the Duma fortunately thwarted) to increase the numbers of the gendarmes under the '87 law: he had certainly been having them trained in the use of Maxim guns for weeks before. But what lent real seriousness to the meeting was the knowledge that one of the greatest living Russian patriots, M. Milyukof, had realized that the time had come publicly to accuse the Premier of that treachery of which every one had long felt morally assured.

From the balconies of the Diplomatic Gallery it is possible to look down into the outer vestibule on the level of the floor of the Duma, where the religious service is held that precedes the opening of any Session. There, within two paces of one another, side by side, together facing the priest, stood M. Sturmer, leaning on his stick, and M. Rodzianko, stalwart and erect, the two men representative of the worst and the best in Russian political life. And during the beautiful prayers for the souls of the departed, added to the service since the beginning of the War, both knelt together, along with the whole assembled company. Thereafter, within a few minutes, the President was thundering in the Duma against the idea of a separate peace in the full hearing of the Cabinet.

After the opening speech, the Premier rose and very deliberately walked out, followed by all the Ministers with one or two exceptions. Of the later speeches we may refer to those of the Ministers. M. Kerensky, Minister of Justice, is a remarkable orator. Very youthful in appearance, he mounted the platform, gripped the sides of the reading-desk firmly with both hands, paused a moment or two until there was absolute silence in the crowded Chamber, and then commenced a sustained attack on the Government. Speaking without note, and passionate with scorn till his voice became harsh and raucous, he looked steadily in front of him all the time, never even deigning to turn towards the two raised boxes on his immediate right reserved for Ministers and now occupied by only one or two, and the assistants of the others, but with short jerky movements of his thumb in their direction merely referring to them with infinite disdain as *"eti liudi"* (these people). As denunciation followed denunciation the protests from the Right became correspondingly violent, and were hardly subdued by the constant agitated use of the Presidential bell calling the House to order. Eventually he was compelled to desist.

Quite different in character was the speech of Professor Milyukoff. Read somewhat closely from notes in a sharp incisive way, with every phrase punctuated by movements of the body or arms, it held his audience from the first word. In Russia, that land of natural human life, you will often notice that if at any public gathering the people in the farther back seats of a hall have any difficulty in hearing some one whom they wish particularly to hear, they will leave their seats in the course of the address, creep up the passageways, and stand close up to the speaker or sit upon the platform at his feet. So was it that day in the Duma. Milyukoff was "saying things." With remorseless logic he impaled the hapless Premier on the horns of the dilemma of stupidity or ill-will. With a certain generosity he attributed the greater part of M. Sturmer's activities to stupidity: "but if there is any ill-will, it is treason; and he must go." And he went—eventually to Copenhagen. Then came the unheeded warning of the murder of Rasputin, and the arrest of the Labor Members of the War Industrial Committee. But the limits of the patience and long-suffering of the Russian people had now been reached, and in a day the country stepped practically alongside of its Allies.

### BY PAUL MILYUKOF

German documents have recently been published containing rules and advice as to the best method of disorganizing enemy countries, of creating disorder among an enemy people, and in general throwing men's minds into confusion. If the Germans had spent all their money and exerted all their influence in Russia for those purposes, they could not have succeeded better than the Russian Government succeeded.

As far back as July 13, 1916, I declared that rumors of treason were spreading through the Russian world, and that these rumors, mounting very high indeed, spared no one. Alas! that warning was not regarded. Now see the result. In the declaration of the twenty-eight Zemstvo Presidents who met at Moscow on October 29, 1916, appears the following statement: "The painful and terrifying suspicions, the rumors of horrid treason, of dark forces working for Germany by trying to create a desire for a shameful peace at the price of the destruction of our national unity—all these rumors and suspicions are transformed into a single certainty. Some enemy hand is secretly directing the affairs of the nation!"

Naturally, these rumors attribute to the Government the opinion that the continuation of the war is useless, and that a separate peace is necessary. How shall the birth of such suspicions be prevented, when a group of hidden personages directs the affairs of State, and when its members at the same time are busy with affairs of basest self-interest?

I have here a copy of the *Berliner Tageblatt* for September 16th, which contains an article entitled "Manouiloff and Sturmer." Its information is false in part. The author of the article has the air of believing that it was Sturmer who put his private secretary, Manasevitch Manouiloff, under arrest. You are well aware that this is not true; you know that all those who aided in the arrest of Manasevitch without informing Sturmer were expelled from office. No, it was not Sturmer who had Manasevitch arrested; on the contrary, he had him liberated.

Perhaps you are wondering who is this Manasevitch Manouiloff? Of what interest is he to us? Manasevitch Manouiloff is a former functionary of the secret Russian police in Paris, who, in his day, furnished the *Novoye Vremya* with piquant details concerning the lives of Russian revolutionaries. Of more interest to us is the fact that he was at the same time entrusted with secret missions. One of these will interest you particularly. A few years ago Manasevitch entered into a series of secret conferences with the Count of Pourtalès, the German Ambassador. The latter offered a large sum, said to be 800,000 rubles, to buy up the editors of the *Novoye Vremya*. I am happy to add that a staff writer on that journal, to whom Manasevitch was first sent, drove him from his apartment. The Count of Pourtalès had much difficulty in hushing up that disagreeable affair.

Such are the missions with which the private secretary of M. Sturmer, Minister of Foreign Affairs, was entrusted. Why was that individual arrested? The reason has long been known, and I tell you nothing new. He was arrested because he was guilty of accepting bribes. Why was he released? That also is no secret. He declared to the examining Magistrate that he divided the proceeds of that bribery with his employer. The article in the *Berliner Tageblatt* mentions two other names: Prince Andronikoff, and the High Priest Pitirim. To the intrigues of the latter is attributed the nomination of Sturmer.

Let me give you a few details about that nomination. I was abroad when I first heard of it. It is mingled with my impressions of travel; and I will tell you quite simply what I learned along the way. You may draw your own conclusions. Scarcely had I left this country a few days after the resignation of Sazonof, when the Swedish newspapers, and later those of Germany and Austria, informed me of the choice of Sturmer as Russian Minister of Foreign Affairs. Here is what the newspapers said.

From the *Berliner Tageblatt*: "The personality of Sazonof gave the Allies a guarantee of stability in matters of foreign policy. In that domain Sturmer is only a 'sheet of blank paper.' He belongs, doubtless, to the circles which regard the war against Germany without any enthusiasm."

From the *Cologne Gazette:* "We Germans have no reason to complain of the change that has taken place in the heart of the Russian Government. Sturmer will offer no obstacle to the desire for peace which from now onward will be born in Russia."'

From the *Neues Tageblatt* of Vienna: "Although it is not now the turn of the diplomats to speak, it is comforting to note that the statesman upon whom lies the burden of having begun the hostilities is retiring."

An editorial in the *Neue Freie Presse* for July 25th is especially interesting in this connection. This is what it says: "However Russified old Sturmer may be, it is nevertheless very strange to see a German directing Russia's foreign policy during a war that had its birth in the domain of Pan-Slavic ideas. The present President of the Council of Ministers, M. Sturmer, has not shared the errors which brought about the war. He has not promised not to make peace without Constantinople and the Dardanelles. In the personality of this Russian Minister of Foreign Affairs we shall find an arm which we can use at our own will; for Sturmer has become a man who satisfies the secret aspirations of the Right, which, before all, desires no alliance with England. He will not declare, as did Sazonof, that it is necessary to annihilate the Prussian military caste."

Whence comes this confidence of the German and Austrian journals that Sturmer, in executing the will of the conservatives, will act against the continuation of the war? It comes from the information furnished them by the Russian press. The newspapers of Moscow have published the memorandum of the "conservative" Government.

This memorandum was sent to the Imperial Great Headquarters in July, just before Sturmer went there for the second time. It does indeed say that we must fight until final victory, but it also declares that we must end the war betimes, otherwise the fruits of victory "will be destroyed by revolution!" This is the usual cry of our pro-Germans.

The Allies have given many proofs in this War that they have admirable perseverance. They have also proved that they were ready for any sacrifice. In this regard they have disappointed the expectations of the enemy, and have surpassed our own. Russia seemed approaching the realization of its hopes, seemed on the point of reaping the fruits of its labors, and of the two preceding Ministries of Foreign Affairs. But at that moment, gentlemen, in place of an experienced pilot enjoying the confidence of all, for this is vital, in that place we find a "sheet of blank paper," an unknown who does not even appreciate the A B C of diplomacy.

The relations that have existed for ten years cannot be destroyed by the caprice of a single person; and the allied press, like our own, had reason to affirm that the change of Ministry could not in any way transform the policy of Russia. But in a thing so delicate as diplomacy there are nuances; there is such a thing as embroidery, lace, delicate drapery, and there is also common sewing. The making of lace is possible only in certain circumstances, under favorable conditions. Well, I have seen the destruction of the most delicate fibers in the embroidery woven by the Allies. I have seen that destruction at London, at Paris. That is what Sturmer has done, and perhaps he had a reason of his own for not promising us Constantinople and the Dardanelles.

I asked myself, by what arrangement is all this change coming? I went to Switzerland to rest a little, but the same obsession pursued me. Even on the shores of Lake Geneva and at Berne I could feel the activities of the old "department" of Sturmer, that of the Ministry of Foreign Affairs and Police. Switzerland is indeed a place where propaganda of all sorts spring up; for that reason it is a good observation post, where one can follow the trail of our enemies' diplomacy. The system of "special missions" also is particularly well developed there; and under cover of these latter appear missions of a peculiar sort. Men said to me: Please ask yonder in Petrograd what the celebrated Rataieff. a former functionary of the Russian secret police at Paris, is doing here in Switzerland. Ask, too, why Ladebeff, an agent of the Russian secret police, has just arrived here; and why he frequents the drawing rooms of certain Russian women who are known for their German sympathies.

One sees that Mme. Wasiltchikoff has her partisans and imitators. She had extensive relations abroad with an Austrian Prince, then with a German Baron. Her salon in the Via Cavour at Florence, and later at Montreux in Switzerland, was well known for the pro-German sentiments manifested there. Now that lady has transferred her household to Petrograd. Apropos of great ceremonies, her name has appeared in the newspapers. I also found fresh traces of her passage through Paris; the Parisians were scandalized by the Germanophile sentiments of this woman, and, may I add, by her conduct toward the Russian Ambassador, though the latter had had no responsibility in the affair.

It is necessary to recall that this woman is the one who directs the career of Sturmer; a few years ago she openly solicited for him a post as Ambassador. I ought to add that this solicitation was considered perfectly ridiculous at the time, and that it had no results.

I do not pretend to have exposed the whole situation as it really exists; but I do assert that a sort of shirt of Nessus envelops certain of our circles and openly favors that propaganda of which Sir George Buchanan spoke so frankly in recent days. It behooves us to start a judicial inquiry like that which was begun in the Sukhomlinoff case. In accusing that officer we had no absolute proofs; it was the examining Magistrate who discovered them. But we had already heard in that case what we hear now, the instinctive appeal of the whole country.

### BY L. J. MAXSE

To-day, thanks to the upheaval at Petrograd, many documents destined to remain forever hidden among the secret archives have come to light. The explanations they furnish are as unexpected as they are valuable. Public opinion, ignorant of the truth, had accepted the most natural explanation and had attributed two capital faults to the Government of Bucharest; but now, to the general stupefaction and indignation, it became evident that, far from being guilty of carelessness and want of foresight, Rumania was the victim of a terrible plot hatched in Berlin in concert with the men of the old régime at Petrograd, enemies of the cause they were called upon to defend.

Irrefutable evidence shows that the date of Rumania's declaration of war and the plan of campaign were forced upon her by the Government of Petrograd, presided over by Messrs. Sturmer and Protopopoff. It is superabundantly proved that these men, who came up against the gentle obstinacy of Nicholas II. every time they tried to convince him of the necessity of concluding "a separate peace," had no other object in view than to put their country into the position of being forced to do so.

The check of the Rumanian intervention, on which many fine hopes were founded, seemed to serve their purpose to perfection. It has been proved now that the offensive of Brusiloff had come to a full stop at the beginning of August. And, still more, his armies were running the risk of being outflanked. Arrested at the passes which debouched into the Hungarian plain by the army of Koewess, General Brusiloff had been obliged to turn the front of his armies to the northwest—toward Lemberg—thus exposing his flank to the divisions which Hindenburg was bringing up against him.

A complete defeat of the Russian armies, for which they would have been responsible to the Emperor, to Russia, and to the Allies, would not have suited these men. The defeat of Rumania, which they could impute to the inefficiency of her army, would lead equally to the same end, without compromising their personal prestige. At any price it was necessary to turn away from the Galician front the storm which was threatening.

So the plan they conceived was put into execution. On July 1st the Imperial Government sent to the Rumanian Government the now famous ultimatum, the brutality of which is equaled only by its perfidy. It was the first document of a correspondence with which the revelations of General Iliesco in the *Matin* have made us acquainted—revelations completed by the publication of Count Czernin's last report in the Austrian Red Book and loyally confirmed by the men of the new régime in Russia. Nothing is more distressing than the reading of this correspondence. On one side the constant reminders of promises, the despairing remonstrances; on the other the haughty, sometimes even injurious, tone, the feigned assurance. "Now or never," says the Russian ultimatum which forced Rumania into the war, "for it must not be hoped that we shall again permit the Rumanian Army later on to make a military promenade and enter Austro-Hungarian territory in triumph."

It was impossible for the Rumanian General Staff to resist the imperious orders of their powerful neighbor, especially as at that moment no help could be hoped for from England or France, both distant and both entirely absorbed by the battle of the Somme. Despite their heroic efforts and their daily successes, the British and French armies had not yet succeeded in their principal object, the relief of Verdun, against which Hindenburg was at that moment preparing his last attack with formidable forces. It was impossible to hope that, under these circumstances, France and England would oppose the wishes of the Russian Government, especially as they were expressed in terms which left no other alternative than to advise the Rumanian General Staff to come to an understanding with the Russian command. France gave a last proof of her solicitude for Rumania in pledging herself to come to her help by a general offensive of the Salonika army, which should begin eight days before the date of the entry of Rumania into the campaign.

The desire of France to help this new ally was so sincere that M. Briand, then President of the Council, breaking all precedents, went so far as to announce in the Chamber the projected offensive of the Orient forces. The treason which unfortunately surrounded this army on all sides rendered it impossible for General Sarrail to carry out this plan at the opportune moment. Warned by the pro-Germans of Athens of the impending attack, the Bulgarian Army made the first move, and, attacking on both flanks, obliged General Sarrail to regroup his forces, which paralyzed his movements. Thus the Rumanian General Staff remained alone to face the Government of Petrograd.

Obliged to yield to the Russian ultimatum and to declare war on the day fixed in it, they asked the Russian higher command for their coöperation in the plan of campaign worked out by them, showing how impossible it would be, with the sixteen divisions, which represented the whole army, lacking heavy artillery, completely unprovided with machine guns, to cover the 600 kilometers of the Danubian front and at the same time attack on the 700-kilometer front of Transylvania. They proposed taking possession of the bridgeheads of Rustchuk and Sistov in order to guard against a passage of the Danube. To hold in check the 200,000 Bulgars, reënforced by several Turkish divisions, whom the Rumanian General Staff knew to be concentrated against the Dobrudja front, they asked for the help of seven or eight Russian divisions.

The answers of Messrs. Sturmer and Protopopoff to these proposals left Rumania no longer any doubts as to the extent of the sacrifice demanded of her. They were opposed to all operations on the Danube, declaring that they had been categorically assured that the Bulgarians would lay down their arms. They took entire responsibility for it. On no account were hostilities to be directed against them. For the same reason they judged it absolutely useless to comply with the request for seven or eight divisions: "Who is threatening the Dobrudja front?" said a message coming from the Russian higher command. And when the Rumanian General Staff insisted on its information, according to which about eight Bulgaro-Turkish divisions were advancing toward this front, a new message arrived, which said that two divisions might be put at their disposal. These indeed arrived. One of them was composed of Serbian, Croatian, and Czech prisoners belonging to Austrian regiments captured in Galicia. As to the machine guns, not one could be procured, and it was only later that M. Protopopoff confessed that he had not been able to deliver them because they had been placed on the roofs of the houses in Petrograd to put down the threatening revolution.

BY RAYMOND RECOULY

While Rumania and Italy were persuaded to relinquish their original neutrality and to join their fortunes with those of the Entente by the same arguments and motives, it was a much slower and more difficult task to secure action from Rumania than from our Mediterranean neighbor. England and France were geographically close to Italy, and they labored in perfect harmony to win her support, knowing that they must succeed and succeed quickly. Italy trusted both these nations, and knew that they would keep their promises. Rumania was in a different situation. France and Russia conducted negotiations with her, and these were not pursued with the same sincerity and unity of purpose. France had a single object in view—to have Rumania's help as soon as possible; and she was willing to promise her in return all that she could legitimately ask—a union under her flag of the Rumanians still living beyond her borders.

Russia, however, was actuated by a different spirit. The Government at Petrograd, and Russian public opinion as a whole, regarded askance the proposal to create a powerful Rumanian state. The Russians were eager to acquire Constantinople. They realized that if Rumania were made too strong she might bar the way to the Dardanelles. Moreover, her growth tended to lessen the importance of the Slav element in the Balkans. She would certainly have the enmity of Bulgaria, for whom Russia, in spite of that country's ingratitude and treachery—past, present and future—still retained a feeling of inextinguishable sympathy and indulgence.

Naturally a proud nation, the Russians looked down on all the Balkan states and attached minor importance to Rumania's aid. They thought her help would amount to little, and that her army was not reliable. They did not like to see France take the lead in negotiations which they felt concerned themselves mainly, since they related to Eastern Europe. They would have preferred to handle the matter alone in their own way. During Russia's early military successes her Government did not want Rumania's help, believing that it would win a victory without her, and that her participation would diminish the spoils. So Russia's negotiators held out against offering Rumania more than insignificant compensation. They haggled, and would consent to annexing only infinitesimal scraps of territory.

In the autumn of 1914, Germany sent a new Minister, Herr von Bussche, to Bucharest. He arrived with his pockets full of money and instructions to secure friends for Germany at any cost. He at once set out to purchase every man whom money could buy. He bought private consciences and newspapers by the wholesale. Our French Minister had little money to meet this new campaign; but he did possess the sympathies of the people. This was especially true of the students, who seized the slightest pretext to parade the streets, shouting: *"Vive la France!"* or to mob the offices and hustle the editors of pro-German newspapers.

In February, 1915, General Pau's visit evoked an enthusiastic demonstration in favor of France. The whole city was a cloud of banners; ladies threw bouquets from every balcony. The streets were black with people, so that it took the carriage of our Minister more than an hour to pass from the station to the Legation.

This gave great encouragement to the war party. But Bratianu's Ministry naturally wished, before acting, to have everything in black and white. Following the precedent set by Italy, Bratianu demanded natural boundaries: the Pruth in Bukowina, and the Danube and the Tisza on the side of Serbia. The first of these demands was promptly opposed by the Russians, who declared they would not give up Czernowitz under any circumstances. France backed Rumania's claim to the utmost. On May 16, 1915, Sazonof's reply arrived. It was uncompromising, although the Russian army was in precipitate retreat across Galicia. When Bratianu learned of this answer, he was stunned. He declared that under the circumstances he would not take the responsibility of advising war. He could not comprehend why Russia, whose army was in such a critical position, persisted in refusing Czernovitz to Rumania. He said: "Russia wishes to remain mistress of the Pruth so as to corner us between herself and Serbia."

Late in the winter and early in the spring of 1916, negotiations were resumed more actively. On the 10th of May, Bratianu told the Minister of France that the King was ready to sign the order for mobilization whenever it was submitted to him. But he insisted that before this was done, a number of conditions should be fulfilled, particulary he must be sure of assistance from the Russian army. By July 6th he was ready to sign the compact with the Allies, subject to the following conditions: (1) That the delivery of munitions begin, and that France and England engage to continue these deliveries, at the rate of three hundred tons a day; (2) that the impending general offensive be not countermanded; (3) that the Russians retain their positions in Galicia and Bukowina; (4) that Rumania be guaranteed against a Bulgarian attack, either by Russian intervention or by an offensive from Salonika.

Neratof, acting Foreign Minister of Russia, telegraphed the terms offering a final agreement. These were the principal conditions Russia made:

"Rumania agrees to declare war simultaneously against all the governments which are fighting the Entente.

"She will employ all of her armed forces against the enemies of the Allies.

"The Allies guarantee Rumania's territorial integrity. She shall be permitted to annex such territories of Austria-Hungary as she may occupy within certain definite limits.

"The frontier between Russia and Rumania shall follow lines specified in detail.

"Rumania shall enter the war not later than August 7th.

"A military convention between the General Staffs of Russian and Rumania shall be concluded immediately.

"In communicating this arrangement to the Rumanian Government, the Minister of Russia has the honor to add that if Rumania does not feel able to enter the war by the date fixed (August 7th), the Allied Powers shall not be bound further by the proposals they have submitted to Rumania."

The reader will see that the Entente rather rushed Bratianu in order to sweep aside his last hesitation. But that gentleman no longer hesitated. He was sure that the King would consent and that the country would support him with enthusiasm.

Since we must pay for everything here below, Bratianu, in avoiding one danger, fell into another. He made an excellent diplomatic preparation for the war. Every treaty was signed, every precaution taken, every frontier drawn to the last detail.

On the other hand, the military preparations were most defective. The Rumanian and Russian General Staffs did not work well together. Rumania's suspicion of the Russians made it the more important that the understanding between the two armies should be clearly defined. In that respect the arrangements were, if I may use the word, "boggled." The results soon made themselves felt. The Russian offensive, instead of advancing, was stopped precipitately. After a brief preliminary success, Rumania, left wholly unsupported, was defeated and invaded.

Early in 1917 I was commissioned by French General Headquarters to inspect the whole Russian front, from Riga to the Caucasus. I reached Jassy toward the end of February, in the heart of a terrible winter. I found many other French officers in the old Moldavian capital, where the Government was then temporarily installed. The intense cold, the universal distress, impending typhus, and all the ills and privations conceivable seemed to have heaped themselves upon Rumania at once.

Relations of the Russians and the Rumanians were far from friendly. The former were inclined to treat the latter as a conquered nation. During a dinner with several of our officers, including General Berthelot, we received the first telegram reporting the revolution in Petrograd. That only added to the disorder and confusion, which thereafter constantly grew worse. The revolution was the reverse of fortune for Rumania. The Russian army speedily became demoralized, until it was an undisciplined horde. Russia was no longer a protector, but a new enemy.

# RUMANIA JOINS THE ALLIES

## HER ARMY INVADES HUNGARY

### AUGUST 27TH

TAKE JONESCU        ION BRATIANU
KING FERDINAND   VON BETHMANN-HOLLWEG

It is typical of the German propaganda system that the moment any neutral joined the Allies, German officials announced with vehement scorn that the offending nation was beneath contempt, had betrayed Germany by falsehoods, had joined the Allies solely for money, and had a dozen other evil purposes beside. So the Chancellor, Bethmann-Hollweg, here judges Rumania. On the other hand, Turkey and Bulgaria, having joined Germany, were always mentioned by her as her "noble and highminded" friends. Their every atrocity is extenuated or denied; and they are given characters above reproach.

These German endorsements and condemnations are too absurd for serious discussion; but it would be well for us to be cautioned by their folly and so avoid running into a similar extravagance upon the other side. Doubtless many mingled motives swayed the Rumanian people when they followed their Government into the War. One essential distinction, however, existed always between those States which joined the Allies and those which joined the Teutons. In seeking the Allies' aid, every State had obviously before it the need of self-defense, the fear that Germany would seize the first opportunity to destroy it as she had destroyed Belgium. Joining Germany was frankly a business speculation, so much chance of profit, and so much of loss. Defying Germany was obviously a matter of life and death, upon which no people and no government would enter without solemn thought and a high resolve.

In such mood did Rumania join the Allies. Her own statesmen will here tell you why. Jonescu had long been the parliamentary leader urging such a course. Indeed he had been forced from office because all the country had not been willing to join him and face the awful risk. Ion, or John, Bratianu had been his rival and successor in office; and at last Bratianu also was convinced of the War's necessity. King Ferdinand came to the throne in 1914 after the War began. He was of German descent; but his wife, Mary, was a British princess and had long espoused the Allies' cause. Both of them were now pushed into action by Russia's insistence. She declared they must be for her or against her.

Immediately upon the declaration of war, the Rumanian army advanced over the border into the Rumanian or "Transylvanian" region of Hungary. There they won a number of small successes, and pushed on as far as the city of Hermanstadt in the south and Bistritz in the north. By mid-September they held about a quarter of Transylvania.

### BY TAKE JONESCU

RUMANIA'S entry into the war is simply the outcome of the entire history of the Rumanian people. A Latin colony established astride the Carpathians between the Black Sea and the Tisza, the Magyar invasion had separated us into two. In spite of centuries of political separation, the intellectual life of all Rumanians has been one and the same, and in every epoch the national aspiration in the two sides of the Carpathians has been for union and a single independent State.

Never before this war has the principle of nationality, the corollary of national sovereignty—that is to say, the right of every people to live according to its own genius—been declared as the foundation of political right in Europe. This principle was first declared by immortal France, but it has been English statesmen of this present epoch who have given it its definite consecration. So, too, are the British people for this principle. Yet more than any conquest do they value being champions of right and liberty. I know no greater good fortune than to be able to assist in the realization of this national ideal while serving at the same time the cause of civilization and permanent future peace. Such is the case of the Rumanian people at this moment.

For two years I never ceased maintaining that if Rumania had nothing to claim for herself she owed it to her own feeling of dignity and honor to draw the sword on the side of the crusaders for the right. The creation of a great Rumania, which will convert us into a State of 14,000,000 inhabitants, is not only a Rumanian but a European interest. We must put Germany into such a position that she will find it materially impossible to start again that tragedy of *armaments à outrance* which fatally led to this monstrous war.

We must put between Germany and the Orient, which she covets, States sufficiently strong and representing military worth sufficiently great to be able to resist all intrigues and sufficiently distant from the German spirit to be by the nature of things soldiers of civilization against German stupidity. Magna Rumania will fulfill these three conditions. With our amazing racial fecundity, we shall have in forty years between Tisza and the Black Sea a State of 25,000,000 inhabitants, and for France, England, Russia, and Italy this will be some recompense for their enormous sacrifices.

### BY ION BRATIANU
#### Declaration of War Delivered to the Austrian Minister in Rumania on August 28, 1916

The alliance concluded between Germany, Austria-Hungary, and Italy, according to the statements of those Governments, had only a conservative and defensive character. Its principal object was to guarantee the allied countries against attack from the outside and to consolidate the state of affairs created by previous treaties. It was in accordance with these pacific tendencies that Rumania joined this alliance.

Devoted to the development of her internal affairs and faithful to her resolution to remain as an element of order and equilibrium on the lower Danube, Rumania never has ceased in her devotion to the maintenance of peace in the Balkans. The last Balkan wars, by destroying the status quo, imposed upon her a new line of conduct, but her intervention gave peace and reëstablished the equilibrium.

For herself she was satisfied with the rectification of her borders which gave her the greatest security against aggression and repaired certain injustices of the Congress of Berlin, but in pursuit of this aim Rumania was disappointed by the failure of the Vienna Cabinet to take the attitude Rumania was entitled to expect.

When the present war broke out Rumania, like Italy, declined to associate herself with the declaration of war by Austria-Hungary, of which she had not been notified by the Vienna Cabinet.

In the spring of 1915 Italy declared war against Austria-Hungary. The Triple Alliance no longer existed and the reasons which determined Rumania's adherence to this political system disappeared.

Rumania remained in the peace group of States, seeking to work in agreement in order to assure peace and to conserve the situation de facto and de jure created by treaties. Rumania then found herself in the presence of powers making war for the sole purpose of transforming from top to bottom the old arrangements which had served as a basis for their treaty of alliance. These changes were for Rumania proof that the object she pursued in joining the Triple Alliance no longer could be attained and that she must direct her efforts in new paths, especially as the work undertaken by Austria-Hungary threatened the interests of Rumania and her national aspirations. Consequently Rumania resumed her liberty of action.

The neutrality which Rumania imposed upon herself in consequence of a declaration of war made independently of her will, and contrary to her interests, had been adopted as the results of the assurances that Austria-Hungary, in declaring war against Serbia, was not inspired by a spirit of conquest or of territorial gains. These assurances have not been realized.

To-day we are confronted by a situation de facto threatening great territorial transformations and political changes of a nature constituting a grave menace to the future of Rumania. The work of peace which Rumania attempted to accomplish, in a spirit of faithfulness to the Triple Alliance, thus was rendered barren by the very powers called upon to defend it.

In adhering in 1883 to the group of Central Powers, Rumania was far from forgetting the bonds of blood constituting between them a pledge for her domestic tranquillity, as well as for the improvement of the lot of the Rumanians of Austria-Hungary. In fact, Germany and Italy, who reconstituted their States on the basic principle of nationality, could not but recognize the legitimacy of the foundation upon which their own existence reposed.

As for Austria-Hungary, she found in the friendly relations established between her and Rumania assurances of tranquillity both in her interior and on our common frontiers, for she was bound to know to what extent the discontent of her Rumanian population found echo among us, threatening our good relations.

For a period of thirty years the Rumanians of Austria-Hungary not only never saw a reform introduced, but, instead, were treated as an inferior race and condemned to suffer the oppression of a foreign element which constitutes only a minority amid the diverse nationalities constituting the Austro-Hungarian States.

All the injustices our brothers thus were made to suffer maintained between our country and the monarchy a continual state of animosity. At the outbreak of the war Austria-Hungary made no effort to ameliorate these conditions. After two years of the war Austria-Hungary showed herself as prompt to sacrifice her peoples as powerless to defend them. The war in which almost the whole of Europe is partaking raises the gravest problems affecting the national development and very existence of the States.

Rumania, from a desire to hasten the end of the conflict and to safeguard her racial interests, sees herself forced to enter into line by the side of those who are able to assure her realization of her national unity. For these reasons Rumania considers herself, from this moment, in a state of war with Austria-Hungary.

### BY KING FERDINAND OF RUMANIA
#### Proclamation of August 28, 1916

Rumanians! The war which for the last two years has been encircling our frontiers more and more closely has shaken the ancient foundations of Europe to their depths.

It has brought the day which has been awaited for centuries by the national conscience, by the founders of the Rumanian State, by those who united the principalities in the war of independence, by those responsible for the national renaissance. It is the day of the union of all branches of our nation. To-day we are able to complete the task of our forefathers and to establish forever that which Michael the Great was only able to establish for a moment, namely, a Rumanian union on both slopes of the Carpathians.

For us the mountains and plains of Bukowina, where Stephen the Great has slept for centuries. In our moral energy and our valor lie the means of giving him back his birthright of a great and free Rumania from the Tisza to the Black Sea, and to prosper in peace in accordance with our customs and our hopes and dreams.

Rumanians! Animated by the holy duty imposed upon us, and determined to bear manfully all the sacrifices inseparable from an arduous war, we will march into battle with the irresistible élan of a people firmly confident in its destiny. The glorious fruits of victory shall be our reward.

Forward, with the help of God!

FERDINAND.

*To the army:*

Soldiers: I have summoned you to carry your standards beyond the frontier, where our brothers are waiting for you impatiently and with hearts filled with hope. The memory of the Great Voivodes Michael the Brave and Stephen the Great, whose remains lie in the earth which you are going to set free, call you to victory as men worthy of the victors of Razboeni, Capugareeni, and Paehna. I have summoned you to fight side by side with the men of the great nations to which we are allied. A desperate struggle awaits you. We shall bear these hardships manfully, and with God's help victory will be ours. Show yourselves worthy of the glory of your ancestors. In the centuries to come the whole race will bless you and sing your praises.

### BY VON BETHMANN-HOLLWEG

Our relations with Rumania before the war were based on the treaty of alliance first concluded between Austria-Hungary and Rumania, and then enlarged by the accession of Germany and Italy. The contracting parties engaged under the treaty to assist each other in case of unprovoked attack by a third party.

When the war broke out King Carlos with all his energy stood up for the idea that Rumania owed to the Central

Powers thirty years of political security and wonderful economic development, and that, therefore, Rumania must support the Central Powers, not only on account of the provisions of the treaty but also for the sake of the country's honor. The late King regarded as sophistry the objection that Rumania had not been informed and consulted in regard to the Austro-Hungarian démarche in regard to Serbia.

But when the deciding session of the Crown Council was held the aged King did not succeed as against the Government, whose Prime Minister, notwithstanding treaty obligations, sympathized with the Entente Powers. A short time later the King died in consequence of the emotions caused by realization that Rumania was a traitor to her allies.

The Rumanian policy was now guided by Premier Bratiano, who attempted to gain riches, without making great sacrifices, at the expense of the party suffering defeat in the war. The main point was to discover in time which party was about to win final victory, in order not to be too late. Nevertheless, during the first year of the war, probably after the fall of Lemberg, Premier Bratiano, leaving his sovereign in ignorance, concluded a treaty of neutrality with Russia. After the fall of Przemysl he thought the time had come to reach an understanding in regard to pay for his Judas-like treason, but the negotiations failed. Russia desired to increase her own vast territory by taking the Bukowina, while Rumania not only coveted this same Bukowina, but also all Hungarian territory as far as the Theiss.

The Russian offensive this spring made Premier Bratiano believe he saw the breaking down of the Central Powers. Accordingly he decided to obtain a share when the robbery of the dead body began. Furthermore, the Entente Powers had a freer hand in conducting negotiations than others. Serbia had been conquered, and the protectors of small, feeble States were no longer obliged to show any consideration for Serbia's former wishes in regard to annexation of territory. They could be more liberal toward Rumania.

In the middle of August Bratiano came to terms with our enemies. He reserved for himself, however, the decision as to the time actual hostilities were to be inaugurated, and attempted to make it dependent on military conditions. The King of Rumania up to that time had repeatedly given the most binding assurances that under all circumstances he would remain neutral. Finally, the Rumanian Minister in Berlin, on the order of the King, gave to me a formal declaration that the King desired to maintain Rumania's neutrality and that the Government was in a position to do so. Premier Bratiano declared to the German Minister at Bucharest, Baron von Bussche-Haddenhausen, that he fully indorsed the declaration of the King.

However, we were not deceived. We were informed continuously in regard to Bratiano's negotiations during August, and constantly directed the King's attention to the secret intrigues of his Prime Minister. The King declared several times that Bratiano was not bound or binding himself to the Entente. As late as three days before the declaration of war the King said to our Minister that he knew the overwhelming majority of the Rumanian Nation did not desire war. To an intimate friend the King declared on the same day in the most categorical fashion that he would not sign an order for mobilization.

On August 26th, the day preceding Rumania's declaration of war, the King said to the Austro-Hungarian Minister that he did not wish war. I add in passing that Bratiano at the same time assured the Austro-Hungarian representative that he had decided to maintain neutrality, and that the outcome of the session of the Crown Council which had been called for the following day would prove the truth of his words.

As late as August 23rd the Entente Powers had not decided at what moment Rumania ought to declare war. We knew this from a most reliable source. The Rumanian army still lacked preparedness, and particularly lacked munitions, as was proved later, at the time of the fall of Turtukai and Silistria.

Then events were precipitated. From information which may be considered reliable it appears that Russia suddenly presented an ultimatum that she would cross the unprotected Rumanian frontier if Rumania did not begin war before August 28th.  Whether this ultimatum was a piece of comedy prearranged with Bratiano, in order to influence the hesitating King, I leave undecided, but the die was cast.

M. Briand, in his latest discourse, praised the beauty and loveliness of Rumania's procedure.  Political conditions of such a nature that orders of Kings and Ministers amount to nothing show the doubtful value of those ideals of liberty, justice, and civilization for which the Entente pretends that it fights.  Since the beginning of the world war Rumania has followed a policy of piracy, depending upon the general war situation.  Rumania's military capitulation will prove as mistaken as her political capitulation to her Entente friends, which already has been proved to have been wrong.  They must have hoped earnestly that Rumania's participation in the war would cause the defection of Bulgaria and Turkey, but Turkey and Bulgaria are not the same as Rumania and Italy.  Firm and inviolable stands their faithfulness as allies, and they have won glorious victories in the Dobrudja.

# REVOLUTION IN GREECE

## STRUGGLE OF THE BULGARS AND ALLIES FOR SALONIKA

### AUGUST 30TH

STEPHEN DUGGAN                                    G. WARD PRICE

### KING CONSTANTINE

Of all the European states which were ultimately drawn into the War, Greece struggled longest to escape its misery by insisting on neutrality. At the first her people's sympathies had been strongly pro-Ally; and only the resolute pro-Germanism of her young king, Constantine, kept her from joining them. The Greek royal family were originally German princelings, but for three generations now they had sat upon the throne of Greece. Hence Constantine was a Greek, but he had been trained in the German army and had married a sister of the Kaiser. His queen, like the German Czarina of Russia, cared more for the land of her birth than for that of her husband.

In the case of the Greek sovereigns, proof has been given since the War that they both espoused the German cause, secretly but completely, and kept Germany fully informed as to their plans and their needs. "Tino," as the German queen and her Emperor brother called the Greek king in their correspondence, gave the Kaiser his positive word that not a single Greek soldier should aid the Allies.

That promise was hard to keep. So many Greeks wanted to join the Ally cause that the king was at length driven to overthrow the constitution and rule by force.

Later, however, as Serbia sank in disaster, the Greek people dreaded a similar fate and lost most of their enthusiasm for the War. There was much rioting on both sides and much distress caused by the commercial pressure by which the Allies sought to bring Greece to join them. In the end the king seemed likely to have his way and to keep his people with him in ostensible neutrality. In May of 1916, however, the king ventured an extreme step; he caused his soldiers to surrender to the Bulgars the Greek fort of Rupel. This was a great help to the Teutons and a dangerous menace to the Allies' army at Salonika. On the other hand, it roused many Greek patriots to furious rage against the king. Hitherto his people had thought of him as a Greek and trusted him. Now they remembered that he was a German.

Some further concessions to the Bulgarians roused the pro-Ally Greeks to revolution. On August 30th the Government which ruled Greece to the end of the War was set up in Salonika under Allied protection. At first it was republican in form.

On September 12th the king took an even further step by surrendering a seaport to the Bulgarians. This so estranged his people that all eastern Greece joined the new republic. The king, how-

331

ever, still maintained his control in Athens.  Not until the summer of 1917 did he find the last vestige of power slipping away from him. He then resigned his crown.  The revolution was complete.

C. F. H.

### BY STEPHEN DUGGAN [1]

WHEN the Great War burst upon Europe the statesman who had become known as the maker of modern Greece, Eleutherios Venizelos, was at the helm of government.  Venizelos had passed most of his manhood in an effort to secure the union of his native island, Crete, to Greece.  He participated in the rebellion against the Ottoman Empire which compelled the powers to intervene and secure autonomy for Crete in 1897.  Under the autonomous government he rendered splendid service as minister of justice in reorganizing the laws of the island, and was finally elected prime minister of Crete in 1910.  When the Greek army officers who formed the Military League assumed control of the Greek Government in 1909 and demanded many governmental changes, including the exclusion of the royal princes from command in the army, Greece passed through a year of anarchy, which finally came to an end only when Venizelos became Prime Minister in October, 1910.  He was as successful at Athens as he had been in Crete, securing the adhesion of the Military League to the new constitution that was adopted, and introducing many reforms in internal administration, which brought upon him the hatred of the political parasites with whom Greece was so plentifully provided.  As soon as Venizelos had secured the necessary reforms in domestic affairs, he turned his attention to the great problem which troubled all Balkan statesmen, the Macedonian question.  His success in foreign diplomacy was as great as in domestic administration.  He was the animating spirit in the organization of the Balkan League, which destroyed the power of Turkey in the First Balkan War, and it was due to his skillful diplomacy that Greece emerged from the Second Balkan War with territorial profits far in excess of any other of the Balkan states.

After the Treaty of Bucharest the foreign policy of Veni-

[1] Reprinted by permission of the author.

zelos was determined chiefly by two principles. The first was the necessity of protecting Greece from a war of revenge by Bulgaria. To maintain this principle he and M. Pashitch, the Prime Minister of Serbia, had committed their countries to a defensive alliance against attack by a third power, and Venizelos made the maintenance of that treaty the corner-stone of his foreign policy. The second principle was the necessity of securing the favor of the maritime powers, France and England. Venizelos believed that the future of Greece was upon the sea and he aimed to strengthen her maritime influence in the eastern Mediterranean. Moreover, he believed that the expansion of modern Greece was to follow the same lines as that of ancient Greece, *i.e.,* to the islands of the Ægean and the shores of Asia Minor. Hundreds of thousands of Greeks dwelt in the coast cities of Asia Minor hoping for the day of deliverance. To realize such a policy demanded the friendship of France and England. Hence when the Great War broke out, Venizelos made no secret of his leanings toward the Entente Allies. Nevertheless when the new session of the chamber opened on October 1, 1914, he declared that Greece intended to remain neutral unless called upon to assist her ally, Serbia.

The great popularity of Venizelos in Greece was equaled by that of King Constantine. Constantine had been compelled by the Military League to relinquish his command in the army in 1909, but had been reëstablished in it after the adoption of the new constitution in 1910. During the Balkan wars he had shown himself to be a brave and capable commander, and for his successes against Turks and Bulgars, especially in compelling the surrender of the fortress of Janina, he had been given the title of Constantine the Victorious. Like his great minister, Constantine was a strong-minded man, and although he was willing that in domestic affairs Venizelos should have practically *carte blanche,* he did not show the same complaisance in foreign affairs as did his father, whom he succeeded in 1913. He had received his military training in Germany, and like many of his general staff, was a firm believer in the invincibility of the German army. He was married to the Kaiser's sister, and that fact, no doubt, had considerable influence with him. He viewed Russia with distrust and like most Greeks looked with concern upon a Russian occupation of Constantinople, an aim that some Russian patriots put forward early in the war. He also shared the antagonism maintained by his countrymen toward Italy, whose ambitions in Albania and the Ægean brought her into conflict with Greece. It is probable that Constantine was personally pro-German at the beginning of the Great War, but there was nothing in his actions or speeches to indicate that he intended to oppose the desires of four-fifths of his subjects to favor, in whatever way was possible, the Entente Allies. In the diplomatic struggle for Greek support which at once commenced at Athens between the representatives of the Entente Allies and the Central Powers, the former had practically everything in their favor. Only unusual blundering could prevent success.

The Central Powers had little to offer Greece in return for a promise of neutrality, but that little was definite and was never diminished. They promised that Greece would not be called upon to undertake hostile action against the Entente Allies and that her territorial integrity would be guaranteed. Their success in securing Turkey's entrance into the war on October 29, 1914, decreased their influence at Athens, for if Greece was to profit by the great struggle, it must be at the expense of Turkey or Albania, or as she hoped, of both, and the success of the Central Powers meant the territorial integrity of both Turkey and Albania. The Entente Allies, on the contrary, after the entrance of Turkey into the war, held out the promise of Greek expansion in Asia Minor in return for Greek support. But at the same time they made the most urgent representations of the need that Greece agree to her own amputation in order to placate Bulgaria. Only in that way was it possible to revive the Balkan Confederation, which would prevent any junction between the Central Powers and Turkey, and would permit of the elimination of the latter from the war. Now the hatred of Greeks and Bulgarians for each other engendered during the Second Balkan War was greater than that between any other Balkan peoples. The territory Greece was urged to relinquish was the rich, fertile district in which was raised the celebrated Turkish tobacco. And of the statesmen Bulgarians looked upon as responsible for their disgrace, no one to them was so blameworthy as Venizelos. Had a group of European powers suggested to Germany, in 1872, that for some common good she return Alsace-Lorraine to France, and that Bismarck undertake the negotiations, the favor with which the suggestion would have been received in Germany and the faith that would have been placed in the proposal by France, offer an analogy to the situation in the Balkans in 1914.

Nevertheless Venizelos considered that the golden opportunity had come to realize Greek ambition for expansion to Asia Minor. On January 24, 1915, and again on January 30, he submitted statements to Constantine suggesting that if by retroceding the Kavala district to Bulgaria the Balkan Confederation could be reëstablished, the sacrifice would be worth while. Greece would be relieved of the fear of an attack by Bulgaria and would receive the vilayet of Smyrna in Asia Minor, which has a population of almost one million Greeks. Venizelos had secured from Sir Edward Grey the promise of Great Britain's benevolent attitude toward the acquisition of Smyrna by Greece. Venizelos afterward stated that the king withdrew the objection which he had at first made to the plan and authorized him to proceed with the negotiations. But early in February the Disconto Gesellschaft made a loan of $30,000,000 to Bulgaria, and although M. Radoslavoff, the Bulgarian prime minister, made a public statement that the loan had not in any way committed Bulgaria to the Central Powers, Venizelos was convinced that Bulgaria had determined to throw in her lot with the Central Powers. Hence he did not make the offer.

On February 19, 1915, the British fleet began its attack upon the Dardanelles forts, and at the same time the Entente Allies invited Greece to participate in the campaign, in return for which she was to receive the vilayet of Smyrna. The proposal was warmly advocated by Venizelos, and early in March the king called a crown council to consider intervention. The general staff of the army was strongly opposed to participation in the Dardanelles campaign. To strip Greece of troops to engage in it would be to open the country to invasion by its worst enemy, Bulgaria. Moreover, the general staff could see no hope of success for the Entente Allies. Before the war, it had worked out a plan of campaign against the Dardanelles and concluded that success would require a very large army to coöperate with the fleet, a far larger army than the Entente Allies had at their disposal. Were Greece to enter the campaign, she would have to bear the brunt of the fighting for a territorial reward which would still have to be conquered. The political consequences also were dangerous. During the First Balkan War, the Turks had driven thousands of Greeks out of Asia Minor and confiscated the property of other thousands. Participation in the Dardanelles campaign would almost certainly have the same effect. So hazardous a step ought to be undertaken only if success were assured. The king refused his approval of the policy of intervention, and on March 7th Venizelos resigned.

Upon accepting office on March 10th, the new ministry led by M. Gounaris issued a statement of policy which implied that Venizelos had negotiated for the surrender of Greek territory to the arch-enemy Bulgaria. This called forth an indignant protest from Venizelos, who a little later demanded that the Government officially deny the implication made in their statement of policy. Instead, the king wrote him a public letter in which he asserted that Venizelos had proposed the cession of the Kavala district to induce Bulgaria to revive the Balkan Confederation. Venizelos then published his memoranda of January 24th and January 30th to prove that he had suggested the cession of the Kavala district only as a last resort, that the king had authorized him to conduct negotiations with the cession as a basis, but that he had not made the offer because of Bulgaria's receipt of the German loan. The king replied on April 6th with another statement denying absolutely that he had ever authorized Venizelos to negotiate for the cession of any Greek territory. Poor Greece! Not only did its two leaders, both respected and admired by the people, wholly disagree as to the policy that the country ought to pursue, but there had developed a personal antagonism between them which boded ill for the country. Meanwhile the French and English press were lauding Venizelos and denouncing Constantine for their respective attitudes upon the Dardanelles expedition. This did not advance the cause of the Entente Allies at Athens. Before deciding against intervention, Constantine as commander-in-chief of the Greek army had carefully weighed the chances of success of the expedition. The total failure of the campaign proved the wisdom of his decision.

As Gounaris was opposed by a majority of the chamber, he first secured an adjournment for a month and then a dissolution. But in the general election of June 13th, despite a strong bid for popular support made in his statement that under no circumstances would he alienate Greek territory, but on the contrary would seek every opportunity to increase it, he was defeated. The Venizelists controlled 186 of the 316 seats in the new chamber. Gounaris delayed the opening of the chamber a month after the time originally fixed and resigned August 16th, when he was decisively beaten in the first important division. A short time previous to his resignation the Entente Allies, alarmed at the rumors of Turkish concessions to Bulgaria in the matter of the Dedeagatch railroad, made a final effort to secure territorial concessions from Greece. This request was flatly refused by Gounaris who, moreover, forestalled any such action on the part of Venizelos by publicly stating that not a single inch of Greek territory would be ceded to Bulgaria. As Venizelos was the only statesman that could command a majority in the chamber, the king on August 23rd reluctantly asked him to take office.

Venizelos' tenure of office, however, was very short. On September 21, 1915, Bulgaria mobilized her army, Radoslavoff stating that the action was not in any way preparatory to war. Venizelos was not deceived, however, and on September 25th ordered the mobilization of the Greek army.

He did more. Under the provisions of the Serbo-Greek treaty of 1913, in case of joint action by Serbia and Greece against Bulgaria, Serbia was to contribute an army of at least 150,000 troops. As Serbia was preparing for the impending Austro-German invasion, the impossibility of her carrying out this provision of the treaty was obvious. Venizelos, therefore, inquired of France and Great Britain whether the Entente Allies would make good Serbia's deficiency. Venizelos was convinced that neutrality would not avert but only postpone war between Greece and Bulgaria. Hence, not only did honor demand fulfillment of the treaty with Serbia, but wisdom also dictated that a war with Bulgaria should be undertaken under the most favorable conditions for a successful outcome, viz., in union with Serbia and the Entente Allies. When troops of the Entente Allies did land at Salonika on October 2nd, Venizelos made a formal protest against their violation of Greek neutrality "to keep the record straight." The Serbo-Greek treaty came into effect only when Bulgaria attacked Serbia, and that had not yet taken place. But Venizelos was preparing for what he knew was about to take place, and after defending his action in the chamber on October 4th, he was sustained by a vote of 142 to 104. The next day he announced his resignation because of the king's refusal to approve his policy.

The king denied, in the first place, that he had ever consented to an "invitation" to the Entente Allies to send troops to Greece. He stated that Venizelos had only informed him that an "inquiry" had been sent to them as to whether they would be willing to replace the Serbian contingent. To the detached student of Balkan affairs, it is futile to attempt to evaluate the relative veracity of Venizelos and Constantine. The two men were in absolute disagreement as to the policy their country should undertake and they were now in such personal antagonism that not only was coöperation between them impossible, but belief in each other's integrity had practically disappeared. When we consider the reasons given by the king and his adherents for his refusal to consent to the cabinet's action we are on more solid ground. The first contention was that according to the provisions of the Serbo-Greek treaty Serbia was not to cede to a third power without the consent of Greece any of the Macedonian territory secured by her in the Second Balkan War. As Serbia had agreed to the proposal of the Entente Allies to retrocede most of Macedonia to Bulgaria, she thereby rendered the treaty null and void. As a matter of fact, Serbia was so convinced of the importance to her safety of the alliance with Greece, that one of the reasons which for more than a year had prevented her acceding to the appeals of the Entente Allies was her resolve to do nothing that would endanger that alliance. She could hardly have agreed to the cession in question without some kind of understanding with Greece. The second contention for the maintenance of Greek neutrality was that the Serbo-Greek treaty was never intended to apply in the case of a European as opposed to a Balkan war; that it was aimed exclusively against a Bulgarian attack upon one of the signatories and could not be expected to function in the case of an attack on one of them by two great military empires. As the treaty was a secret pact, the provisions of which have not been divulged, one is left his choice of accepting the king's interpretation or that of Venizelos, who contended that to desert Serbia was a violation of the spirit and intent of the treaty.

The fact is that the arguments of the adherents of Constantine for maintaining neutrality were not his real reasons. Although Greece had obtained a great extension of territory by the Balkan wars, her resources had been strained almost to exhaustion. The Great War was rapidly enabling her to recover. The mercantile marines of France, Italy and Great Britain were engaged chiefly in the transportation of troops and munitions, and that of the Central Powers had disappeared from the seas. Greece was rapidly securing a monopoly of the carrying trade of the eastern Mediterranean and did not wish to take a step that might hinder that development. The chief reason, however, for the king's decision was that prestige and power were with the Central Powers. When Venizelos resigned on October 5, 1915, the Dardanelles expedition had totally failed, the Anglo-French "drive" in the Champagne had accomplished nothing and Von Hindenburg had driven the Russians from Poland. There is no reason to doubt the sincerity of the king's belief that intervention on his part would result not only in the rapid overrunning of Serbia by the Central Powers, but in the destruction of Greece. He is a good soldier and at the beginning of December, in an interview with the correspondent of the Associated Press, stated: "Certainly the Allied expedition to the Balkans is doomed to failure if undertaken with no more men than are now there or on their way. The minimum army that can hope to accomplish anything in the Balkans is 400,000. As that number is not being sent, that is no proof that it is Greece that must suffer—Greece that must pay the penalty for the failure of the Allied Balkan venture."

This prediction was soon verified. The advance of the Anglo-French army up the Vardar valley into Bulgarian Macedonia ended in a fiasco. The army would have been annihilated but for the willingness of its commander to retreat into Greek neutral territory. The Bulgarians stopped on the frontier, anxious to avoid offending Greece, while the Anglo-French forces hastened to Salonika, where they engaged feverishly in digging themselves in. Though the great majority of the Greek people were pro-Ally, there can be little doubt that the king's decision met with their approval. The Entente Allies were undoubtedly trying to force Greece to exchange a safe neutrality for risks that might be fatal. Not the king's obstinacy but the Allies' stupidity brought about the desertion of Serbia by Greece. The Entente Allies were always rich in promises, poor in performances. The king could never have prevented Greece from abiding by the treaty of 1913, had the Entente Allies not made it evident that they expected Greece to stake her destiny on the campaign, to push forward her army in advance of Allied assistance. The Greeks were thoroughly aware that Serbia early in the summer had suggested that the Entente Allies send troops to its support and that the troops were not forthcoming. They had no reason to suppose that their own experience would be different.

It might have been a fortunate thing for Greece and for the Entente Allies also, had the latter evacuated Salonika after the failure of the Vardar campaign. The Central Powers understood that Greece with its long seacoast and insular possessions could not afford to enter the war against the Entente Allies, but they did demand that as a neutral state Greece should intern their enemy who had been defeated in Bulgaria and had retreated into Greek territory. But by that time the benevolent attitude of the Entente Allies to Greece had given way to one of coercion. When Venizelos resigned on October 5, 1915, he was succeeded by Alexander Zaimis. His ministry existed, of course, at the sufferance of Venizelos, who commanded a majority of the chamber. When Bulgaria attacked Serbia on October 14th, Zaimis refused to enforce the Serbo-Greek treaty and on October 17th declined Great Britain's offer of the island of Cyprus in return for active Greek military support. As Venizelos had permitted the ministry to exist only provided the question of war was merely one of time and not of doubt, he brought about the defeat of the ministry on November 4th, by a vote of 147 to 114. The king then called M. Skouloudis to office, dissolved the chamber, and called for new elections on December 19th. Now not five months had passed since Venizelos had received the approval of the people and secured a majority of the chamber, as the result of a general election. In the meantime, a large part of the electors had been called to the colors, and as Greek soldiers cannot vote when in service, a new election could not be at all representative of the will of the people. Venizelos, therefore, declaring that the king had launched upon a policy of arbitrary government and that his action was unconstitutional, requested his followers to abstain from voting at the election to show their disapproval of the king's policy. The result was that the Skouloudis ministry, the fifth in the year 1915, secured a majority of the chamber, which was elected by a minority of the voters.

The Skouloudis ministry, while professing to maintain an attitude of benevolent neutrality toward the Entente Allies, firmly opposed any of the latter's demands that would result in a breach of strict neutrality. The press of the Entente Allies, therefore, soon adopted the position of Venizelos that the existing Greek Government was unconstitutional, and demanded that France, Great Britain and Russia enforce the treaty of 1864, whereby "Greece under the sovereignty of the Prince of Denmark and the guarantee of the three courts forms a monarchical, independent and constitutional state." As Greece was no longer a constitutional state, the press of the Allies demanded that the guaranteeing powers perform their duty by intervening to secure such a state—which meant, of course, the return of Venizelos to power. Just what liberal England, Napoleonic France, and autocratic Russia had in mind by the term "constitutional state" when they negotiated the treaty of 1864, it would be hard to say. It must always have had a very vague meaning, for when the army under the Military League really subverted the constitution in 1909, none of the guaranteeing powers hinted at intervention. But the exasperation of the Entente Allies at the recalcitrant attitude of the Skouloudis ministry gradually overcame Sir Edward Grey's reluctance to sanction any dealing with Greece which might be interpreted in neutral countries as smacking of "Prussianism." Lack of space permits only an enumeration of the chief incidents which gradually transformed the attitude of the majority of the Greek people from one of enthusiasm for the Entente Allies to one of ill-concealed hostility.

In December, 1915, the Entente Allies demanded of Greece that it give formal assurance that the Allied troops be in no case disarmed or interned and be granted full freedom of action; also that all requisite railway facilities be placed at the disposal of the Entente Allies for the transport of troops and supplies. The Greek Government declared its readiness to concede such facilities as would not transgress the limits prescribed by the observance of neutrality. As this answer was unsatisfactory, the Entente Allies ordered a commercial blockade of the Greek coast, which was maintained until the Greek Government yielded. This action antagonized not only the influential commercial class, whose vessels could neither enter nor depart from Greek ports, but also large numbers of the poorer people, who suffered from the advance in the price of food products.   On January 11, 1916, the Allies assumed control of the island of Corfu as a place of recuperation for the Serbian troops that had escaped annihilation.   The Greek Government maintained that the territory of one of the Allies, Italy, was near enough for such a use and objected to the violation of Greek neutrality.   In late March the Allies took control of the island of Cephalonia as a naval base.   In April they requested permission of the Greek Government to transport the recuperated Serbian army by rail to Salonika in order to avoid the danger of submarines.   The Central Powers protested that compliance with the request would be regarded by them as an unfriendly act and the request was refused.

On May 26th occurred the most serious of all the untoward incidents, one which went far to convince the Entente Allies that the Greek Government was working in the interests of the Central Powers.   The commander of the garrison of Fort Rupel, the strongest of the forts on the northeast frontier, surrendered to the Bulgars after telegraphing to Athens for instructions.   The government that had once asserted that it would never cede a foot of Greek territory to Bulgaria defended its action on the twofold ground that resistance would be useless, and that in view of what the Allies had already done in Greece, it could not without inconsistency have acted otherwise in applying the principle of neutrality. Moreover, it stated that it had secured, not from the Bulgarian but from the German Government, a written promise to restore the forts in good condition.

The Entente Allies looked upon the surrenders of Rupel and the neighboring forts as evidence of a deliberate agreement by the Greek Government with the Central Powers to shut up the allied troops in Salonika.   In conjunction with the belief that the Greek Army would strike them in the rear if they commenced operations, the surrenders certainly had the effect of immobilizing the half-million men concentrated by the Entente Allies in the neighborhood of Salonika.   The Entente Allies, therefore, determined to take precautionary measures.  The only reasonable precautionary measure was to act upon the suggestion of some of the Allied press and hold the king responsible. Instead, the Entente Allies proceeded to punish the whole Greek people. They not only resorted to a commercial blockade of Greece, but laid an embargo upon Greek vessels in their ports. At the same time the ministers of the Entente Allies presented a note to the Athens Government in their position as the "Protecting Power of Greece," making a clear distinction between the Greek people and the Greek Government, which had "evident collusion with the enemies of the Allies." The note demanded: (1) complete demobilization of the Greek army; (2) a new ministry pledged to show the real benevolent neutrality to the Allies that had been promised; (3) immediate dissolution of the chamber and fresh elections within the time limit provided by the constitution; and (4) dismissal of police officials that had insulted the Allied legations and oppressed peaceable citizens. This demand refers to certain police officials of high position believed to be in the pay of the Central Powers and guilty of oppression of Venizelists. The Greek Government protested indignantly in a note to the Department of State at Washington against the interference with their commerce. The note stated that the Allies not only had blockaded the Greek coast, but had seized Greek ships which they sometimes turned into transports for their own purposes. As a result the Greek sea trade had been ruined and the Greek people deprived of necessary food supplies. Nevertheless on June 28th the Greek Government acceded to the four demands of the Allies.

The surrender of Fort Rupel and the other forts on the Bulgarian frontier was a strong blow to the prestige of Constantine. The street demonstrations that occurred upon receipt of the news showed him that public opinion was against the government's tame surrender and would not back him in withstanding the Allies' demands. Hence he yielded. But each demand of the Allies in violation of Greek neutrality not only met with a hostile reception, but when accepted, was carried out with reluctance and incompleteness; e. g., the army was never completely demobilized. The attitude of the Allies on the other hand was always characterized by vacillation. At one time it was peremptory, at another apologetic. The Allies were determined to prevent the Central Powers from reaching the Greek coast at all hazards, but instead of securing their object by adopting a bold policy with the king, they pursued a policy of pinpricks which injured his subjects more than himself and gave him the position of a martyr. On September 4, 1916, the Allies demanded that the Greek Government hand over to their representatives the telegraph and postal systems, on the ground that they were being used in the interests of the Central Powers by the notorious Baron von Schenk and other German agents in Greece. Moreover, they insisted that Von Schenk and his confrères be arrested and expelled. The king's adherents had no difficulty in pointing out that German agents were active in the United States, Spain and other neutral countries, and that the Allies made no protests to the governments concerned.

On September 12th occurred an event which gave the Allies an opportunity to settle the status of Greece in their own favor and nevertheless retain the sympathy of most of the Greeks. On that day the Bulgarians occupied the Greek seaport of Kavala, and the garrison of 10,000 troops was sent to Germany as "guests." This event roused the greatest indignation throughout Greece. The Greek garrison at Salonika had revolted upon the surrender of Fort Rupel, and in union with discontented civilian elements they, on August 30th, established the "Provisional Government of Macedonia."

The revolt now spread to most of the Greek islands, and the kingdom was soon divided between two governments: the Royalist, which maintained authority over most of old Greece, and the Nationalist, which controlled the territory acquired by the Balkan wars. The latter region was the one in which the influence of Venizelos was strongest, and on September 20th he issued a statement in which he said he "would wait a brief time yet to see what the government purposes to do before deciding on the course it will be best to adopt in the event that Greece does not enter the war." As the government apparently purposed to do nothing, on September 25th Venizelos, Admiral Condouriotis, commander of the Greek navy, and a considerable number of army and navy officers and civilians of influence left Athens, and after making a tour of the islands, landed at Salonika, where Venizelos became the real head of the "Provisional Government of Macedonia."

BY G. WARD PRICE

Rupel is a black word with our Army in the Balkans. When the Bulgars suddenly advanced and took over from the Greeks (by previous secret arrangement) the fort that commands the Struma valley, they threw a five-barred gate across the only way by which we might later on have been able to advance into Bulgaria. The Bulgars stopped the gap we might have gone through. They put themselves across the path of any advance northward, and on the flank of any advance eastward. Since then the wall of strong positions over against us has been complete, and to achieve anything on what later became the British sector of the front it was made practically inevitable that we should first attack the strong position of Rupel.

Why did not the French, whose troops were on the Struma at the time, seize and hold Fort Rupel before the Bulgars got there? It is a question that has been often asked. Certainly we had plenty of reasons to expect that they would advance on the fort. What restrained the French General Staff from occupying it, however, was that, with the limited forces which General Sarrail had at his disposition, it would only have been possible to send a regiment (say 2,000 men) to hold it and the mouth of the defile which it protected. This would not have prevented the Bulgars from coming down in force, and the destruction or the capture of the isolated garrison thrust far out in advance of the main Allied Army would have been a defeat for us and an injury to our cause.

It was on the morning of May 26th that the Bulgarian force sent to seize Rupel appeared in the valley of the Struma. At first it was reported as one brigade strong, then as one division. The infantry of the force seems to have consisted of three whole regiments and part of another, and there was also artillery, three companies of German sappers, and some Uhlans.   The enemy came in three columns, of which the center one moved on Rupel.   The fort had a Greek garrison, of course, the Greek Army being still in occupation of Serres and Demir Hissar, and as the Bulgars approached the Greeks fired a few shells at them—a *pro forma* resistance evidently—to which the Bulgars made no reply, but instead sent at noon a white flag to demand the surrender of the fort.   The officer in command said that he could not give it up without orders from Athens, so a delay was granted for these to be obtained, and at 2.30 p.m. the telegraphic order came that the Greek garrison was to evacuate the fort and withdraw to Demir Hissar.   So the Greek flag was hauled down and the Bulgarian one hoisted.   The Bulgars and Germans signed an inventory of the contents of the fort, and told General Bayeras that they only wanted it for defensive purposes, to stop an Allied move northwards.   A telegram to the Athens Government from General Bayeras, who commanded the 6th Greek Division at Serres, which came to the knowledge of the French General Staff, goes far to confirm the idea that Rupel was surrendered by King Constantine to his friends and our enemies by deliberate previous collusion.   "The Germans and Bulgars arrived at Demir Hissar station this morning to occupy it," telegraphed the General a day or two later.   "I told them that I could not hand over the station without previous reference to you, because the transference of Demir Hissar station was not comprised in the treaty."

Only a year later, in July, 1917, did it become known, from the disclosures made by the reëstablished Venizelist Government in Athens, that, immediately before handing over Fort Rupel to the Germans and their Allies, King Constantine's Government had obtained (as the price of it) a loan of £3,000,000 from the German Government, while at the same moment, with characteristic duplicity, it was trying to avail itself of the long-suffering benevolence of the Allies to get another loan of £5,000,000 out of them.

Demir Hissar station was occupied immediately after

Rupel, treaty or no treaty, and the Bulgarians, crossing the Greek frontier at other points, waited only until they were ready to make a simultaneous push on the other flank of the Allied front before carrying the zone of their occupation down to Kavalla, so that it enclosed our positions in a great arc. At Kavalla part of the garrison under Colonel Hatzopoulo went over to the side which had always had their sympathies and were carried off to Berlin for "training." Colonel Christodoulo, who had brought down a contingent of anti-Bulgar Greeks from Seres, got across to Thasos Island and so back to Salonika, where he was received by the population with hero-worship, and later became the first General of the Venizelist forces. Salonika, as a part of New Greece, was indeed much perturbed by the invasion of the Struma valley by the Bulgars. Her townspeople remembered by what precarious means Salonika had become Greek, and they knew that the Bulgars aimed, and aim still, definitely and ardently, at recapturing the coveted port in which their troops temporarily set footing during the first Balkan War. There was a large public meeting of protest against the action of the Greek Government, held in Salonika, which the Royalist municipal authorities tried in vain to prevent, and from that time a feeling of resentment and apprehension grew among the townspeople and the officers of the garrison until it brought about the "Revolution" of August 30th.

Following upon the Bulgarian descent into Greek territory, and their seizure, by connivance with the Greek Government, of the fort of Rupel, General Sarrail (on June 3rd) seized the control at Salonika of the services of communication and of the police force of the town. The step was one essential to our military security. It was the knowledge which reached the French General Staff of the telegram to the Greek Government, proving its complicity in the advance of the Bulgarians against us, that armed Sarrail's hand. His reply to the surrender of Fort Rupel was the proclamation of martial law at Salonika and throughout the zone of the Allied Armies, and the military occupation of the public buildings of the town. With the swiftness and decision which are characteristic of Sarrail's actions, the step was taken on King Constantine's birthday, the preparations for the celebration of which were hastily called off as French patrols with fixed bayonets suddenly appeared before all the public buildings and at every street corner. The civil administration of the town, except Posts and Telegraphs and police, was left in the hands of the Greeks, but several officials who had been particularly active in their hostility to the Allies, such as Troupakis, the head of the gendarmerie, were expelled.

I will not go into the question of the blockade of the Greek coast by which we brought pressure to bear on Athens. That was a political matter ordered in the first place by the French Minister of Marine, the French Government acting as the delegate of the Allies in the relations of the Entente with Greece. Several times troops were embarked at Salonika to go and lie off Athens ready to land if the Greek Government proved obstinate. Dense secrecy prevailed, of course, about these movements, and rumors of the greatest variety about their destination would spring up in the town like mushrooms after rain.

As a result of these demonstrations, we won some pseudo-concessions from the Royalist Government at Athens. Thus after June 21st, when we threatened to occupy the capital, the king agreed to demobilize his army—but he proceeded to arm civilians, who formed bands of irregulars in our rear just as capable of giving us trouble as Greek uniformed troops would have been.

At length, at the end of August, 1916, came the "Salonika Revolution." This was an outburst of the indignation of the Greeks of Macedonia against the simultaneous invasion of still larger tracts of both Eastern and Western Macedonia by the Bulgars, which took place in August, when they occupied Florina and Banitza and advanced to Lake Ostrovo in the west and pushed on to Kavalla in the east.

By a sudden and rather dramatic upheaval, such as appeals to the Greek temperament, allegiance to King Constantine and the Athens Government was renounced by the majority of the Salonika garrison and population and the resistance

of the Royalist minority was overcome after five minutes'
fighting in the dark. The "Revolution" had the distinct
advantage for the Allies of clarifying the situation. The
transference by the revolutionaries of their adherence from
King Constantine to the Entente made General Sarrail's
authority supreme in Salonika. And after that there was
no more trouble.

A revolutionary feeling had been growing in Macedonia
ever since the Greek troops, under orders from the Athens
Government, abandoned Fort Rupel and a considerable extent of Greek territory to Bulgarian occupation. The jeal-
ous hatred which is the chief feature of the international
relations of the Balkan races was stirred to frenzy, and a
really bitter feeling of indignation sprang up and grew
against the pro-German king and his Ministers; nor was this
indignation based solely upon sentiment. Well-founded
apprehension had no small part in it. The graves were still
fresh of the victims of the Bulgarian massacres at Doxato,
in the very district which was now tamely surrendered to
them. The hopes of this Greek pro-Ally party which was
forming at Salonika had been raised for a moment during
the last week of August by the news from Athens that General Dousmanis, Chief of the General Staff, the arch-enemy
of the Entente, and principal pro-German plotter, had lost
his post, and been replaced by General Moschopoulos, who
had previously commanded the Greek Army Corps at
Salonika. But though Moschopoulos had been personally
friendly with the Allied Staffs, he was above everything a
professional soldier, anxious not to forfeit his post for
political reasons, and he quickly came into the orbit of King
Constantine and the pro-Germans with whom he had to work
in Athens.

And the last circumstance which encouraged the pro-Ally
party at Salonika to pass from sympathy to action was the
fact of Rumania's entry into the war.

It must be remembered—though the recollection is bitter
now—that it was then expected with confidence that this
event marked the beginning of the triumph of our Balkan
campaign. Bulgaria would be crushed by a converging

attack from both sides. Russia—mysterious, but with her strength as yet undoubted—would begin an irresistible offensive at the same time; the Allies at Salonika would march victoriously forward through the Balkans. There would be redistribution of territories and a recasting of frontiers, and from all this, Greece, as the pro-Ally party at Salonika felt, would be shut out and left without a friend in the world.

So on the afternoon of August 30th, a proclamation suddenly appeared on the walls of Salonika, addressed to the Greek people and the Greek Army and signed by Colonel Zimbrakakis, the leader of the movement, by Colonel Mazarakis, by the Venizelist deputy for Seres, and half a dozen other lesser personages, over the title, "Committee of National Defense." In brief, what they said was, "The present state of affairs has lasted long enough. The surrender to the Bulgars of Greek forts and territories is a betrayal of the fatherland to foreign interests. The time has come for Greece to place herself by the side of the Powers of the Entente, who have always been her friends." The proclamation urged the Greek soldiers at Salonika to reject all further orders from Athens and to join the Allies in driving the Bulgars off Greek soil.

The news spread through the town that the Greek gendarmerie—largely Cretans, and therefore Venizelists—had joined the movement in a body, and that the officers of the three Greek regiments at the barracks were holding a meeting to discuss their attitude. Meanwhile Colonel Zimbrakakis, at the head of the gendarmes, all wearing a blue and white silk armlet, which was to be the badge of the Revolution, and followed by a nondescript crowd of volunteers, hastily equipped with any weapons available, marched through the town to offer his services and theirs to General Sarrail. The side-street in front of French Headquarters was packed with an excited crowd, for the Greek loves political demonstration above any form of entertainment. Colonel Zimbrakakis made an impassioned speech from horseback amid loud cheers of "Zito!" then went in to offer the support of his adherents to the Allied cause for the liberation of Macedonia. Sarrail accepted the proffered services, having already been in the habit of taking Greek volunteers into the French Army since the Bulgars came into Greece. At the same time he issued a general warning that he would intervene if public order were disturbed. Though there was no definite repudiation of loyalty to the Greek Crown, I heard many cries from the crowd of "Down with the King!" and there was a feeling in Salonika that night that trouble was in the air. All British troops were ordered out of the town at dusk, but everything remained quiet until 4.30 a. m. next morning.

My own quarters when in Salonika happened to be in a house looking directly on to the broad parade-ground which lies in front of the main barracks, and I was suddenly awakened by a violent rifle-fire very close at hand. One always thinks instinctively of aircraft nowadays when disturbed by explosive noises at night, but this tumult evidently required another explanation. It was a pitch-black night. I went out on to the veranda at the back of the house to find the whole of the parade-ground flickering with the flashes of rifles. Bullets were flying to every point of the compass. Some hit my house, which was at right angles to the line of fire, others fell in Allied camps a mile away. Then came much whistling and shouting and the firing gradually died down and stopped. But the creaking of wheels and the noise of footsteps and lowered voices told of the presence of a good many men. It was evident that the revolutionary gendarmes were attacking the Royalist infantry and cavalry in their barracks.

Dawn came in an hour or so, and the position grew clearer. Overnight the revolutionary gendarmes had demanded the surrender of the barracks by the cavalry and infantry that occupied them. The officers of the latter refused, and when the time fixed by the revolutionaries for the evacuation of the building arrived there was some shooting. Everything, however, was soon patched up and the Royalists withdrew.

## BY KING CONSTANTINE OF GREECE
His Statement of January 14, 1917, Addressed to Neutrals

All we ask is fair play. But it seems almost hopeless to try to get the truth out of Greece to the rest of the world under present circumstances. We have been sorely tried these last two years and we don't pretend to have always been angels under the constant irritation of the ever-increasing allied control of every little thing in our own private life—letters, telegrams, police, everything. Why, do you know that my sister-in-law, Princess Alice of Battenberg, was only permitted to receive a telegram of Christmas greetings from her mother in England by courtesy of the British Legation here?

Moreover, by taking an active hand in our own internal politics, England and France especially have succeeded in alienating an admiration, a sympathy, and a devotion toward them on the part of the Greek people that, at the beginning of the war, was virtually a unanimous tradition. I am a soldier myself and I know nothing about politics, but it seems to me that when you start with almost the whole of a country passionately in your favor and end with it almost unanimously against you, you haven't succeeded very well. And I quite understand how those responsible for such a result seek to excuse themselves by exaggerating the difficulties they have had to contend with in Greece—by talking about Greek treachery and the immense sinister organization of German propaganda that has foiled them at every turn, and so on.

The only trouble with that is that they make us pay for the errors of their policy. The people of Greece are paying for them now in suffering and death from exposure and hunger, while France and England starve us out because they have made the mistake of assuming that their man, Venizelos, could deliver the Greek Army and the Greek people to the Entente Powers whenever they wanted to use Greece for their advantage, regardless of the interests of Greece as an independent nation.

There are just two things about our desperate struggle

to save ourselves from destruction that I am going to try to make clear to the people of America. The rest will have to come out some day—all the blockades and censorships in the world cannot keep the truth down forever. Understand, I am not presuming to sit in judgment on the Entente Powers. I appreciate that they have got other things to think about besides Greece. What I say is meant to help them do justice to themselves and to us, a small nation.

The first point is this: We have two problems on our hands here in Greece—an internal one and an external one. The Entente Powers have made the fundamental mistake of considering them both as one. They said to themselves: "Venizelos is the strongest man in Greece and he is heart and soul with us. He can deliver the Greeks whenever he wants to. Let us back Venizelos, therefore, and when we need the Greek Army he will turn it over to us."

Well, they were wrong. Venizelos was perhaps the strongest man in Greece, as they thought. But the moment he tried to turn over the Greek Army to the Entente, as if we were a lot of mercenaries, he became the weakest man in Greece and the most despised. For in Greece no man delivers the Greeks. They decide their own destinies as a free people, and not England, France and Russia together can change them, neither by force of arms nor by starvation. And they have tried both. As for Venizelos himself—you had a man once in your country, a very great man, who had even been Vice-President of the United States, who planned to split the country in two and set himself up as a ruler in the part he separated from the rest. I refer to Aaron Burr. But he only plotted to do a thing which he never accomplished. Venizelos, with the assistance of the allied powers—and he never could have done it without them —has succeeded for the time being in the same kind of a seditious enterprise. You called Aaron Burr a traitor. Well, that's what the Greek people call Venizelos.

The impression has been spread broadcast that Venizelos stands in Greece for liberalism and his opponents for absolutism and militarism. It is just the other way around. Venizelos stands for whatever suits his own personal book.

His idea of government is an absolute dictatorship—a sort of Mexican government, I take it. When he was Premier he broke every man who dared to disagree with him in his own party. He never sought to express the will of the people; he imposed his will on the people. The Greek people will not stand that. They demand a constitutional Government in which there is room for two parties—Liberals and Conservatives—each with a definite program, as in the United States or England or any other civilized country, not a personal Government, where the only party division is into Venizelists and anti-Venizelists.

The other thing I wanted to say is about the effect of the so-called German propaganda in Greece. The Entente Powers seem to have adopted the attitude that everybody who is not willing to fight on their side must be a pro-German. Nothing could be falser in respect of Greece. The present resentment against the Allies in Greece—and there is a good deal of it, especially since the blockade—is due to the Allies themselves and not to any German propaganda. The proof of it is that when the so-called German propaganda was at its height there was little or no hostility in Greece toward the Allies. It has only been since the diplomatic representatives of all the Central Empires and everybody else whom the Anglo-French secret police indicated as inimical to the Entente have been expelled from Greece, and any German propaganda rendered virtually impossible, that there has grown up any popular feeling against the Entente.

Part of this is due to the Entente's identification of its greater cause with the personal ambitions of Venizelos, but a great deal has also been due to the very unfortunate handling of the allied control in Greece. When you write a personal letter of no possible international significance to a friend or relative here in Athens, and post it in Athens, and it is held a week, opened, and half its contents blacked out, it makes you rather cross—not because it is unspeakable tyranny in a free country at peace with all the world, but because it is so silly. For, after all, if you want to plot with a man living in the same town you don't write him a letter. You put on your hat and go to see him. Half the people in Greece have been continually exasperated by just this sort of unintelligent control, which has irritated the Greek people beyond telling.

The fact of the matter is that there is even now less pro-German feeling in Greece than in the United States, Holland, or any of the Scandinavian countries. And there is far less anti-Entente propaganda in Greece even now than there is anti-Hellenic propaganda in England, France and Russia. The whole feeling of the Greek people toward the Entente Powers to-day is one of sorrow and disillusionment. They had heard so much of this "war for the defense of little nations" that it had been a very great shock to them to be treated, as they feel, very badly, even cruelly, for no reason and to nobody's profit. And more than anything else, after all the Greek Government and Greek people have done to help the Entente Powers since the very outbreak of the war, they deeply resent being called pro-German because they have not been willing to see their own country destroyed as Serbia and Rumania have been.

I have done everything I could to dissipate the mistrust of the Powers, I have given every possible assurance and guarantee. Many of the military measures that have been demanded I myself suggested with a view to tranquillizing the Allies, and myself voluntarily offered to execute. My army, which any soldier knows could never conceivably have constituted a danger to the allied forces in Macedonia, has been virtually put in jail in the Peloponnesus. My people have been disarmed, and are to-day powerless, even against revolution, and they know from bitter experience that revolution is a possibility so long as the Entente Powers continue to finance the openly declared revolutionary party of Venizelos. There isn't enough food left in Greece to last a fortnight. Not the Belgians themselves under German rule have been rendered more helpless than are we in Greece to-day.

Isn't it, therefore, time calmly to look at conditions in Greece as they are, to give over a policy dictated by panic, and to display a little of that high quality of faith which alone is the foundation of friendship?

# MACKENSEN'S BRILLIANT RUMANIAN CAMPAIGN

## RUMANIA MISLED AND BROKEN

GENERAL WOLLMAN    GENERAL MACKENSEN
WINIFRED GORDON

Rumania entered the War under a triple misconception. First, Russia had promised her ample support, so she thought her northern frontier secure; whereas in reality she received from Russia only a mere shadow of support, which was worse than useless, since it lured the Rumanian army into dangerous positions. Second, Russia had assured her that Bulgarian neutrality was fully pledged, that the Bulgars would not fight their Slavic brethren. Hence Rumania thought her southern or Bulgarian frontier needed no defense. Third, Rumania supposed Germany to be exhausted by Verdun and the Somme, and quite incapable of lending Austria further aid. It was under this triple misunderstanding that Rumania, immediately on declaring war, sent her troops across her northern border to the invasion of the Hungarian province of Transylvania.

Germany had been awaiting this very opportunity. Her prestige had been disastrously lowered upon the western front; she would retrieve her fame by a brilliant and easy victory in the east. Hindenburg's ablest lieutenant, Mackensen, now raised to the rank of Field Marshal, was sent secretly to Bulgaria. With a few German troops and a mass of Bulgars and Turks he suddenly attacked the exposed Rumanian southern border. The forces hurriedly sent to oppose him weakened the Rumanian army in Transylvania.

A second Teuton army now appeared in Hungary and, on September 19th, checked the advance of the Rumanians at Hatzeg. Meanwhile a third column of Teutons marched secretly through eastern Transylvania and got between the Rumanian army and its own country, seizing the border passes of the mountains. The Rumanians, with their lines of communication partly cut, had much ado to regain their own country, and only did so after heavy losses.

By mid-October the Teutons were invading Rumania from the north, while Mackensen's main army was advancing from the south. On October 22nd he captured Constanza, Rumania's only seaport. After this the Rumanian resistance stiffened, and more Russian troops came to her aid. But on November 17th the northern Teuton armies under General Falkenhayn won a decisive victory at Tirgujiulij. This enabled them to sweep straight across central Rumania and unite with Mackensen's forces. These now fought their way across the Danube, and Rumania's defeat was manifest. Her western provinces were occupied by the enemy and from every direction except the northeast the Teuton armies were gathering round her capital. Its fall and the subsequent Rumanian resistance are left for another picture.

### BY GENERAL WOLLMAN
#### Semi-Official German Statement

THE Rumanian declaration of war against Austro-Hungary on August 27, 1916, was followed on the next day by a declaration of war against Rumania by Germany. On August 29th, General von Falkenhayn was transferred from his position as Chief of the General Staff for "service elsewhere." In his new capacity as commander of the Ninth Army, von Falkenhayn immediately marched against the Rumanians who had crossed the mountains into Transylvania, drove them back, and during September wrested from them the Szurduk, Vulcan, and Red Tower passes. During October the Rumanians, helped by the Russians, put up a desperate resistance to von Falkenhayn's further advance, and the month was spent in heavy fighting with victory first for one side, then the other. In the meantime, immediately after war was declared on Rumania by Turkey and Bulgaria, Mackensen had gone to Bulgaria and thence led an army composed of German, Bulgarian, and Turkish units from the Varna-Rustchuk line over the border into Rumania by way of the Dobrudja.

Under the delusion that Bulgaria would not declare war against her and might even break with the Central Powers, Rumania had sent the bulk of her forces to the Transylvanian frontier, leaving the Bulgarian front, except for some Russian reënforcements, weakly held. This mistake, made at the very beginning of the campaign, affected the whole course of the struggle, and after Mackensen's success in the Dobrudja, could never be retrieved.

Mackensen's object, which was to occupy the Dobrudja and thus block the Russians from their shortest road to Constantinople, was accomplished in a comparatively short time. One smashing blow after another was delivered against the allied Russians and Rumanians. The bridgehead at Tutrakan on the Danube was attacked on September 4th, and captured on the 6th, at a cost to the enemy of 22,000 men. On the day that Tutrakan fell, a Rumanian division hurrying to the rescue was routed at Sarsinlar by the west wing of Mackensen's army, which subsequently took 30,000 prisoners and much war material.

On the eastern wing furious Russian attacks in the region of Dobritch led to heavy fighting. This ended on September 7th with the complete defeat of three Russian-Rumanian-Serbian divisions. As a result the Rumanians voluntarily evacuated Silistria, and, pursued vigorously by Mackensen, retreated along the whole front in a northerly direction. Between Lake Oltina and Mangalia the arrival of four fresh Rumanian divisions and some additional help from the Russians enabled the fleeing enemy to make a stand, but his resistance was broken in a few days, and on September 14th he was driven back to the general line Cuzgun-Cara Omar, forty kilometers north of Dobritch.

Here also his stay was short. Beaten almost to annihilation, he soon continued his flight to prepared positions between Rashova, Cobadin, and Tuzla, twenty kilometers south of the old Trajan wall and the railroad from Cernavoda to Constantza via Megidia. On this line he was able to stand under the protection of Rumanian regiments drawn from Transylvania and of Russian troops sent by sea to Constantza.

As announced in the *communiqués* of September 20th and 21st, the battle now came to a standstill. After the line was stabilized, the Bulgarians, who had particularly distinguished themselves on the east wing, erected on their front as a threat to the Russians and a sign of their own confidence a huge placard bearing the inscription "Mackensen leads us."

The results of Mackensen's victorious progress up to this point were important. Eight Rumanian divisions had been taken prisoner or terribly shattered; the Russian forces sent to aid Rumania had been so often defeated that their fighting power was badly shaken; and positions on the lower Danube flanking Wallachia and the national capital had been won. In addition, any invasion of the southern Dobrudja by the enemy had been rendered impossible, and his main army on the Transylvanian front had been weakened by the withdrawal of troops which it could ill spare. These were now shut up behind Trajan's wall. The Rumanians were compelled to wage war upon three fronts.

Before undertaking further operations, Mackensen's army needed time to repair the losses which had been incident to the delivery of its mighty blows and to replenish its war material. Heavy artillery, in particular, was required for the reduction of the enemy's strongly fortified position, and this could be brought up only with the greatest difficulty owing to the lack of good rearward lines of communication. The enemy, on the other hand, had the advantage of the railroad which ran behind his front.

The Rumanians used the pause in the battle to make a feeble attempt in the first days of October to cross the Danube farther up and fall upon our army from the rear. As an inadequate force was detailed for the venture—some fifteen battalions of infantry without artillery support—and Rahovo, the place chosen for the crossing, was midway between our two points of support at Tutrakan and Rustchuk, the undertaking failed completely. A German-Bulgarian force sent hurriedly up from Tutrakan practically annihilated the attacking battalions. The few who got back to the north bank of the river fled to Bucharest, where they caused a panic among the inhabitants.

During October the battle for the passes on the Hungarian border developed steadily in our favor, but no military events in the Dobrudja were reported until the twentieth. After that, there were frequent bulletins about the war of position on the Trajan line, where both sides were extremely active. Each day brought new successes to Mackensen's army. One after another the enemy's points of support, including Constantza, the chief Rumanian seaport, fell into our hands, until a break through and enveloping movement put us in possession of Cernavoda and the whole Russian-Rumanian position. Communication between Wallachia and the sea by way of Constantza was cut. That the Rumanians despaired of restoring the line was proved by their blowing up the great bridge across the Danube west of Cernavoda.

After being driven out of the Trajan line, the enemy was pushed farther and farther into the northern corner of the Dobrudja. Finally, however, he received reënforcements from the hinterland over pontoon bridges and reached prepared defenses, where he compelled us to settle down again to a war of position. When events had reached this stage, that is, on November 24th, the telegraph gave out this brief but highly significant piece of news: "Forces from Mackensen's army group have crossed the Danube in several places."

The plans for this undertaking were so well thought out and the coöperation of the different groups so carefully and secretly arranged that it was carried out almost without losses. In the misty early morning of November 23rd the advance party gathered at several places in the vicinity of Svistov and set out upon the river, which at this point is nearly two kilometers wide. The enemy on the north bank was taken completely by surprise. There was therefore no interruption to the transference, on pontoons and barges towed by motor boats, of additional infantry and some batteries, who built up the position into something like a bridgehead. On November 24th, under the protection of these forces, the construction of a bridge capable of bearing the heavy artillery was begun; in twenty-two hours it was finished, and on November 25th, at five o'clock in the morning, the bridge was open to traffic.

As soon as the penetration of the Danube front was an accomplished fact, Mackensen's German-Bulgarian-Turkish army could coöperate closely with von Falkenhayn's Ninth Army, which was advancing from the boundary passes of the north and west. The despairing attempts of Russian and Rumanian divisions to hold off or to turn aside the fate that threatened, availed them nothing, in spite of their great sacrifices. After the decisive three-day battle on the Argesh the capital of Rumania surrendered without a struggle. On December 6th, his birthday, Field-Marshal von Mackensen entered Bucharest amid the joyful greetings of the liberated German and Austro-Hungarian inhabitants and of the Rumanians who were friendly to Germany.

From now on the Field Marshal drove the fleeing enemy ever farther to the eastward between the Danube and the mountains. Bands of Bulgarians crossed the river at Tutra-kan on December 8th, and at Fetesti on the 14th, and thrust at the enemy's flank. The fortified positions on the Jalo-mitza, on the Buzeu, and on the Putna could not halt our invincible troops. At Nanesti-Fundeni on the line of the Sereth and at Braila-Vadeni the Russians lost great numbers in dead, wounded, and prisoners. Their efforts were vain. Coöperation between Mackensen's army and that of the Archduke Joseph, who was driving the Russians out of the mountains into the Moldavian plain, was perfect. Not until the winter cold had a paralyzing effect on friend and foe did the fighting slacken.

During the winter the two opposing armies were en-trenched in Wallachia and Moldavia on both sides of the Sereth and its right hand tributaries, and in the Dobrudja on both sides of the branches of the Danube. Their advanced posts and artillery clashed occasionally in minor engage-ments. Galatz, the important point of support of the en-emy's wing, was constantly bombarded by our heavy artil-lery. The Sereth marked a goal beyond which our army command did not mean to go; for the critical point of the War was no longer to be found in Rumania. The danger there had been obliterated.

### BY GENERAL MACKENSEN

#### Letter Addressed in the General's Own Hand to His Troops

The troops who in the Dobrudja, in the mountains that form the frontier between Transylvania and Rumania, and in Wallachia defeated the Rumanian army so decisively that this army was broken up and compelled to seek refuge behind the protecting Russian troops and fortresses on the Sereth, will be accorded in the future even higher recognition for their achievements than they have already received.

March 3, 1917.                                    MACKENSEN.

BY WINIFRED GORDON

Russia had assured Rumania that there was little to fear from Bulgaria, as the latter would never be willing to fight against her Slav mother Russia. It seems incredible that any one could have put faith in the traitorous character of the Bulgarian, or in the crafty scheming fox who occupies the throne, and who was using the negotiations between his Government and the Rumanian Minister at Sofia regarding neutrality as a pretense to gain time for his attack, using these diplomatic maneuvers in true Teutonic style as a cloak to conceal the dagger beneath.

But the Prime Minister Bratiano, strange to say, did not believe in the duplicity of the Bulgarian Government, and thought it possible to avoid war. Thus a grave political miscalculation determined the course of the campaign.

The element of surprise counted considerably in the first great successes for the Rumanian Army. She was able to throw her forces well over the Carpathians, crossing at eighteen points, and to penetrate deep into the enemy's country before the latter could assemble in force, even had the latter had at her disposal sufficient men and material to release from her other fronts for this purpose—a condition the Allies did not believe to be possible. Of the four Rumanian armies, the third, under General Aslan, was left to watch the Bulgarian frontier, while the other three—the first, under General Culcer; the second, under General Averescu, and the fourth, under General Présan—were to operate on the Carpathians.

During the first few weeks the Rumanians made a rapid advance, all opposition being overcome. The Central Powers had been taken by surprise, and had as yet no time to bring up reënforcements to arrest the victorious march forward, since the élan of the Rumanian troops was at its highest, fighting as they were now on what was once their own territory, and where their kinsmen are held under the iron hand of the Magyar.

The Czech regiments sent to oppose these Rumanian units simply walked right over to them, so glad were they to join those fighting against the Magyar tyrants—"The Prussians" of the Dual Monarchy; and indeed as a Deputy said in the Hungarian Parliament, "they just disappeared without any one being able to say where they went!"

The Tornos, the Tolgyes and the Rothen Turm passes were in turn forced, the railways and frontier towns occupied, and the Rumanian Army was debouching into the wide country of rolling hills and valleys—the well-loved land—while Hermannstadt was being menaced.

It was a triumphant success, and the hopes of the little nation beat high. But their slender forces, in a country both mountainous and difficult and covering a frontier of no less than three hundred miles, were widely separated, making it hard to establish communications. It must be remembered they had not yet reached the river Maros, which in itself would have given them a position of comparative security.

The enemy meanwhile with furious energy and aided by his splendid railway system was preparing a deadly counterstroke, of which the Rumanians with their limited and scattered aëroplane service were unable to gauge either the extent or full importance.

It was at this moment that the risky nature of the strategic plan began to make itself felt. Bulgaria had held her hand until Mackensen, who was in the Balkan area, had been able to make his military preparations and assume command of the armies on the Bulgarian frontier. Within five days of Rumania's declaration the Slav Judas, Ferdinand of Coburg, ruler of Bulgaria, had once again sold his honor and declared war on Rumania and on his country's liberator, Russia. General Jostoff, the Chief of the Bulgarian Staff, a man of patriotism and honor, who was strongly opposed to the German domination of his country, was, following the notorious Enver Bey tradition, "removed," his body being found riddled with bullets. Such indeed are the rewards for men of this stamp in countries where Germany teaches "Kultur"!

Mackensen was the first to strike. Massing his troops with great speed he fell on the scattered Rumanian forces defending the fortresses of Turtukai, and Silistria in the Dobrudja, the reduction of which would open the way for a quick advance to the great bridge and railway over the Danube at Cernavoda, linking the port of Constanza with the capital. Turtukai, though defended by fortifications, had been left with a very inadequate number of troops. The utmost gallantry was displayed by the defenders, who were seriously handicapped and at a most serious disadvantage on account of the superiority in men and guns which the enemy possessed. Though vigorously contesting every inch of ground under the most terrific fire, and repulsing the enemy again and again, they were eventually overwhelmed, and the fortress fell on the 6th of September, just ten days after Rumania's entering into the war.

This was a very serious reverse for Rumania, as the fortress covered the crossing of the Danube. On the Bulgarian side the river bank stands high, dominating the low Rumanian bank opposite, and the advance from this point to the capital is only thirty miles. As a consequence of the fall of the fortress of Turtukai, the evacuation of Silistria, a little further to the east, was decided on, on the ground that the garrison being insufficient would have merely fallen into a trap. The loss of these two important fortresses, within two weeks of the opening of the war, was a disastrous check, and placed a very anxious aspect on one portion of the campaign.

Meanwhile the Transylvanian armies had been weakened by the transference of some of their not too abundant forces for the defense of the Dobrudja, and the withdrawal of General Averescu, the ablest of their generals, to command the army there, which now found themselves involved in serious difficulty.

Rumania's equipment was inadequate for a war which she had hoped to limit to the Central Powers alone, but which had now developed into one against four nations, Germany, Austria, Bulgaria and Turkey, all combining to surround and crush our gallant little Ally, who was still awaiting the promised artillery and support from Russia. Guns, machine guns, aëroplanes, field telephones, rifles, etc., were alike lacking to meet the wants of the long line of thirteen hundred kilometers on which she was conducting two campaigns simultaneously, and to combat the gigantic fighting machine elaborated by the enemy during two years of war and continual experience.

The Rumanian Army consisting of only *sixteen* divisions was now having to face *thirty-seven* divisions, accompanied by an overwhelmingly superior armament, *twenty divisions of which belonged to the élite of the German Army.*

Rumania's two years of neutrality had not availed her much, for the Powers, uncertain as to her decision, would not assist her with supplies, and it was only by the long, roundabout way through Russia with its interminable delays and demoralization that she could get any munitions at all. Furthermore, the hopes she had built on the promises of a steady flow of these from Russia were not fulfilled. The treacherous pro-German Sturmer Government at Petrograd held up supplies and absolutely vital necessaries, with the consequence that the brave little nation, cruelly isolated in this distant corner of Europe, was for the most part left alone to meet the combined attack of the four Powers.

With Turtukai and Silistria in German hands, Mackensen's aim was now to push on to the great Carol Bridge at Cernavoda (which means Black Water), the only bridge over the Lower Danube for a distance of six hundred miles. By capturing it and the railway across it, he would sever Rumanian access to the Black Sea, as well as cut through Russia's road to the Balkans. The bridge is one of the longest in the world, and counting the causeways is twelve miles long and cost £1,500,000 to build. The railway was built in 1882 under Turkish rule, by an English company, and cuts through the wonderful old wall of Trajan at several points.

The greater part of the Russian 47th Army Corps and the Serbian division were now supporting the Rumanians in the Dobrudja, the whole under the command of the Russian General Zayonchovski, the Serbian division being composed of Jugo-Slavs forced to fight in the Austro-Hungarian Army and taken prisoners by the Russians. These soldiers were a splendid lot, and begged to be allowed to fight on the side of the Allies and to strike a blow for their kinsmen. They fought with stubborn tenacity all through the campaign, winning the admiration of both Allies and enemy alike.

Mackensen, even with his war experience and superior troops, vastly superior artillery, and aëroplane service, which gave him inestimable advantage over the Rumanian forces who were practically without "eyes," encountered the fiercest opposition. The defenders contested his advance with the greatest pugnacity and valor. Even the German report admitted that "fierce and fluctuating battles have taken place, the enemy defending himself with great stubbornness." So much indeed was this the case that they were able to inflict serious reverses on the enemy at Kara Orman, where they lost eight guns and a high-born officer, Prince Henry of Bavaria, nephew of the king. The Rumanians drove the invading armies back in complete confusion. Mackensen's boast of the "crowning mercy" that was to be his—the Cernavoda bridge—was still out of reach.

Apropos of the death of this Prince, it is said that just before he expired, conscious that his death was not as that of other men, he murmured, *"Noblesse oblige."* These words were applauded by the German nation, who overlooked the fact that they were the last words spoken by a scion of a Royal German House, and were those of their traditional but always chivalrous foe, France.

The Rumanians, unable to bring up sufficient reënforcements, were too exhausted to pursue their successes. All through October battles swayed, alternately success coming first to one side, then to the other, the Rumanians fighting with fury and desperation to arrest the enemy advance on their port of Constanza.

Their forces were still further depleted by some divisions being withdrawn to the Carpathians, where the passes were being seriously threatened. Towards the end of September Mackensen, strongly reënforced by Turkish and Bulgar divisions, was able to seize his advantage, and after a fierce resistance to cut the connection between Cernavoda and Constanza, the latter coming within range of the German guns and unable to be held. The Rumanian troops withdrew under cover of the fire of the Russian fleet in the Black Sea, and amid a wild storm of wind and rain the Bulgars entered the city. Everything had been destroyed, including the great stores of grain and oil, and the enemy found little beyond some hundreds of empty railway trucks and a few locomotives. By this Rumania lost her only seaport and the principal lines of communication with Russia were cut.

The Transylvanian campaign had been launched on the assumption of surprise, and unpreparedness on the part of the enemy. An historian has described it as a "gamble between two conditions of unpreparedness," in view of the political conditions and the poor equipment of the Rumanian Army for the heavy tasks awaiting her. Austria had, however, the luck to hold the better card. Thanks to her splendid system of strategic railways, her ally, Germany, was able to summon to her support large forces from Verdun, the Somme, and the Riga fronts, while Turkish and Bulgarian hordes rolled up from the south on the brave but unfortunate little country, which found it could count but little on the promised assistance from Russia.

The forces arrayed against her consisted of over nine hundred thousand war-seasoned troops, picked Bavarian Alpine corps—sturdy highlanders accustomed to mountain warfare—and a great mass of artillery, the whole under the command of General von Falkenhayn. The Rumanian forces were depleted by having to send several divisions to the Dobrudja. They were short of big guns and had no experience of mountain warfare, for since the outbreak of war in 1914 they had been unable to practice maneuvers there for fear that they might excite the apprehension of the Central Powers and have them misconstrued as a threat.

The early days in October saw the great German offensive in the Carpathians launched. Brusiloff's advance in Galicia had been checked, and the ill success on his left wing was soon to be followed by disastrous consequences for the Rumanian offensive. Supported by an overwhelming preponderance of artillery, the Austro-German command delivered blow after blow with deadly effect.

The Rumanians fighting desperately reeled under the titanic onslaught of massed guns and superior forces and were forced to retreat towards the passes. Slowly, bit by bit, all the ground they had won had to be given up, and soon the fifteen thousand prisoners that they had taken and their depleted forces were all that remained to them of the great adventure.

In the rocky gorges and precipitous roads of the Carpathian passes she braced herself sternly for a desperate defensive. Amid the blaze of color, the glorious beauty of early autumn, a fierce resistance took place in the narrow defiles, defended as strongly as the slender resources of the Rumanians allowed.

High up on the ledges of the narrow defiles ran the steep winding roads on which the Austrian high-explosive shells were blasting their way; hundreds of feet below brawled the streams.

Again and yet again the valorous Rumanians wrested success from the enemy and drove him back. In the Jiu valley they inflicted a crushing and humiliating defeat on those fiercest of Teuton fighters, the Bavarians, who fled in utter rout. They left immense stores behind them, only snatching time to shoot 1,300 of their horses, which they hastily buried in a gigantic funeral mound before escaping on foot through the ravines. General Dragalina, one of Rumania's exiled sons from Transylvania and a most daring and capable commander, was severely wounded here and succumbed later to his injuries. He was a brave, strong personality and greatly beloved by his men.

But these and other brilliant counter-offensives of the gallant little Rumanian Army could not stem the onward sweep of the Teutonic hosts, who had burst through the mountain passes and were pouring into the wide rich plains of Wallachia, this treasure land of grain in Eastern Europe.

Rumania had hardly faced the disastrous fall of Constanza and the Cernavoda bridge when the rude shock of the fall of Craiova, the chief town of Ollenia, "the millionaires' city," as it was called, forced them to realize the imminent peril of the nation. Out-gunned, out-manned, the splendid peasant soldiers of our Ally rose to the crisis with the true spirit of soldiers, defending their country with desperation, and as the German reports admit, "with unsparing energy."

The small Orsova group stubbornly holding on to its positions at the Iron Gates of the Danube was left far behind, as the main Rumanian Army retreated, and found itself in the rear of the advancing enemy forces. Completely cut off and isolated from the main army, this valiant detachment of seven thousand men under General Anastasiu, stubbornly fighting, tried to escape the doom that they knew was certain. But they resolved to sell their lives dearly, harrying unceasingly the rear troops of the enemy forces and menacing their transport traffic on the Danube.

This wonderful retreat lasted three weeks, and so courageously and determinedly did they fight to the last that they even earned the praise and admiration of the enemy, who reported that "amidst continuous fighting and delivering repeated counter-attacks the Orsova group withdrew slowly to the southeast, constantly resisting and fighting for the honor of its arms."

Decimated and lacking in everything but their superb courage and daring which resisted to the bitter end, the gallant remnant, under its heroic General Anastasiu, were forced to surrender at Caracalu two days after the fall of Bucharest.

Meanwhile on the Danube frontier Mackensen had been able to force a crossing at Giurgevo and was now marching northwards to coöperate with the armies advancing from the west under Falkenhayn, the objective being to close in on the capital.

Whilst destroying Giurgevo, the Bulgarian forces under his command gave full rein to the hatred and savagery of their dour natures. In a few hours nothing was left of the once prosperous little town but scenes of wanton destruction and piles of grewsome corpses—old men, women, children, girls! What the flames did not spare was wrecked by the fury of these heartless brutes, who in the way of the *furor teutonicus* of their predatory masters had nothing to learn, and in the matter of murder, rape and savagery could even give them points.  They were well aware of Germany's order that "Rumania should pay in full the expenses of her invasion."

The German Socialist and Labor paper, the *Arbeiter Zeitung,* crowing with satisfaction over the misery of the devastated peasantry, remarked:

"Our troops could not possibly have marched at this rate had not Rumania so much cattle, so many geese, pigs and poultry.  The Wallachian plain is covered with thriving villages very different from the poor hamlets in the mountains on the northern border of the country.  The invading forces live here in great style."

The extreme gravity of the moment was incontestable. General Averescu, now in supreme command of the Rumanian Army, gathered together all the forces he could muster for a last stand on the river Argés and a decisive battle, on which the fate of Bucharest would depend.

It was now that the soldiers of the Czar—two divisions, a small part of the long-promised help—made their first appearance in Wallachia, although this was three months after the commencement of hostilities, at a time when the little nation was mourning the tragic loss of more than half her kingdom.  Bleeding and exhausted, she was facing a formidable foe flushed and exalted with success, and supported by a crushing preponderance of both artillery and men.

The narrow line of the river Argés, on which Averescu was giving battle, presented no formidable obstacle, being not much more than a wide ditch.  Nevertheless, General Présan delivered a counter-stroke in the hope of driving a wedge between the army of Mackensen and the German center under Kühne.  Within an ace of achieving his purpose, he repulsed the enemy, throwing him across the river Neaylovic and defeating the Turkish division as well as the main body of German-Bulgarian troops, resulting in the capture of fifty guns and some thousands of prisoners.

But success was dashed from his grasp, for espionage was rampant, and the whole place infested with German civilians domiciled in the country, of whom fifty, disguised in Russian uniform, were arrested, tried and shot in one day.

General Présan, desperately pressed and anxiously awaiting the expected reënforcements which were purposely delayed through the culpable negligence of a subordinate officer, found treachery on every side. General Socescu—a naturalized German whose real name was Sosek—commanding a division, left his post at night at nine o'clock without authority, and, in the midst of this supreme crisis, went to Bucharest. The position occupied by his troops was attacked by the enemy at 9.30, the line was pierced—General Présan's at one time victory was turned into a crushing defeat of the Rumanian armies—and the way to the capital lay open!

For Rumania these were indeed terrible days of anxiety. Bit by bit the heroic army were forced back, fighting stubbornly under overwhelming odds, exhausted, decimated, lacking everything, yet constantly winning a grudging acknowledgment of valor and resistance in the enemy's reports.

The treachery of General Socescu and the consequent defeat of the Rumanian armies had fallen on the capital like a thunderbolt. The excitement in these bitter days of winter was indescribable. The cry: "The Germans are coming" filled the populace with terror.

But with unquenchable hope and faith they waited— with sinking hearts they waited and hoped. Where was the promised help from Russia? Only two divisions had arrived. Where was the Brusiloff offensive in Galicia that was to draw the enemy off? The advance from Salonika? But the Allies were too busy parleying and believing in the false protestations of neutrality of another traitor, Constantine, once of Greece. And Sarrail, immobilized and paralyzed for lack of men, munitions and railroads, could not advance for the promised assistance.

Rumania stood at bay facing her martyrdom alone. A tense pause seemed to hang over Europe as it watched the mortal struggle of the little nation, the cup raised—to be drained to its bitterest dregs.

# THE VERDUN COUNTER-ATTACK

## A FRENCH DASH REGAINS THE LOSSES OF MONTHS

### OCTOBER 24TH

### GERMAN OFFICIAL STATEMENTS
### MARSHAL HINDENBURG   THE CROWN PRINCE
### FRENCH AND BRITISH EYE-WITNESSES
### GENERAL DUBOIS

The great German attack upon Verdun had slackened, as we have seen, in July and August. By fall the front there was scarcely more active than other portions of the trench line. Then on October 24th the French commander there, General Nivelle, launched a sudden and most successful surprise attack. Fort Douaumont and much of the surrounding region, which the Germans had battled for months to win, were wrested from them in a single charge. Over a front of four miles the French advanced to a depth of two miles. Fort Vaux, the companion defense to Douaumont, was then assailed, and in less than a week the Germans were driven from it. This double success in a region where almost every rod of advance had once been heralded as a victory, was a striking triumph. So valuable did it seem to the French that General Nivelle was, in December, made Commander-in-Chief of all the French armies in France, taking the place of Joffre, who retired.

Naturally, the Germans sought to belittle their loss of the historic Douaumont and the ground they had toiled so desperately to win. Moreover, General Ludendorff, since the War, has admitted that he framed his official bulletins to "keep up the morale" of his soldiers. Whether falsehood was the most effective way of accomplishing this may be open to question—but it was the German way. Hence in giving Ludendorff's contemptuous dismissal of the French "local" success, we have placed before it the account of Colonel Frobenius, the semi-official German historian, and also a memorandum by General von Zwehl, the commander on the spot. This was received by Ludendorff just before the attack. We give also the more honest and generous review by Marshal Hindenburg as he summed up the French attack in his Memoirs. The pathetic protest of the nominal commander at Verdun, the Crown Prince, crying that all this was not his fault, closes this not uninteresting conflict of German accounts of Verdun.

The intense earnestness of the French spirit in the assault is then presented by a French staff officer; and the wide triumph of the Ally world over the victory is voiced by the British newspaper report that follows. Before October 24th the Verdun position might have been regarded as a mere lull, a resting point from which Germany would again resume her advance. After October 24th, Verdun ranked as a great defensive victory for France. Germany, to win the ancient stronghold now, would have to begin operations all over again, almost from the beginning. On December 16th the French, now under General Mangin, made another similar assault and won back another section of territory even larger. In both of these counter-attacks the French used new cannon of great destructive power, and their loss in men was comparatively small. This increase in artillery force and the resulting conservation of human life was one of the most notable features in the approaching superiority of the Allies.    C. F. H.

### BY COLONEL FROBENIUS

IN the Battle of the Somme the English and the French indeed succeeded as far as their avowed object of relieving the French defenders of Verdun was concerned. The Germans, in order successfully to resist the onslaughts at the Somme, were compelled to draw heavily upon their artillery before Verdun, thus enabling the French there to proceed to counter-attacks.

It was not unknown to the Germans that the defenders were preparing to recapture forts Vaux and Douaumont. The artillery preparation for the attack began on October 21st, the attack being directed, on October 24th, from the lines on the heights of Haudromont over the crests at Fleury, and from Vaux-Chapitre toward Damloup. Against the troops stationed within the area Douaumont-Vaux, consisting of 28 battalions and 10 reserve battalions, together with 130 batteries, the French launched three divisions with an additional infantry regiment joined to each wing.

The attack of the troops, which had been long and carefully detailed, succeeded. On the 26th the German position, including the third line, was in the hands of the French. Fort Douaumont, which, in consequence of the bombardment was afire and had become untenable, had already been evacuated on the evening of the 23rd. Only Fort Vaux held out until November 2nd.

A cessation of the combats, now supervened, the Germans meanwhile occupying positions farther back, their operations remaining unmolested by the enemy. The French wished to renew the attack with the utmost rapidity, yet the artillery fire accompanying the attack of the 24th had so devastated the region to be traversed that it was found necessary first to make the roads leading to the newly won positions passable. The transportation of the heavy artillery was not completed therefore until December 11th, so that the preparation for the new attack could not begin before that day.  The goal was the line Bezonvaux Forest from Courières Farmhouse over Chambrettes, Louvemont, Vacherauville.  Consequently the attack had to be made in the form of a wide diversion to the left.

Four divisions began the attack on December 15th, and, after several bloody encounters, succeeded, on the 18th, in attaining their goal.  With this second undeniable success the defenders of Verdun remained content for the time.  As the Germans also had no motive for continuing the attacks, the heavier combats here ceased for the winter.  The fighting activities were not resumed until March, 1917.

### BY GENERAL VON ZWEHL

*A memorandum delivered to the commanding general just before the French attack*

The value of Fort Douaumont, leaving aside the great political importance of its possession by us, lies in the possibility of our artillery dominating the terrain in front of it, thanks to the excellent observation posts in its armored turrets.  We can only prevent a surprise of our first line by its means.  Moreover, to a certain extent, the fort gives our reserves good shelter two kilometers from our first line.

According to information from agents a French attack on the Verdun front is to be expected.  Our battle position must be held at all costs.  Infantry and machine guns must be ready to repulse French attacks at any moment.  The greatest number of grenades must be carried to the front line, the reserves and machine gun reserves at Thiaumont-Hang and Ablain-Schlucht and Minzenschlucht must be prepared to go to the front line at any moment.

### BY GENERAL ERICH VON LUDENDORFF

*Announcement from German Headquarters immediately after the attack*

The projected withdrawal of the first line in the Douaumont-Vaux sector of the front to prepared positions was accomplished on Wednesday night.  Although the French, favored by foggy weather, were able on October 24th to advance just at the time when this withdrawal was in progress, and thus obtained a local success, the methodical retreat of the troops from Vaux Fort was carried out on the night of November 1st without the attention of the enemy being aroused. Moreover, at dawn on November 2nd, the deceived French opened fire on Vaux Fort and maintained it into the daylight. French assaulting columns made an attack into space and discovered the fort had been abandoned.

The forts of Douaumont and of Vaux played an important part in the battle of Verdun so long as they remained as French forts in the hands of the defenders. In order to weaken the Verdun position they had to be rendered inoffensive; deprived of their fighting means and largely destroyed, they possessed only a limited value for the assaulting party from a tactical point of view immediately the attack upon Verdun had been interrupted. Further, they gave the French artillery excellent objectives. In consequence of local gains by the French in the neighborhood of the former Fort of Douaumont the importance of Vaux Fort to the German troops had become less than nil and there was no reason to make great sacrifices for the maintenance of this advanced position. As also the ground near Vaux was not suited for defense toward the south, the fort was abandoned and the German battle line was carried back to a more favorable line which had long ago been prepared. It is less visible and less exposed to the enemy's artillery fire. It is well to add that the abandonment of Vaux Fort is devoid of any important effect upon the situation before Verdun.

### BY MARSHAL HINDENBURG

#### From his Memoirs after the War

Our rôle as supreme directors of these battles was simple. For lack of men we could not contemplate the idea of a relief attack either at Verdun or the Somme, however strong were my own inclinations for such a measure. Very soon after I took over my new post I found myself compelled by the general situation to ask His Majesty the Emperor to order the offensive at Verdun to be broken off. The battles there exhausted our forces like an open wound. Moreover, it was obvious that in any case the enterprise had become hopeless, and that for us to persevere with it would cost us greater losses than those we were able to inflict on the enemy. Our forward zone was at all points exposed to the flanking fire of superior hostile artillery. Our communications with the battle-line were extremely difficult. The battlefield was a regular hell and regarded as such by the troops.

When I look back now, I do not hesitate to say that on purely military grounds it would have been far better for us to have improved our situation at Verdun by the voluntary evacuation of the ground we had captured. In August, 1916, however, I considered I could not adopt that course. To a large extent the flower of our best fighting troops had been sacrificed in the enterprise. The public at home still anticipated a glorious issue to the offensive. It would be only too easy to produce the impression that all these sacrifices had been incurred in vain. Such an impression I was anxious to avoid in the existing state of public opinion, nervous enough as it already was.

We were disappointed in our hopes that with the breaking-off of our offensive at Verdun the enemy would more or less confine himself to purely trench warfare there. At the end of October the French opened a largely-conceived and boldly-executed counter-attack on the eastern bank of the Meuse, and overran our lines. We lost Douaumont, and had no longer the strength to recover that field of honor of German heroism.

For this attack the French commander had abandoned the former practice of an artillery preparation extending over days or even weeks. By increasing the rate of fire of the artillery and trench-mortars to the extreme limit of capacity of material and men, only a short period of preparation had preceded the attack, which had then been launched immediately against the physically exhausted and morally shaken defenders. We had already had experience of this enemy method of preparation for the attack in the course of the long attrition battles, but as the herald to a great infantry attack it was a novelty to us, and it was perhaps just this feature which doubtless produced so important a success.  Taking it all round, on this occasion the enemy hoisted us with our own petard.  We could only hope that in the coming year he would not repeat the experiment on a greater scale and with equal success.

### BY CROWN PRINCE FREDERICK WILLIAM

From his Memoirs, abridged

When the situation at Verdun became so acute that, in view of the futility of the sacrifices I felt unable to sanction the continuation of the attack, I reported personally to the Kaiser and made written representation to the G. H. command.  Thereupon the Kaiser adopted my view and granted the desired cessation of the attack.  After the resignation, on August 29th, of General von Falkenhayn, the head of the Commander-in-Chief's General Staff and of the Operation Department, the orders to cease attacking were issued by Field Marshal General von Hindenburg on September 2nd, 1916, together with instructions to convert into a permanent position the lines that had been reached.

The newspaper at home were cruelly unjust to me in this, representing me as responsible for all the bloodshed. They even called me "the laughing murderer of Verdun." Our soldiers at the front knew better.  A dozen incidents showed their affection for me, and their knowledge as to where the responsibility really lay.

### PERSONAL NARRATIVE OF A FRENCH STAFF OFFICER

From the slopes of Souville I have seen victory climb and crown Douaumont.  Our modern battles afford no spectacle; they are cruel and mysterious.  There are big empty spaces dotted with shell holes and cut with long furrows which mark the soil as the veins make marble patterns on the hands.  There are columns of smoke from bursting shells, a line of shadows that creeps close to the earth and disappears.  Those who are in the battle never know anything more of it than one episode.  But the victory of October 24th—I saw it before me like a living being.

Souville Hill is the only one of all the heights around Verdun which reaches the altitude of Douaumont.  Between these two rival heights rises Fleury Ridge.  Beyond, upon the crest, lies the Fort of Douaumont. I so often looked at this landscape of hill and ravine that I had it in my eyes when on the morning of October 24th I took my post at Souville, but my eyes looked for it in vain. A thick fog prevented my seeing anything except the nearest tortured slope and here and there a mutilated tree trunk.

The fog, however, was by no means inert. It seemed as though it was being stirred about and labored by the constant and invisible flight of shells. Their whistling was so continuous that instinctively I looked up as though I had expected them to form a vault of steel above my head. Our artillery was pounding the enemy's positions, and I recalled the terrible days of the end of February when the shells were rushing upon us. This time it was the opposite impression that I got, an impression of our definite superiority. The guns with their thousand voices gave a prodigious concert in the fog, and I tried to analyze its skillful orchestration, to identify the strident plaint of the "75's," and the big bass of our heavy howitzers. I asked myself if we would attack in spite of the obscurity? Would it not be disastrous and prevent the guns from accompanying our advancing troops with their fire? On the other hand, might not the fog increase the elements of surprise? Knowing the hour fixed for the attack, I looked at my watch, and while waiting I gradually grew more and more anxious with the fear of postponement of our trial and the adjournment of our hopes. I knew that the operation had been minutely arranged and that our troops had been marvelously trained, but I also knew the disproportion of the forces to be engaged and the daring of the undertaking. Three divisions entrusted with the duty of dislodging seven divisions from formidably organized positions! It was a daring undertaking, but one conceived in the proportions of a masterpiece, and one which was to be carried out so precisely that once it had been executed it seemed quite simple.

I had upon me the Order of the Day of General de Passaga, in which he stimulated his men by recalling the prowess of the neighboring division. I took it out of my pocket and I chewed it over and over again as a horse does his oats.

During the long wait it was to me a song accompanied by
the orchestra of guns.  On the positions which I knew so
well I reviewed the divisions ready for attack.  From Haudromont quarries on my left to Douaumont Fort in front
of me lay Guyot de Salins' division with its Zouaves, its
Tirailleurs, and the famous colonial regiments from Morocco which retook Fleury on August 17th.  To the right
lay the Chasseurs of Passaga's division, and still further
to the right, towards Vaux and Hardaumont, the fantassins of Lardemelle.  I imagined them for I could not see
more than fifty yards in front of myself.  I also imagined
and not without anxiety, the German order of battle, the
number of battalions in first and second line, the trenches,
the supplementary defenses, the redoubt, Thiaumont work,
Haudromont quarries, and at last, and above all, Douaumont
Fort.  How could our men get the better of such human and
material obstacles?

Every now and again I pulled out my watch.  Eleven
o'clock!  Eleven-twenty!  Eleven-forty!  The time fixed!
Had the attack, which I ought to have seen rise up and roll
down the ravine and then sweep over the opposing slope,
had it been launched?  Had the artillery lengthened its fire?
It was impossible to know.  At eleven-fifty on the right I
heard the tick-tick of machine guns.  If machine guns were
in action the attack must have been launched.  If machine
guns are firing our men have been seen and are meeting
with resistance.  Then I heard them no more.  The roar of
the guns drowned everything and again I go through uncertainty and anxiety.  At the command post where I went
from time to time news was at last coming through.  The
start was magnificent.  The first objective is reported to
have been reached already.  The men are organizing their
positions.  They are going to get on the move again.  They
are off.

An aëroplane-motor hums over my head.  The pilot is
flying so low that it looks as though he is going to touch me.
I see the enormous bulk of his machine loom gray through
fog.  He comes down still lower.  I was told later on that
the pilot had been able to shout out *"En avant"* to our men

and that a conversation had thus been exchanged between heaven and earth.

Towards two o'clock a strengthening wind begins to worry the clouds, following them, chasing them away, turning on those which take their place, and finally rending them and putting them to flight just as a storm drives clouds off a mountain pass. In the intervals of their flight first a slope, then a crest, appears. At last I begin to see. I recognize Fleury crest, the ravine of Chambitoux, the slopes of Douaumont, and then Douaumont itself. The clouds are now flying so fast that in a second their ranks are broken and the landscape stands out with the astonishing clearness which precedes or follows bad weather.

Through my artillery glasses I could count the shell holes. They are all full of water. What a time our men must have had if they went through there! The landscape is not dead. Over there on the slopes of Douaumont earth-colored men are moving about. To the left and to the right they are marching in Indian file. They are advancing, climbing, and gradually getting nearer their objective. At last there is one whose silhouette stands out upon the sky as clearly as if a shadow show. Others are going down a gorge. They are going to be seen. They will be mown down. Don't show yourselves like that. It is crazy. They are moving, and turn, describing a vast circle around conquered Douaumont as though they were dancing a "farandole" of victory. I want to shout. I must have shouted, but I did not hear the sound of my own voice in the noise of bursting shells, for the German riposte had not been long in coming and shells are bursting. I must have shouted, for my teeth shut upon some earth splashed up into my open mouth by a shell, which had just fallen close to me. Douaumont is ours. The formidable Douaumont, which dominates with its mass, its observation points, the two shores of the Meuse, is again French.

### BRITISH POPULAR NEWSPAPER REPORT

There are two ways of looking at the brilliant victory gained yesterday by the French at Douaumont. You may say that Verdun wanted more breathing-space, more elbow-room, before settling down for the winter, for there is no denying the fact that the Germans were uncomfortably close. In that case it has already secured a great part of its objective. As the result of one day's magnificent fighting it has reconquered a strip of territory which it took the enemy months to win.

They have made a wonderfully satisfactory start. They have proved that they have the power of conducting successful offensive operations on a large scale on two widely removed sectors of the line at one and the same time. That will give the enemy food for thought.

From what I saw at Verdun on the day preceding the advance, and on the day itself, it was perfectly evident that our Allies have at their command behind the lines in advance of the fortress an immense reserve store of guns. Over a breadth and depth of many miles the whole country was swarming with troops, and guns and ammunition and aëroplanes were everywhere. The fact that the battle was going on all day over a front of about five miles made no difference whatever to the streams of convoys moving to and fro along the roads leading to Verdun from the south. The men in billets in the various villages, the Annamite and Senegalese and French road-menders, the thousands of soldiers busied in a thousand and one different ways in the block of country behind the line where the regiments engaged in the attack were fighting, were all going on with their ordinary work for all the world as if nothing out of the common was on foot. There seemed to be quite as many troops marching away from the scene of action as towards it. There was no extra excitement, no fuss, no disorder, no hurrying up of reserves. Everything had been carefully and systematically prepared well in advance of the day. All that was necessary had been done. Some days before the attack, General Nivelle's army had been strongly reënforced. The rest depended on the thin blue line in the front trenches, the incomparable work of the gunners, and the daring of the airmen.

The actual artillery preparation began rather more than

a week ago.  Then came a succession of wet days, as the result of which the men whom I saw coming back from the trenches were plastered with mud from head to foot and had become a line of khaki instead of a line of blue.  The attack was consequently postponed till one or two bright days (cold enough, even before the arrival proper of winter) made it once more practicable.  On Monday, when I arrived at Verdun, the French guns and aëroplanes were particularly active.  The resumed preliminary bombardment was in full swing.  The air was clear, the sky was blue, a rather cold sun was shining brightly, and, though towards evening a thick mist rose from the Meuse and hindered accurate observation of the effects of the gunfire, the rest of the day was admirably suited to the French plans.  Those in the know were very chary of giving any but the vaguest hints of the nearness of the coming event.

But the Germans themselves must have been uncomfortably aware of what was in store for them.  About a third of the batteries with which they bombarded Verdun up to and beyond the beginning of the Somme offensive had been displaced, or at all events had for a considerable period of time been silent.  With the rest they replied to the incessant fire of the French guns with all the vigor at their command and sometimes with the nervousness born of apprehension.  On the evening before, for instance, owing to an entirely groundless alarm of an infantry attack, they suddenly opened a barrage fire with no fewer than 83 batteries, all firing at once.

All day long on Monday and till late in the evening, when I was obliged to come away, the fierce duel went on, the French shells falling on the ridges north and northeast of the town, the German round the French batteries on the nearer slopes of the ridges and in the valleys and ravines between them.  In Verdun itself only two or three at the most exploded while I was there.  The enemy had other things to think of than the additional mangling of those shattered ruins, and as for bombarding the citadel, they might as well try to shell the moon.

But outside the town on those northern heights, on and

behind which half a million German soldiers and what was left of the Crown Prince's military reputation have perished, the continual roar of the guns and the flashes and smoke clouds of the shells were—both in themselves and for what they might mean—a magnificent and cheering sound and spectacle.  And all the time overhead the aëroplanes, the splendid, dauntless, far-seeing eyes of the French Army were calmly carrying on their invaluable part of the common work, sometimes poised apparently without motion high in space, utterly disdainful of the black smudges of shrapnel bursting all round them as a German battery burst into a furious rapid bombardment, sometimes whirring noisily as they darted swiftly towards earth to deliver their messages.

On Tuesday, the day of the attack, the weather changed again, to the disadvantage of our Allies.  The sun was hidden by a thick blanket of clouds, the air was thick and heavy with moisture, and a river mist added to an occasional drizzle of rain, blotted out the outlines of all but the nearest hills.  All the conditions seemed to be as unfavorable as possible to an infantry attack, and it seems to me more than probable that that was the view taken by the enemy.

But this time there was to be no holding back.  The attack was carried out as it had been arranged.  After seven hours' severe fighting, the French once more gained the mastery of the fort which has cost so many hundreds of lives, and undid the whole of the work which the Germans have done since February 25th.

On the left of the five-mile front the attack began from what was the most advanced and most northerly point of the French line, at the Côte du Poivre and the quarries of Haudromont, about two miles east of the Meuse at Vacherauville.  Between this point and Thiaumont, a distance of a mile and a half, the first advance carried the French infantry about a mile to the road running west from Douaumont to Bras, up the ravines of Couleuvre and La Dame.  In the next section troops starting from Fleury moved almost directly north towards Douaumont, up and to the left of the Ravine Chambitoux and took the Bois de la Caillette, so that the way to Douaumont was now open on both sides, and further to the right the attack was pushed forward in a straight line between Douaumont and Bezonvaux till it nearly reached the Fort of Vaux midway between them.

As far as I can gather, the French generals themselves were astonished by the rapidity of the advance, and during the afternoon extended their objective to include the capture of Douaumont. Artillery and infantry fought together in perfect combination with magnificent courage and resolution. That, for one who has seen them lately, was a foregone conclusion. The French have recently been described as a tired army. Nothing could be further from the truth. Their *entrain* is as fine as it ever was and their experience immeasurably greater. Personally, I have seen no tired troops among them. Even the mud-caked *poilus,* fresh from a long night in the trenches, some of them nursing frostbitten feet, are full of go and determination, and when you see them after a few hours or days *en repos* behind the lines, with clean uniforms and faces, they look as if nothing could stop them.

On Tuesday nothing did. It was beautiful to watch the regularity of the advance. In all directions, from behind and in front and from both flanks, the batteries were pouring their hurricane of steel on those long, low hills in front. Gradually, as the afternoon wore on, the explosions of the French 75-shells and the double German barrage-fire behind and upon or in front of the attacking troops moved steadily farther and farther up the ravines and slopes. On the crests of the farther ridges, from Haudromont to Douaumont, and well past it to the right, huge pillars of black smoke kept shooting up from the ground, and two or three times a dense volume of white smoke, colored red by flame, shone out for some time against the sky as a giant incendiary shell set on fire some explosive or inflammable material. And all the time in the middle distance, between the French field batteries and the burst that outlined the position of Douaumont and the retreating Germans, shell after shell churned up the ground over which the infantry fight was advancing, and filled the air with yet other clouds of earth and stones and smoke.  Steadily, foot by foot and trench by trench, but with extraordinary rapidity, those splendid French infantry advanced, driving the enemy before them—for, remember, when the attack began the opposing trenches were, as always, close up to each other—and, taking 3,500 prisoners by the way, till at last, after a final severe struggle round Douaumont Fort, they shot all of its defenders who refused to surrender and won it back for France.

I asked General Dubois to give me in a few words his own idea of the strength of the place, and this is what he wrote:

### Statement of General Dubois

"The most striking thing at Verdun is the pitiable and lamentable failure of the German effort against all the military organizations of the town.  Their present certainty that they will soon be definitely compelled to retire (this was written the day before the advance on Douaumont) leads them from time to time, as has happened again within the last few days, to redouble the fury of their bombardment.  But it is trouble lost.  During eight months nothing has given way, nothing has been seriously injured in the vitals of the defenses.  The old *enceinte* of Vauban and the citadel itself are unharmed, in spite of the storm of 380 shells and projectiles of other calibers which have been showered upon them.  Quite the contrary—and it is hardly necessary to say so—the whole time which has passed since the beginning of the attack has been made wonderful use of in putting Verdun in a state of solidity of resistance of which the Germans have no idea.  This considerable reënforcement of the means of defense would have very much surprised them if their assault had succeeded.  Lastly, the bombardment itself—a detail which is not without its piquancy—has on more than one occasion facilitated the execution of important works.  A 380 shell is sometimes very valuable; it can do the work of 50 men for eight days.  That is the way in which the Germans, without suspecting it, have collaborated in the defense of the fortress.  It is also one of the reasons, and not one of the least original, why they will never take Verdun."

# SERBIA REBORN

## THE NEW SERBIAN ARMY CAPTURES MONASTIR IN SERBIA

NOVEMBER 19TH

### G. WARD PRICE

Serbia, as our previous volume told, was completely captured by the Teuton powers in 1915. Most of its army was destroyed and the remnant who escaped across the mountains were so ravaged by disease that they seemed specters rather than men. Italian ships saved them, Italian supplies nourished them, and they were placed upon the Greek island of Corfu to regain their strength.

Now, in the fall of 1916, they were once more healthy, and were most eager for revenge, especially upon their most brutal enemies, the Bulgarians. Hence they were sent to join the Ally forces at Salonika under the French general, Sarrail; and here they were given the opportunity to fight their way back into Serbia if they could, breaking a passage through the hated Bulgarians.

How they accomplished this is here told by a British observer on the spot. Their first goal was Monastir, the chief city of southern Serbia. This they recaptured on November 19th, and immediately thereafter they reconstructed there a Serbian Government.

Gradually, in the course of the next two years, these Serbs fought their way northward over the martyred Serbian ground until once more all Serbia was theirs. It was a long and bitter task. Yet from the moment Monastir was recaptured the new Serbia was reborn, the Serbia which seems now to have before it a fair and prosperous future.

### BY G. WARD PRICE

THE Franco-Serbian counter-offensive started on September 11th and met with very satisfactory success. The Serbs had in line the whole of their Third and First Armies under General Vassitch and Voivode Misitch respectively. Their Second Army remained where it had been since before the Ostrovo battle, further round on the right, facing the Bulgars among the steep, scrub-covered mountains of the Moglena. And in coöperation with the Serbs, at the northern end of Lake Ostrovo, was practically the whole French force in the Balkans, with a contingent of Russians. The

Serbs were also supported by French heavy artillery, having no guns of their own bigger than 120 mm.

I returned immediately after witnessing the attack on the Macukovo salient to the Serbian front. By this time, September 18th, the Franco-Serbian Army had pushed forward to within a few miles of Florina on the left wing, their new line running in a northeasterly direction from there back towards Kaimakchalan. The Serbs took back thirteen miles of lost ground in three days. The Gornichevo pass and the village of Banitza, on the main road to Monastir, had been regained, and as you drove along it you passed ample evidence that the Bulgarian retreat had been considerably hurried. Abandoned guns, to the number of nine, and thirty limbers, lay by the side of the road. The victorious Serbs had not yet had time to drag them away. All the rubbish that a hastily retreating army leaves behind was scattered right and left. Bullet-pierced caps and helmets, greatcoats, broken rifles, ammunition pouches, marked the trail of the retreating enemy, and from the top of the hill at Banitza, where the road drops steeply down to the plain, you could see the Serbian infantry spread out on the green turf, each in his little individual shelter-trench, while the enemy shrapnel burst above and among them; and beyond, right away in the distance, loomed faintly the white minarets and walls of Monastir, their goal on the threshold of Serbia, gleaming faintly through the haze, like the towers of an unreal fairy city. There was to be much fighting during the next two months in this green plain of Monastir, across which the enemy had already constructed two strong lines of defensive works before he started on his advance to Ostrovo.

And this is the moment to say how effective a contribution towards the success of the Serbian advance from Ostrovo was made by the English M.T. companies, which had been lent to the Serbian Army, the Serbs having no M.T. organization of their own. If I remember rightly, there were at this time three Ford companies of 100 lorries each and one 3-ton lorry company attached to the Serbians. Serbian generals have frequently avowed in their Army orders how impossible it would have been for them to press so closely as they did upon the heel of the Bulgars but for the self-regardless assistance of the officers and men of these M.T. companies. The drivers threw themselves into the work of punching those little Ford vans up appalling hills like the Gornichevo pass in a truly sporting spirit. It was up to them to see that the Serbians fighting on ahead were not let down for lack of ammunition and that as many of their wounded as possible should be brought back down to railhead at Ostrovo. They worked for forty-eight hours on end without stopping, over roads crowded with troops and guns, cheerfully giving up food and sleep during the push. Some of the gradients up which they took their loads were so steep that the petrol would not flow into the carburetor, and the only way the cars could get up these parts was by a sort of waltzing movement, the weary but determined driver twisting his van sideways across the road every few yards to get another gasp of petrol, and then making on up the slope a little further, until his engine was on the point of stopping, before repeating the maneuver. Perhaps the worst of the many bad runs which these Ford companies undertook was the one from the side of Lake Ostrovo up to the village of Batachin on the slopes of Mt. Kaimakchalan. I made one journey up it, and though it was once my fortune to chase an aëroplane across the Swiss Alps in a 100 h.p. racing car, climbing Kaimakchalan in a "flying bedstead" of a Ford was a sensation yet more vivid. As the car zigzagged up the hairpin ladder of the yellow road one was haunted by an incongruous memory of how

> "The blessed Damozel lean'd out
> From the gold bar of Heaven."

For, indeed, one might have been on some celestial balcony. Ostrovo Lake, with its ragged fringe of trees, and the sandy flats upon its shore, lay far below, almost sheer beneath one. And looking down upon the roofs of the next convoy of cars following, they seemed more like an orderly string of ants than of vehicles as big as one's own.

There is a belt of splendid beech forest halfway up Kaimakchalan, but beyond that the bare mountainside stretches nakedly on to its cap of almost perennial snow. Its surface is like Dartmoor drawn up at an angle to the sky, and right on the top, where the north slope drops sheer away to the Cerna valley, stand the white frontier stones that mark the boundary of Serbia. From here there is a magnificent outlook across a great confused stretch of rocky hills, which from this height appear no more important than the wrinkles on a plaster contour map.

It was on this vantage ground above the clouds, with the country they were fighting to win back laid out in full prospect before their eyes, that the Serbs fought their fiercest battles with the Bulgars. The Bulgars had such casualties that one battalion of their 46th Regiment mutinied. Little entrenching was possible on the stonebound mountainside. In clefts and gullies, behind outcrops of rock or under shelter of individual heaps of stones collected under cover of the dark, the soldiers of these two Balkan armies, not unakin in race, with languages closely related and histories that are a parallel story, faced and fought each other with savage and bitter hatred, under the fiercest weather conditions of cold and exposure. The wind there was sometimes so strong that the Serbs said they "almost feared that the trench-mortar projectiles would be blown back on to them."

There could be little artillery at that altitude to keep the battle lines apart. Mortar, bomb and bayonet were the weapons that worked the slaughter on Kaimakchalan, and so fiercely were they used that Serbs would reach the ambulances with broken-off pieces of knives and bayonets in their wounds. You came upon little piles of dead in every gully; behind each clump of rocks you found them, not half-buried in mud or partly covered by the ruins of a blown-in trench or shattered dugout, but lying like men asleep on the clean, hard stones. The fish-tail of an aërial torpedo, the effect of whose explosion had been magnified by flying clouds of stony shrapnel, usually furnished evidence of the nature of their death. Not only for days but for weeks after dead Bulgars lay there, preserved in the semblance of life by the cold mountain air, looking with calm, unseeing eyes across the battleground that had once been the scene of savage and concentrated passion and activity, and then lapsed back again into its native loneliness, where the eagle is the only thing that moves. Some still held in their stiff fingers the bandage they had been putting to a wound when death took them; here was a man with a half-eaten bread-crust in his hand. On others you could see no sign of hurt. They must have been killed by the shock alone of the explosion of that aërial torpedo whose black fragments lie among them— killed, too, at night probably as they waited for the dawn to start fighting once more. In other places you would find bodies of Serbs and Bulgars mixed together where they had met with the bayonet. Yet on none of the dead faces that you looked into did you see the trace of an expression of anger or fear. They slept dispassionately, calmly, as if finding in death the rest and release from suffering that war had so sternly denied them.

Meanwhile, in the broad corridor of flat green turf that leads northward from Florina to Monastir the Serbs and French fought unremittingly to drive the Bulgars further. Delay was caused to our advance by the fact that the Bulgars in their retreat blew up the railway viaduct across the gorge at Eksisu; and the need of pausing while the French wheeled round into line at Florina to conform with the right-angled change of direction necessary for the advance on Monastir allowed the enemy time to settle into his Kenali trenches which held us up for six weeks more. A preliminary Bulgar stand was made on a line that ran through Petorak, Vrbeni and Krusograd.

It was open fighting in the fullest sense of the word. From the crest of one of the rolling ridges of grass you could watch the movement of every individual infantry soldier from the time he got up at the foot of your hill, through all his two-mile advance in skirmishing order across the bare plain, until he reached the enemy wire, which was clear to see with glasses in front of the black copses of trees that surround the villages of Petorak and Vrbeni.

Once during that fighting, on September 19th, I saw a Bulgarian attempt at a cavalry charge. It was only an affair of two squadrons and it was swept away by machine guns, the body of the young captain who led it being found afterwards on the ground. But cavalry charges are rare now, and an open flat country like this plain of Monastir, where you could gallop till your horse dropped dead without meeting any obstacle more formidable than a drainage-ditch, was a rare setting for one. The Serbian infantry were scattered in the open, not in a continuous trench-line, but in those little *trous individuels,* like the beginnings of a grave, which each man digs for himself. The Bulgar guns were shelling them with shrapnel in a half-hearted way. It seemed a slack sort of battle-day. Then one noticed an indistinct little black blob moving about on the edge of Vrbeni wood four miles away. The glasses revealed it as horsemen, formed in two separate bodies. Could it be that they were going to charge? Evidently, for they began to move towards us, keeping their close formation for a little, then opening out on to a wider front. They trotted on a little distance in this way, with shells beginning to drop in their direction from batteries which had noticed the unusual phenomenon. The trot broke into a canter and then the two squadrons suddenly strung out into another formation, a long diagonal line, and lengthened into a gallop. It was a gallant sight, and when the Serbian machine guns began a rattling fire that eventually stopped the charge, one's sympathy seemed drawn somehow to the horsemen. For one thing a mounted man coming down is much more dramatic a sight than a foot-soldier falling. Horse and man, if it is the horse that is hit, go sprawling and rolling over, or if the man is shot and falls from the saddle, the horse either comes galloping on riderless or else rushes wildly away on his own; whereas when you watch an infantry advance you cannot tell which men are dropping because they are hit and which are only taking cover or lying down to get breath. Those Bulgar horsemen never got up to the Serbian infantry. As soon as they were within a thousand yards the leading files of the diagonal lines withered away before a hail of bullets from rifles and machine guns; they could never have seen the troops they had been sent to attack, and indeed the whole thing seemed a very futile and unpractical sort of enterprise to have undertaken at all. What was left of the two squadrons

frayed out into a line that became more and more ragged
till it just broke off, and the survivors, wheeling round, gal-
loped back for Vrbeni wood again.

The right use for cavalry in modern war was shown a
little later, when the Serbs forced the passage of the Cerna
River. That was part of this same battle for Monastir,
but occurred when we had got a little further forward and
the Serbs were pushing on to the right of the town so as
to threaten the enemy line of communications and force him
to abandon the place.

The continuous trench-line which the Bulgars had built
across the plain of Monastir ran in front of Kenali and then
mounted a conspicuous sandstone bluff forming the left
bank of the Sakulevo River, the line of which it followed
till it reached the Cerna at Brod. East of Brod the Cerna,
hitherto open on one bank to the flat plain of Monastir, enters a valley between rocky mountains as it begins to turn
north again. On the corner which the Starkovgrob heights
make on the southern bank of the river, like a high bastion
looking out over the Monastir plain to the west and across
into the welter of stony hills beyond the Cerna to the north,
the commander of the Serbian Morava division had fixed his
battle observation post. There you could stand among pin-
nacles of rock and watch every move of the fight across the
valley. Alongside you, concealed by the crags, French field-
guns pounded the stony heights that rose like an unbroken
wall beyond the river, where, dotted about among the huge
bowlders, you could see the Serbian infantry clambering upwards to the assault. To make their horizon-blue coats more
distinguishable against the slate-colored rock so that the
French gunners and their own should not drop shells among
them, every man had a square of white calico fastened to his
back and the leader of each section carried a little flag, so
that the steep slopes opposite were dotted with moving points
of white.

Brod, the village on the river bank, was burning and had
been abandoned by the enemy. Veliselo, the squalid little
hamlet above it, hiding in a pocket of the mountains, was
the Serbians' next objective. And suddenly, as we watched

the Serb infantry climb upward among the rocks with their
screen of friendly shells creeping on ahead of them, a number of little black figures sprang into sight on the hillside
above and went racing off among the rocks towards Veliselo.   It was the Bulgars in retreat.   And soon Veliselo
itself, whose thatched mud huts were plainly to be seen, began to show signs of panic-stricken activity.   A string of
Bulgarian carts started pouring out of the further end. With
your glasses you could see stragglers running into the village, dodging about among the houses and then out along the
track beyond, on the trail of the retreating column.   The
Bulgars were in full flight for their next prepared position
among the mountains behind.   To cut off as many as possible
before they got to the protection of the new line the commander of the Morava division ordered up the Serbian cavalry.   They appeared from behind us down in the plain below on our left—a long column trotting and cantering alternately in a dry stream-bed.   While they followed that
the Bulgar and German gunners on the rocky slopes beyond the Cerna could not see them, but soon they had to leave
it and strike for the river bank across the open.   It was a
splendid spectacle—a half-mile column of horsemen cantering over the grass.   Shells began to fall about them, now on
this side, now on that.   One or two men fell, hit by flying
fragments, but the rest swept on and crossed the Cerna with
a mighty splashing.   Brod, the village on the other side,
was already on fire and a bombardment of it was begun
by the enemy to hinder the Serbian cavalry from passing,
but they formed up under the cover of the river bank and
then squadrons began to set off on individual adventures after
the flying Bulgars.   One of them captured a whole enemy
battery, limbers, gun-teams and all.

While the Serbians were thus fighting with gradual success upon the right of the Monastir sector the French made
one or two frontal attacks upon the Kenali trenches in the
flat plain, and the Russians had some rough fighting among
the mountains that stretch westwards to Lake Prespa.   These
attacks, of which the chief was that of October 14th, were
not successful, for the Kenali lines were made with all the

skill and thoroughness of positions on the Western front, while we had nothing like the same weight or quantity of artillery at our disposal to smash them. So that when the Serbs carried Kaimakchalan and began to get on in the loop of the Cerna River on one flank of the Kenali lines, in such a way that if they won much more ground they would succeed in turning the defenses of Monastir, General Sarrail withdrew troops, both French and Russian, from his left wing to strengthen his right, and put these French reënforcements under the orders of Marshal Misitch, commanding the Serbian First Army, who proved worthy of his confidence. The tactics which led finally to the recapture of Monastir were, in fact, maneuvering and pressure along the whole of this sector, combined with a definite attempt to pierce the enemy front at one point, this effort being made by the Serbs, to whose persistence under most severe fighting conditions the credit for the winning back of their own city belongs.

As November drew on, the heavy autumn rains converted the trenches in the Kenali plain into a swamp of the utmost wretchedness. There had been no progress there, but meanwhile the Danube Division, among the snow on the heights in the Cerna loop, had taken, first Polog, then Iven, and finally got up halfway the steep side of Hill 1212, one of the main positions in this confused tangle of mountains, which, however—as is the heartbreaking way of the Balkans —is dominated in turn by the next height, Hill 1378.

On November 14th an offensive was ordered along the whole line from Kenali to the Cerna. Two brigades of French infantry attacked Bukri and what was now the Kenali salient at noon. Three bayonet assaults were met by such heavy machine-gun fire that they failed; but at 2.30 the attack was renewed and two Bulgar lines at Bukri were carried and held against two counter-attacks—all this in teeming rain, penetrating cold and the worst mud conceivable. The result was at last to force the Bulgars out of the Kenali line, which they had held for two months, and back on to the next prepared position on the Bistrica River, five miles behind, towards Monastir.

The Serbs made prisoners in this fighting no less than twenty-eight German officers and 1,100 other ranks—a big haul for the Balkans, where the Germans are used only as stiffening for especially threatened positions. These captives cursed the Bulgars freely, saying that they had bolted and let them down.

On November 17th the Serbs carried both Hill 1212 and Hill 1378 beyond. On that, two days later, without further pressure, the Bulgars suddenly left the Bistrica line and abandoned Monastir itself, falling back down the road to Prilep.

Like many things long and earnestly awaited, the evacuation of Monastir finally came as something of a surprise. It seemed when the winter rains and snow began as if we should hardly get there before the spring. Even the night before the city was actually evacuated, when I was riding back to Vrbeni from a visit to the Serbian sector of the front with some English Staff officers, and we saw an enemy column marching out of Opticar village on the Bistrica, while earlier in the afternoon we had also noticed a string of wagons crossing the Novak bridge to the other side of the Cerna, it only seemed as if the Bulgars were moving troops from their center to reënforce their hard-pressed left. I slept that night in a shell-riddled house in Vrbeni, which I had shared with some French officers who had moved on since the Kenali lines had fallen. It was a dingy, rickety place, its shattered windows carefully patched with sheets of German maps and a penciled screed on one of the doors to say that it was "reserved for three Staff officers of the map-making section of the Staff of General Mackensen's Army."

Next morning, wading out into the river of fluid mud which served as the main street of Vrbeni, I met a Serbian cavalry officer on horseback, clearly in a mood of some excitement, who waved his hand and shouted: *"De bonnes nouvelles! De bonnes nouvelles!* Monastir is taken; the town is in flames!"

It was not the first time that people had assured me with equal emotion of the capture of Monastir, but though one still felt doubtful, it was the least one could do to go and see. So the mud-caked Ford car was turned out with all speed, and I started along the well-known and terribly bad road that led towards Monastir—twelve or thirteen miles ahead.

As usual, the road was crowded with every sort of transport, from creaking, solid-wheeled, bullock-drawn ox-carts that the supply service of Charlemagne's army might have used, to three-ton motor lorries, skidding and splashing through the mud. On either side were spread camps and bivouacs and dumps and depots of every kind; heaps of carcasses of meat, mounds of petrol tins, piles of long black cylinders of gas for the observation balloon, timber, tin, wire, carefully scattered supplies of ammunition.

One thing caught the eye at once as the presage of a day that would live in history. The most perfect triple rainbow I ever saw hung over Monastir, spanning it in a brilliant arch of color. One foot rested on the mountains to the west, where the Italians had been fighting shoulder to shoulder with the Russian and French troops in the plain; the other was planted on the rocky heights beyond the Cerna, from where the Serbs, worn by much hard fighting, were looking down upon the city which their dogged determination had done most to win.

As one got nearer to what the night before had been the enemy's line on the Bistrica, the Monastir road became less and less thronged. And here the ability of the German road-engineers forced itself upon the attention by a remarkable contrast. Presumably there had been as much traffic along the road up to their front line as along that which led to ours, and the weather had certainly been the same for both. Yet while our part of the Monastir road had a surface like rock-cake covered with mud of the consistency of porridge, directly you passed into what had been until that morning the German lines, you found yourself on a hard, smooth surface as good as an English road at home.

The enemy retreat had been skillfully arranged. At three o'clock in the morning the sentries in the new French line opposite the Bulgar trenches on the Bistrica had seen a great fire start in Monastir. It was the barracks, which the enemy had set burning. Then, a little later, the French patrols reported that the enemy front trenches had been found empty in several places. The Bistrica line was accordingly occupied along its whole length, the Russians wading the stream breast-high, and the Allied force began to feel forward to get into touch again with the retiring enemy.

By seven o'clock the advanced patrols reported that the town seemed unoccupied. They were then at a distance of two miles from it, and as Prince Murat, a young French cavalry officer and descendant of Napoleon's general, at the head of some mounted scouts, approached the town he caught sight of the last German battery making off.

At first it scarcely seemed as if there were any civilian population in Monastir, but they were only hiding in their shuttered houses, and when the French marched in many of them came out and threw flowers or hung up French and Serbian flags, which they must have hidden somewhere all the twelve months the enemy was there. The British consulate flag—the Union Jack with an official "difference" in the center—had been tucked away in a mattress all that time.

I turned into what used to be the "Imperial and Royal Austro-Hungarian Consulate" in the main street of the town. In the hall, littered with broken packing-cases and other signs of hurried departure, were two placid-faced French Sisters of St. Vincent de Paul, with their white-winged headgear as stiff and spotless as if they were in a peaceful French country town instead of a newly captured Macedonian city. They had come there to try and reclaim their piano, which some German officers had commandeered and carried off to their quarters at the consulate.

The nuns said they had organized a hospital at their convent, which had been under the supervision of German medical officers; seventeen dying Germans had been left behind in their charge when the army retreated the night before. "The Germans were correct but brusque," said one of the Sisters. "The Bulgars were——" And she made an expressive little grimace.

# RUMANIA RALLIES IN HER MOUNTAINS

## THE CAPTURE OF BUCHAREST

### DECEMBER 6TH

CONSTANTINE ANGELSCU        COLONEL SHUMSKY
QUEEN MARIE OF RUMANIA

Though known to her people as Marie, the Rumanian queen was christened Mary. She is a British princess who married the German-Rumanian Prince Ferdinand and succeeded with him to the throne. She has, however, completely identified herself with her people and is as beloved by them as was their former queen, the authoress known to the world as Carmen Sylva. Queen Marie tells here of her own tragic experiences in the defeat and rally of her countrymen. The official Rumanian outlook as to the extent of the disaster is furnished by Dr. Angelscu, the Rumanian Minister to the United States. Russia's estimate of the situation is given by Colonel Shumsky, the most noted of Russian military critics. Naturally he makes the most of what his own country finally accomplished in Rumania's aid.

Bucharest, the Rumanian capital, was occupied by the Teuton forces under Marshal Mackensen on December 6th. The Government and the army had, however, escaped by flight. The northeastern section of Rumania is very mountainous, and there the still resisting soldiers found a refuge. Russia, at their back, furnished them supplies; and they were thus enabled to hold about a quarter of their country, the poorest and most rugged quarter, free of the invaders. Their battle line became a portion of the long Russian line which formed the eastern front.

### BY CONSTANTINE ANGELSCU

Rumanian Minister to the United States. His Official Statement Issued at Washington in October, 1917

THE first phase of our entry into the great struggle was fraught with immense sacrifices and sufferings. Our front, more than 1,200 kilometers (750 miles) in extent, had to be defended by us single-handed, for the help we had been led to expect did not arrive. But the courage of our soldiers did not fail.

Unhappily, we sustained losses amounting to over 50,000 killed and 150,000 wounded. And that was not the full extent of our calamities. There was our retreat in Mol-

davia, the heartrending exodus of the inhabitants of the
occupied territories, rich and poor, old men, women and
children, abandoning their homes before the advance of the
hated enemy; and our enforced destruction of the oil wells
in Rumania, representing hundreds and hundreds of millions of francs in value, as well as of our stores of cereals
and our factories, to prevent their falling into the hands of
the invaders. To these indescribable misfortunes were added
other sufferings which culminated in an epidemic of ex-
anthematic typhus, which claimed an immense number of
victims.

In spite of all this, however, my country did not lose
faith, but remained profoundly attached to the common
cause. Our sorely tried army awaited with passionate ardor
the moment when it could turn the tables on the enemy, and
when that moment came in 1917 it did so in most magnificent fashion. In the battles of Marashesti men were seen
to throw away their steel helmets and their coats, and, thus
freed, fall on the enemy with tremendous fury. Many are
the heroic deeds that have been related of them.

When, in consequence of the condition of internal affairs
in Russia, the order came from Petrograd to stop the Rumanian offensive, our officers and men wept from disappointment. Later Mackensen assumed the offensive. His
object was to conquer Moldavia also on the occasion of the
first anniversary of the entry of Rumania into the war,
and, once in the possession of the whole of Rumanian territory, the Germans had the intention of proclaiming a new
régime. They reckoned without the valor of the Rumanian
soldier. As a matter of fact, Rumania saved the eastern
front. The offensive of Mackensen was definitely broken,
and the Rumanian Army, with our chivalrous King at its
head, was absolutely confident that it was no longer possible to break through the Rumanian front.

### BY COLONEL KONSTANTIN SHUMSKY

The German armies advanced upon Bucharest in three
groups. The northern was under General von Falkenhayn,
the former Chief of Staff; the western, under General von

Delmensingen; the southern, under Field Marshal von Mackensen. Falkenhayn's army was the last to advance. Before it started Delmensingen's column was at a point twenty-six miles west of Bucharest and Mackensen's army was eight miles south of the city.

The advance of Falkenhayn to support the other two marked the decisive moment in Germany's Rumanian campaign. Falkenhayn after much severe fighting reached the railroad at Titu, twenty-six miles north of Bucharest. The three enemy groups then formed a half circle around Bucharest, which was held by the Rumanian armies. The Rumanians slowly withdrew, some toward the northeast and some to the east, in the direction of the Moldavia-Bessarabia frontier. Bucharest was gradually evacuated.

Falkenhayn's army, which was moving from north to south toward Bucharest, sent forces hurriedly eastward, in an endeavor to seize Ploesci, an important railroad junction, valuable for the retreating Rumanians. The next important railroad junction is Buzeu, by occupying which the enemy might cut the Rumanian line of retreat from Bucharest to the Moldavian region. This might compel the withdrawal of the Rumanians to Galatz, that is, to the Moldavian-Bessarabian frontier, and thus cut the Rumanian army in two parts—the Moldavian part and the southern part somewhere east of Bucharest.

This menacing possibility made the German move against Ploesci of vital importance, perhaps more important than his move on Bucharest. The Rumanians, therefore, vigorously guarded the road to Ploesci-Buzeu, and held Falkenhayn's army back from Ploesci until Bucharest had been completely evacuated.

On December 6th at noon the Rumanian rearguard, covering the departure of the main forces, evacuated the last of the eastern forts of the Bucharest circle, Ploesci was evacuated at the same time. In this way the Ploesci-Buzeu line was occupied by the enemy, and the Rumanians began to fall back from it to the east, in the direction of Buzeu and Galatz.

The Germans followed up the retreating Rumanians

with great energy and determination.  They felt that from
a military viewpoint, the capture of Bucharest had fallen far
short of complete success, since the main objective, the Rumanian Army, itself had successfully withdrawn.  Hence
Falkenhayn once more sent a considerable force along the
Ploesci-Buzeu highway, in the attempt to deliver a blow
against the center of the Rumanian battle line.

The Rumanians vigorously resisted this attempt to break
their center between Ploesci and Buzeu; and the Rumanian
rearguard continued to defend their position by vigorous
counter-attacks.  As a result the Rumanians, during the
first half of December, held a new line to the east of
Bucharest.  It extended from the Danube opposite Silistria
to the frontiers of Moldavia and Transylvania.  Consequently, the Rumanian front ran nearly north and south,
from Bukowina to Silistria.

Falkenhayn did not succeed in capturing much spoils.
Neither did he succeed in trapping the Rumanian Army, or
even any considerable number of Rumanian soldiers.  According to the German bulletin of December 4th, the captives did not exceed 10,000, with twenty-six guns.  This
must be considered a quite inconsiderable booty, in comparison to the half million men engaged on either side.  It is
true that Bucharest was evacuated, but the Rumanian
armies left Bucharest in perfect order.  Hence, while the
Teutons gained possession of Bucharest and Ploesci, they
did not succeed in delivering a serious blow at the Rumanian
Army.  Instead, the Rumanians made a vigorous resistance
on the new battle line east of Bucharest.

Falkenhayn's main success was the shortening of a front
725 miles long to 270 miles, a great strategic success; but
the effort to keep the Rumanian Army out of Moldavia
failed.

Neither the strategical position of the armies nor the
character of Bucharest as a fortified place permitted a determined defense; it would have been a mere repetition of
the disastrous sieges of Liege, Namur and Antwerp, hammered to nothing by Germany's heavy artillery.  It would
have been still more unwise to shut the Rumanian Army up

in the fortress. The Rumanians came to a wise decision, saved their army and effected a junction with the Russian battle line, forming its left flank, on the section between Bukowina and Silistria.

Notwithstanding the cold and the mud, the warlike efforts continued. Falkenhayn extended his wide movement to the east of Bucharest, from Ploesci to Buzeu. From this, it is possible to judge of Falkenhayn's real intention. After seizing Bucharest, he transferred the center of his advance to the north, planning to carry out a larger purpose. He hoped to capture Buzeu before the Rumanians had passed safely beyond it. Thus he would cut them off from the Russians. This plan failed, because of the coöperation of Russian forces, especially the Russian cavalry.

As was announced in our Russian bulletins, large forces of Russian cavalry advanced before Buzeu, and succeeded in checking Falkenhayn's attack. The cavalry fought both mounted and dismounted. Digging trenches, and turning machine guns on the enemy, they compelled him to change from a marching column to fighting order, and to attack in regular form. The cavalry waited until the enemy was fully prepared, then mounted and hastily withdrew to the next position in the rear. There the same tactics were repeated. Whenever possible, mounted attacks were made by separate detachments of cavalry, further delaying the advance of the enemy.

This sort of cavalry work involves self-sacrifice, vigor and great speed. It was admirably accomplished by our Russian horse before Buzeu, and gained for the Rumanians time to withdraw in good order from Buzeu and further south, from Bucharest to Galatz.

Thus, by means of a series of obstinate conflicts, a new battle line was occupied sixty-six miles to the east of Bucharest, in a straight line running from Moldavia to the Danube. This front had a continuation in the Dobrudja, where similar attacks were made by the enemy with considerable forces.

Falkenhayn's main objective was gained; yet he continued his forward movement. His purpose now was less strategic than political. He planned to give such an impression of "uninterrupted victories" as would strengthen the hand of German diplomats in the game they were preparing to play, the making of peace proposals on the basis of another great German victory.

### BY QUEEN MARIE OF RUMANIA

Distances are so great and communication so difficult, that very few details of our troubles and trials reach other countries. We are completely isolated from all our Allies, except Russia, and have had to stand unheard-of hardships because relief could only be offered us from one side, and that side needed all its resources for itself.

The winter that lies behind us is as one of the most fearful nightmares man ever dreamed. There is no suffering that my people have not been called upon to endure, no fear, no sorrow, no pain—every misery, both moral and physical, had to be borne at once.

And I, their Queen, suffered with them, struggled with them, wept with them, shared and understood their every grief.

I too had to leave a home I loved, I too had to flee before the invading foe, had to forsake the new-made grave of the little one who was torn from me whilst the enemy was flooding my land on every side.

All have I known of mortal anguish, of days when hope became less and less, till the last shred had to be surrendered —my child and my country both at once.

The remembrance I keep of those days is of a suffering so great that it almost blinded me; I was as one wandering in fearful darkness wondering how much anguish one single heart can bear; black waves seemed to be rushing in upon me threatening to drown me, yet I was quite calm and continued living and working as though my heart had not been torn from my breast.

Strong ties of sympathy had always bound me to my people, but since the extraordinary misfortunes we have undergone together, our mutual affection has turned into deep and comprehensive love.

The grief that God sent me whilst so many were mourning rendered me strangely dear to their hearts; I had suddenly come quite close to them—they felt in me a comprehension of their own woes that had not been mine before.

An immense tide of sympathy flowed from their souls to mine, giving me strength to bear bravely every sacrifice, and not to give way to selfish despair. Tragedy had come upon us, recrimination would but weaken us, complaint lessen our courage—nothing was left to us but dumbly to bear our Fate.

Winter came and with it retreat; hunger came and sickness and death in every form.

One town after another had to be surrendered, ever smaller became our country, a cruel exodus encumbered the remaining provinces; our riches, our pride, our hopes had been torn from us, and like a troop of emigrants we had to try and find place for our weary bodies and for our sorrowful hearts.

Each thing we thought we could count upon crumbled before the inflow of an enemy ten times too strong for us, who knew all about war whilst we were ignorant and had everything to learn. Nowhere were we safe; all the help that had been promised us was not forthcoming, we had nowhere to turn to in our agony, and the deadliest of winters was closing in upon us before we knew if we could remain there where we had pitched our tents!

Amidst this constant fear of further invasion we had to gather our courage and our wits so as to improvise hospitals, house refugees, feed and clothe our retreating troops, all this with the feeling that next day perhaps our efforts would be in vain, that the work so painfully accomplished would fall into the enemy's hand!

All our stores, our hoarded treasures, our food, corn and oil had been torn from us by the rapid advance of the foe; all that remained to us of our once blooming country were but a few provinces, the poorest, those upon which in the days of abundance we had counted least.

That was but the material side of our distress, and to that must be added every anguish, every grief of departure and separation, the leaving of loved homes, the haunting pictures of devastation, fire and ruin, of abandoned graves and of dying heroes who could not be saved.

With a fresh wound in my own heart I stood amidst the turmoil. I myself empty-handed—I myself a refugee! What had been mine lay behind the line of fire—also the lonely little grave lay there, belonged now to the enemy, and with it all the torturing remembrance of my child's illness and death. He was my youngest, my baby, and just the most helpless had I to forsake!

But there was no time to cry over a personal grief, in the hour of disaster so much depends upon the leaders not losing their heads.

To piece together that which is broken is no easy task; if your house falls down around you, at first your only wish is to sit on its ruins and weep. It is then that those whose love and courage are greatest must come forward and help. Those too grievously smitten cannot immediately lift up their heads, and very gentle must be the hand that endeavors to lead them back from darkness to light.

For a while I thought that the effort would be beyond my strength, such was the hopeless discouragement that had taken possession of every heart. No good news came to gladden our spirits, only tidings of defeat, disaster and distress, and winter lay over everything like a pall of despair.

Then little by little hands were stretched out to help. French and English doctors offered their assistance and with them many nurses and sisters whose devotion has no name.

Little by little we began building up what had fallen; at first only those whom adversity cannot crush showed the way, then others joined in—till imperceptibly a great new effort was born, and with that effort, new courage and new hope.

It were too long to relate all the weary work of this past winter, a whole volume of want and suffering, of devotion and charity would not suffice. So many single incidents rise before me, so many faces, so many efforts, and alas! so many death-beds that I hesitate which to describe.

There is too much to tell, too many pictures haunt me,

pictures of what was, what is, and of what we hope one day will be.

I look back and see visions of my country as for twenty-three years I have known it, peaceful, blooming, full of abundance, its vast plain an ocean of waving corn amongst which diligent peasants move to and fro gathering in the harvest, the land's dearest pride. I see its humble villages hidden amongst fruit trees, I see the autumn splendor of its forests, I see the grand solitude of its mountain summits, I see its noble convents, corners of hidden beauty, treasures of ancient art, I hear the sound of the shepherd's horn, the sweet complaint of his ditties. I see long roads with clouds of dust rising from them, many carts in a file, I see gayly clad peasants flocking to market. I see naked plains and long stretches of sand by the sea.

I also see our broad, proud Danube rolling its many waters past quaint little villages and boroughs inhabited by motley crowds of different nationalities, past towns of which the rising industries are a promise of future wealth. I see our port of Constanza with its bustle, its noise and its hopes.

Then on August 27, 1916, the call to arms—War!

I see the ardent faces of my young soldiers going off gayly to battle—I see the trains leaving, the flowers that decorate the cannons, horses and men—I hear the tramping of passing regiments, shouts of enthusiasm, words of exultation.

I see the first wounded in the hospitals of Bucharest, white beds, many faces all turned towards me, eager hands helping; I inspect everything, go everywhere. I have my own hospital in our palace, I too am full of hope.

For a while, a very short while, the news received from our armies is good, awakes wild enthusiasm, awakes dreams of glory in many a breast. Then the first ill tidings, a shadow on the expectant faces—a shadow over the town in spite of the blue sky above!

After that there are still days of hope and confidence, days when the first illusions seem to take form once more, but through it all I have the strange presentiment that my country will have to drink to the dregs the bitterest of cups.

Airships and Zeppelins become a haunting dread by night and by day; our country being narrow, the ground is good for such cruel sport. Death is poured down from the skies into the streets, women and children are slaughtered without number, and as though in defiance of the laws of God, the days they choose for their death-raids are the days when heaven is bluest and the sun shines most brightly.

Having been designed by the enemy as principal culprit, it is the house out of town where I live with my children that they single out for special punishment, and on a glorious autumn morning they throw seventy-two bombs upon dwelling and garden where it is known that my little ones are usually to be found. But on that day God did not wish another crime to be added to their lists!

Ever darker are the clouds gathering around our heads, with anxiety we look for the help that was promised us; Sarrail's advance in the south? The Russians' offensive in Galicia? Russian reënforcements in the Dobrudja? But we wait in vain; no good tidings from any side, and the Germans have not yet straft enough!

Surely this proud little country that had defied her must learn its lesson and be laid low in the dust. And as in the time of the great flood, our small, struggling country is threatened from all sides at once. Our frontiers are endless, without reënforcements our own resources are too small, we begin to realize the inevitable results if help does not come soon enough.

But my cup is not yet full—amidst all the turmoil and growing anxiety my youngest child sickens and all our efforts cannot save his life. During three mortal weeks we struggle to keep him, but Death rules supreme over the world. It is not to be. On All Souls' Day, my last born, my little Mircea, passes away—and the voice of the cannon sounds closer every day.

After that, for a while all becomes dark. I grope about as one who has lost her way. Only one thing remains to me, the intense desire to alleviate suffering around me, to go there where despair is greatest, to drown my own grief in the grief of others, to move in places where my own tears can be shed without shame.

So I begin wandering about in all parts of the country that have remained to us. On all sides I hear the dreaded voice of the cannon calling out its message of death and destruction.

I penetrate as far as they will allow me to go, I hunt up those freshly brought in from battle; as in a ghastly dream, I move from bed to bed.

Every form of suffering do I see; the last look of nameless dying do I carry away in my heart, and all the while I have the absolute certainty that my country is becoming smaller and smaller—I am in a hurry, I want to go everywhere—everywhere before it is too late. But in a sort of frenzy of grief I know that all my love, all my devotion cannot hold back the advancing feet of Fate.

Then comes flight! The cruel hour of parting from our capital, of parting from our home, our hospitals, from the little grave so freshly dug—flight!

For weeks we live in the train, not sure how far we must go to be safe; but one only thought moves me: put the living out of danger, then return once more, only once more to the grave of the dead!

But it is not to be—even that consolation is denied me —Bucharest falls, I can no more return to my dead.

My people know that I am absolutely unafraid of contagion, therefore more than ever was I claimed amongst them during this cruel epidemic. I penetrated into the most infected corners, giving everywhere, trying to carry a little hope and help into the most forsaken holes of misery.

I think that few queens have had the privilege to get so near their people. I have really gone amongst them, there where very few go. I have both health and good-will and an inexhaustible desire to console them, to sustain them and to awake hope in their hearts.

Certainly there were days when everything seemed impossible, when the material difficulties were such that the most energetic spirit quailed before the morrow. At those hours it was to me as though I must stand a while quite still, squaring my shoulders, concentrating all my strength so as to lift a weight almost beyond what a single man can carry. Thus we struggled on from day to day, from hour to hour. "Faith removeth mountains"—I had Faith!

How often here in Jassy—when going from hospital to hospital, trying to overcome always new difficulties, trying to supply ever new wants, did my thoughts turn to my own hospital in Bucharest, in the large roomy halls of the palace where I had everything I could want—I remember the white beds, the good food, the many helpful hands, eager ladies, books in plenty, music, flowers—a lost paradise indeed!

Here I had no house of my own to turn into a hospital. It was more useful to divide my material and energies, sustaining those already existing. It is a harder way of doing good, less personal, less satisfactory, needs greater abnegation, brings less comfort to one's soul, but in this case I knew it was best.

My ear had to be open for each cry of distress, my hand always ready to succor or to give, all my energies strained so as to encourage the efforts others were making. I had to go everywhere, see everything myself.

I was almost a stranger to the town of Jassy, thus I gained their confidence, by the way I worked with them. I by degrees stole into their hearts.

Those who have never seen them have no notion of what Rumanian roads can become in winter, of how difficult is all circulation, how communication becomes an effort almost beyond human strength—and this winter was a winter of terrible snow and frost.

Part of our army had to be quartered in small, miserable villages, cut off from everything, buried in snow, transports were almost impossible, untold of hardships had to be borne. All my energy and good-will could not take me to places where neither motor, sledge, nor carriage could go—I knew that there was want and sickness in those villages, but it was only towards springtime that I could reach them with infinite difficulty, often having to quit my motor and doing the rest of the road on foot.

That was the hardest work of all, that going about in those fever-stricken hamlets, where the patient troops were herded together in wretched mud-huts alongside of the few remaining peasants.

Food was scarce, hardly any wood for heating, soap was a thing almost not to be found, linen was a luxury of better days—illness in every form broke out amongst the soldiers and many died before we could give sufficient aid!

Ah! Indeed, I have seen death and misery very near—I have moved about amongst them, have felt the despair of my helplessness, have tried with insufficient means to do wonders, but alas! against sickness, cold and hunger good-will alone did not suffice—not to be numbered were the graves that overfilled the cemeteries; like a wood, the rough crosses grew up side by side.

And yet how much more ghastly is the fate of those in the invaded part of the country, where no help can penetrate.

Here I can at least get to my people—visit them or send them food, aid, comforts—but there in the dear regions we have lost, what may their sufferings be? Who succors them? Who consoles them? Who helps them to hope?

The enemy must have taken everything from them, forcing them to work against their own brothers, and probably he scoffs at their misery, trying to make them doubt the love of those who had to leave them to so cruel a fate!

That thought is the hardest of all! And to be so helpless—to have no news, no details, to be entirely cut off!

I feel it is a rambling tale, the tale I have told—it is as though I had written in a trance—maybe I have often repeated myself, yet I have only said half of what I had to say. One day perhaps when this period of suffering will be a little more distant I will more clearly be able to write the history of these days of distress.

# THE GERMAN TREATMENT OF PRISONERS

VIERORDE                          MAJOR C. VANDELEUR
              RUSSIAN GOVERNMENT REPORT
ROBERT YOUNGER                    DANIEL McCARTHY

That the Germans did to a wide and even terrible extent mistreat
their prisoners of war there is unhappily no question whatsoever.
Rumors of this began to spread through the Allied countries in 1915;
but not until late in 1916 were the black facts clearly established by
official investigation and convincing proof. Then the protest was
world-wide and under the influence of neutrals, and especially of the
United States, the worst abuses were done away with.

Daniel J. McCarthy, official investigator for the United States,
made a detailed report and afterward published a book describing
what he had seen. His summary of conditions is given here; and
as he certainly was not trying to exaggerate, his report may be considered as presenting the best possible side for Germany. The full
extent of excuse to which he goes is that the crimes were not national,
that the better class of Germans supposed the prisoners were being
well-treated, and that the guilt thus falls chiefly on only a few military
commanders. Of course this is only another way of saying that militarism had poisoned Germany to the very soul.

On the other hand, in reading such statements as that of the Russian Government, here presented, the reader would do well to bear
in mind that the Government wanted to excite its people against their
foes and therefore resorted to the primitive but effective method of
painting these foes at their worst. That is to say, the very worst
examples of mistreatment seem to have been picked out and emphasized.

The general truth is thus rather to be gained from such documents as the personal experiences of Major Vandeleur, here narrated
under oath, or the report of Mr. Younger, who conducted a British
Parliamentary inquiry and here presents in carefully restrained fashion
the conclusions drawn from a mass of testimony as to conditions in
the worst and most deadly of all the prison camps, the "typhus-
camp" at Wittenberg.

In brief, the indictment against the Germans in this matter seems
to come under three heads. First, the Government had long taught
its people to despise other races; now it encouraged them to hate
the others and especially the English. The result was a coarse mistreatment of prisoners by the German public, which seems to other
races the most disgraceful and disgusting feature of the whole. This
mistreatment rarely resulted in loss of life, and was a shame far
more to those who enacted than to those who suffered it. The first
evidences of this coarse spirit may be seen in the picture of the

treatment of Belgian prisoners in our earlier volumes, in the commands of General von Bissing, and in Lissauer's "Hymn of Hate." The spirit was kept alive by the German press and even by the German "intellectuals" through the appeal of such poems as that of Vierorde, here reprinted.

The second indictment is against the German soldiers, trained in brutality as we have seen, and especially against the German officers. These deliberately ruled their prisoners by a brutal terrorism in which beating and starvation were the mildest punishments, and a deathblow even at the hand of a savage or stupid sentry was sure to be condoned. Moreover, German commissariat officers deliberately trafficked in the starvation of their prisoners. The food officially assigned them was often shown them, weighed as though for cooking, and then sold to German civilians, who eagerly bought it at high prices. A meaner form of thievery can scarcely be imagined.

The third indictment is the most serious of all; for it is not against the coarseness of a people or the brutality and thievery of a soldiery, but against the intellectual and political leaders, the so-called "upper classes," the "nobility" of Germany. From these leaders there came repeated orders that prisoners should be treated harshly, and even that prisoners were undesirable nuisances and had better die. Hence came the abominable overcrowding in transit, the abominable sanitary arrangements, the deliberate abandoning of a prison camp to disease. That there was also misery suffered by Germans in Ally prison camps, none would deny. During the War, Germans talked much of the "horrors" of British prisons, but afterward abandoned all serious charges of this sort. Since the War, they have specially directed attention to certain French camps where the rule seems to have been harsh if not savage. But the worst individual cases evidenced by German testimony never for a moment approach the fully established and customary German methods pictured here.                C. F. H.

## BY VIERORDE

### Germany, Hate!

O my Germany, into thy soul thou must etch a deep and indelible hate;
  This hate thou hast lacked for a long, long time.
Retribution, vengeance, fury are demanded;
  Stifle in thy heart all human feeling and hasten to the fight.

O Germany, hate!
Slaughter thy foes by the millions
And of their reeking corpses build a monument.
  Let it reach the clouds.

O Germany, hate now!
  Arm thyself in steel and pierce with thy bayonet the heart of every foe;

No prisoners! Lock all their lips in silence;
  Turn our neighbors' lands into deserts.

O Germany, hate!
  Salvation will come of thy wrath.
Beat in their skulls with rifle-butts and with axes.
  These bandits are beasts of the chase, they are not men.
    Let your clenched fist enforce the judgment of God.

BY MAJOR C. B. VANDELEUR
Sworn Testimony of a Captured British Major Who Escaped in 1915

The narrative begins at the French city in the invested district to which he was first sent, on October 13, 1914.

"At Douay I was detained on the square in front of the Hôtel de Ville with a sentry over me, and was subjected to continual abuse and revilement. On the arrival of the other prisoners we were all confined in a large shed for the night. No food, except a little provided by the French Red Cross Society, was given, also no straw, and we spent a terrible night there, men being obliged to walk about all night to keep warm, as their great-coats had been taken from them.

"On October 17th, in the morning, the French Red Cross people gave us what they could in food, and did their very best, in spite of the opposition from the Germans. At about 2 p. m. on the same day we were all marched off to the railway station, being reviled at and cursed all the way by German officers as well as by German soldiers. One of our officers was spat on by a German officer.

"At the station we were driven into closed-in wagons, from which horses had just been removed, 52 men being crowded into the one in which the other four officers and myself were. So tight were we packed that there was only room for some of us to sit down on the floor. This floor was covered fully 3 inches deep in fresh manure, and the stench was almost asphyxiating. We were thus boxed up for thirty hours, with no food, and no opportunity of attending to purposes of Nature. All along the line we were cursed by officers and soldiers alike at the various stations, and at Mons Bergen I was pulled out in front of the wagon by the order of the officer in charge of the station, and, after cursing me in filthy language for some ten minutes, he ordered one of his soldiers to kick me back into the wagon, which he did, sending me sprawling into the filthy mess at the bottom of the wagon. I should like to mention here that I am thoroughly conversant with German, and understand everything that was said. Only at one station on the road was any attempt made on the part of German officers to interfere and stop their men from cursing us. This officer appeared to be sorry for the sad plight in which we were. I should like also to mention that two of the German Guard also appeared to be sympathetic and sorry for us; but they were able to do little or nothing to protect us.

"Up to this time I had managed to retain my overcoat, but it was now forcibly taken from me by an officer at a few stations further on.[1]

"On reaching the German-Belgian frontier the French prisoners were given some potato soup. The people in charge of it told us that none was for us, but that if any was left over after the French had been fed we should get what remained. This is in accordance with the general treatment of British prisoners by the Germans, who always endeavor to attend to our necessities last, and to put us to as much inconvenience and ill-treatment as possible. We subsequently got a little soup and a few slices of bread amongst 25 British prisoners in the same wagon with me.

"On October 18th, early, we arrived at Cologne, and the four officers and myself were removed from the wagon and, after some delay, sent on to Crefeld.

"I said that 52 prisoners were in the wagon with me when we left Douay. These were: [here follow the names of five officers, 15 English soldiers and 32 French civilians of all grades of society.] It is difficult to indicate or give a proper idea of the indescribably wretched condition in which we were in, after being starved and confined in the man-

[1] It is scarcely necessary to emphasize that this taking of a prisoner's clothes is as unusual as it was wholly unnecessary. The Germans at this time had more clothes and spoils of every sort than they could possibly make use of or even carry away. Food also was super-abundant.

ner stated for three days and three nights. As is well known, one of these wagons is considered to be able to accommodate six horses and 40 men, and this only with the doors open so as to admit of ventilation. What with the filth of the interior, the number of people confined in it, and the absence of ventilation, it seemed to recall something of what one has read of the Black Hole of Calcutta. To give an idea of the state of mind to which we have been reduced, I got one of the better-class French prisoners to secrete a letter to my wife in the hope that he might be able to get it out to her when he reached his destination, as these French civilian prisoners were being treated better than ourselves. They all expressed great pity for the way in which we were being treated.

"I found out that the wagon in front of us was full up with English soldiers. This particular wagon had no ventilation slit of any sort or description, and men were crowded into this even worse than they were in the wagon in which I was. They banged away continually on the wooden sides of the van, and finally, as I supposed the Germans thought that they might be suffocated, a carpenter was got, who cut a small round hole in one of the sides.

"I am strongly of opinion myself that this brutal treatment of British officers and men on their way to a place of internment is deliberately arranged for by superior authority, with the object of making us as miserable and despicable objects as possible.

"I would especially call attention to the barbarous way in which British soldiers are being treated in the various laagers of the Germans. The information which follows has been obtained from the British orderlies who came to Crefeld as servants, and also from English and French medical officers who had been in the camps. The men all had their greatcoats, and in many cases their tunics as well and their money, taken away from them, and are in great need of clothing, especially underclothing. It appears that the Germans supplied them with wooden clogs when their boots were worn out. The men state that they slept on straw which had not been changed for months, and was quite sodden and rotten. All the men who came as orderlies were crawling with vermin, and half of them were suffering from the itch. The medical officer had to isolate these men before they could be employed as servants. I was also informed that the feeding arrangements for the British soldiers were very bad indeed, and as the men had no money to supplement their rations, they were in a half-starved condition, which their appearance corroborated."

## RUSSIAN OFFICIAL INQUIRY REPORT

Whatever mitigation of the treatment of Russian prisoners in Germany may have now been secured by the Russian Government's threat of "similar treatment" to German prisoners in Russian hands, the behavior of the Germans to their captives on the East Prussian front and the Mazura Lakes region at the beginning of the war was of the same kind as that experienced by British, French and Belgians in the West.

Russians made prisoners were generally deprived of their overcoats, boots and everything else of any value by German soldiers, and even by German officers. They were sent on foot to the nearest railway station. The slightly wounded had to walk. During such marches no food was given them. They had to eat raw potatoes, turnips and carrots which they tore up in the fields along the route, and for getting these vegetables they were beaten and ill-used by the Germans of the escort. The senior subaltern of the 21st Siberian Regiment—Raphael Kochurovsky—witnessed the shooting of a wounded Russian prisoner by a German soldier for leaving the ranks to pick up a half-rotten turnip lying in the road.

The peaceful inhabitants along the route traversed in Germany showed the greatest hostility towards the prisoners, whom they reviled as "Russian swine and dogs." Women, and even children, threw stones at them and spat in their faces. At Allenstein the crowd struck the wounded men, pulled their mustaches, and spat in their faces. Entrained, they were conveyed in cattle-trucks with dirty, stinking floors, with a thick layer of dung. The normal load per truck was 80 to 90 men. The trucks were so overcrowded that it was impossible to sit or lie down. Before the train started the trucks were tightly closed and the prisoners had to obey the calls of Nature where they stood, using their caps for the purpose and throwing them out afterwards through the small window, which also served as the only means of ventilation.

The atmosphere in the trucks, as all the prisoners who have returned home declare, was frightful. Men were half-suffocated; they fainted away and many even died. Hunger was their constant companion. A mug of bad barley coffee and a small piece of bread in the course of two or three days—this was all the prisoners had to satisfy their appetites. The pangs of hunger were only intensified, instead of being appeased, when the train stopped and the trucks were opened to exhibit the prisoners to the public at the stations, where victualling arrangements existed for the German soldiers. The latter were then regaled with abundance of food and drink before the very eyes of the famished Russians looking out of the trucks.

Vasili Tretiakov, a private in his Majesty's 3rd Life Guard Regiment of riflemen, has related a case which it would be difficult to believe were it not told by an eye-witness. At one of the stations the truck was opened in which Tretiakov and 80 or 90 men altogether were being conveyed into the interior of Germany. Having received no food for two days, the Russian prisoners, who fully expected to get some bread at this station, were gazing with hungry and longing looks into the distance, when they saw women dressed as Sisters of Mercy distributing bread and sausages to the German soldiers. One of these sisters went up to the truck in which Tretiakov was standing, and a Russian soldier at the door stretched out his hand for something to eat, but the woman simply struck it and smeared the soldier's face with a piece of sausage. She then called all the prisoners "Russian swine," and went away from the side of the train.

The extent to which the Germans have cultivated the art and means of cruel mockery may be seen in an incident of which Nicholas Eichem, a soldier of the Life Guard Regiment of Keksholm was a spectator. At Neidenburg the Germans harnessed a Russian officer to a machine gun and made him drag it through the streets of the town accompanied by the jeers and jibes of the inhabitants.

On August 28th, during the fighting in the region of the Mazurian Lakes, in East Prussia, the Germans captured about 300 Russian soldiers, including Gabriel Piskunov, a junior subaltern, and privates Ivan Abramov and Kozma Nazarov. All the prisoners were first of all searched and relieved of their money and everything else of any value. Then the Germans picked out all the Russians who were distinguished by wearing medals and crosses, and shot them dead on the spot. The rest were made to tramp to Letzen. Those who lagged behind were goaded on with the butt ends of rifles, and when some fell down quite exhausted the men of the German escort dispatched them at the point of the bayonet. Along the road they were reviled by the natives, who also pelted them with stones and sticks, and German cavalrymen in passing by stabbed them with their lances without the least cause or reason. In this way the prisoners were forced to march the whole day without food or drink. In the evening they reached Letzen, and were entrained in goods wagons or trucks, which had just been evacuated by horses; 80 or 90 men were crowded into each truck, with closely-shut doors, and thus they were conveyed to Stendal. The journey took two days, and all that time the prisoners were not once let out of the trucks, or allowed to taste even the usual thin black coffee. At Stendal they were taken to a concentration camp, in which about 10,000 men were interned. According to the accounts given by the prisoners, the life there was frightful. They were so badly fed that many died of ill-nourishment and exhaustion, while the strongest men among them became so feeble that they might have been knocked down by a child. The German sentries treated the captives with the utmost rigor and cruelty. For the slightest mistake or offense they were beaten with the butt ends of rifles, tied up to a post for several hours at a time, and attacked by watch dogs.

Three witnesses escaped on May 31st, and on June 29th managed to cross the frontier into Holland, where they were well treated, and sent to London. Thence they traveled back to Russia.

Joseph Dashkevich, a soldier in the Life Guard Regiment of Keksholm, was picked up by German stretcher-bearers on the third day after a battle near Lodz and taken, together with three other wounded Russians, to the nearest farmhouse. They were put into a stable with the cattle, thrown down on to the dung, and in spite of their entreaties to have their wounds bandaged, so as to keep them clean, the German sanitary officers went away, leaving the wounded Russians without any medical assistance or attendance. The cattle shed in which the wounded men were lodged took fire from an artillery shell. The Germans leisurely led out the cattle and brought out things of no value, but only when the fire had spread very considerably did they proceed to drag Dashkevich and another of the wounded Russians out of the flaming building. The two others remained inside and were burnt alive.

The Germans have made wide use of the compulsory and unpaid labor of their prisoners of war. The hardest and dirtiest work was given to the Russian and the English prisoners. The French were treated more considerately.

The prisoners were set in parties of a hundred at a time to dig canals, hew down timber, carry logs and dig trenches. The hardest work was that of draining swamps and tilling and harrowing the fields. From 6 o'clock in the morning till 8 o'clock at night prisoners had to work, standing barefooted in water up to the knees, in digging canals for the drainage of marshy soil. . . . In tilling the fields they were harnessed in batches to plows and harrows, and thus taking the place of cattle, and being treated like cattle. If they sat down to rest they were driven back by a whip or the butt end of a German soldier's rifle. Any prisoner who refused to work was beaten senseless. Jacob Kalichkin, 27th Regiment Siberian Riflemen, was a spectator of the way in which a whole party of Russian prisoners were beaten, and ten of them beaten to death, for refusing to dig trenches in front of Kalisch.

In addition to the beatings very frequently inflicted with the whips with which the German sergeants, subalterns and soldiers holding sway in the camps were abundantly furnished, there were a number of cruel and humiliating "disciplinary punishments." Prisoners were kept on bread and water, they were made to stand with uplifted arms, they were made to kneel with bare knees on broken bricks, to drag heavy loads round the barracks until they were thoroughly exhausted and so forth. For the most part the forms of punishment favored by the Germans remind one of the tortures of the middle ages.

Offenders were tied up high with ropes or wire to posts, so that their feet barely touched the ground, and in this position they were left for 3 or 4 hours. In 20-25 minutes the blood began to rise to the head, copious hemorrhage took place from the nose, mouth and ears, the unfortunate man gradually grew weak, lost consciousness, and was only prevented from falling down by the ropes or wires which held him to the post.

According to the evidence of prisoners who underwent that kind of torture, it was frightful. The rope and wire cut into the body, causing unbearable suffering and for a long time after being liberated the victim was "unable to come to himself." All the body ached and a general weakness rendered any movement impossible.

Not infrequently prisoners were stretched over a barrel and beaten with sticks and whips with thongs of gut until they completely lost consciousness.

There is another form of punishment, invented by cultured Germans, which does not, at first sight, appear to be very dreadful, but which those who had the misfortune to experience it declare is in the highest degree painful. The men to be punished were led out on to an open space, placed back to back, and in this position they were tightly bound together, the rope enveloping the body from head to foot. The men thus lashed together were left standing until one of them fainted away and pulled down the other.

These disciplinary punishments were inflicted at the discretion of German sergeant-majors, under-officers, and even private soldiers, who were apparently given uncontrolled power over the honor, health, and lives of the prisoners.

On the night of May 7, 1915, in the camp of Wittenberg, seven Russian prisoners were shot for applying to the commandant with a request for better food. This execution was carried out in the presence of Serge Demin, a private in the Grenadier regiment of Kiev.

In the camp at Schneidemühle, where there were 12 degrees of frost, a German officer, who was making an inspection, ordered the prisoners to come out of their barracks dressed only in their shirts, without the bed covers, which served them instead of the overcoats taken away from them when they were captured. One of the Russian prisoners, not waiting till the inspection was quite finished, ran off to get into his barrack out of the cold, but the inspecting officer sent a revolver bullet after him and killed him on the spot.

When the news of the defeat of the German troops at Warsaw spread through the camp at Schneidemühle it caused a pleasant animation among the Russian prisoners. The Germans being annoyed at the reverse, made the prisoners strip naked and kept them in the frost for several hours while they jeered at them and thus revenged themselves for failure at the front. This cruel case, which one would rather not believe, is vouched for by Semen Yashenin, a private of the 291st Trubchevsky Regiment, who was one of the victims.

A terrible case of cruel mockery of a defenseless enemy is related by Private Paul Kreshchenko-Kravchenko. One of the Russian prisoners, a Georgian by origin, tried to escape, but was caught and brought back to the camp. The Germans fastened a chain round his neck and drove him into a dog kennel, where he could neither sit nor lie down. Each time the guards were relieved the fresh soldier placed on duty at this post dragged the unfortunate Russian out of the kennel by the chain, struck him several blows and then drove him back. This torture lasted for two weeks.

Acts of cruelty, extending to causeless murder, were quite common occurrences in the concentration camps.

The camp at Schneidemühle was divided into four sections, and it was forbidden to pass from one section to another. Conversation between prisoners interned in different sections was also forbidden. For not observing this rule one of the Russian prisoners was killed by a German sentinel in the presence of Vasil Stemberg, a private in the 255th Regiment of Akkerman, who has related this disgusting case.

Private Artemius Shneir, of the 22nd Regiment of Nijni-Novgorod, relates that one of the men from his own regiment was tied up to a post every day for two weeks, because in one of his letters addressed to Russia he described the hard fate of prisoners in Germany.

One of the Russian prisoners picked up a rotten mangel-wurzel, which had been thrown away near the camp fence, and began to eat it, contrary to the orders of a sentinel, who at once shot the offending prisoner dead on the spot. The dead body was put into a coffin and deposited in the center of the camp, with the inscription in Russian: "Shot for disobedience to a sentinel." For the further edification of the prisoners they were brought out of the barracks and made to walk for two hours round the coffin containing the corpse. Besides other evidence of this fact, it has been attested by Private Alexander Kuznetsoff of the 218th Gorbatovsky Regiment.

The senior under-officer of the 87th Infantry Regiment, Paul Samsonov, has told how he saw a German sentinel in the camp of "Frederichsfeld" kill a Russian prisoner with two shots from his rifle, because the Russian went into another part of the camp and asked a French prisoner for a piece of bread.

One of the Russian prisoners who was very hungry took a few raw potatoes from a load and began to eat them. This was observed by a German sentinel, who stabbed the prisoner in question in the side and he died the next day. This was witnessed by Fedor Vostriakov of the 208th Loreisky Regiment.

Napoleon Yadvershis, a private in the 107th Moloden-chensky Regiment, certifies that in Schneidemühle 70 Russian prisoners, working in the kitchen of the camp, were stretched out in turns over a barrel and severely beaten with sticks because one of them gave a piece of meat to a Russian prisoner.

There is much more evidence; and in a letter in our possession a returned British prisoner was moved to pity their lot as worse in some instances than that of the British.

BY ROBERT YOUNGER

Official Report to the British Government on the "Typhus-camp," Wittenberg

The camp at Wittenberg is built on a flat, sandy plain, devoid of trees or shrubs. The total area of the camp is 10½ acres, and is subdivided into eight companies or compounds, intended to be separated from each other, but not so in practice. Every compound contains on an average six wooden bungalows, in which the men are housed, each bungalow in turn being divided into two compartments or barracks, originally constructed, it is believed, to accommodate 120 men. In fact, however, there were frequently, before and during the epidemic, 180 to 200 prisoners in a barrack, so that the overcrowding was most serious. In the early stages of the war and during the fever the camp was very full. The British prisoners numbered between 700 and 800. There was a much larger number of French and Belgians, but the Russians always greatly preponderated over all the others. It is believed that before and during the progress of the typhus there were at least 15,000 prisoners in the camp, and there may have been as many as 16,000 or 17,000— an enormous population for so restricted an area as 10½ acres. The winter of 1914-15 was extremely severe and the cold at Wittenberg intense, but the heating arrangements for the camp were altogether inadequate. Although there were two stoves to each bungalow, frequently during the winter there was a great shortage of fuel, while the stoves were so constructed that it was only if they were both constantly stoked with all the coal they could possibly hold that a bungalow was reasonably warmed. Often there was no coal for either stove, and the temperature was so low that the men had always to keep every window shut to husband what little warmth there was, and this greatly aggravated the evil of the overcrowding.

The medical and surgical arrangements were under the charge of Oberstabsarzt Dr. Aschenbach and his German assistants. At the outbreak of the epidemic there were no British medical officers at Wittenberg. There were a number of Russian and there may have been some French doctors; of this the Committee are not certain. The arrival of the British medical officers at the camp came about in the following way. From the month of November, 1914, 13 English doctors had been detained at Halle. They were none of them required for attendance upon their own men, and it is difficult to understand how, consistently with the Geneva Convention, their continued detention was justifiable. Indeed, in direct defiance of the provisions of that Convention, these doctors were treated as ordinary prisoners of war, and the Committee cannot resist the suspicion that they were deliberately detained by the German authorities so that they might be made available, if need be, for work of danger in relief of their own staff. Be that as it may, after three months' wrongful detention, these doctors were, on February 10, 1915, informed that they were to be distributed among the other German camps, and particularly that 6 were required for the camp at Wittenberg. By arrangement among themselves, the 6 sent there were Major Fry, Major Priestley, Captain Sutcliffe, Captain Field, Captain Vidal and Captain—then Lieutenant—Lauder. No reason was given for the order that they should go to Wittenberg, and it was from the guard on the train that they first heard of typhus there. On arrival at Wittenberg they were marched to the camp. They visited the different compounds. They were received in apathetic silence. The rooms were unlighted; the men were aimlessly marching up and down; some were lying on the floor, probably sickening for typhus. When they got into the open air again Major Fry broke down. The horror of it all was more than he could for the moment bear.

The epidemic broke out in December, 1914. Thereupon the German staff, military and medical, precipitately left the camp, and thenceforth until the month of August, 1915, with the exceptions detailed later on, no communication was held between the prisoners and their guards except by means of directions shouted from the guards or officers remaining outside the wire entanglements of the camp. All supplies for the men were pushed into the camp over chutes. The food for the hospital and medical officers was passed in on a trolley over about 20 yards of rail, worked by winches at either end, so as to avoid all contact between the prisoners and the outside world. No medical attention during the whole time was provided by the German staff. And the spread of the typhus, when it came, was much facilitated by a camp regulation, not confined to Wittenberg, which enjoined that prisoners of all nationalities should be mixed together. Normally, there was only one mattress for every three prisoners, and every British prisoner was compelled to have one French and one Russian prisoner to share his mattress with him. And the German authorities, although they were not ignorant of the danger, did nothing to prevent or minimize the spread of infection. That they knew it might become general throughout the camp is undoubted. German non-commissioned officers warned the French, shortly before the outbreak, of the risk, and, when during the course of the typhus, Captain Vidal, in order that its spread might be restricted as much as possible, asked a German officer, himself standing safely outside the camp, if the remaining healthy English could be placed together in one compound, his request was insultingly refused. Of the four officers left on February 11th at the camp itself, Captain Lauder alone survives, and the conditions as he describes them during the period between February 11th and March 7th are full of horror. The wonder is that any prisoner escaped infection.

When Major Priestley arrived at Wittenberg Camp the allowance of bread was 1 kilog. loaf for ten men. Breakfast for the men, he says, consisted of black (acorn?) coffee and bread. The bread contained a high percentage of potato and was most unpalatable. Sometimes a thin soup was given for breakfast in place of coffee. The midday meal consisted of a soup made of potato flour, horse-beans, soja flour, some form of grease, and a minimum of meat. Men would go days without finding any meat in their bowl. Sometimes the midday soup contained a powerfully smelling sun-dried fish, at other times dried plums, etc. In the evening there was more thin soup containing margarine. Before the outbreak there was a men's canteen at which bread and some other articles could be bought, but this was closed with the departure of the German guards on the outbreak of the typhus, and was not reopened until after their return when the epidemic was over. Then the camp food improved, but since the month of May the English had become largely independent of it, for from that time they mainly subsisted on parcels sent them from home. No parcels, however, reached the camp until May, and the German food previously supplied was, apart from its bad quality, quite insufficient to maintain vitality or enable an ordinary man to resist disease.

During the first month the food ration for each patient was half a petit pain and half a cup of milk each per day. The only soup to be got was from the camp kitchen, but that came up in a wooden tub without a cover, and it arrived at the hospital—so one of the prisoners says—full of dust and dirt. It was hopeless diet for patients in a fever. In truth, the ration was not a ration at all; it was a pretense. It was not even possible to give the patients warm water with their milk. The camp conditions were too much for each of the four medical officers who were left there; two of them, Major Fry and Captain Sutcliffe, very soon sickened, and they died of typhus about a month after their arrival. Captain Field was attacked later by the disease and also died. There is no doubt that the condition to which the camp authorities had reduced the camp and the prisoners they had abandoned was directly responsible for the deaths of these devoted men. Lieutenant Lauder was finally stricken with the disease on March 7th, after having for three days, with a temperature due to typhus, stuck to his work, there being no one then to take his place. He alone of the officers attacked finally recovered. When convalescent he bravely resumed his duty. There were then about 1,000 cases of typhus in the camp, and fresh cases were coming in at the rate of about 50, and sometimes more, a day. There were at that time about 150 British cases.

The British sick were lying scattered amongst the French and the Russians, both in the compound No. 8 and in the other compounds of the camp. Being sometimes dressed in French, Belgian, or Russian uniforms, they were difficult to recognize. They were lying in their clothes on the floor, or on the straw mattresses above described. In the beginning there were no beds in compound No. 8; there were not even, as has been shown, mattresses for all. Major Priestley saw delirious men waving arms brown to the elbow with fæcal matter. The patients were alive with vermin; in the half-light he attempted to brush what he took to be an accumulation of dust from the folds of a patient's clothes, and he discovered it to be a moving mass of lice. In one room in compound No. 8 the patients lay so close to one another on the floor that he had to stand straddle-legged across them to examine them.

Captain Vidal's description is even more appalling. It was impossible, he says, to obtain bedpans for the British patients, and consequently in cases of delirium, and even in less serious cases, the state of the mattress was indescribable. Even such a thing as paper for sanitary purposes was almost unprocurable. The difficulty in the way of obtaining sufficient drugs and dressings was for a long time extreme. Camphorated oil, Captain Lauder says, could never at Wittenberg, contrary to his experience in other German camps, be secured in adequate quantity, yet this was practically the only stimulant available. Day after day a list of medical requisites would be sent out, and only a third of the things requested would be supplied. Bed sores were common. In several cases toes or whole feet became gangrenous, and sufficient bandages were not available to dress them. One

of the patients now returned to this country, Private Lut-
wyche, of the 1st Battalion Royal Scots Fusiliers, had in
May to have one leg amputated below the knee, and in July
the other leg amputated at the same place, in both cases owing
to gangrene. Had dressings at the proper time been available both feet would in all probability have been saved.
And his case does not stand alone. The officers are quite
satisfied that the *post* typhus gangrene, which was so common, was largely due to the fact that for so many patients
there were neither socks nor anything else to keep their feet
warm. In the earlier stages of the epidemic there was practically no hospital clothing available for the prisoners.

In all this work Major Priestley, Captain Vidal, and
Captain Lauder were splendidly supported by the many English prisoners who volunteered as nurses. Many of these
devoted men caught the infection and died of the fever.

On one occasion only during the whole course of the epidemic did Dr. Aschenbach enter the hospital, or even the
camp. His visit took place about four weeks after Major
Priestley's arrival, and after some kind of order had been
evolved. He came attired in a complete suit of protective
clothing, including a mask and rubber gloves. His inspection was brief and rapid. For his services in combating
the epidemic, Dr. Aschenbach, it is understood, has been
awarded the Iron Cross. Some of the German guards outside the camp were infected by prisoners to whom, contrary
to orders, they persisted in selling things. These men were
placed by the Germans in a hospital outside the camp, and
one of the German medical staff, an Alsatian, as it happened,
was sent to attend them. At a later stage in the outbreak
this young man came to the hospital, but simply to take bac-
teriological specimens for research work at Magdeburg. He
helped in no way. With these exceptions no visit was paid
to the camp during the whole outbreak by any member of
the German Medical Service. Yet for months the plague-
stricken camp was starved of the barest necessaries of existence and of the simplest drugs, and was not even provided with surgical dressings for the patients' wounds. We
are therefore compelled to look elsewhere for an explana-

tion of the criminal neglect of which, as it seems, the German authorities were guilty. And it is found in the history of the administration of the Wittenberg Camp from the very commencement. Incredible as it may seem, the action of the officers and guards in precipitately deserting the camp and thenceforth controlling its caged inmates with loaded rifles from the outside, was only in keeping with the methods and conduct of these men throughout. The cruelty of the administration at Wittenberg Camp from the very commencement has become notorious. Savage dogs were habitually employed to terrorize the prisoners; flogging with a rubber whip was frequent; men were struck with little or no provocation, and were tied to posts with their arms above their heads for hours. Captain Lauder reports that many of these men went so far as to look upon the typhus, with all its horrors, as a godsend; they preferred it to the presence of the German guards.

And the callousness during the outbreak even of so prominent an officer as Dr. Aschenbach is illustrated by an incident related by Captain Lauder. Shortly after their arrival at the camp, Major Fry, with Captain Lauder, was begging Dr. Aschenbach, standing outside the entanglements, for some medical requisite urgently required. One of his staff with Dr. Aschenbach was apparently favorably inclined towards the request, but it was curtly refused by Dr. Aschenbach, who turned away with the words *"Schweine Englander."* An incident like that, with all it implies, speaks volumes.

The effect of such methods as have been described were manifest even on October 29, 1915, when, as has been stated, Mr. Lithgow-Osborne visited the camp. In his report of that visit, after remarking that the authorities of the camp regard their prisoners as criminals whom fear alone keeps obedient, Mr. Osborne proceeds: "In no other camp have I found signs of fear on the part of the prisoners that what they might say to me would result in suffering to them afterwards."

Mr. Gerard, speaking of his visit of November 8th, says: "The impression gained after careful examination of the camp and long conversations with the prisoners was even more unfavorable than I had been led to expect."

We are forced to the conclusion that the terrible sufferings and privations of the afflicted prisoners during the period under review are directly chargeable to the deliberate cruelty and neglect of the German officials whose elementary duty it was, in the words of the Geneva Convention, to respect and take care of these men, wounded and sick as they were, without distinction of nationality, but who acted as if neither that Convention, nor even the ordinary instincts of humanity, had any place in their scheme of things.

## BY D. J. MC CARTHY [1]

Widespread contact with the best elements of the German people, the middle, the working and the farmer class, gave the impression that they wanted the prisoner of war to be cared for properly and that they believed this was being done. The passion and race hatred that led at times to irresponsible, brutal and cruel actions to the British prisoners of war in the early days of the war had given way after two years of contact to a sane attitude, so much so that the officers could go on their walks freely in Germany, and the prisoners of war to their work or on the farms with little or no cause for complaint. The exceptions to this were in the mines and in the workshops.

The people expected their government, I think, to act decently, and I think the central civil government tried to meet the problem fairly, and as far as it was able did meet it in a general way in a fair and satisfactory manner. The administration of the problem was, however, in the hands of the Army, and the Army Corps Commanders felt themselves more powerful than the Central Government. On general subjects such as the industrial problem, working camps, etc., and in all military matters they acted independently. In technical matters they were advised by their own staff experts. I have already stated in connection with the desertion of the typhus camps, that I did not believe this repre-

[1] Reprinted by permission from "Prisoners of War in Germany," copyright by Moffat, Yard & Co.

sented the spirit or ideals of the German medical profession. The professional army surgeon of Europe, as differentiated from the civil surgeon or physician, is a different individual. The army surgeon, whether he likes it or not, is a part of a distinctive military machine. Sooner or later he realizes that he is an essential part of the machine; comes in time to look on problems from a military angle; is concerned more with the health and efficiency of his men than with the reconstructive work after they have been rendered unfit in the service.

During the first year of the war, when the military surgeon was dominant and before sheer necessity forced thousands of civilian doctors, many of exceptional position and brain power, into the ranks, he was more interested in keeping his line of communication open, to get the sick and wounded out of the way to some distant point than he was in the fortunes of the individual case. He was proud not to have his hospitals full with opportunities for helping the wounded, but rather that his hospital was empty, ready for any emergency of sudden attack or defense. He was thinking more as a soldier than as a doctor. He had grown to look upon the wounded as incubus, and to assume the military point of view to send men and munitions and supplies and food to the front, and if, when opportunity and means offered, to get the wounded back for treatment. Not that this point of view did not have its own value; war means men and guns, not doctors and wounded men who cannot fight. But that was the military point of view as contrasted with the purely humanitarianism of the civilian doctor.

One can imagine how far afield, in such a machine as the German Army, such an idea could be carried. It was just such a point of view that led whoever was in charge to order or consent to the order for sending the wounded prisoners of war to the camp at Minden. The German profession, no less than the German people in reference to the general problem, would not have willingly and knowingly consented to such a perverted view. They were, however, without knowledge of such occurrences, and would have been powerless had they the knowledge.